1-73 Bus 1

Sharon Zankich
245-0849

Business, Society, and Environment

McGraw-Hill Series in Management

Keith Davis   Consulting Editor

Business, Society, and Environment:

Social Power and Social Response

Second Edition

Keith Davis, Ph.D.
Arizona State University

Robert L. Blomstrom, Ph.D.
Michigan State University

McGraw-Hill Book Company

New York	Kuala Lumpur	Panama
St. Louis	London	Rio de Janeiro
San Francisco	Mexico	Singapore
Düsseldorf	Montreal	Sydney
Johannesburg	New Delhi	Toronto

This book was set in News Gothic by
Monotype Composition Company, Inc.,
and printed on permanent paper and
bound by The Maple Press Company.
The designer was Joan O'Connor; the
drawings were done by John Cordes,
J. & R. Technical Services, Inc. The
editors were Richard F. Dojny and
John M. Morriss. Les Kaplan
supervised production.

Business, Society, and Environment

*Library of Congress Catalog Card
Number 75-136176*
07-015522-4
234567890   MAMM   7987654321

To Sue and Marge

CONTENTS

PREFACE

The earth is traveling through space at a high rate of speed, and changes within the whole social system on the earth seem to be moving about as fast. If business wishes to remain viable and potent in its role as a major social institution, it needs to be flexible and relate to these new conditions. That is what this book is all about. It seeks to relate business to its external culture, that is, to the whole social system. It takes a system point of view, relating business to ecology, pluralism, and social power. Hopefully, the discussion also is challenging and constructive, showing how mankind's institutions work together to achieve a better *quality of life* for all of us.

It is a myth to think that we understand business just because we see business in operation every day. Experience shows that many people know about its *practices,* but too few know and understand its *social role and relationships.* In this book we hope to challenge the reader to give more thought to these latter items.

We have designed this book for college students, business managers, and others interested in institutions in our society. In universities and colleges the book is suitable for courses in Business Policy, Business and Society, Social Responsibility of Business, Management Responsibility in Society, and other integrative courses. We have sought to present illustrations, problems, and cases to make ideas more meaningful and practical. We have also tried to achieve a readable style, avoiding the technical language of specialized volumes written for one particular discipline. Another objective has been to include a discussion of multinational business in order to show how the concepts we are developing apply to global business systems.

We are grateful to many people who have helped with this book. Without them we could not have completed it. We especially thank several of our colleagues who have discussed these ideas with us and provided critical comment for different chapters of the book. The administrative support of Deans Glenn D. Overman and Kullervo Louhi and Dr. Harold E. Fearon has been encouraging. The help of our research assistants and typists has been essential; these include Mrs. Patricia Welch, Patricia Gill, Janet Martin, Cynthia Olson, Marilyn Paine, and Theodore Kinkel. Finally, we are grateful to our wives and families for their encouragement.

We hope the result will be worthwhile to you, the reader.

Keith Davis   Robert L. Blomstrom

Business, Society, and Environment

PART ONE

THE INTERFACE OF BUSINESS AND SOCIETY

CHAPTER 1

BUSINESS IN A DYNAMIC SOCIETY

It is now recognized that the direction of business is important to the public welfare, that businessmen perform a social function. . . .

ROBERT D. CALKINS[1]

What we seek is not a problem-free society but a problem-solving society. . . .

HERBERT D. DOAN[2]

As twilight settled over a suburban Maryland community, the president of a small wholesaling firm talked in quiet tones with his sales vice-president. They were trying to decide what to do next with an alcoholic salesman. On earlier occasions they had warned him and referred him to a community agency, which he refused to see, but his problem had persisted until it was seriously affecting sales in his district. Was his work a precipitate cause of his problem? Should more corrective action be tried? What action?

Not many miles away in a high-ceilinged government office, three administrators with the National Aeronautics and Space Administration were implementing a program change that required a private contractor to lay off or transfer some three hundred men. They knew that the change was unexpected and would materially affect the economy of a community near the work site. What standards of action should be expected of the contractor in this situation? What standards would he actually apply? Would he cause political repercussions for this sensitive government activity? Was this situation a joint contractor-NASA responsibility?

Across the Atlantic in Africa the general manager of a British subsidiary tossed restlessly in his bed, wondering whether to reduce prices of a retail product in an overpriced, semicartelized market. With his new

---

[1] Robert D. Calkins, "The Problems of Business Education," *The Journal of Business,* January, 1961, p. 4.
[2] Herbert D. Doan, "Controlling Society's Social Weeds," *Chemical Engineering Progress,* May, 1969, p. 30.

production facilities he was sure he had the lowest costs in the country and could win any price war that developed. Competitive economics dictated a price cut, but from the *total view* would this decision be wise? How would the community and government react to a price war? How would his labor union react if he caused layoffs of its members in competitors' plants? What about effects on investors in native plants of this capital-poor country if he bankrupted a few native businesses in this price war?

The three incidents just discussed represent only a moment in time in a day involving thousands of similar decisions concerning business and its environment. Each new day brings thousands more new decisions, and so does the next—and the next. Business managers throughout the world are busily trying to make socioeconomic systems function effectively, and they continually face decisions involving the environment outside the firm.

This "world beyond the company gate" is the subject of this book. Going by the name "business and its environment" or "business and society," it is defined as the relationship of a business institution to values and institutions outside its own formal organization. This book is, in short, a study of institutional relationships from the reference point of business: How does business affect society, and how does society affect business in our modern, complex world?

SOCIETY AS A SOCIAL SYSTEM

A Systems Concept

The complex relationship of business to its environment becomes evident when expressed in terms of a systems concept. The idea of system provides a means of understanding the dynamic variability of business's interactions with other parts of society. In an ultimate sense every action which business takes is related to the external world around it; and, in turn, everything which occurs in the external world is related to business. If we can identify the significant relationships business has with its external world, we can relate business effectively to that larger framework we call the social system. In this manner we can better understand the contributions which business and society make to each other. This knowledge should provide managers with better inputs for making socially effective decisions. It should also give society a better understanding of the mission business has in the social system, as well as better criteria for determining how well business achieves its mission.

What Is a Social System?

All systems are not social systems. There are mechanical, biological, and chemical systems and other types. A system is a combination of interrelated parts operating as a whole. It becomes a *social system* when it relates to people. It follows that a *social system* involves people and/or their organizations in relationships consisting of some observable whole. Normally the system is seeking certain human objectives. A corporation or a local parent-teacher association is a social system seeking objectives. At a different level so is a national association of corporations or parent-teacher organizations. Each has the following typical social system conditions.[3]

A Processing Sequence Directed toward Objectives

Each system has inputs of various types, such as information, economic resources, and employee loyalty. It then processes these inputs to form outputs which are intended to contribute to its objectives. Thus each system has inputs, processors, outputs, and objectives.

Parts Which Make an Interrelated Whole

The important point about a systems concept is that it allows us to see something as a *whole.* This gives us more understanding of the role played by the different parts and of the workings of cause and effect in the system. Each part has its own function. It is "doing its own thing," which may be entirely different from what other parts are doing, but it is in some way affecting the whole. An example is the biological system known as the human body in which the eyes perform one function and the hands another. An additional point, already evident, is that the parts in the system are *interrelated,* affecting each other in various ways through their inputs and outputs among themselves.

Dynamic and Stabilizing Tendencies

A social system is understood to be *dynamic.* This is one of its important characteristics. People contribute to this dynamism because they are living, thinking, acting beings. They add the variability and uncertainty of human behavior to systems, making social systems a difficult challenge for administrators who must manage them. Life does not hold still for organizations or persons.

In spite of its dynamic nature a social system tends to operate in some degree of *equilibrium,* which means a degree of accommodation and working harmony both among its parts and with its external environment. Equilibrium is interpreted as a dynamic, continuously floating balance of interacting forces rather than a static state of complete harmony. It is like a quiet ocean filled with moving sea life and waves, all operating in a balanced system. However, when a typhoon builds towering waves that are destructive or the water becomes so polluted that sea life is dying, we would at some point conclude that disequilibrium is occurring. In the same manner a business needs to maintain satisfactory equilibrium, both internally and externally, in order to survive and make reasonable progress toward its objectives. If its internal parts are working against one another, they are dissipating their energies in friction among themselves,

---

[3] Systems concepts are probably well known by most readers of this book, but we believe it desirable to review these concepts in terms of business and society.

and the organization is weakened. Likewise, if an organization lacks working harmony with its external environment, its progress toward objectives is reduced or entirely stopped.

Normally an organization maintains effective equilibrium by continuously taking corrective action as minor imbalances occur. It can do this because the people within the system have the human capacity to make choices and partly determine the future for the system. This internal and external self-correcting tendency is called *homeostasis*. Social systems may live in perpetuity. Unlike man, they do not have to die. And unlike man, they do not necessarily age. A social system can be stronger at an age of 100 years than it was at an age of 25 years. It is capable of self-renewal indefinitely, provided its leadership and membership have the capabilities to keep it serving the broader society of which it is a part. As we shall see, the idea of homeostasis is important for business organizations as they try to maintain themselves in a constantly changing, sometimes hostile environment.

Subsystems

A system such as an individual business is also part of a larger system, which is part of an even larger system—and so on, until all interrelated parts have been related in terms of the largest known system. When one refers to a smaller system in relation to a larger one, the smaller system is called a subsystem. Thus, something is a whole system from one point of view, but a subsystem from a larger point of view. The subsystem is also called a lower-order system, compared with the larger one which is a higher-order system. In this manner, systems exist in hierarchies from lower order to higher order.

A local laundry illustrates the relation of systems and subsystems. This one business is a subsystem of an association of local laundries. The local laundries are part of a larger system called the laundry industry, which is a part of the service industry (as distinguished from the mining industry, for example). The service industry itself is a subsystem of the larger system we call business. In turn, business is a subsystem of the larger system we call society.

The laundry is also a subsystem of other system hierarchies, such as a community named Rockford or all local business as represented by the Rockford Chamber of Commerce. Likewise, the laundry has its own social subsystems, such as the managerial group or the truck drivers.

To be sure, the laundry is not alone in an isolated world. It is tied to other social systems in a multitude of ways.

The systems concept suggests that the most productive analytical approach to understanding systems is to begin one's analysis from the view of as large a system as possible, because this view gives a clearer understanding of the role and contribution of all the subsystems involved. This is one of the reasons why business is giving more attention to relations with its broad social environment.

Interface with an External Environment

A system such as an individual business relates to other businesses and social groups throughout society. This area of contact between one system and another is the system *interface*. Areas of interface are important because they are sources of inputs into the system. These inputs give it additional resources and provide it with information feedback which enables it to take corrective action to maintain equilibrium with its environment.

For example, the manager of a large manufacturing branch plant was asked to speak at a luncheon of a local ministerial association which consisted of ministers from most churches in the community. He was asked to discuss what his company was doing locally to improve employment and promotion of disadvantaged employees. This meeting and speech provided an interface between the branch plant and the ministerial association.

The trade-offs of information, power, and other values which occur at the point of interface are called *social transactions*. These transactions maintain a process of social exchange in the system in the same way that economic transactions provide economic exchange in the economic system. In the example just mentioned some of the social transactions probably included the following. From the company to the ministers came an explanation of the values it held and the actions it was taking, a redefinition of company image in the ministers' minds, an image of the quality of leadership of the manager himself, and a view that the company alone could not solve this broad social problem. From the ministers to the company came an image of their ability to view problems realistically, their capacity to understand business problems, their moral commitment, and the implied threat of their power for moral persuasion in the community. Assuming these social transactions, would you consider this to be a productive social exchange? Have both parties profited from the exchange, or has one profited at the expense of the other? These are the kinds of questions which can be asked about all social transactions.

In the luncheon transaction just mentioned, the manager was acting to maintain his organization as an *open system*. So was the ministerial association. Each was acting as an open social system by accepting influence from its environment and, in turn, exerting its own influence externally. The influences it receives are social inputs, and those which it gives are social outputs. It is evident from this definition that business organizations are open systems in interaction with such external groups as customers, labor unions, government, community agencies, and others. Research supports this view. After a thorough study of the changes of ten companies over a period of many years, one researcher concluded that "these data imply that forces external to the organization itself instigate and moderate many of the dominant structural changes."[4]

[4] William H. Starbuck, "Organizational Metamorphosis," in R. William Millman and Michael P. Hottenstein (eds.), *Promising Research Directions*, Bowling Green, Ohio: The Academy of Management (Bowling Green State University), 1968, p. 132.

A CLIMATE OF SOCIAL CHANGE

Modern society presents business with immensely complicated problems that it did not have formerly. One hundred years ago the three incidents mentioned at the beginning of this chapter would hardly have been relevant to a business discussion. Societal relationships in those days were simpler than they are today, and even the meager complexities that did exist were usually overlooked. Decisions were clear-cut. If a man could not perform his work (the alcoholic incident), dismiss him; if a contract was canceled, lay off the men; and if you can do so, price your competitor out of the market. Each action was considered "in the public interest" because of its favorable effect on costs and prices according to the "invisible hand" of economics described by Adam Smith.[5] If matters of community values were raised, a suitable answer was the "Bah! Humbug!" of Ebenezer Scrooge in Charles Dickens' A Christmas Carol.

Most of modern civilization's intricate problems appear to derive from fast change which upsets the delicate equilibrium of a complex social system. It is clearly a system relationship in which social, educational, technological, and other types of change are closely interwoven. Change increases the disequilibrium among social institutions, thereby usually increasing the friction among them. This condition, in turn, requires much larger inputs of effort, resources, and knowledge in order to restore some sort of workable equilibrium.

An Age of Discontinuity

Our modern civilization, according to Peter Drucker, is experiencing more than an age of change. It is passing through an *age of discontinuity* in which change is so severe that it will create whole new institutions and significantly alter existing institutions. The four discontinuities are:[6]

1 Technological innovations such as the computer and television, which are having major effects not only on business but on the whole world.

2 Development of a world economy of one market but without suitable institutions for handling it, with the one exception of the multinational corporation.

3 A pluralistic social system in which social tasks are mostly entrusted to large institutions.

4 Most important of all, there is a knowledge revolution which has made knowledge the crucial resource of society.

Each of these ideas will be discussed further in our book, and the development of pluralism is one of the major frameworks of this book, as will be discussed in Chapter 2.

[5] Adam Smith, *An Inquiry into the Nature and Causes of the Wealth of Nations* (1776), New York: Modern Library, Inc., 1937, p. 423.
[6] Peter F. Drucker, *The Age of Discontinuity: Guidelines to Our Changing Society*, New York: Harper & Row, Publishers, Incorporated, 1968.

An Example: Jet Air Travel

Consider the changes wrought by one small part of the technological revolution—jet air travel. With jet air transportation, people from around the world have been brought into frequent contact. They begin to see the strengths and weaknesses of their own communities and nations and to increase pressures for change therein. At the same time the simple fact of their travel gives cause for new international business to service them with rental cars, hotels, transportation, airports, and similar facilities. Whole new areas have been opened to large numbers of tourists, such as Hawaii, the South Pacific, and the Caribbean. In turn, these areas experience a new economic outlook, changes in real estate values, higher capital and educational needs, and other developments.

In some cities jet aircraft have significantly altered the demography and business practices of a city. Formerly the downtown area was the business center, having developed around a railroad or port because it was the hub of commerce in earlier days. Now the downtown area is decaying, and often the hub of activity is centering near the airport and near freeways which are conveniently located to it. An example is the substantial expansion of hotels, business offices, and manufacturing on both sides of the Los Angeles International Airport.

Social Problems Are Complex

We have been considering only a few of the "ripples" in the lake of civilization made by one development—jet air travel. When the world's many other changes are combined with this one, we begin to see the massiveness of forces tending toward disequilibrium. Each of these changes is interfacing with most or all of the others, making new demands upon old institutions, upsetting the relationships among institutions, and even creating needs for new institutions. How in this immensely complex interface can society maintain and enlarge the desirable values of life, such as justice, equality, freedom, and virtue? The task is a massive one.

Some idea of the difficulty of existing problems may be seen by multiplying an index of change by indexes of other main problem areas. Let us assume that change is six times as rapid as it was a century ago. Multiply this by urban decay and congestion which is three times as serious, and so on, using a seriousness-complexity index for each item mentioned. The result is as follows:

INDEX	ITEM
6	Rate and complexity of change
×3	Urban decay and congestion
×4	Racial and ethnic unrest
×3	Implications of poverty
×9	Pollution
×5	Drug abuse

INDEX (cont.)	ITEM (cont.)
×2	Inflation
×2	Crime
	(etc.)
38,880	Index of current problem seriousness and complexity compared with a century ago.

The index is obviously overstated because these conditions exist in a system relationship of interaction, rather than in a simple multiplicative sequence. Furthermore, the items in the index are of unequal significance to society, and they have not been weighted accordingly. Nevertheless, there is some multiplicative relationship among the items; so the index is a mathematical way to illustrate the growing seriousness of social problems. For example, urban decay has undoubtedly increased racial unrest, and pollution has increased urban decay. The important point is that modern social problems are grossly more difficult and complex than those of a century ago, so old solutions are unlikely to work with these new conditions.

On the other hand, society does have some new solutions for these new conditions because it is more capable of solving social problems than it was a century ago, and business has contributed substantially to this capability. These improvements may also be multiplied in an index of problem-solving capability, which can be compared with the index of problem seriousness to get a relative understanding of how capably and quickly society may solve some of its problems.

INDEX	ITEM
15	Available capital resources
×8	Increased technological capability
×3	Improved understanding of social forces
×3	Better educated citizens
×30	Increased per capita income available for solving problems
	(etc.)
32,400	Index of current problem-solving capability

Two additional ideas arise from this analysis. One is that business is directly involved in these problems, as will be discussed throughout this book. Business is both a contributor to pollution and a developer of devices to prevent pollution. It is a part of the urban community, and in general is part of the whole fabric of society. A second idea is that, since these problems are complex and institutionalized, certain business skills are needed for solving them. Business has the know-how to manage complex institutions and bring productivity and order out of chaos. It knows how to train and develop people, to get them to cooperate, and to produce technological change effectively. Its record is imperfect like that of all institutions, but it stands high among all of them in these areas of competence.

As a result of the pace and complexity of change, social disequilibrium appears to have become more severe in recent years, raising the nagging threat of major social breakdown. In symbolic terms, the candle of time burns shorter. It also stands as a beacon of light brightening the way for society's leaders and followers to give their finest talents to solving the problems ahead. In the darkness, waiting for the candle to dim, the forces of social collapse are lurking. Their allies are the winds of emotionalism and ignorance which flutter and threaten the candlelight. What is needed is a quieter, problem-solving atmosphere provided by rational men with proven modes of action. As mentioned in one of the quotations introducing this chapter, we are seeking a problem-solving society, not a problem-free society.

BUSINESS AS A SOCIAL INSTITUTION

Institutions are established by society for social purposes, and business is one of these institutions. The economic nature of business is well established in literature and the public mind. Likewise the technology of business is evident at every turn. What is often overlooked is the fact that business is also a social institution, performing a social mission and having a broad influence on the way people live and work together. As stated in the Calkins quotation introducing this chapter, the direction of business is important to public welfare, and businessmen do perform a social function.

Definition of Business

Viewed in a broad way, the term *business* typically refers to the development and processing of economic values in society. Normally we use the term to apply to the private (nongovernment) portion of the economy whose primary purpose is to provide goods and services to customers at a price, but lines of distinction are getting hazy as business and government overlap their functions in organizations such as the Communications Satellite Corporation and the Tennessee Valley Authority. In addition, *business* is a term applied to economic and commercial activities of institutions having other purposes, such as the business office of an opera association. The Metropolitan Opera Association, for example, negotiates with labor, invests capital, and makes layoffs in ways similar to those of private business. So also does the Tennessee Valley Authority.

Let us consider further the Metropolitan Opera Association of New York City. Its primary social mission is artistic and cultural; however, in 1969 it failed to meet its September 15 opening date because of labor troubles.[7] Its executive committee determined that it could not open until labor contract settlements gave it some basis for predicting expenses and knowing that it could operate throughout the season in order to recoup its costs. The preceding year it had ended the season with a $3.5 million deficit.

The Opera Association is a social system composed of subsystems, one of which is a business system. Presumably the musicians were qualified and prepared to perform if business issues could be settled. Music was the Opera Association's primary mission; however, the mission was delayed because of a failure in one of its lower-order systems, the business function. In today's organized society even artistic activities—at least the major ones—require a successful business function.

The Ecology of Business

Our modern view of business in society is an ecological one. Ecology is concerned with the mutual relations of human populations or systems with their environment. It is necessary to take this broad view because the influence and involvement of business are extensive. Business cannot isolate itself from the rest of society. Today the whole society is business's environment.

In taking an ecological view of business in a system relationship with society, three ideas are significant in addition to the systems ideas already presented. The three ideas are values, viability, and public visibility.

Values: A Source of Institutional Drives

Businesses, as well as other social institutions, develop certain belief systems and values for which they stand. These values derive from a multitude of sources, such as the mission of business as a social institution, the nation in which a business is located, the type of industry in which it is active, and the nature of its employees. For example, the people in a steel mill might have entirely different views toward steel import quotas and labor unions than the people in an engineering research organization.

Over a period of time, values become institutionalized, meaning that they are accepted by a large number of people in the organization. Sometimes these values are an official policy, but more often they are merely an informal understanding among people in the organization. The values are, of course, held in different degrees by each person in the organization, and some persons do not support certain values at all; nevertheless some values become generally accepted as institutional ones. With regard to business and society these values perform two important functions. First, they become guides for employee decisions in the interface of business and its environment. Second, they become strong motivators for people in a business. Thus they become a key factor in the system relationship of business with society. They are discussed further in Part Two, "Business Ideology."

[7] "Discord Keeps Met Curtain Down," *Business Week*, Nov. 8, 1969, pp. 34–35.

Viability: The Drive to Grow

In discussing social systems we presented the ideas of equilibrium and homeostasis. These were, respectively, the drive to maintain working harmony with the environment and the capacity to take corrective action to restore harmony. There is an additional thought which these ideas may imply but which they do not state explicitly, and we believe it merits separate emphasis because of its significance in modern business. The thought is *viability*, and it implies something more than the maintenance of harmony and continuity for the business. Viability means the drive to live *and grow*, to accomplish potential not yet reached, and to achieve all that a living system is capable of becoming.

People bring viability to the business system. They seek growth. Thus, the system which they operate can move beyond simple maintenance and achieve growth in the quality and quantity of services it renders. In a world of hunger and ignorance, growth has become a key focus for social development.

One author has developed the thesis of *counterpoint*, which means that in order to keep competitive and growing a business must constantly strive to upset the same equilibrium it is trying to achieve. This creates a state of dynamic tension between the forces of change and stability. This tension exists both in headquarters and in operating areas. Although it is a seeming contradiction of effort, counterpoint is necessary in order to maintain the viability of the organization in a changing world.[8]

Business Viability

History shows that business is remarkably viable in response to change. It has operated as a substantially more open system than a number of other institutions, and this openness has stimulated its response to change. Generally it has responded faster than educational institutions, the military, the church, or the judiciary. Some areas in which it has been especially progressive are technology, migration to frontiers, improved working conditions, and international development. As far back as the Jamestown colony of Virginia, business was a prime mover in developing the New World.

Since modern society is experiencing unusually major social changes, business is diligently seeking a viable accommodation to these changes. To accommodate may be costly, in the same way that new technology has required expensive factory alterations, but failure to accommodate would be even more costly because business's significance as an institution would decline as a result of its inability to meet human expectations.

Accommodation does not imply direct conformity to existing culture, for business is always transmitting values *to* society as well as receiving values *from* society. In fact, if business is to be a viable, vigorous institution in society, it must initiate its share of forces on its environment,

[8] Neil W. Chamberlain, *Enterprise and Environment: The Firm in Time and Place*, New York: McGraw-Hill Book Company, 1968.

rather than merely adjust to outside forces as a bucket of quicksand does. Every business needs a drive and spirit all its own to make it a positive actor on the societal stage rather than a reactor or a reflector. To expect business to be otherwise is to deny it the opportunities available to other institutions.

In connection with adaptation, one of the shallowest criticisms that can be made of business is that fifty or one hundred years ago it had some practices, long since changed, which by today's standards are considered "bad." For example, it is said that business used to employ workers twelve hours a day, which is "proof" that businessmen were heartless villains. To evaluate this situation rationally, we must ask whether this historical practice was out of line with needs and practices of that time in history. Did business "villains" and shopkeepers work less than their employees or less than farmers or government workers? And was productivity so low that longer hours were necessary in order to maintain reasonable subsistence? Historical events need to be evaluated in terms of historical conditions and standards. For example, businessmen 100 years ago did not use atomic energy, which "proves" how technologically backward they were—or does it? Actually, criticisms of this sort are merely evidence of business progress and adaptation.

Public Visibility: The Glass House

A powerful pressure for business adaptation to society is the public visibility of business compared with other institutions. *Public visibility* refers to the extent that an organization's activities are known to persons outside the organization. The activities may be directly observed, such as polluting smoke seen coming from a smokestack or purchase of a product which is deficient. Activities also may be indirectly communicated by news media, neighbors, and other sources. The importance of public visibility is that it makes business activities subject to public examination, discussion, and judgment. If acts are not known, they cannot be judged.

Since business is an advertiser, a major employer, and a supplier of customers—to name just a few of its activities—its acts are widely visible much of the time. It is an open system. It lives in a glass house. In contrast, penal institutions are substantially closed systems which have much less public visibility. They are isolated spatially and socially, serve a limited membership, and restrict communication by means of minimum mobility. They have little contact with outside society, and they have changed very slowly over history.

Public visibility is different from the idea of public image often mentioned in public relations. Public image refers to what people think about an organization's acts, while public visibility refers to the extent to which its acts are known. A business may have high visibility and either high or low image. Similarly, it may have low visibility and either high or low image.

A striking illustration of business visibility occurred in the winter of 1969 when a drilling accident caused crude oil to leak in the Santa

Barbara Channel of California. It was a catastrophe because it despoiled some coastal areas and damaged property and wildlife. Newspapers around the nation discussed it week after week. There were severe criticisms of business, lawsuits against businesses, and political crises concerning the event.

At that time one of the authors was in Los Angeles, 60 miles south of Santa Barbara in the direction which ocean currents flow; so he went to beach areas near Huntington Beach to see if oil pollution had reached this far. As he approached the beach, an unpleasant odor was evident one to two blocks away, affecting homes and apartments near the beach. Upon reaching the beach on this warm, sunny day, he found it bare of people for over a mile in each direction, except for one man walking his dog. Sure enough, there were temporary signs every 100 feet saying "WARNING. Beach pollution. Do not enter." This beautiful place was desolate. There were not even any seagulls, and a resident stated the pollution had either killed them or driven them away. The pollution, however, was *not* oil pollution. It was *sewage pollution!* Because of heavy rains, some municipalities that had storm sewers and sanitary sewers interconnected in order to save money were dumping large amounts of raw sewage into the ocean because their systems were overloaded.

In Santa Barbara the pollution was caused by private business; in the Los Angeles area it was caused by municipal government. Since the oil companies were following federal standards for ocean drilling, the worst accusal that could be made was carelessness and poor planning. The same accusals could be applied to the municipalities. In both instances metropolitan areas were affected, but the Los Angeles pollution, especially the odor, seemed to affect a large number of homesites and people. In both cases the pollution was temporary, but in Los Angeles it was more of a health hazard.

The important point about these two events is that the business pollution received the adverse publicity because of the greater public visibility of business. Considering the whole situation, there seemed to be no reason to judge the Santa Barbara pollution as being more serious or more willful than the Los Angeles pollution; however, the national press gave the business pollution the adverse publicity. Regardless of arguments about what is and is not news, or what is fair or unfair reporting, the simple fact is that the business pollution received much publicity, while the municipal pollution did not. This is business's glass house.

Management's Awareness of Its Social Involvement

One final question which must be asked is: Are businessmen aware of their business's interface with society and social involvement in it? Five years ago when we wrote the first edition of this book we detected only a glimmer of awareness and interest, but conditions have changed significantly since that time. In the words of a top government adviser the spreading social awareness of the United States business community "is certainly among the most significant developments of the last few years."[9] There is a corporate social revolution which is supplementing the corporate technical revolution that dominated business life from 1940 to 1965.

Assuming that a corporate social revolution is developing, we need to examine its causes and consequences and will do so in subsequent chapters. Is this a desirable trend? Will it dilute the economic efficiency of business? Will it lead to confusion of objectives among social institutions? Will it place excessive power in the hands of business managers? Will it produce false expectations which cannot possibly be fulfilled, thus eventually damaging the image of business? Is it a temporary fad? *Will it produce results?* As with any new development, this one has its critics. John K. Galbraith said in a speech before New York's City Club that "private enterprise and private investment are being aroused to their responsibilities—as they have *without result* a hundred times before."[10]

As with any group of free social institutions, the new social awareness exists in varying degrees among businesses, and some lack it entirely. There are many businessmen who show little concern about the public interest, but the significant question is: What is the dominant trend? There will always be exceptions. Social awareness is especially concentrated among large corporations; and since they dominate the business system, it is important to know the views of their top managers concerning the priority of social problems which involve business. These priorities are reflected in a *Fortune* survey of over 300 chief executives from the 500 largest industrial corporations and 50 largest banks in the United States. These executives were shown a list of social problems and asked to designate the ones which deserved "top priority" for business involvement. The four problems given most emphasis were: supporting education (62 percent), combating air and water pollution (58 percent), ensuring equality of opportunity for minorities (57 percent), and employing the hard-core unemployed (54 percent). Urban issues, conservation of natural resources, political reform, and decentralization of social, economic, and governmental institutions also received strong emphasis.[11]

Another study covered fifteen large manufacturers normally producing about eight percent of the gross national product, and it reported that all of them had given more emphasis to external relations during the last ten years.[12] Executives in charge of external relations usually reported to the top executive officer and always had direct access to him. The firms were engaged in long-range planning to anticipate and deal with major external issues. One firm, for example, established a corporate relations committee to look ahead and recommend policy on external affairs. It included five executives of vice-presidential rank or above.

[9] Quoted in Alan L. Otten, "Doing Good," *Wall Street Journal* (Pacific Coast edition), Mar. 18, 1969.
[10] Quoted in *Public Affairs Review*, Oct. 17, 1967, p. 4. Italics in original.
[11] Arthur M. Louis, "The View from the Pinnacle: What Business Thinks," *Fortune*, September, 1969, p. 94. See also a survey of over 100 corporate chief executives in Stuart A. Taylor, "Is Management Truly Involved in the Urban Crisis?" *Business Horizons*, April, 1969, p. 42.
[12] Paul E. Holden and others, *Top Management*, New York: McGraw-Hill Book Company, 1968, pp. 14–16.

VIEWING THE WHOLE BUSINESS SYSTEM

Chris Argyris states that all organizations have three essential core activities. These are (1) achieving objectives, (2) maintaining the internal system, and (3) adapting to the external environment.[13] Typical books on management and organization tend to emphasize the first two core activities; however, our book is directed primarily toward the third: adapting to the external environment. We shall discuss the importance of this environment in management policy making and decision making.

Our objective in this book is to integrate as many as possible of the disciplines and value systems affecting business so that we can examine the business environment as a whole. The total system is generally something different from the sum of its parts. Consider an animal dissected and described in a laboratory. Even if the parts are sewn back together, they do not restore the living animal and show its living responses as a system. A similar situation exists with the business system. We recognize that this book cannot truly picture a living business system, but at least its emphasis will be integrative rather than functional.

This is not a book on business ethics, but rather an analysis of business in its social environment. One influence in that environment is ethics, but there are many other influential factors. When it is necessary to discuss ethical norms, we plan to cover different points of view wherever practical so that each reader can make his own decisions. This book, therefore, does not offer a normative ethic of what business *ought* to do to be right with the world. Rather, it offers a discussion of how business and society mutually interact in performing their functions.

In the remaining chapters of Part One we discuss some of the frameworks by which business relates to society, such as pluralism, technology, social change, and social responsibility. We also examine the business and managerial roles in the social system. In Part Two we discuss business ideology, including its historical development and the individual's relationship with the organization.

In Part Three we relate business to some of its major publics, such as government, owners, customers, and labor. Part Four, "Business and the Community," moves into some of society's most current and controversial issues which involve business. Some of the issues covered are urban problems, disadvantaged citizens, the interface with education, relationships with art and the professions, and pollution. Then, in Part Five we discuss the broader involvement of business in social change in an international world. A concluding chapter offers some interpretations of what is happening and where trends may be leading.

SUMMARY

The subject of business and its social environment covers relationships of a business institution to the broader society outside its own formal

---

[13] Chris Argyris, *Integrating the Individual and the Organization*, New York: John Wiley & Sons, Inc., 1964, p. 120.

organization. This is a complex relationship which a systems approach may aid in understanding. The systems approach implies a processing sequence directed toward objectives, parts which make an interrelated whole, dynamic and stabilizing tendencies, subsystems, and interface with an external environment.

The social institution of business operates as an open system and is especially concerned with values, viability, and public visibility. The modern social environment presents business with a complex age of discontinuity, and businessmen are gradually becoming aware of their social involvement in it.

STUDY GUIDES FOR INTERPRETATION OF THIS CHAPTER

1 Is the relation of business to society and the environment worthy of serious thought and study? Explain.

2 What are the benefits to business and to society which can be achieved by using a systems framework to analyze their relationships with each other?

3 In terms of business, society, and its environment, discuss the Santa Barbara and Los Angeles beach pollution mentioned in this chapter.

4 What is the difference between a social discontinuity and routine social change?

5 What decision would you make for each of the three cases introducing this chapter? Give reasons for your decisions.

CHAPTER 2

A PLURALISTIC SOCIETY

A society capable of continuous renewal would be characterized first of all by pluralism—by variety, alternatives, choices and multiple focuses of power and initiative. We have just such pluralism in this society.

JOHN W. GARDNER[1]

Today's society and polity are pluralistic.

PETER F. DRUCKER[2]

A subsidiary of one of the largest 500 companies in the United States bought several thousand acres of ranch land in order to develop it. The plan was to develop a seaside resort with hotels, a leisure-living community among rolling hills, golf courses, an airstrip for light airplanes, some new farm land, and a large "green belt" of land permanently dedicated to the county government to be kept in its natural state. The plan for land use was carefully devised and reasonable. No industrial zoning was proposed.

The land purchase was easy compared with the hornets' nest of controversy which surrounded the land's development. Conservation groups protested that the land should not be developed at all, but should be reserved for public use. The conservationists and a group of sports fishermen joined in opposing the seaside resort, because they felt it would mar the rugged beauty of the coastline and perhaps pollute a popular fishing area. Farmers who had property within two miles of the airstrip claimed that noise from airplanes would disturb them and frighten their cattle. Another group of farmers insisted that the added farm land and population would increase water use so much that the underground water table on which they depended might be depleted. A historical group insisted that agreements be made to protect certain old homesites and other

[1]John W. Gardner, "Toward a Self-renewing Society," *Time*, Apr. 11, 1969, p. 40.
[2] Peter F. Drucker, *The Age of Discontinuity: Guidelines to Our Changing Society*, New York: Harper & Row, Publishers, Incorporated, 1968, p. x.

points significant to the history of the state. A group of hotel managers in the nearest resort community insisted that a new resort was not needed, because there were not enough tourists for two resorts. A labor group argued that zoning must provide adequate low-income homes and apart- ments near the expensive hotels and leisure-living homes so that workers in the hotels and shops would not have to travel long distances to work.

There were also various government groups to negotiate with, such as the State Water Resources Board and the County Zoning Board which had to give final approval for the project. Several lengthy zoning controversies developed, such as whether streets in residential areas should have expensive concrete curbs and gutters with sidewalks. After nearly a year of delays, one company executive observed, "In spite of our experience in this field, we didn't know what we were getting into."

What the company was "getting into" was a pluralistic community in which organized groups were representing the special interests of groups of citizens. This chapter discusses some of the interest groups interacting with business and then examines the elements and modes of operation of a pluralistic society.

INTEREST GROUPS INTERACTING WITH BUSINESS

Increasing Social Complexity

Centuries ago business was a rather uncomplicated relationship involving only a few interest groups, and it had been that way throughout history. There were owners who supplied the small amount of capital needed, employees who performed the work, and customers who purchased the products, as shown in Figure 2–1. Government and religion stood weakly on the side performing their political and moral regulatory rules, and their influence was relatively minor. In very small businesses such as a

Figure 2–1 Business complexity centuries ago and today.

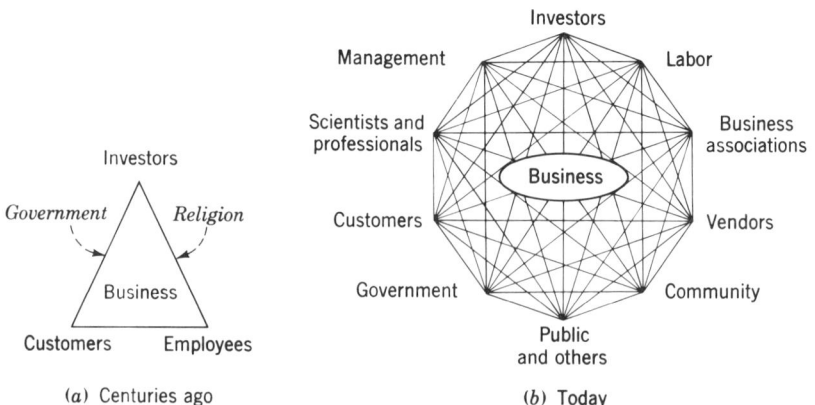

(a) Centuries ago

(b) Today

"mom-and-pop" grocery store, the employee supplied his own capital, and he and his family operated the store, so even the separate ownership role was bypassed. There was a direct relationship only between the owner-employee and his customers. There are even today many shops of this type, but in advanced nations most commerce is achieved by larger organizations with entirely different and more complex modes of action.

During the last two centuries, revolutions in science, education, productivity, and culture developed in a way that expanded institutions and interest groups until the social system became significantly more complicated. Each group in the system developed its own specialized activity, which then had to be integrated with other activities to make the system function effectively. Many of these groups are active participants in the business environment as shown in Figure 2-1b, which is more complex than Figure 2–1a.

The purpose of Figure 2–1b is to portray most of the groups directly involved with business, and the words "Public and others" at the bottom of the chart are intended to represent the idealized norm which we call the public interest and all other groups which relate to business. Some of these other groups are agriculture, minority groups, conservationists, journalists, news media, educators, nonprofit foundations, churches, and medical services. In the example reported at the beginning of this chapter, most of the groups fit the classification "Public and others," since the business was not yet operating in the community.

A Community of Competing Groups

The president's suite in today's business is less a place for autocratic decisions than a place for reconciliation of the multitude of competing interests impinging on business. Although the number of competing interests demanding reconciliation has expanded greatly, cultural guides to help an executive make the right decision have hardly expanded at all. In addition to the expanded *number* of interests pressing on business, the *kinds* of decisions needed and the cultural conditions for them have changed drastically but without corresponding changes in cultural guides for business. The result is that modern managers develop a *social vertigo* trying to balance all interest groups because they cannot relate to enough familiar points of reference. Like a pilot flying blind, they become disoriented and confused because the familiar horizon is gone; consequently, they are quietly searching for more guides such as professionalism and the idea of social responsibility.

Likewise, the passengers in the airplane—who in this instance are the publics of business—rise in confused disharmony because they have lost the horizon also. What is the social purpose of business? Upon what pillars does its legitimacy of power rest? What functions should it perform? How can society judge the effectiveness of its performance?

One company president comments as follows about the myriad pressures on a president: "If we used more accurate signs than we do, the sign on his door would not say 'President,' but would read, 'Department of Pushing and Tugging, Pulling and Hauling.' "[3] Without a doubt we expect a modern business to be:

A better place for investment
A better place to work
A better supporter of ethical ideals
A better company to buy from
A better company to sell to
A better taxpayer and supporter of government
A better neighbor in the community
A better contributor to social goals, public interest, and human progress

The unique development of modern business life is competition among institutional interest groups, as shown in Figure 2–1b. Economic competition in the marketplace has been diluted by social competition among various business claimants seeking higher economic payouts, more prestige, power, and other benefits. Competition has moved partly from the marketplace to committee rooms, business offices, and legislative halls. The old competition was judged by precise, impersonal economic standards of conduct, but the new competition is based upon social standards which are vague, nebulous, and overrun with personal views and emotions. The old competition was primarily among persons acting individually, but the new competition is among interest groups and institutions which act for people as a collective community. They may act as much for power and institutional survival as they do for people.

The Changing Role of Business Clients

The interest groups which deal directly with business and, therefore, have a direct claim to certain outputs from it are the *clients* of business. Examples are customers, stockholders, and employees. The role of these clients has been changing in a dramatic fashion during the last century.

OWNERS   Even the traditional ownership role has changed to an investor role. As large organizations have increased their dominance of business, one or a few persons can no longer supply the capital needed. The result is that ownership has been dispersed through stock markets to millions of persons who think more like investors than owners, as will be discussed in the chapter concerning ownership claims on business. Of equal importance is the fact that business investors in modern society are changing from individuals to institutions. Individuals place their money in mutual funds, insurance plans, pension plans, trust funds, and other institutions, which then invest the funds as representatives of millions of small savers. These institutions have tens of billions of dollars invested

---

[3] John L. McCaffrey, "The Boss's Bosses," *The Management Review*, November, 1954, p. 712.

in corporate stocks, and each year they increase their investments. In the 1960s, individuals—the historical capitalistic investors—became net sellers on major stock exchanges, while institutions became net buyers.[4]

MANAGEMENT   The relationship of ownership to management has also changed. One or two centuries ago the principal owners of business were also its managers. Ownership vested a person with symbolic powers of leadership which were substantially related to his property rights. He knew best how to manage his resources. Even when his leadership faltered, this turn of events was considered an exception to the rule, rather than a denial of the unity of owner and manager. If any conflict arose between owner and manager roles, it was internal, to be resolved within the person and never exposed to public consideration.

Today, as shown in Figure 2–1b, management is more a differentiated role, semiprofessional in nature, with accession by competence rather than ownership. In many large enterprises the entire top-management group owns less than five percent of the company's assets—sometimes less than one percent. Management has become a distinct type of work with its own educational programs, literature, and criteria for achievement.

LABOR   As management changed, so did labor. In early times employees acted primarily as individuals in their relationships with owner-managers. Increasingly, however, employment became governed by group contracts negotiated by labor unions. The union arose as a separate institution with its own power groups and institutional interests. As an example of these evolving institutional relationships, a common term in personnel management today is *labor-management* relations, not employee-owner relations. Employees today find their employment conduct bound by management's rules, management-union contracts, and union rules, all of which are surrounded by a firm canopy of government intervention. In the crush of institutional claimants upon business, individual needs of employees are apt to be bypassed, as will be discussed in a later chapter.

SCIENTISTS AND PROFESSIONALS   Historically, labor unions have represented mostly manual skills; and as civilization became more advanced, the burgeoning scientific-professional-intellectual groups tended to develop separate institutional interests. In the 1960s labor-union membership stabilized and actually declined as a proportion of the labor force (less than 25 percent), while membership in scientific and professional occupational groups expanded dramatically. In the same manner that owners and managers differentiated their roles, it appears that manual workers and intellectual workers are developing separate institutional claims on business, as shown in Figure 2–1b. This growth of professional groups has been one of the most striking business developments in recent years.

[4] For example, see the historical trends reported in Daniel Seligman and T. A. Wise, "New Forces in the Stock Market," *Fortune*, February, 1964, pp. 92–95; and *Business Week*, June 5, 1965, p. 110.

BUSINESS ASSOCIATIONS   In the same way that employees have joined together for their own interests, businesses have formed a multitude of business associations to serve the interests which they have. The result is a more complex web of customs and relationships. The extent of involvement of even small businesses is illustrated by a local automobile agency in an urban community.

Ruskin Automobile Agency joined the local chamber of commerce in order to cooperate with other businessmen in community affairs. It was a member of a local credit bureau which served businessmen by providing customer credit ratings. With other businesses it had helped organize a Better Business Bureau to investigate and expose shady business practices because it was especially concerned about their effect on the used car market. Each of the three associations mentioned was also affiliated with a similar national association.

At the national level Ruskin Agency was a member of the National Automobile Dealers Association in order to represent its industry group to manufacturers and others. It also belonged to the National Federation of Independent Business, which sought to protect small business interests. Recently it joined the American Management Association, a nonprofit group concerned with training and development, in order to encourage growth of several of its managers. There were also other business-related associations to which it belonged.

CUSTOMERS   At first glance it might seem that the customer is the same as always, but his role also is changing, as will be discussed in a later chapter. He is more sophisticated and he has more choice, but at the same time he needs more protection because technological complexity reduces his power to judge product quality at the time of purchase. In general, there is a tendency for his sovereign power to be lost to the producer as products become more complicated.

VENDORS   Modern business also gives vendors a more significant role than they once had. Increasing scientific complexity requires business buyers to work closely with their vendors to develop better schedules, methods, and product reliability. Major buyer-vendor relationships are long run rather than consisting of a single commercial transaction. Sometimes deliveries are rescheduled or a part redesigned to fit a vendor's capabilities better. Vendors frequently have service representatives in buyers' plants, and buyers have their technical representatives in vendors' plants. When there is a powerful buyer purchasing a major part of a vendor's output, the buyer often acts responsibly to help the vendor maintain competitive efficiency and stable schedules to avoid layoff and bankruptcy. Large mail-order houses and automobile manufacturers, for example, have actually served as management consultants to improve vendor business practice.

GOVERNMENT AND THE COMMUNITY   The increased role of government in modern business is well known and is discussed in a later chapter. The community, shown separately from government in Figure 2-1*b*, represents all *local* interests—including local government—in a business's employment community, and is discussed in Part Four of this book. The community is definitely one of the growth areas in business's relationship with its environment.

THE PUBLIC INTEREST   It may appear strange that the public interest is separated from government and community in Figure 2-1*b*; however, neither government nor community—nor any other group—is sure to represent the public interest at all times. The "public interest" is an abstract, general term used to describe the greatest good for the greatest number. Where government is involved, powerful dictators, inept bureaucrats, or power-hungry politicians may work against the public interest rather than for it. We cannot say that Hitler represented the public interest merely because he represented government. Similarly, a community may serve its own interests to the detriment of other communities; hence it cannot always act in the public interest. The public interest is actually an idealized norm which all people use to judge the acts of others. Most institutions claim to represent the public interest most of the time. The problem is that their views of public interest may differ.

ELEMENTS OF A PLURALISTIC SOCIAL SYSTEM

The relationships described in connection with Figure 2–1*b* represent a *pluralistic society*, in which diverse groups maintain autonomous participation and influence in the social system. Business is influenced by these groups in its interface with them in the system. In turn, again at the points of interface, business exerts a countervailing influence on them. As indicated in both quotations introducing this chapter, pluralism is a basic reality of the modern business culture. The significance of this reality for business is that pluralism defines the fundamental framework within which business must live and grow. Unless businessmen understand the "rules of the game" by which pluralism operates, they are handicapped in their efforts to make business a viable social institution. This is their environment. They must know it in order to perform their roles as leaders. Whether they prefer pluralism is not the issue. It, like the weather, is here. For this reason much of this book relates to how business deals with relationships, power, and responsibility in a pluralistic society.

Some of the major elements of pluralism are discussed in the following paragraphs. Emphasis is on pluralism in the social system (social pluralism), for pluralism within a system of government (political pluralism) provides a slightly different context, although the basic ideas still apply.

Diversity of Interests

In pluralism there are numerous economic, political, educational, social, artistic, and other groups developed by people to promote their welfare.

Social organization into one institution

Social organization into many interacting institutions

Social organization into an infinite number of persons

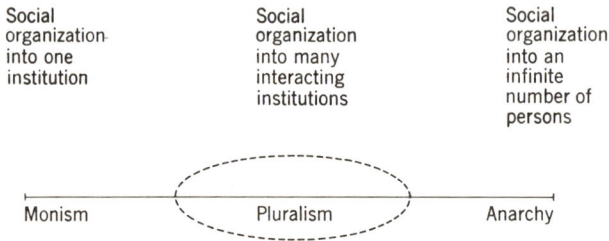

Monism   Pluralism   Anarchy

Figure 2–2   Pluralism occupies a middle ground on a continuum from one to an infinite number of social units.

There are, therefore, many different points of view represented in the interface of these groups. As shown in Figure 2–2, pluralism occupies a broad middle ground on a social continuum from monism at one extreme to anarchy at the other. Monism requires that all men's affairs be operated by one absolute social institution which satisfies all of their needs. It is a social system with a monolithic, centralized power structure. The other extreme, anarchy, implies an unorganized society in which each person pursues his own interests without regard for others. Pluralism, operating between the extremes, decentralizes social power by dispersing it to a variety of institutions performing different social functions.

Institutional Specialization

Pluralism is an institutional concept. It recognizes that although people act individually in their interests, they also form institutions which act as agents to represent these interests. Since there is a diversity of interests among people, they tend to form specialized institutions which operate in relatively restricted areas of activity, leaving other needs of clients to be supplied by other institutions. One reason for this is that specialization appears to be more efficient socially in the same way that labor specialization has proved itself more productive economically.

In modern society large institutions have arisen to dominate nearly every field of activity. Peter Drucker observes, "Historians two hundred years hence may see as central to the twentieth century what we ourselves have been paying almost no attention to: the emergence of a society of organizations in which every single social task of importance is entrusted to a large institution."[5]

Multiallegiant Man

In connection with institutional specialization, each person specializes his own interests and contributions, so he relates to many institutions in order to fulfill all his needs. In other words, he divides his needs and assigns different need fulfillments to different institutions. The result is that no business, labor union, or other pluralistic organization can claim

[5] Drucker, *op. cit.*, p. 171.

a person's full loyalty to the exclusion of all other organizations. Writers in labor relations refer to a worker's "dual allegiance" to management and union;[6] however, in terms of the total business environment a better term to apply is *multiallegiant man* because he allocates his allegiance among many institutions.

In a drug firm, for example, one chemist may be a member of management, a chemical-society member, an investor in business, a consumer, a Boy Scout leader, a member of the local community, and so on. He does not depend on only one institution representing his social class to supply most of his needs. Whatever conflict exists is not primarily a class conflict, but is a result of institutions trying to resolve different role needs which have been assigned to them by a common population. The chemist may have different expectations as a consumer, investor, and manager; however, this conflict is not between three classes of different people.[7] Rather, it is conflict among his own diverse expectations as represented by various institutions to which he is allegiant.

When a person relates directly to an organization in a client role, he is making a *role investment* in it. This investment may consist of time, tangible goods, status, security, or other values useful to him. For example, a business owner may risk his prestige and reputation in a shaky venture. The venture's economic risk is minor to him compared with possible loss of prestige and self-esteem in the event of failure. Similarly, a customer invests his time, economic resources, and judgment. If his purchase does not meet his expectations, he may be more angered by his mistake in judgment than by his economic loss. Thus men sometimes will fight about a dollar or a word, but on another occasion they will lose $1,000 with a smile because their social investments in each situation are different.

In making his investment in an organization, a person trades off some of his values in expectation of reciprocal benefits. Thus, he makes a social transaction in which he gives something and gets (or expects to get) something in return. The return which he expects from his investment is a *role benefit*, gain, reward, or payoff. It comes to him because of his performance in one or more roles. It, like his investment, may consist of any kind of value which the organization provides him. It may vary in amount, certainty, and other ways. If the organization's payoff of benefits is less than he expects in relation to his total investments, he will bring pressure on it to increase benefits. Or he may reduce his investments to bring them more in balance with his benefits. He may even withdraw from any further involvement with the organization.

The sequence of a person's investments, benefits, and possible actions is shown in Figure 2–3. Although a person's role investments and benefits are not fully quantifiable, for purposes of illustration it is assumed that

[6] Theodore V. Purcell, *Blue Collar Man: Patterns of Dual Allegiance in Industry,* Cambridge, Mass.: Harvard University Press, 1960.
[7] According to Eells and Walton, this is one element of pluralism which Karl Marx could not understand. He perceived only class conflict. See the chapter on "Pluralism" in Richard Eells and Clarence Walton, *Conceptual Foundations of Business,* Homewood, Ill.: Richard D. Irwin, Inc., 1961, pp. 360–379.

Individual	Investment role	Units of investment	Organization	Required units of benefit: a "fair" return from —	Actual units of benefit: a "fair" return from —	Possible action
Need structure	Social	3	A	3	2	Stop relationship
	Civic	5	B	5	7	Satisfaction Perhaps increase investment
	Employee	18	C	18	18	Satisfaction
	Economic	4	D	4	3	Pressures

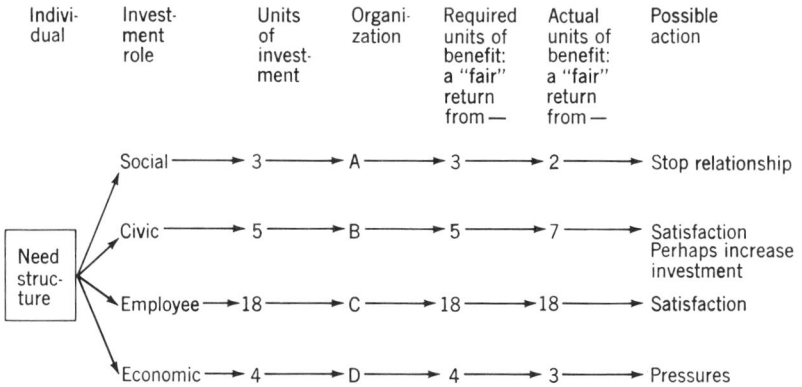

Figure 2–3 An individual's role investments, benefits, and possible actions regarding four organizations.

they are. In Organization A the individual's benefits were inadequate, and he eventually withdrew from the organization. Organization B returned him higher benefits than he expected, so he was satisfied and considered increasing his investment in it. Organization C, the one in which he had the largest investment, returned a fair benefit, but one that was not proportionately as high as Organization B. In Organization D his benefits were not adequate, and he brought pressures to increase them.

A Relatively Open System

The elements of pluralism imply a relatively open system in which there is substantial social exchange among organizations at their points of interface. Some of the modes of interface are cooperation, bargaining, and competition. Both cooperation and conflict are built into the system by the fact that each organization has a specialized interest and constituency to serve. One company president comments, "Coping with pluralistic objectives, most of which are conflicting, has indeed become the *sine qua non* of industrial management." He adds that, although managers will never be able to satisfy all the claimants on business, their constant striving to do so may be their greatest contribution to society.[8]

Diffusion of Power

Since there are many institutions functioning in an open system, pluralism implies a diffusion of power among many decision makers. By means of diffused power, pluralism is "as much opposed to the ambitious pretences of a James Stuart (the king can do no wrong), as it is to the Rousseauian version of democracy (the collectivity can do no wrong)."[9] No power center is completely independent to do exactly as it wishes, but

[8] Raymond H. Mulford, "Pluralism Redefined," *Saturday Review*, Jan. 13, 1968, p. 33.
[9] Eells and Walton, *op. cit.*, 1961, p. 363.

each has some autonomy. This condition suggests that progress is made through communication, innovation, negotiation, compromise, and consensus rather than by monolithic decision making.

Pluralistic systems are thought to be especially innovative and flexible because their multiple areas of power and initiative provide alternative choices to society. The society possesses a capability for continuous renewal, as stated by the first quotation introducing this chapter, and can therefore avoid aging and deterioration. Whether it does do so is dependent on the quality of its leaders and its citizens. Business leadership, therefore, becomes a valuable social asset.

Joint Venture

Since there is diffusion of power, major social institutions such as business are able to marshal sufficient resources to perform their function only by developing a joint venture among a number of groups. That is, groups pool their capabilities and resources to accomplish an objective. The spirit of joint venture is developed by focusing on mutual interests and superordinate goals. Business, for example, is a joint venture of investors, managers, workers, communities, and others. Although these groups offer diverse inputs and expect diverse outputs from the venture, they join together in order to gain additional rewards from organized group effort. For example, the investor seeks more return on investment, greater security of investment, and pride of ownership. The manager seeks status, a feeling of contribution, and self-esteem from a job well done. Without capital and workers he could not manage. The worker seeks an opportunity to use his skill, social satisfactions, and higher pay. Working as an individual without associates, management, and extra capital, he might derive less of these desired benefits. Observe that the rewards expected in joint ventures are not only economic; they usually are also social and psychological. No man—even a poor one—lives by bread alone.

Limited research indicates that it is, indeed, difficult for business to meet the different expectations of those involved with it. A study of ninety-seven small businesses examined their ability to fulfill the needs of the following groups: community, government, customer, supplier, creditor, and owner.[10] There were only small correlations of satisfaction among the groups, and some correlations were negative. Customer satisfaction did correlate positively with supplier and owner satisfactions. Owner and community satisfactions also were positively correlated. The study shows that business cannot maximize for any group, so it adopts a policy of reasonably satisfying several system components.

In summary of this section, pluralism is a complex social system not easily understood; however, some of its major elements are diversity of

[10] Frank Friedlander and Hal Pickle, "Components of Effectiveness in Small Organizations," *Administrative Science Quarterly*, September, 1968, pp. 289–304; and Hal Pickle and Frank Friedlander, "Seven Societal Criteria of Organizational Success," *Personnel Psychology*, Summer, 1967, pp. 165–178.

interests, institutional specialization, multiallegiant man, a relatively open system, diffusion of power, and joint venture.

OPERATION OF A PLURALISTIC SYSTEM

Claimants on Business

In the operation of a pluralistic system, clients are not the only ones who can make claims on a business—or any other organization. Since pluralism is a system relationship, all social units are interconnected, and any unit which believes that its interests are even indirectly affected by business can become a claimant on it. The system relationship gives the unit an "indirect investment" in the business which justifies a claim. Claims are made by such means as publicity, appeal to government, use of influence, and trade-offs with other institutions which are in a more favorable position to bring pressures. An illustration follows.

A lumber company decided to cut certain redwood timber which it had owned for years. Conservationists who were opposed to this action felt that they could exert very little direct pressure on the company, so they chose to work indirectly. They enlisted the support of businessmen in two nearby towns by convincing them that the forest was an important tourist attraction which would become more significant in future years as affluent people spent more money on recreation. They worked with county and state governments to try to have part of the land dedicated as a public recreational area. They also issued news releases about the situation and set up a speaker's bureau to furnish speakers on the subject to any available group.

Claimants may also arise more or less involuntarily, not as a result of organization in advance, but from a series of events which begin to close in on their interests.

George Sykes's home adjoined a farm in a modest subdivision on the edge of a Midwestern city. He assumed that further subdivisions eventually would be developed on the farm. Three years after he bought his property he and his neighbors learned that a national manufacturer had taken a purchase option on the farm and was seeking industrial zoning in order to build a large foundry and forging shop on part of the property. Quickly he and his neighbors organized to prevent the industrial zoning, or as a minimum to get a buffer area of intermediate zoning established on that portion of the farm which was nearest their homes.

Discussions of business issues in the past have tended to focus on business members (such as employees) and other direct clients (such as vendors). Now, however, the indirect claimants on business are getting a larger share of attention. One reason is that society is becoming more urbanized and crowded so that pollution, industrial noise, and similar matters are suddenly becoming critical; in a rural society they were a minimum concern. Another reason is that individuals and institutions have become more specialized and interdependent than they used to be, so more people are affected by business in more ways and more often. A third reason is that our systems way of thinking is providing more evidence of the intricate ways in which business is related with all parts of society.

Social Constraints on Institutions

Since pluralistic institutions have autonomy, social constraints are required to integrate them into the system and check unbridled power. The most evident constraint is law, both legislative and administrative. Business is especially affected by administrative law, which consists of decisions and rules made by regulatory commissions and administrators, such as the Interstate Commerce Commission, Federal Communications Commission, Internal Revenue Service, and National Labor Relations Board.

Another constraint is the countervailing power of other institutions which respond to excesses by increasing opposing pressures. This means that the institutions partly regulate each other as a result of their diffused power.

The cultural values and norms established by society are also powerful constraints. Even though most are unwritten, they become known and accepted ways of relating to one another and doing business. Sometimes these norms are formalized, such as professional standards and the concepts of social responsibility and constitutionalism, which are discussed in a later chapter.

A constraint sometimes overlooked is the freedom of participants to withdraw their support of an institution. This always stands in the background as a threat. For example, if customers go elsewhere and better workers take other jobs, a business cannot function effectively.

Good Intentions Are an Inadequate Constraint

One point is certain. Good intentions alone are not a sufficient constraint on institutions in a pluralistic society. Some of society's most autocratic institutions and destructive actions have developed out of high purposes. Noble objectives sometimes deteriorate into cults or into obsessions about the interests of certain groups, completely disregarding the interests of others. Leaders believe so strongly in their noble purposes that they assume they are absolutely right. The result is that they adopt a *two-valued orientation,* meaning that they see a situation as all right or all wrong, and neglect the intermediate areas between the extremes. Their obsession with one group or situation leads to social division and ignoble purposes in the manner of George Orwell's *Animal Farm:* "All men are equal, but some are more equal than others."

The Senate Agriculture Committee, for example, held hearings concerning farm labor, during which it was reported that oranges and lettuce were rotting in fields because farm labor was not available. Then a spokesman for a religious-action group testified: "As to the precious lettuce rotting in the fields, I can't squeeze out even a single tear of grief.

I think people are more important than lettuce."[11] Granted that people are more important than lettuce, does this fact make his view "right" and that of the produce growers "wrong"? Did the speaker recognize more than a two-valued orientation in this complex economic and social problem? Did he show concern for people who grow lettuce and people who want to eat it, or was he concerned only for those who harvest it? Did he recognize the waste of human effort already invested that occurs when produce is unharvested? Did he recognize the connection of human wants with gross national product, productivity, and waste? Did he honor equally the employment desires of all people?

Even though the motives of an individual or group are indisputably exalted, this does not make them reasonable or accurate in their interpretations of business and its environment. Business relationships are intricate, complex systems in which a two-valued orientation rarely applies, and we shall try to take a broader viewpoint in this book—but we hasten to add that we do think people more important than lettuce! We also believe business cannot dispense utopia. Business can, however, help create conditions which contribute to human progress. That alone is a mission of great significance. Its successful performance will mean that we will have socially responsible managers exercising business statesmanship, no matter what we call them or think about them.

Does Pluralism Serve the Public Interest?

Although most analysts agree that pluralism exists, there is much less agreement about whether it effectively serves the public interest. There are allegations of concentrated economic power and inadequate constraints on power use. Groups often make trade-offs for mutual accommodation to each other's interests with minimum regard for public interest. As the saying goes, "You scratch my back, and I'll scratch yours."[12]

There are also charges that the psychological focus of pluralism is undesirable because it emphasizes power as a means of accomplishment rather than ability. In addition, it is suggested that diverse interest groups make it difficult for society to marshal its resources toward unified objectives and that energies are wasted in friction among the groups.

Each of these allegations has some truth in it, but there are also strong opposing views. One detailed analysis shows that dominance by an economic elite is an ideological fiction not supported by the facts.[13] It is also shown that one of the strengths of pluralism is that it offers more diffusion of power than other social options do. Though there is emphasis on power, cultural constraints keep the institutions focused on the functional power "to do," which is a useful social power compared with the less desirable power "over" others which some social systems emphasize.

[11] United Press International news release, *Arizona Republic*, Jan. 17, 1965, p. 4-A.
[12] Significant and popular historical examples have been A. A. Berle, Jr., and Gardiner C. Means, *The Modern Corporation and Private Property*, New York: The Macmillan Company, 1932; and C. Wright Mills, *The Power Elite*, Fair Lawn, N.J.: Oxford University Press, 1956.
[13] Arnold M. Rose, *The Power Structure*, New York: Oxford University Press, 1967.

Finally, although friction does exist, there is growing evidence that some friction stimulates innovation and keeps a system more flexible for change. Since all social systems have faults as well as benefits, the question is not whether pluralism has faults. Of course it has. The more accurate question is: Does the system maintain the greatest net balance of advantages over disadvantages compared with alternative systems?

Criteria for Appraising Worthiness

There are a number of useful criteria for appraising institutional worthiness and effectiveness in a social system. These criteria are culture-bound in the sense that they have arisen partly out of the Judeo-Christian ethic of American society; however, they have a broad base of worldwide support. They will be mentioned at points of application throughout this book.

In essence the most desirable social institutions are those which provide an optimum combination of the following criteria:

1 An open system. Systems theory suggests that an open system provides free flow of information among components of the system, and it maintains flexibility by providing an optimum number of social choices. Both information and flexibility are essential for viability in a world of change.

2 Participative organization. Reasonable opportunity is provided for members to participate in maintaining and changing the system. This is psychologically desirable to stimulate motivation and commitment. It is also the essential element of social and political freedom.

3 Productivity. This means net outputs of any type which are valued more than inputs. It forces institutions to emphasize capable performance instead of bureaucratic power. Unless each institution provides outputs over inputs in the long run, it is wasting society's limited resources.

4 Distributive justice. This is a reasonable distribution of outputs to persons and groups in relation to their inputs. It provides a sense of fairness, and it rewards those who are willing to invest their social resources.

5 A power-responsibility balance. Those who exercise power have responsibility and accountability to society for their use of that power. This encourages the just use of power and provides a criterion for reallocating power when it is not responsibly used.

These five criteria are certainly not all of those necessary for evaluating institutions, but they do constitute five of the more desirable long-run values which society expects from its institutions.

Does Pluralism Have a Social Ideal?

For long-run viability the mere fact that a system exists and works satisfactorily is not enough. It needs to represent a social ideal or mission toward which all can work. Critics say that pluralism is merely American pragmatism represented by a pragmatic balance of power rather than a definable ideal.[14] Although pluralism is often pragmatic in its *operations,* its *philosophy* represents an open system of search for social truth. Expressed in a single word, *truth* is the utopian ideal of pluralism. Social truth arises from looking at an issue from many points of view and then delicately balancing the values in those points of view. As C. West Churchman explains in his award-winning book, truth in the social sciences is reached only by viewing something from as many points of view as possible, whereas physical science has truth only when there is one unerring, proven view of reality.[15] This fundamental ideal of pluralism should not be underestimated. Pluralism provides a view of the whole system, instead of leaving society bogged in subsystems such as economics, humanism, management science, and law. It seeks to "tell the whole story" and come closer to the whole truth. Though the pluralist ideal cannot be reached perfectly, it is there; and it is a key reason why pluralism is achieving growing viability in this generation.

The pragmatic operational modes of pluralism, such as an open system, are designed to bring to issues as many different points of view as possible. Also, the organizational form which establishes multiallegiant man forces him to broaden his personal outlook. As he evaluates his different role investments in separate institutions, his thinking broadens to include the points of view represented. By diffusing power, society also broadens the base of inputs into the system and tries to assure that no institution will monopolize knowledge in the system. The result is both a broader society and broader individuals, hopefully bringing more knowledge and viewpoints into the system so that truth may be more nearly achieved.

The ideal of social truth is a worthy one in the history of man; therefore the social truth sought by pluralism can hardly be dismissed as mere pragmatism.

SUMMARY

Pluralism defines the environmental system within which business operates. Many autonomous interest groups influence business either as direct clients or indirect claimants, and, in turn, business influences them. Major elements of pluralism are diversity of interests, institutional specialization, multiallegiant man with role investments in many institutions, a relatively open system, diffusion of power, and joint venture. Its social ideal is truth achieved by examining issues from many points of view. Although pluralism has its weaknesses, it displays viability as an open, flexible system, with a capability for self-renewal. In any case, it is the current business environment which businessmen need to understand in order to perform their roles as leaders.

[14] William G. Scott, "Technology and Organization Government: A Speculative Inquiry into the Functionality of Management Creeds," *Academy of Management Journal,* September, 1968, pp. 301–313.
[15] C. West Churchman, *Challenge to Reason,* New York: McGraw-Hill Book Company, 1968. This book won an Academy of Management book award in 1968.

STUDY GUIDES FOR INTERPRETATION OF THIS CHAPTER

1 The beginning of this chapter described a corporation's efforts to develop certain ranch land. As the corporation's local manager on the site of this development, how would you respond to each of the groups mentioned? Why?

2 Define social vertigo, pluralism, business claimant, multiallegiant man, role investment, and two-valued orientation.

3 Explain each of the major elements of a pluralistic social system.

4 From your own point of view evaluate the usefulness of the five criteria suggested for appraising social systems.

5 Discuss the social ideal of pluralism and how it is applied operationally.

PROBLEMS
"AN OPEN LETTER TO THE FARMERS"

In a midwestern state the farmers typically burned field stubble after harvest of a certain crop. The crop was a major economic contributor to communities in some parts of the state. During one summer, unfavorable weather combined with heavy burning to produce a pall of heavy smoke which hung over half of the state for two weeks. It irritated eyes and lungs and at times was so thick that it interfered with highway traffic. Complaints mounted from highway users, medical groups, city persons, and others. Legislators became alarmed and introduced a bill banning field burning. Although the legislation failed, it created animosity between city dwellers and farmers.

In a rural town of less than five thousand population, a group of businessmen became concerned because they felt this animosity had harmed business relations with farmers. Working through a chamber of commerce committee they arranged to place an advertisement in the local newspaper. It read in part as follows:

AN OPEN LETTER TO THE FARMERS
From our conversations with other citizens of the community, we know that those of us listed below represent only a fraction of the people who share our feelings on the recent field-burning legislation.

We sympathize with you. . . . We not only sympathize—we stand ready to help in any way we can to bring about a workable solution to your dilemma. Granted: Air pollution must be eliminated. But we feel that lightning-fast legislation, singling out and virtually closing an entire industry, is not the answer. Especially when no alternate solution is offered.

Our silence in these past weeks has not meant that your city neighbors were not aware of your problem. Or that we "don't care" about its solution. Perish the thought! You are our neighbors—our friends—our relatives! Our destinies are intertied by bonds of understanding that go back many generations. We cannot and WILL NOT forget that agriculture has been the foundation-stone and backbone of this community.

Names of many of the town's major businesses appeared at the bottom of the advertisement. One of the names was that of a statewide bank which had a branch in the town. No person at the bank had prior knowledge of the advertisement, but its name was included routinely by a clerk because it was a member of the town's chamber of commerce, even though the name "chamber of commerce" did not appear in the advertisement.

When the advertisement appeared, many local citizens protested to the branch manager that the bank was "taking sides," and some threatened to withdraw their accounts. Other protests were made to executives in the home office. Some protests came from influential bank clients who represented interests favoring the legislation. Others complained about the bank's lack of neutrality.

1 Appraise the objectives and methods used by the advertisers and relate them to pluralism.

2 Discuss the manner in which pluralism operated as a part of the bank's environment in this episode. Who were the interest groups involved? Was public interest served?

THE BAN ON IMPORTED AUTOMOBILES

During the 1960s imported automobiles gained an increasing proportion of the market in the United States. The United Steelworkers union estimated that 20,000 steelworkers lost their jobs because of imported steel and steel products. The steel industry as a whole experienced relatively hard times and low profit margins. There was a feeling in the industry and the union that more should be done to encourage use of steel products made in the United States.

On January 1, 1970, a large branch works of one of the nation's top steel producers announced on bulletin boards and in widely circulated memos that no imported automobiles would be allowed inside the plant gates. The company said that visitors, vendors, and others who drove imported automobiles to the plant would be provided with transportation inside the plant if necessary. A company spokesman said the action was taken because the plant had "a considerable stake in the continued success of domestic auto companies, which are its best customers."

Production workers were not affected by the ban, because they parked their cars in a company lot outside the main plant area; however, a local official of the United Steelworkers said he agreed with the company's action. He added, "We'd like to see all foreign-made cars banned from the U. S."

An observer added that the idea was not new, because manufacturers and unions in the ailing hat industry had insisted for years that those doing business with them must arrive wearing hats.[16]

1 Appraise the company decision—and union agreement—in terms of pluralism. Select the major investment groups in this decision and identify the role investments of each.

2 Was the public interest served in this decision? Explain.

[16] "Foreign Cars Get Bumped in Birmingham," *Business Week,* Jan. 10, 1970, p. 29.

CHAPTER 3

THE BUSINESS ROLE IN THE SOCIAL SYSTEM

> The pluralistic role of profit-making and of social involvement, then, seems to be an inevitable condition of the future. But making the two factors jibe is tricky.
>
> BOB R. DORSEY[1]

> *The modern corporation has evolved into a social as well as an economic institution.* Without losing sight of its need to make a profit, it has concerns, ideals, and responsibilities which go far beyond the profit motive.
>
> THEODORE C. SORENSEN[2]

A ragged group of student activists was pressing hard against the police barricades across the street from a San Francisco hotel. A trained tactical police force separated them from the hotel itself. The students were chanting revolutionary slogans and shouting accusations at businessmen inside the hotel who were attending a meeting of the Fourth International Industrial Conference sponsored by Stanford Research Institute and the National Industrial Conference Board. Those attending included presidents or chairmen of over one hundred major United States corporations and heads of over fifty of the largest companies of other nations such as Italy, Mexico, Belgium, Germany, and Sweden. They talked about their past mistakes and their long-run obligations to society.

Outside the hotel the activists wanted to change the world. "You are the enemy," one of them shouted at the businessmen. Inside the hotel the businessmen also spoke of changing the world, and their focus was the same as that of the students—meeting human and social needs. "The reformist fervor permeated the meeting," a reporter observed. Although no businessman was heard to return the accusation, "You are the enemy," one of them did comment, "I find this particularly ironic at a time when business and the general run of college students have moved closer together than ever before in their desire to satisfy the wants and

---

[1] Bob R. Dorsey, "Making the Future Our Business," *Advanced Management Journal,* July, 1968, p. 8.
[2] Theodore C. Sorensen, "Public Obligations and the Private Corporation," *Saturday Review,* May 14, 1966, p. 24. Italics in original.

needs of people the world over."[3] Were the top businessmen and students really enemies? Or were they allies whose common ground was not yet recognized by the students? The students wanted action. The business leaders were men of action on an international basis.

Meanwhile, in another city (although probably something similar was happening in San Francisco), a laborer received a postcard saying that he could win some valuable prizes by calling at the office of a high-pressure sales firm. He and his wife and two young children arrived at the office about 7 P.M. and were told that they would have to submit to a sales presentation on housewares before they could receive their prizes. Then for the next four and one-half hours they were bombarded with high-pressure sales pitches by two men. Sometime during the marathon sales session they were given steak knives and promised other inducements if they would sign an installment contract for nearly $500 worth of merchandise, much of which they did not need. As the hour approached midnight, their resistance was so low they finally signed. The salesman placed the goods in the car trunk, and they were still there a few days later when the husband called the firm to ask it to take back the merchandise. The company refused; it had already assigned the contract to a finance company.

The two incidents illustrate many factors concerning business's role in the social system: a wide variety of business practice, differences between large international corporations and small businesses, conflict and misunderstanding concerning business's role, evolving viewpoints of this role, and difficulties in getting high-level ideals translated into lower-level business operations. This chapter compares the traditional economic role of business with the new social role which seems to be emerging. Business capabilities for this new role are discussed along with the potential risks and gains involved. Functional analysis is presented as a concept for evaluating which activities can be performed better by business than by other institutions in a pluralistic social system.

The incident of high-pressure salesmanship is not a pleasant one.[4] Certainly business has its share of shady characters operating on the fringes of acceptable behavior or even in violation of law, but the same observations apply to other institutions. All human institutions are subject to the frailties of human nature; however, a description of these frailties does not explain the basic role of any institution in society.

THE TRADITIONAL BUSINESS ROLE

Institutions Serve Social Purposes

All institutions are tools of society. They are established by society, and in the long run they continue to exist with the consent of society. Each

[3] "San Francisco, 1969," *Forbes*, Oct. 15, 1969.
[4] The final results were not as negative as they appear, because a pluralistic society provided other alternatives for the laborer. He appealed to a legal aid society which threatened legal action. This caused the sales firm to cancel his contract and take back the merchandise before any money had been paid. However, his long-run attitudes toward business deteriorated as a result of this experience.

institution is viewed as a social asset for performing some purposeful, constructive role. These facts do not prevent unethical behavior, poor quality, or straying from goals (even with the best of intentions); nevertheless, the social role remains to guide the institution's actions.

An institution's social role is not forever rigid. It will gradually evolve over a period of time in response to human needs. It may change its way of working with people, its manner of relating to other organizations, the activities it performs, and in a host of other ways. All of these changes relate to its attempt to meet human needs and remain viable in the system. As it operates, people in society are evaluating it according to certain criteria, such as those mentioned in Chapter 2: an open system, participative, productive, just, and balancing responsibility with power. These criteria may also change, initiating strong pressures on the institution to amend its activities to conform more successfully to the new criteria. In this dynamic manner, traditional practices give way to new practices, which in turn eventually become traditional and give way to even newer practices. These conditions describe the evolution of business's role, as well as the role of other institutions.

A Traditional Focus on Economic Productivity and Profit

The traditional focus of business has been almost exclusively economic. All other activities were strictly sidelines to be dabbled with when they became urgent through indirect effects on profit. This role has been strongly supported by the doctrines of classical economics which argued that, through strict emphasis on economic values in a free market, maximum human benefits would result because goods and services would be produced efficiently. These goods and services were desperately needed by a poor and hungry society.

Both theory and practice concentrated on economic profit as the ultimate measure of a firm's success in its role. In this model, economic values were the only ones accounted for and owners primarily provided the capital to produce these values, so emphasis was mostly upon obligations to ownership, rather than to other business claimants. This heavy emphasis on one client group and on one measure of performance caused questions to be raised about business performance as people began to think more in terms of a systems concept.

In reality, few people in society would deny that business should be "profitable," provided this term is interpreted to mean net gains of all types in relation to inputs of all types. Obviously business or any other institution wastes social resources unless it can provide outputs greater than inputs; and the greater the net gain, the better it is for society. The principal issue in modern industrial society, and the key to the evolving role of business, is differing expectations of what kinds of outputs should be emphasized and what groups should receive them. People want the outputs, but they want them in the form of broad social benefits along with economic profits.

This new broader demand for general benefits poses a new role for business. The result is that business managers, as the responsible agents of business, find themselves answering to many types of investors having both economic and noneconomic expectations. The idea of pure competition and maximizing economic profit appears most workable on college blackboards! As soon as the systems concept is made a part of the business environment, economic profit becomes only one of many values produced by the system. The question is: Does business have the leadership and flexibility to respond successfully to these new expectations?

On the other hand, economic profit cannot be rationalized out of the system, because this opposite extreme would equally ignore the systems concept. Economic deprivation and want in much of the world are evidence that economic profit is a social need. It is needed as a valid measure of productive use of capital, a criterion for allocating resources, and a just benefit for economic investors whether they are state citizens or private investors. For example, a significant international development has been Russian experimentation with the Liberman Plan starting in the 1960s. Russian economist Yevsei Liberman argued that industry should be judged at least partially by its return on capital, and a few factories have been freed from central planning to pursue this "novel" measure of efficiency. Apparently the Russian economy was deficient in this type of social measure and needed to give it more recognition in order to serve public needs.

The systems concept implies that what is needed is a balanced view which recognizes the need for economic profits along with social benefits (in a sense, social "profits") for those affected by business. Thus, it is appropriate to refer to a *balanced profit concept,* a *socially profitable business,* or a *socially beneficial business.* All of these phrases mean that a business is providing both social and economic outputs greater than inputs in a manner which reasonably serves the expectations of claimants on business.

AN EVOLVING BUSINESS ROLE

As society changed, it was inevitable that business's role within it would need to be reconsidered. In advanced nations, for example, business's enormous success in producing goods and services led to widespread material affluence. Precisely because of business's success, economic output took a lower priority on the scale of social needs. People began to ask, "Since business has been so successful in meeting our economic needs, could we expect similar success if we gave it a major role in solving some of our pressing social problems such as urban blight?" They also asked, "Has business's concentrated drive for economic results contributed, either knowingly or unknowingly, to the social problems which have top priority today?"

Some Insights from Systems Thinking

A systems framework has been particularly helpful to businessmen in perceiving their broader socioeconomic role. Businessmen feel more comfortable working in a rational analytical framework, and systems concepts provide this type of framework. Businessmen are beginning to see that they cannot isolate their business in an economic cocoon because they have a systems interface with society. They realize that a healthy society is necessary for healthy business. If there is social decay, business will tend to decay also; therefore, poor home environments and crime in the streets are likely to be reflected in employee performance and crime in business.

Systems insights also help businessmen see the extended social effects of regular business activities. For example, when businesses move into new communities they now cooperate more with other agencies to assure that facilities such as roads, private housing, schools, and cultural centers are available. They want to be sure that their arrival does not overload community facilities and that their employees will have a desirable community in which to live.

An example of systems thinking, in this instance without operating cost to the firm, is an isolated mining company which built a hydro-electric dam to supply its mines with power. It owned all the adjoining property and water rights, so it could have closed the property to public use. Looking beyond its own needs to those of its community, it saw that the lake was needed as a recreational area. Working with government, it built roads, picnic areas, and boat ramps and opened the area to the public for recreation. Private businesses were given leases to establish boat docks, snack bars, and related service facilities. Income from the leases paid for maintenance of the entire property.

Profit Making and Social Involvement

The preceding discussion suggests that modern business's role is evolving into a combination of profit making and social involvement, as indicated by the two quotations introducing this chapter. If this is happening, it is a major change in business's role. It is an age of discontinuity, not routine change. It may cause a reallocation of activities which are appropriate to business enterprise. If so, the changes which are occurring will be of major social and political significance. There will be both opportunities and dangers for business. New organization structures and new reward criteria may be required in the firm in order to recognize social contributions along with economic ones.[5]

As a minimum there is some recognition of the influence of social goals on business decision making. The real question is not whether social goals will influence business decisions and cost. Instead, the question is how much will this influence be? One author gives social and economic goals equal rank in decision making. He states, *"To realize its full promise in the world of tomorrow, American business and industry—or, at least, the vast portion of it—will have to make social goals as central*

[5] See the special issue of *Daedalus,* Journal of the American Academy of Arts and Sciences, on "Perspectives on Business," Winter, 1969; and Elliott Haynes, "Executives Wanted: Innovators and Risk Takers Only Should Apply," *Columbia Journal of World Business,* May–June, 1969, pp. 10–12.

to its decisions as economic goals; and leadership in our corporations will increasingly recognize this responsibility and accept it."[6]

Reasons for Business's Social Involvement

Whatever the extent of business's social involvement, there must be some reasons for it, because it appears to be happening with the consent and even at the request of society. The first reason is a negative one. It comes from the failures of other institutions. Many people are frustrated with these failures. They have poured massive resources into public education, but school dropouts, marginal literacy, and student aimlessness remain. (Can business give meaning to a person's education?) For decades they have provided resources for sociologists, psychologists, and others to care for criminals and take corrective action, but the crime rate increases and penitentiaries remain places of horror. (Can business reduce criminality and reform criminals through job structure?) They have seen cities deteriorate under the leadership of urban government, public welfare, and public housing. (Business can build automobiles. Can it also build cities?) They have seen social programs degenerate into politics and graft. (Surely business can promote the better men and keep the books straight, or can it?)

Whatever the justification for these failures, some people who are frustrated by them are turning to business. Viewpoints are along the following lines:

"Give business a try. Maybe they can come up with some new ideas."
"Let business have a role. They couldn't do any worse!"
"Who else is left? We've tried all the others!"

Many of these comments are exaggerated and not very flattering to business. They are made more out of desperation than reason. Many of the people who make them have exorbitant expectations of perfection in human institutions, so business will probably fail in their eyes as the other institutions have done. On the other hand, the issue which they raise remains as a nagging question: Have we performed poorly with some social problems precisely because we have not used business's capabilities for solving them?

Business Capabilities for Social Involvement

The other reasons for business involvement are more positive because they relate to apparent capabilities which business has. One reason is capability by association. Since business has had rather phenomenal success in economic areas, perhaps it could be similarly effective in social areas. But will economic capabilities transfer to social areas? Another reason, and a significant one, is that business does have a substantial pool of management talent, functional expertise, and material

[6] Sol M. Linowitz, "Public Affairs: The Demanding Seventies," *Looking Ahead*, p. 2, National Planning Association, May, 1966. Italics in original.

resources. Probably it is without peer in all three of these resources. Institutions that work in social areas seem to be especially deficient in management talent, and business is known worldwide for its investment in this resource.

An additional reason is that business values focus on productive increase of resources, while many other institutions give more emphasis to conserving and distributing existing resources. For certain social problems productive use of limited resources is grossly needed. Perhaps business's productivity-and-growth orientation can make a contribution.

Business also is known for its capacity to innovate and introduce change. It is flexible, willing to experiment, and less bound by bureaucracy than many institutions. One analyst of business and society comments, "Change may well be the most significant output of a business system."[7] Another observes that among all social institutions business is the one which exists to make and manage change. Most other institutions exist primarily to slow it down.[8] Innovation is sorely needed regarding many social problems. Could business innovate socially as well as economically?

A further reason for business involvement is that it has environmental conditions favorable to the solution of some kinds of social problems. Its work is reality-oriented, so the disadvantaged student who could not tolerate the abstractions of public school may find that business gives him a feeling of accomplishment. Those who are semiliterate may want to improve in reading, writing, and mathematics, since having a job gives them purpose in learning. Similarly, on the job a minority employee may for the first time in his life feel that he is an equal on a team. Business as an employer can provide a climate for action, reality, teamwork, purpose, and a feeling of doing something useful.

Finally, business is especially capable in dealing with underdevelopment internationally. Politically it is more of a free agent than government; hence it is less bound by protocol and bureaucracy. It can be flexible and productive. This is one area where its capabilities are proven. If governments could accomplish what private business has already accomplished in tying nations together culturally, socially, and economically, it would be hailed as a near utopia in political progress. Pan American Airways, for example, can establish operating bases and effective business procedures in nation after nation, and then transport people among nations, indirectly achieving social interchange and cultural understanding as a part of its *business* activities.

Sears, Roebuck, and Company, a major retailer, may quietly achieve greatly improved retailing and employment practices in a community, and it may encourage fast development of local industry to supply it with quality products—something which neither *local* government nor a foreign government would be able to do because of political interferences. Similar comments could be made about International Telephone and Tele-

[7] Joseph W. McGuire, "The *Finalité* of Business," *California Management Review*, Summer, 1966, p. 92.
[8] Peter F. Drucker, *The Age of Discontinuity: Guidelines to Our Changing Society*, New York: Harper & Row, Publishers, Incorporated, 1968, p. 236.

graph Company, Sony Corporation, Unilever, Shell, Nestlé International, and a host of other businesses. All have been successful in creating wealth for more people outside their home nation, improving social interchange, improving productivity, and bringing world cultural understanding.

Risks of Social Involvement

Businessmen perhaps should be flattered that so many people are turning to them for aid with social problems; however, there are many risks involved. The risks exist for society as well as for business. Businessmen are not sure how far they should commit themselves and their firms. A major reason is that they may lack the perceptions and skills to do the job. Their outlook is primarily economic and their skills are the same. Can they broaden their outlook and will their skills transfer? Can business really do the job? Is it better equipped than government and other institutions?

Since many persons have high expectations of business, in working with social issues it will be difficult to live up to expectations, and failure will provoke strong disenchantment with business. From business's point of view it might be better not to risk a chance of lowered public image. Does not business have enough to do in meeting the economic expectations of society? There is, additionally, an uneasy feeling that many of the problems people would assign to business are not really solvable, which would make business the scapegoat of this social exchange.

Another risk is that involvement in social goals might dilute business's emphasis on economic productivity, divide the interests of its leaders, and weaken business in the marketplace, with the result that it would accomplish poorly *both* economic and social roles. The result could be that business would lose economic powers and functions to other institutions. Perhaps business's involvement should extend only as far into society as its economic interests reach. In this way it will not be out of its area of capability, yet it will still be broadening its viewpoint in terms of social implications of its decisions. Following is an example.

A recreation equipment manufacturer decided to manufacture and market mobile homes. It had the resources, know-how, and market outlets to do the job. In examining the extended effects of this new product, it discovered that mobile home parks would be needed by purchasers of its mobile homes. Further study showed that mobile home parks were in a stage similar to motels thirty years earlier. A large number of them were small, unsightly, poorly managed, and lacking in sewage and other facilities. More mobile homes might aggravate existing conditions.

Rather than back away from the situation, the firm did begin manufacturing mobile homes, but it invested even more resources in developing and managing large mobile home parks which were attractive community assets and efficiently managed. They had underground power lines, sewage facilities, recreational areas, and adequate privacy for each homesite. These parks were profitable operations for the firm. They were also community improvements.

A further risk, related to the preceding one of divided interests, is the simple matter of economic costs of social involvement. As presently constituted, many social goals do not pay their own way in an economic sense; therefore, someone must pay for them. Business has very substantial economic resources, but these resources will quickly dwindle into economic impotence unless they are self-renewing. Although business can invest small amounts of its resources in social obligations, as it has done in the past, it cannot really commit major economic resources unless these resources will be renewed during the term of the commitment.

A typical solution to this problem is for government to require business to meet certain standards, thus passing social costs to the consumer. Another approach is for government or other institutions to pay business for its assistance toward specific goals, such as training of hardcore unemployed. The reasoning is that this same social task will be an economic cost to government, but business can perform the task more effectively, so the public interest is served by paying business to perform it. A more creative approach is for business to find ways to link economic returns with social goals. This has been done with literacy training of one's own employees, pollution control through by-product recovery, and reclaiming blighted areas for homesites and recreational use. With business's creative ability, it will probably generate more of this kind of integration of social and economic interests.

An additional risk is that business social involvement will lack a broad base of support from others in society. Although many persons wish business to be more involved, others oppose the idea. There is lack of agreement among the general public, among intellectuals,[9] and even among businessmen themselves. Some feel that social activities combined with economic activities will give business an excessive concentration of social power. Some are opposed to business in general, and consequently they oppose any extension of its activities. Others philosophically support pluralism and believe that business involvement in social areas will give it further powers which will erode the institutional division of powers now existing in pluralism. Regardless of the reasons, the fact that there is divided support for business social involvement means that it will operate somewhat in a hostile environment which could hamper its effectiveness in social areas. In social affairs it will have even more public visibility in its glass house than it does in economic affairs.

Gains from Social Involvement

To offset the risks, there are many gains which can be expected from business involvement in social issues. Through involvement business can expect to broaden its own outlook and gain maturity as an institution. This maturity should be a long-run asset to business. Assuming reasonable success in its broader role, business will improve its public image and broaden its base of support.

[9] For example, see Edward S. Mason (ed.), *The Corporation in Modern Society*, Cambridge, Mass.: Harvard University Press, 1959.

To the extent that business can improve society, it establishes a better environment for its own operations. Its recruits will be better educated and more capable. It will have a better community, freer of pollution, crime, and blight, one which allows its employees to come to work with fewer frustrations and "chips on their shoulders." Reduction of social problems should also reduce burdens on government, causing a possible reduction in taxes and even a reduction in detailed, expensive government regulation of business in social areas. There are also some areas of social involvement that business will be creative enough to make as economically profitable as traditional business has been. Even with unusual success, not all of these gains are likely to occur; however, each stands as a challenge and an opportunity for business.

Based upon social needs, business capabilities, and the risks and gains of business involvement, it appears certain that business will become more active in social aspects of its environment. Pressures are very strong because society needs all resources and skills that are available. There is grave danger that business will be persuaded to overcommit itself. In spite of business's capabilities, there is abundant evidence that far too much is expected and even demanded of business. In the system "everything is related to everything else"; so there are no simple problems, and few of them yield to low-cost solutions. Business's toughest job in social areas may be convincing the public of its limitations.

FUNCTIONAL ANALYSIS TO DETERMINE AREAS OF BUSINESS ACTIVITY

One reason for social involvement is simply that, compared with other institutions, business has resources and capabilities which make it a better institution for certain social purposes. For the same reason, in some other areas business will be less involved or relatively uninvolved. In job training, housing, and minority employment, for example, it is capable of taking a leading role. In education its role may be substantial in areas such as vocational education, but on the whole its role probably will remain secondary to government's.

Functional Analysis

Since business will have variable involvement in different social needs, how will the extent of its involvement be determined? One helpful approach is *functional analysis,* which compares social priorities with institutional capabilities for serving them and then assigns the most important priorities to those institutions most capable of performing them. In this manner society should be able to make the best use of its resources by using the specialized capabilities of different institutions. This process supports pluralism by dividing social tasks among institutions. It also means that no single institution "owns" any function for all time. Situations may change, making other institutions more capable within the framework of the new conditions. Following is an example.

In 1968 Congress made the Federal National Mortgage Association (nicknamed "Fannie Mae") into a private corporation after it had been a government agency for thirty years. Fannie Mae was founded during depression years to feed money into the mortgage market at a time when business was weak and unable to do so. Eventually financial business became stronger and government processes became more cumbersome, so Fannie Mae was transferred to private ownership with some government ties.

A report one year later indicated that the transfer, although still incomplete, had proved quite satisfactory for all concerned. Fannie Mae had streamlined operations, improved efficiency, and increased profitability so much that its stock price rose vigorously. It went through its first functional test successfully; in the credit pinch of 1969, it was able to feed more money into the mortgage market than it had been able to do in a similar pinch in 1966 when it was a government agency. In summary, "The career of the one-time government girl, Fannie Mae, now that she has turned to private enterprise, is proving an eye-popping success."[10]

A movement in the opposite direction occurred early in United States history when there were many private toll roads. Gradually it became evident that the need for personal transportation could be better served by tax-supported free public roads, so they became the predominant form of highway. Private industry, however, continued to build most of the roads because it appeared to be functionally more efficient and free of political encumbrances.

The Long-run View of History

When history is viewed in terms of centuries rather than years, the transfer of functions among institutions appears to be normal instead of revolutionary. It is the means by which society relates new conditions to institutional capabilities. Medical services originally were provided by spiritualists and witch doctors. Gradually they became a concern of religious orders, charitable institutions, government, and the physician operating as an individual professional person. In recent years government and large business are assuming more dominant roles. Hospitals are being managed by business-oriented administrators, rather than physicians. Large business is establishing franchised nursing homes. (Compare these with the alternatives of a county poor farm or public mental institution for senile persons fifty years ago. Which is likely to be more effective today?) And even individual physicians are now organizing into medical corporations with their associates.

In the area of employment, 200 years ago employees were primarily the concern of their employers. Often the relationship was personal, and sometimes it was paternalistic. Gradually government assumed more functions in this area. Now both government and business share this function with labor unions.

A classic example of changed conditions which respond to functional analysis is postal service. Centuries ago government was clearly the

[10] "Privacy Becomes Fannie Mae," *Business Week,* Aug. 30, 1969, p. 44.

proper institution to operate postal service, although there were exceptions, such as the famed Pony Express of the American West which existed for eighteen months. The power of the state was necessary to maintain privacy of personal communication and to protect mail from highwaymen and pillage. The service was also a necessary activity of government in order to maintain control and coordination among its separated branches. Official documents had to be transported securely. Today, however, the postal service has become a vast business organization in competition with other communication businesses. It is trying to operate like a business, while remaining fettered to political and bureaucratic restrictions. To keep viable it needs massive amounts of capital which it cannot get through the political machinery, and electronic breakthroughs now offer economical alternative means of communication. These changing conditions caused a presidential commission to recommend in 1968 that the United States Post Office be reorganized into a semipublic business free of political controls. Two generations ago this recommendation would have been considered radicalism and political heresy.

A major development in the mix of business and government functions was a sharp swing in the 1960s toward a larger business role in functions that traditionally were considered in government's domain. This swing developed in Europe as well as the United States.[11] The Director of Studies at the Royal Institute of International Affairs in London comments, "One has the impression nowadays that the dialogue between the corporation and the state consists largely of a simple assertion by the former: 'Anything you can do, I can do better.' And the claim is widely conceded by the public, indeed by many of the servants of the state itself. This is a remarkable reversal of roles compared with two or three decades ago."[12]

Criteria for Functional Analysis

In assessing which institutions are the better ones for performing functions in a pluralistic social system, a number of criteria may be used. Following are several important ones.

1 Social effectiveness—predicted satisfactions of clients and others concerning benefits
2 Economic efficiency—predicted performance of an institution's function without waste of resources
3 Resources—depth of resources available, alternative uses for those resources, and need for new resources if new functions are performed
4 Innovative and creative capacity; flexibility
5 Capacity to move with deliberate speed, without delay

[11] For example, see the discussion of denationalization of Volkswagen and other firms in Germany in James C. Baker, "Popular Capitalism through 'Peoples Shares' in Germany," *Columbia Journal of World Business*, March–April, 1969, pp. 63–67.
[12] Andrew Shonfield, "Business in the Twenty-first Century," in *Daedalus, op. cit.*, p. 191.

6 Predicted negative by-products—
a Community, economic, and other dislocations caused by the institution's taking a function
b Risks to the institution's survival and viability caused by its new activity

These criteria may be illustrated by a brief comparison of small business and large corporations to determine the probable extent of their social involvement. Large business has a capacity to move with deliberate speed in terms of carefully reasoned plans, long-run cash flow, and professional management. It also has a depth of resources probably unparalleled in modern history. Although these resources have alternative economic uses, they are flexible enough for partial diversion if social priorities dictate this and if ways are devised to renew these resources as social functions are performed. Further, the economic role of large business particularly qualifies it to work with large and economically related social priorities, such as urban housing and job training.

Small business, on the other hand, has limited resources which are more likely to confine it to local projects and those of smaller dimensions (although not necessarily of lesser importance). Its acceptance of social involvement will be more variable, because it will be substantially influenced by the personal attitudes of its owner-managers. It probably will be more innovative in taking fresh approaches to social problems because it affords a means of entry for persons with new ideas.

John Wilson is one of three investor-organizers of a small business devoted to literacy training of adults. He is an educator who has worked all his life with government rather than business, and, in fact, he has been somewhat disdainful of business. In this instance, however, Wilson feels that public schools provide inadequate environment and methods for literacy training of adults. He feels a deep need to take action now, using new methods and greater flexibility than public education seems able to provide. The main benefit or reward which he seeks in this situation is the feeling that he is using his skills more fully to provide a public service. He knows this area is crowded with others performing similar services, so he expects to compete. He has competed in the realm of ideas all his life, and in this instance he believes his ideas are better. He perceives business as the best social organization to achieve his purpose, and he is willing to risk his capital and other values to achieve his goals.

Wilson's choices reflect functional analysis to determine which institution is most appropriate to perform a particular social function. He chose business because he felt it was the best institution to do the job. He does not believe that business is the *only* institution which can provide literacy training for adults, but he does feel it is the desirable one in this situation.

The Mission of Business

A viable role for business ultimately depends on its having an institutional mission which is acceptable to society. *Mission* defines the social purpose of business; it is business's reason for being. It legitimizes role performance in the system. It represents the benefits which *society as a whole* seeks from business, rather than the benefits which are sought by particular clients such as owners and employees.

The mission of business is typically considered to be efficient provision of goods and services for society. This mission can be easily interpreted to include the idea of social services; however, the public historically has equated goods and services with a materialistic philosophy. In the long view the mission seems to be evolving somewhat, so new statements of the business mission are being sought. One observer comments that the ultimate purpose of business is *progress* and that this is an understandable purpose, relatively well documented.[13] Progress does express business's broad social purpose, but it requires more specific definition because society wants all institutions to seek progress in some way.

What kind of progress distinguishes business from other institutions? What is really different about business? It appears that business's distinguishing feature is its social assignment to marshal and apply society's resources productively at a point of performance. It is a doer, an executor, and an accomplisher. It is action-oriented toward serving general public needs. This thought is represented by the phrase *productive implementation,* because business is the implement for much of society's work accomplishment, both social and economic. Further, business focuses on working in a productive manner, that is, innovating to improve outputs in relation to inputs. Accordingly, the evolving business mission is a special kind of progress; it is progress through productive implementation of social resources toward useful projects as defined by society. All institutions can be said to implement, but not as their primary purpose in the productive, innovative way that business does. They have other primary purposes. Educational institutions provide knowledge; religious institutions give spiritual guidance about how knowledge shall be used; and government provides justice among social components as well as priorities for social progress. Business, in turn, becomes the major social institution for progress through productive implementation of these ingredients. It is results-oriented.

SUMMARY

The business role traditionally has focused on economic performance in the production of goods and services, but this role gradually is evolving toward a more social orientation. Business is recognizing that it is part of a system in which society desires both economic and social benefits in its interface with business. There are strong pressures for more business social involvement. Business has certain capabilities for making a contribution, and potential gains are evident, but there will also be risks for both business and society. Functional analysis is a useful tool to determine the areas most appropriate for involvement. The mission which

[13] McGuire, *op. cit.,* pp. 89–94. See Mason, *op. cit.,* for further discussion of the business mission.

legitimizes business involvement is that it is a productive implementer of social resources toward useful projects. Thus it contributes to progress.

STUDY GUIDES FOR INTERPRETATION OF THIS CHAPTER

1 Discuss with other persons whether they view business as the enemy of social change, as the student did in the incident at the beginning of this chapter. Try to analyze their ways of thinking, and report to class the results of your experience.

2 Compare the traditional role of business with the modern social role which seems to be evolving.

3 Compare the capabilities which business brings to social problems with the capabilities that other major institutions appear to have.

4 What are the risks and potential gains that may arise from more social involvement by business?

5 Explain how functional analysis can help determine the areas for most effective business involvement in social affairs.

PROBLEM
INDUSTRIAL PRODUCTS COMPANY

The purchasing manager of Industrial Products Company is Mr. Hale Drury. Industrial Products Company is located in a metropolitan seaport having over one million population. The company processes certain imported raw materials for sale to other manufacturers.

Recently a metropolitan crime commission which was appointed by the mayor to study crime in the community issued a report which emphatically and directly linked a local trucking contractor with the Mafia and with crime and corruption on waterfront docks. The report shows in detail how this firm seems to operate more efficiently (i.e., with lower costs) by paying bribes to give its trucks preference at the docks while other trucks wait, by collecting protection money from ship lines to prevent pilferage and damage on the docks, by collecting similar protection money from competing truckers to prevent pilferage and accidents, and by other practices.

For the last seven years Mr. Drury has purchased all contract trucking through the alleged Mafia-linked trucker because his bid price for services is about two percent lower than that of other truckers. Annual contract trucking purchases exceed $200,000. The trucker's services have been consistently high quality, clearly equal to the services Mr. Drury could expect from other truckers.

The company policy manual for Mr. Drury's department includes the following statement: "The mission of the Procurement Department is to ensure that all products, materials, and services are purchased at the lowest cost and best terms possible. To accomplish this mission, all appropriate steps may be taken, including renegotiation, value analysis, and changing vendors."

Mr. Drury believes the crime commission report is accurate, and he personally is much opposed to the Mafia and other organized crime. Although Drury is concerned, he is not sure what to do. He believes that if he awarded next year's contract to any other trucker which bid higher, his company would suffer some unfortunate trucking accidents, delays in delivery, pilferage, and other difficulties, in addition to paying more for trucking services. He is not sure management would support an award to a higher bidder solely on the basis of the crime commission's allegations.

1 If you were Mr. Drury, what would you do, why would you do it, and how would you go about it? (For some useful analysis, see Charles Grutzner, "How to Lock Out the Mafia," *Harvard Business Review,* March–April, 1970, pp. 45–58.)

CHAPTER 4

TECHNOLOGY AND SOCIAL CHANGE

> Modern power is based on the capacity for innovation, which is research, and the capacity to transform inventions into finished products, which is technology.
>
> J.-J. SERVAN-SCHREIBER[1]

> For the old capitalists controlled only money; the new managers control science and technology, which are immensely more powerful than money itself.
>
> BENJAMIN M. SELEKMAN[2]

On July 20, 1969, civilization made perhaps its greatest technological breakthrough when it placed two men on the moon and later safely brought them back to earth. This was a daring and exciting adventure which quickened men's minds to the wonders of technology and the universe. It was an impressive example of business's cooperation with other pluralistic groups to build and operate an effective system of people and equipment. It also illustrated how fast technology is advancing, because twenty years earlier most persons would have viewed this event as wild science fiction.

There is no doubt about it. Mankind is living in its greatest age of technological breakthrough, and business is intricately involved in it. Estimates were made in the 1960s that 90 percent of all the scientists who ever lived were still alive.[3] This figure suggests in an approximate way that society is now in the process of absorbing about 90 percent of the total technological change it has had. The result is that business is in the midst of a massive task of absorbing technology on a scale never before experienced. Technological change has become the *norm* instead of the exception. Because business has successfully applied new tech-

[1] J.-J. Servan-Schreiber, *The American Challenge,* New York: Avon, 1969, p. 240. Translated from the original French, *Le Défi américain,* Paris: Editions Denoel, 1967.
[2] Benjamin M. Selekman, "Call for Business Statesmanship," *Harvard Business Review,* July–August, 1962, p. 22.
[3] Billy E. Goetz, "Avoiding Managerial Obsolescence," *California Management Review,* Spring, 1965, p. 91.

nology in the past, we expect that it will do so again, but this expectation should not blind us to the magnitude of the job. The statement from *Alice in Wonderland* is almost a truism for organizations in a technological society: "You have to run as fast as you can to stay where you are."

This chapter discusses some of the characteristics and effects of technological change and business's involvement with it. Modern technology has given managers new powers, as indicated by the quotations beginning this chapter. It has also given them new responsibilities, such as translating technology into productivity and managing the creative spirit.

ABUNDANT TECHNOLOGY

Throughout history technology has pressed onward like a glacier, overturning everything in its way and grinding all opposition into dust. Its unrelenting power has overcome all who tried to stand in its way. In eighteenth-century England, for example, a band of unhappy workers known as Luddites challenged the Industrial Revolution by roaming the countryside, smashing machinery and burning factories. From their narrow viewpoint, machines were enemies taking away jobs and freedom and harming mankind. But the Luddites were soon overcome by the benefits brought by the same machinery they opposed. They sank into oblivion, just as their more modern successors have done. And we know now that they were largely mistaken. Though the Industrial Revolution created new problems, it was a great advance in the history of man.

The glacier of technology grinds on toward progress because of man himself. Man, having tasted the fruit of knowledge, cannot suppress his desire for it. He forever seeks to expand knowledge of his environment.

Business Applies Technology

As soon as new knowledge exists, man wants to apply it in order to reap its benefits. At this point business becomes important because *business is the principal institution which translates discovery into application for public use.* Printing, housing, education, and television are all dependent on business activities to make them work productively. Society depends on business to keep the stream of discovery flowing into useful goods and services for all mankind. Less-developed countries have learned that scientific discoveries mean very little to them unless they have competent business organizers and managers to produce for their people what science has discovered. Developed countries have learned that their progress stops unless they operate a business system which contributes to discovery and uses discovery to produce for their people.

In further support of the role of business in technological development, a university study of 900 key inventions in this century reports that in most cases growing markets stimulated invention, rather than invention coming first and creating a market. In all but a few cases "market was the mother of invention." [4]

[4] What Is the Key to Progress?" *Business Week*, May 16, 1964, p. 132.

A Service Economy

In an agrarian economy the majority of the labor force is employed in farm work in order to produce food to sustain life. With the arrival of the Industrial Revolution, many nations gradually advanced from an agrarian society to an industrial one in which the labor force was employed predominantly in factory production and related work. Business was so successful in applying technology in factories that by the 1960s the United States became the world's first *service economy*.[5] This means that the majority of the labor force became for the first time employed in retailing, banking, insurance, and related service occupations, rather than in direct production work such as industry, farming, and construction. Production is no longer the primary user of manpower or the central economic and social problem.

The service economy is an event of great significance which should at least be equivalent to the Industrial Revolution in its effects throughout society. It will affect the distribution of occupations, educational patterns, leisure time, and other areas of society. For example, the size of service units tends to be small compared with factory units, even though corporate size may remain the same. The striking growth of the franchise movement in the 1960s is a reflection of the development of service industry. Service industries have also shown themselves to be resistant to unemployment during recessions; therefore, their dominance in the economy should help reduce employment fluctuations during economic swings.[6]

Concurrent with the service economy an "electronic revolution" began to dominate technological change. The focus of technology in the Industrial Revolution was on forming and making material products. In the electronic revolution the focus has changed to storage, processing, and transmission of images and information. This new era of technological breakthrough and social influence is represented by television and the computer. It is producing massive changes in service areas such as education, entertainment, medicine, and banking. Electronic technology may keep you alive in a hospital. Or, it can catch you if you try to forge a check!

Barbara walked into a branch bank and tried to open an account by depositing a check. She had what she thought was a foolproof system, because she was going to open small accounts in several banks on the same day, write overdrafts against them, and then leave town at once before she was caught. Unfortunately she was not aware of some of the bank's operations.

The bank was a subscriber to a private business which operates a check verification service. The business stores information about 11 million persons in its computer, filing the information according to each

---

[5] Victor R. Fuchs, *The Service Economy*, National Bureau of Economic Research General Series, no. 87, New York: Columbia University Press, 1968; and Gilbert Burck, "The Still-bright Promise of Productivity," *Fortune*, October, 1968, pp. 134ff.
[6] U.S. Department of Labor, Manpower Administration, *Assessing the Economic Scene*, 1969, p. 6.

person's driver's license number. When Barbara tried to make her deposit, the bank clerk checked with the verification service, and its computer reported that Barbara was a felony suspect wanted for trying a similar scheme in another part of the state. A surprised Barbara was arrested by two patrolmen before she could leave the bank.[7]

SOME GENERAL EFFECTS OF TECHNOLOGY

Effects of Technology Are Pervasive

When technology is applied by business or any other institution, its effects are frequently widespread. They reach far beyond the point of immediate impact of the technology, and they have both desirable and undesirable results. The dominant climate becomes one of change and then more change. In a dynamic society technology operates as a multiplier, not as an additive, because it acts in a system relationship with other parts of society. Thus, invention of the wheel led to perhaps a dozen or more applications rather quickly. These applications, in turn, may have affected fifty other parts of the system and led to several additional inventions which similarly influenced society as multipliers.

The automobile serves as an example. It could not have been invented much earlier because hundreds of inventions had to precede it, such as improvements in metallurgy, vulcanization of rubber, electrical generation for sparkplugs, and refining of crude oil. Once these inventions existed, the automobile almost had to be invented, because there was a market for faster transportation than horses and bicycles and more individualized transportation than the faster trains offered.
    When the technological breakthrough of the automobile did occur, its effects were pervasive throughout society. It had a profound effect on the whole ecological system. It changed the living habits of people, including their buying habits, the location of their homes, their independence, and their patterns of courtship. It increased the number of supermarkets and helped create drive-in movies. It expanded land areas allocated to roads, increased traffic to wilderness areas, and added pollution to the air. By means of the automobile truck, it altered shipping patterns and manufacturing locations. Hardly any area of society was untouched by the automobile.

Higher Productivity

Perhaps the most fundamental effect of technology is greater productivity of both quality and quantity. This is the main reason that most technology is adopted. In a hospital the objective may be qualitative in terms of maintaining life with electronic monitoring equipment regardless of costs. In a factory the objective may be quantitative in terms of more production for less cost.

Some of the changes in technology have been striking. Nylon filament is extruded at 4,000 feet a minute, which is one-half million times faster

[7] "Los Angeles Company Helps Catch Crooks with Wary Computer," *Wall Street Journal* (Pacific Coast edition), May 12, 1969, p. 1.

than a silkworm produces silk. A good glassblower with a helper could make some fifteen hundred light bulbs a day, but a single machine can produce 132,000 bulbs *an hour.* Another dramatic example of productivity increase is the telephone system. It is estimated that if the telephone system of the 1960s depended on manual operation as used in the 1930s, every woman in the United States over eighteen years of age would need to be employed in telephone work to handle the volume of calls being made in the 1960s.

Benefits of technology are reflected in the rising factory production indexes of advanced nations. These indexes reflect higher standards of living and different ways of living for hundreds of millions of people. Using the 1957 to 1959 average as a base of 100, the indexes of representative nations in 1969 were as follows:[8]

Japan	402
Italy	236
West Germany	190
Canada	184
France	180
United States	172
United Kingdom	137

Although technology *in general* has been successful in bringing a better quality and quantity of output, in specific instances it often does not do so. Sometimes management is swayed by the enthusiasm of a functional specialist and adopts a change without adequate evaluation. It discovers later that the projected savings did not materialize because the specialist overlooked costs outside his field. When extended economic costs are included, savings dwindle or disappear; and when social costs are added, the change may be clearly unwise in its totality.

A petroleum company made an analysis of one of its regional offices handling credit-card accounts. This office employed 500 persons and handled $25 million annually. An accounting study showed that the office could be abolished and all accounting done by a computer in the national office of the company at a saving of $75,000 out of an annual regional office cost of $500,000.

This saving appeared to justify centralization; however, investigation disclosed other factors affecting the decision. If the change were made, mail contact with customers would be slowed three days by regular mail or one day if air mail was used at an additional cost. Since no other jobs were available at the regional office, it was estimated that 325 employees would need to be moved to other offices including the central office. These costs were not computed in estimating the saving. Some other employees would be laid off or retired, which would incur additional costs of dismissal or early retirement benefits. As a matter of fact, the central office was in a large city in expensive office space, and no further space was available. Space would have to be leased or new facilities built.

[8] John O'Riley, "Appraisal of Current Trends in Business and Finance," *Wall Street Journal* (Pacific Coast edition), May 12, 1969, p. 1.

Furthermore, fixed costs resulting from equipment lease cancellations at the regional office were not counted. Also omitted was the necessity for simultaneous operation of both offices during the changeover period. The company personnel director also observed that salary costs were generally higher in the national office, and he predicted that persons who transferred would soon get sizable increases in order to bring their salaries into line with those of other employees and to allow for living costs in their new community.

Considering the total picture, management decided that the saving would be less than $10,000 and that in terms of total economic and social costs to the company, the change would be unwise. It was not made.

System Complexity

An evident effect of technology is complexity. The modern washing machine does a better job than the old washboard and tub, but when it breaks down, it requires a specialist for repairs. And it may break down more often because of its complexity. The same reasoning applies to a complex production system. In November, 1965, for example, an equipment failure on a power network in the northeastern United States caused a power overload and opened circuit breakers nearby. In turn, a larger system became overloaded because of interties with other power systems. At once almost the entire northeastern United States and part of Canada were gripped in a giant power failure which lasted throughout the night and into the next day. About twenty million people were affected. Gasoline stations could not pump gas, traffic lights stopped, elevators hung between floors, and so on. A localized problem on one circuit ballooned into a regional problem affecting other areas because of the intertie. Under conditions of this type, management is under great pressure to keep the whole system working all the time.

Also because of complexity, failure of one part in a system such as an airplane or a space ship can abort the whole operation for the long run. The Apollo spacecraft system has over one million parts, and they all must function properly. Reliability of performance, therefore, assumes new significance. It is possible that technology eventually will lead to simplicity and small independent operational units, but that condition is far into the future. Meanwhile, more complexity in work and product systems is expected. Business is developing zero-defects programs in order to maintain reliability under these conditions.

Unless the more complex system can be maintained reliably, it is not better than the system it replaces. Hans Christian Andersen in "The Nightingale" tells of an emperor who depended on a mechanized nightingale to sing its beautiful song. Its clockwork was so good that he banished the real nightingale. But eventually the clockwork failed and was discovered to be so complex that it could not be repaired. Again he came to depend on the real nightingale Though technology is complex like the mechanical nightingale, we expect that man will be able to keep it "singing" for his benefit without having to return to old production systems.

Capital Requirements

Another effect of technology is its insatiable demand for capital. At the turn of the century, an investment of $1,000 for each worker was adequate in a factory, but today investments in pipelines and chemical operations exceed $100,000 for each worker. Capital needs become staggering when considered in terms of new jobs. Assuming a moderate investment of only $10,000 for each worker and using forecasts of 20 million new jobs needed in the United States in fifteen years, $200 *billion* of new capital is needed. This figure does not include expenditures for capital replacement to keep the existing labor force employed. These developments require business to generate large amounts of capital and engage in more long-range planning and budgeting for capital use.

Further, the magnitude of investment units is increasing. An old factory could increase production by adding units of one machine at $1,000 and one man at a time. A modern factory having an integrated production system may discover that expansion is possible only in system units having twenty machines and much supporting equipment costing $3 million. The output potential of the system unit is likewise much greater than that of the one machine in the old factory. These conditions mean that expansion which permits idle capacity over an intermediate term is often technologically correct and in the public interest from a cost viewpoint. Expansion at the rate of consumer use, allowing no idle capacity, would be costly or not feasible technologically. Idle capacity, therefore, is not necessarily a social ill. During periods of business growth and technological change, wise use of resources requires investment in system units which will have idle capacity.

The changes that are occurring place new responsibilities on management to keep abreast of technology in order to be sure it is using investor funds in the best way. Further, management needs to reconsider organizational objectives to be certain they are broad enough. The wagon firm which looked upon itself as only making wagons has gone out of business, but the wagon firm which saw its objective as providing consumer transportation equipment could move into automobile and aircraft manufacturing. The attrition of technology is evident from a comparison of lists of the 100 largest manufacturers in 1909 and 1959. Less than one-third of the 1909 firms are on the 1959 list. In other words, advancing technology initiates action on management requiring adjustment, just as much as it does in the more publicized cases requiring workers to adjust.

More Emphasis on Research and Development

As technology has advanced, research and development (R&D) has become a giant new function in business. Research concerns the creation of new ideas, and development concerns their useful application. Direct research and development expenditures in industry in 1960 were over $10 billion, and these expenditures increased to about $30 billion by 1970. These figures do not include billions of indirect expenditures such as planning and introducing new products. Much R&D work is supported by government contracts, but private industry is also risking large amounts of its own money.

Effective management of R&D is an important business responsibility because R&D brings social benefits through increased productivity. Comparative research among countries of the world shows that R&D investment is closely related to economic growth. This international study concludes: "It is suggested that the civilian economy will continue to benefit from further increase in the fraction of national income devoted to R&D, even if the increase is at the expense of more conventional uses of investment funds."[9]

R&D has become so important in some companies that it is ranked along with production and sales as a primary function, or "line function," of their business. No longer do they only produce goods and sell them. With accelerated technology, many companies now develop goods, produce them, and sell them. In some instances R&D becomes the primary emphasis of an organization, with production secondary. Research and development becomes the largest department, having more employees than either production or sales. Its salary budget is larger, and it assumes an active voice in the councils of top management. The traditional industrial order of priorities shifts from production to R&D. The assumption is that new products must be developed in order to keep abreast of competition and that if something useful can be developed, production and sales will develop normally. R&D, therefore, becomes the key to market leadership in many situations.

New Expectations from Customers

Affluent citizens with new wants are another result of advancing technology. Now supplied with the necessities of life, affluent customers spend more money on semiluxuries such as boats and country homes. Having the power to buy more things, they are not going to buy more of the same things. They want something different. Many of them are becoming independent, demanding adaptation of products to their unique needs. Already there are hundreds more models of cars and combinations of accessories than in the days of the Model T Ford. Demand is expanding even for custom semihandcrafted automobiles, and this market is being served by customizing shops, custom parts wholesalers, and specialized magazines. Society has come almost full circle from handicraft production to standardized mass-production items and back to semicustom production of some products, even though these custom items are constructed largely from standardized parts. The factory of the future may be like an organ console, having a complex, integrated system from which an operator produces infinite combinations of products in the same way that an organist produces a variety of sounds.

[9] Herbert K. Weiss, "Some Growth Considerations of Research and Development and the National Economy," *Management Science*, January, 1965, p. 393.

Side Effects of Technology

In the same way that a lifesaving antibiotic may have side effects, technology also has system side effects. When they are negative, they become social costs. From society's point of view these social costs need to be calculated in the cost-benefit analysis of every proposed social change. Very often some of these social costs are overlooked because the persons who work with technology do not think broadly enough of its system effects. However, even among the broadest thinkers, system effects frequently are not predictable. There is not even agreement concerning whether a particular technological change will result in net social costs or social benefits.

For example, how will television affect types of political leadership, morality of youth, mass propaganda, and cohesion of the family? No one is sure. Looking even more broadly, will teaching machines psychologically condition students in a way which causes them as adults to respond like robots to political propaganda, thus losing their democracy to a dictator? Will medical diagnostic and monitoring machines so dehumanize medicine that they will cause more ills than they cure? There is no way to know; hence, as we use these devices, we need to be continuously alert to feedback about negative side effects so that corrective action can be initiated.

A fact frequently overlooked is that technology can be used to correct side effects which exist. It is not unidirectional; it can be corrective as well as causative. For example, technology does cause pollution; however, technology can also be used to reduce pollution from both machine and human wastes. Technology does contribute to urban blight, but it can be used to increase beauty and make it easier for people to live in cities. It has already done so. For example, the smoke from one electric generating plant serving 100,000 homes is much less than the smoke from fireplaces in a similar number of homes in earlier days—and it can be better controlled. Further, the waste from one city sewage plant is much less than waste, stench, and disease in cities without sewage facilities.

Indeed, technology is creating all sorts of new situations to which people are reacting in unique ways. The technological revolution causes an associated social revolution. The problem with technology is that it moves so fast that it creates problems before society is able to work out solutions. For these reasons business firms associated with technological change have been supporting public research on the subject in addition to their own private research. Notable is a ten-year study at Harvard Business School financed by a $5 million grant from International Business Machines Corporation. The project seeks ". . . to identify and analyze the primary and second-order impacts and effects of technological change on the economy, business, government, society, and individuals."[10]

In summary, technology is changing the entire structure of civilization. With regard to business, more competition is expected from distant geographical areas and from nontraditional fields. The life-spans of many

---

[10] "A $5-million Search for Answers," *Business Week*, July 4, 1964, p. 84.

products will decline because of technological obsolescence. Many new and unusual business opportunities will develop, but it will be more costly to take advantage of them because of the effort required for research and development. Companies which fail to keep up will be wiped out by technologically superior firms. Traditional management will be inadequate for success unless it is coupled with technological progress. These conditions will increase risk and cause disturbing economic dislocations as industry shifts with technology. For these reasons, government will continue to play an overriding role in regulating technological change and interfacing with business in other ways in order to maintain system effectiveness, as discussed in later chapters. Technology also has a major impact on employment patterns, as is shown in the following section.

TECHNOLOGY'S INFLUENCE ON EMPLOYMENT PATTERNS

Increased Real Wages

Perhaps the most significant employment effect of technology is that it tends to increase real income for employees. This result is especially evident in advanced industrial nations. Figure 4–1 shows that, in spite of inflation, real average hourly wages of nonfarm employees in the United States increased approximately 60 percent from 1947 to 1968. This is significant progress in less than one generation.

Upgraded Job Skills

Part of the increase in wages arises from a redistribution of job skills required for the work force. Jobs generally tend to be upgraded as

Figure 4–1 Technology contributes to the steady rise in real earnings of wage employees in the United States. Source: U. S. Department of Labor, Manpower Administration, *Assessing the Economic Scene,* 1969, p. 2.

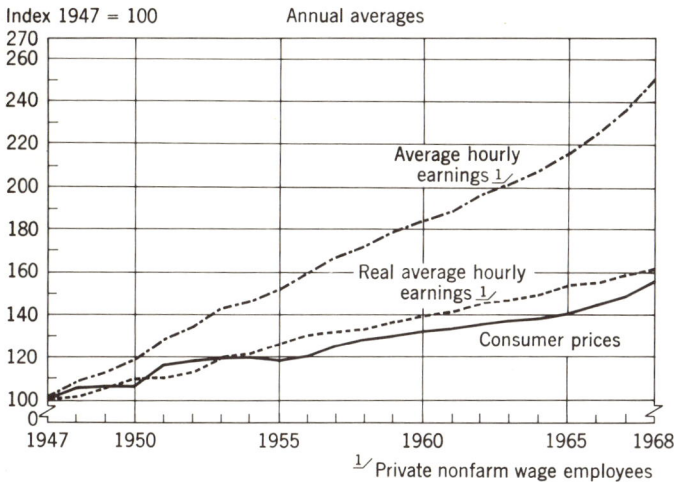

Index 1947 = 100   Annual averages

Average hourly earnings [1]

Real average hourly earnings [1]

Consumer prices

[1] Private nonfarm wage employees

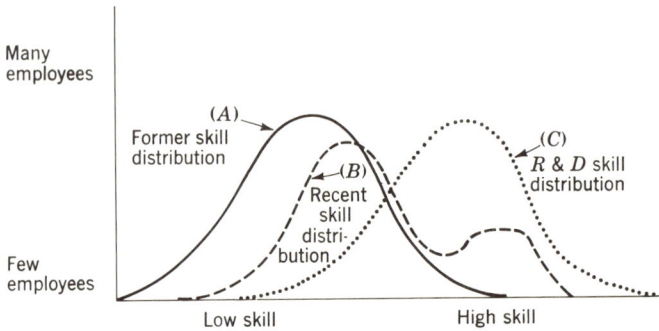

Figure 4–2 Changes in skill distribution in a business required by advances in technology.

machines perform more routine tasks. The job that required a day laborer now requires a craneman, and the job that formerly employed a clerk now requires an accountant. A generation ago the typical factory had a range of skills approaching curve A shown in Figure 4–2. This curve was shaped like the normal curve of intelligence among people. Being matched to people, it suggested that an adequate supply of labor would be available at all levels of business in the long run.

In modern business the curve has moved toward the right, higher in skill, as shown in curve B. And in many oragnizations the skill distribution has become bimodal, as shown by the second top on the curve. Many scientific and professional people are required in research, development, planning, and other specialized work, creating the secondary bulge toward the skilled end of the scale.

Curve C represents the skill distribution which is developing in firms oriented toward research and development. Even though these firms manufacture products for sale, much of their effort is devoted to development and to building prototypes. In some of these the number of engineers, scientists, and college-graduate specialists exceeds the total number of other employees.

More Scientific and Professional Workers

The increased number of intellectual workers represented by curves B and C has placed new responsibilities on business for managing the creative spirit, sometimes called "maverick management." Historically, the scientist worked in a small laboratory at his own pace, usually in an academic setting, but more and more he is working for big organizations, both private and public. Most certainly he performs best in a work culture different from that of the assembly line.

Creative and intellectual workers expect relatively high job freedom. They are motivated by opportunities which offer a challenge for growth and achievement. They are less motivated by the expectations of higher formal authority than by their own professional interests and perception of opportunities. Their orientation is *cosmopolitan,* toward their profession and the world outside their organization, rather than *local,* depending primarily on the reward structure of the firm itself. Although they are a part of the company work culture, they are just as much a part of a separate scientific culture operating beyond their organization's boundaries. Under these conditions they have an organizational rootlessness which increases job mobility.

Business is adjusting its supervisory practices to meet needs of intellectual workers. Some companies have established dual promotion ladders so that distinguished technical people can rise to ranks and receive salaries that are equivalent to those of managers. Flexible work schedules are allowed. Profit sharing is provided to give the creative person a financial stake in the ideas he creates and to discourage his rootlessness. Attendance at professional meetings and writing professional articles are supported. In further response to the intellectual worker's cosmopolitan interests, he is allowed to teach part time or is given special assignments.

In fact, research covering industrial, government, and university scientists discloses that the more productive scientists are those who spend part of their time in teaching, administration, or other nontechnical work. In other words, the more productive scientists spend less than full time on technical activities. Although a cause-and-effect relationship is not proved, it appears that diversity in the scientists' work situations actually enhances their performance. Having broad and cosmopolitan interests, they thrive on variable conditions. At a minimum this research suggests that the more productive scientists have an expectation of broad duties and gravitate toward them.[11]

Scientific and other specialized workers comprise the *technostructure* of modern organizations, and more or less govern them through control of their decision-making processes. This condition exists regardless of what pattern of authority is shown on the organization chart. According to John Kenneth Galbraith the technostructure "embraces all who bring specialized knowledge, talent, or experience to group decision-making. This, not the management, is the guiding intelligence—the brain—of the enterprise."[12] Technostructure is a convenient term, although a broad one, for emphasizing the pervasive influence of technology and specialization in organizations.

Since the majority within the technostructure of most organizations are likely to be technically trained persons, care must be taken to assure that they do not become a *technical elite* dominating business and social decisions. They are the experts concerning the technical feasibility of their proposals. Their expertise in this area cannot be questioned, so they may become impatient with people who stand in the way of a technically feasi-

[11] Frank M. Andrews, "Scientific Performance as Related to Time Spent on Technical Work, Teaching or Administration," *Administrative Science Quarterly,* September, 1964, pp. 182–193. For further details on managing the creative spirit, see the special issue on professionals in organizations, *Administrative Science Quarterly,* June, 1965.
[12] John Kenneth Galbraith, *The New Industrial State,* Boston: Houghton Mifflin Company, 1967, p. 71.

ble project. However, their expertise may be the factor which limits their broader view of social effects. Business managers, therefore, have a responsibility to assess pluralistic views *within* the firm, as well as viewpoints from pluralistic groups outside the firm, when making decisions about the use of technology. Decisions concerning technological changes are social decisions rather than narrow technological decisions. This requires socially responsible decision making by socially conscious managers.

Changes in Management

Technological advances seem to be increasing the proportion of managers in the labor force. The labor saving of technology primarily displaces lower-level workers, while the cadre of managers remains the same or even increases. Assume, for example, that a department before automation has ten managers and ninety workers. Its ratio of managers to workers is 1 to 9. As a result of automation ten workers are laid off, but the management cadre is not reduced. The ratio of managers is now 1 to 8. If one specialized manager is added, the ratio of managers increases to one manager for each 7.3 workers. This change in ratio can move fast. In one department of seventy employees the ratio of managers to workers was 1 to 35 before automation but 1 to 8 after automation.[13] Meanwhile, the new firms which are developing also need managers. The result is that the proportion of managers in industrial society is inching upward, compounding the existing managerial shortage. This condition is one of the reasons business is giving more effort to management development.

The manager shortage is likely to get worse before supply is able to catch up with demand. The business investment in training and education above the worker level is high and will continue to grow. Likewise the community investment will grow. Since management is a key factor in making other resources productive, it is beginning to receive priority in economic and social development. It, along with high-level technical manpower, constitutes a "takeoff" investment which enables other resources to be used more productively; consequently, modern technology requires higher training for most types of work. One study reports: "The proportion of national income devoted to human resource development is likely to rise in all countries that are growing."[14]

Advancing technology requires more *biprofessional and multiprofessional managers.* These are men who are professionally trained in management and also in one or more intellectual specialties which they need in order to understand the environment they manage. Examples are physics and management, and biochemistry and management.

An unusual illustration of the need for a multiprofessional manager is the pharmaceutical firm which spent several months seeking a man who

[13] Otis Lipstreu and Kenneth A. Reed, "A New Look at the Organizational Implications of Automation," *Academy of Management Journal*, March, 1965, p. 26.
[14] Frederick Harbison and Charles A. Myers, *Education, Manpower, and Economic Growth,* New York: McGraw-Hill Book Company, 1964, p. 186.

had degrees in both biology and advertising, professional training in management, and a Ph.D. They wanted this man to manage their advertising department. They found him and paid the price required to move him from his present employer.

The trend toward multiprofessionalism places more responsibility on business to support education and training because preparation of this kind of person is expensive. Fortunately, technology's greater productivity eases the burden of the costly education which it requires.

Employment Dislocations

It is often reasoned that technology causes unemployment because one of its purposes is to reduce labor costs. Others insist that technology's effect is neutral or that it increases job opportunities. The main reason for these differences of opinion is that some people are thinking about an individual firm (with either a short-run or long-run outlook) while others are looking at a larger economic system. In an individual firm technological change does displace jobs and require readjustments. The individual worker who thinks that technology may abolish the exact job he now performs is probably correct. Jobs are changing, and relearning is required. Even whole departments may become unnecessary as a result of technological advancement. In the long run a firm's technological changes may increase job opportunities because of higher efficiency which improves competitive ability, but in the short run jobs are displaced.

Looking at the whole economy, the view is different. The overwhelming weight of evidence is that technology is not a cause of unemployment in the total system. Based on his study of employment statistics, the United States Commissioner of Labor Statistics concludes: "Technology as such does not result in a net loss of jobs in the economy."[15] The reason is that technology permits human labor to be allocated to more efficient uses, but it does not destroy the need for labor as long as any human wants remain unfulfilled. If technology causes unemployment, then jobs should decline as productivity increases in an economy, but this does not occur. As stated in a research study prepared for the Senate Committee on Labor and Public Welfare, "The great majority of professional economists today agree that we simply cannot have any such thing as permanent technological unemployment."[16]

From the broader view of international business, technological improvement in one country may reduce its labor costs, thereby adversely affecting the trade of another country where technology is advancing at a slower pace. In this instance, technology increases job opportunities where it occurs, indirectly penalizing other nations which fail to use it. Technology thus becomes a worldwide pressure for productivity improvement.

[15] Ewan Clague, "What Employment Statistics Show," *Automation*, April, 1964, p. 55.
[16] Charles C. Killingsworth, "Automation, Jobs and Manpower," in *Nation's Manpower Revolution*, Hearings before Subcommittee on Employment and Manpower, Senate Committee on Labor and Public Welfare, 88th Cong. 1st Sess., 1963, part 5, p. 1,461.

The difficulty with technology is not that it destroys men's jobs for all time (permanent technological unemployment) but that it creates jobs which people are not yet prepared to fill. The bargain which technology strikes with a man is to take one job and offer him in return another one for which he may not be qualified. It places a burden of training and education on the employee, the firm, and the nation. The poorly educated, the aged, and other marginal employees are the first to be dislocated, but they are often the ones least able to adjust. In economic terms, by requiring workers to be better prepared in order to contribute fully, technology increases the marginal productivity of skilled and intellectual work, while decreasing the marginal productivity of unskilled and manual work.

An individual organization can usually retrain employees who are ready and able to respond, and large firms usually have done this, but those who are unable to respond flexibly constitute a larger social problem that requires assistance from other pluralistic groups. Society faces the immense task of motivating these persons, for without help they become the hard-core unemployed and the "untrainables." Without realizing it, the high school dropout has set his own job ceiling before he ever starts to work!

Some persons display a *technophobia* in which they view technology as a great terror which will cast poorly educated workers into permanent unemployment and reduce all workers to obedient servitude to machinery. They foresee a day when workers, having lost all their individuality, will drift uselessly under the care of giant electronic machines. This wide variety of views is a normal condition when people with different perceptions try to predict what an unknown social force will do at some future time. As is usually the case, future events will probably range somewhere between the extreme views.

A Shorter Workweek and More Moonlighting

Labor philosophy strongly favors a shorter workweek, so in the long run workers are likely to take part of their productivity gains in the form of fewer hours of work. At some point of economic affluence additional leisure time becomes more important to many workers than additional income. However, not all of them desire a shorter workweek. Some have strong drives to work because of the psychological satisfactions they derive from it compared with leisure. Others find that, even though they are more affluent, their wants have increased at a faster pace. The result is that many workers will choose second jobs, usually part-time and often in employment areas which they like. This activity is called moonlighting. Statistics of the United States Department of Labor show that millions of workers engage in it, even though it complicates their work schedules, interferes with their home life, and divides their loyalties.

Assuming that wage employees do secure a shorter workweek in the future, will others follow? What about physicians, shopkeepers, research workers, and teachers? Surveys show that persons in these groups often work close to fifty hours a week. In many instances they will find it difficult to reduce hours because of demands made on them or because of their personal enthusiasm for their occupations. The distinct possibility exists that two standards for work hours may develop. Some occupations, especially intellectual work, may tend to hold a long workweek, while other occupations gravitate toward a shorter workweek. Those on the longer week may have schedule flexibility, compared with closely controlled schedules for those on a shorter workweek. Employees then will have a measure of choice concerning whether they wish to take the fruits of productivity in more pay or more leisure. Since there is no basis for assuming that all persons want a shorter workweek, this flexible arrangement permits adaptation to different desires. It also burdens organizations with additional planning and scheduling responsibilities.

As the workweek decreases, a large number of employees will engage in what we call *public moonlighting,* which is semischeduled, responsible assistance with public-service activities of a community. Usually five to ten hours a week is given without pay or with token payment for expenses, because the person is working to satisfy his idealistic drives more than his economic ones. Since his own family is now economically cared for, he feels he can afford to give himself more directly to others. Examples of public moonlighting are devoting Saturdays to youth council work, providing social work ten hours a week in a hospital, or working eight hours a week on a city beautification committee.

It is not often recognized that many of the public-service activities which are found in the United States—activities which are not directly productive of basic goods—exist because of wealth produced by a technological society. An impoverished economy can hardly support well-equipped hospitals for all its people or aid for retarded children. Likewise productivity is essential to support mass cultural activities, such as community museums and symphonies, as distinguished from culture for a small elite. As these activities expand in society, some of them—such as a two-hour noon committee meeting—will conflict with work schedules. Additional responsibility will be placed on employers to support these developments by permitting flexible working hours. One way to do this is to develop broadly trained men who are interchangeable on jobs within the system, in the same way they would interchange in case of sickness absence.

SUMMARY

When we begin to see the intricate relationships of technological developments to each other and to many institutions, we realize that technological change is not a simple creation of business alone. Business responds merely as a system component. However, business is perhaps the primary agent for technological change, so it has major responsibilities for proper introduction of change. The system in the United States is now a service economy in an electronic age.

The effects of technology are pervasive throughout the system, producing both favorable and unfavorable results. Managers operating within the technostructure delicately balance specialized points of view in order to make broad decisions which are socially responsible. This need for breadth increases the demand for multiprofessional, socially-conscious managers.

STUDY GUIDES FOR INTERPRETATION OF THIS CHAPTER

1 Assuming that the swing to a service economy will continue, discuss its potential effects during the next twenty years. Present current manpower data or other information to support your discussion.

2 What do you consider to be the three most favorable effects of technology (a) in the whole society and (b) in your local community? Explain why you chose each. Do likewise for the three most unfavorable effects.

3 Discuss and chart the shift in job skills as technology advances.

4 It has been suggested that a law be passed prohibiting any business from making a technological improvement which results in the layoff of an employee (i.e., the laborer must be retrained and transferred within the business). Appraise the merits of this proposal as it applies to a pluralistic society.

PROBLEM
PEABODY ELECTRONICS ASSOCIATES, INC.

Peabody Electronics Associates, Inc., is an electronic firm which markets a number of consumer and industrial items. One of its industrial products plants which employs 1,700 persons is located in a town of 50,000 persons about fifty miles from any large metropolitan area or major university. This location was chosen seven years ago because the plant uses mostly semiskilled labor, which was plentiful in the community, and the factory building of a bankrupt firm was available for a ten-year lease.

Recently the home-office research department made a technological breakthrough in design of the principal product produced in this branch plant. The new design will have much greater reliability and cost about one-half of what it does now; however, the labor force will be reduced 72 percent and will consist mostly of skilled workers and scientific personnel. Capital costs will increase fourfold, and the existing building is unsatisfactory because expensive, especially designed equipment and buildings will be required. During preliminary planning for the new facilities one scientist explained that the existing location would be unsuitable for a permanent plant, because scientific personnel would feel that a location this distance from a major university would hinder their opportunity for personal growth through education.

1 Evaluate from a social system point of view the alternatives available to this firm, and recommend the appropriate course of action with reasons supporting your choice of action.

CHAPTER 5

THE MANAGERIAL ROLE

The managerial role, in contrast to many other professional roles, tends to be defined in terms of a system of *multiple clients*.

EDGAR H. SCHEIN[1]

The objective of management is stewardship, including stewardship of human assets.

H. G. HENEMAN, JR.[2]

Consider the situation of John Jones, a chemist promoted to laboratory manager. As a chemist, he usually knows when he is right, but as a manager he cannot be so sure. His decisions are restricted by social norms such as profit, justice, and human relations, none provable by laws of physical science. His new managerial role requires him to think beyond his narrow specialty of chemistry and even beyond the firm itself. When he is asked to decide whether a dangerous drug is ready for market tests, he needs to weigh new value systems before making his recommendation. What about danger to human life and the effect on the company's reputation and profits? Although he uses scientific facts in his decision, they are of less influence than when he acts as a chemist only.

The case of John Jones is a typical one. Managers are the main linking pins between business and its environment, so their decisions need to be related to the values and expectations of the claimants in the social system. For this reason we can reach a better understanding of the business-environment interface by discussing how managers perceive their role in different parts of the world and the types of activities managers perform in relating business to society. Then in Part Two of this book we discuss the ideological values applied by managers in executing their managerial role.

[1] Edgar H. Schein, "The Problem of Moral Education for the Business Manager," *Industrial Management Review*, Fall, 1966, p. 9. Italics in original.
[2] H. G. Heneman, Jr., *Personnel Audits and Manpower Assets*, Minneapolis, Minn.: University of Minnesota Industrial Relations Center, 1967, p. 11.

MANAGERIAL-ROLE BEHAVIOR

Role is a fundamental idea in understanding social systems because all persons therein act in role relationships to each other. William Shakespeare described role, in his famous passage from *As You Like It*, as follows:

> All the world's a stage,
> And all the men and women merely players:
> They have their exits and their entrances;
> And one man in his time plays many parts.

Role is social behavior oriented to the patterned expectations of others. A manager perceives himself in a certain job which establishes a set of relationships with others, so he acts partly on the basis of what he thinks is expected of him. In other words, society's expectations influence his behavior. He becomes socially conditioned to act in a way which is consistent with the job of "manager."

The managerial role requires different conduct with different people rather than uniform conduct. One pattern of conduct is required with a subordinate, another with a fellow manager, and another with the local mayor; yet all three are managerial-role actions. Since these role variations are expected, managers need to develop role sensitivity for appraising each situation and do role thinking to select the most appropriate action.

Managers Have Similar Perceptions of Their Role

The most significant fact about the managerial role is that managers' perceptions of it appear fairly uniform throughout the world, especially in industrially developed nations. Kerr and others, on the basis of international studies lasting a decade, developed evidence that industrialization tends to cause a uniform work culture, including the managerial role. Generally speaking, as industrialization advances, there is a move toward more democratization of employee and managerial roles.[3]

A study of role perceptions of higher managers in Israel and Australia, nations with distinctly different industrial heritages, reported substantial agreement between the two countries.[4] Cross-cultural comparisons showed that role perceptions and work values were similar on most items surveyed. The study concluded that similar institutional pressures act on managers in both countries to promote similarities in attitudes and perceptions.

---

[3] Clark Kerr, John T. Dunlop, Frederick H. Harbison, and Charles A. Myers, *Industrialism and Industrial Man: The Problems of Labor and Management in Industrial Growth*, Cambridge, Mass.: Harvard University Press, 1960. See also A. Inkeles, "Industrial Man: The Relation of Status to Experience, Perception, and Value," *American Journal of Sociology*, vol. 66, 1960, pp. 1–31.

[4] The Israeli-Melbourne correlation was .79, significant to the .01 level, and the Israeli-Sydney correlation was .54, significant to the .05 level. Y. Rim and Bilha F. Mannheim, "Factors Related to Attitudes of Management and Union Representatives," *Personnel Psychology*, Summer, 1964, pp. 149–165.

One comprehensive study covered written responses of 3,641 managers in fourteen countries.[5] Research showed general uniformity in role perceptions regardless of country, although there were moderate cultural variations. Many differences tended to group around clusters of nations having a common cultural background. Separate clusters existed for northern European, southern European, Anglo-American, and developing nations, while Japan stood by itself. These variations show that cultural traditions do affect role perceptions, partly offsetting technological pressures for uniformity.

The study of fourteen nations extends the Kerr study just mentioned by showing that even managers in developing nations have similar perceptions of the managerial role. Since both technology and culture are different in developing nations compared with advanced ones, but managerial-role perceptions are similar, this suggests that there is something other than technology which encourages similar role perceptions. Perhaps this additional factor is the functions which the manager must perform to accomplish his job. As he performs these rather similar functions, such as planning and organizing, they eventually encourage him to perceive his role in ways which are rather uniform although still culturally conditioned.

Further evidence of managerial similarities in developing and advanced nations is revealed in a survey of 215 Indian managers in Bombay and 230 United States managers in Philadelphia.[6] It was thought that since the Indian managers were reared in a strongly authoritarian culture with wide class differences and were supervising a different quality of labor in a less technological environment, they would be much more authoritarian than their counterparts in the United States. Although there was a tendency in this direction, the difference was not significant. The researcher concluded that the managerial perceptions of the two groups were substantially congruent.

Perceptions Are Similar in Different Ownership Situations

Another possibility is that managerial-role perceptions vary according to different types of ownership control, such as private industry, government, and unions; however, research discloses that managers in various types of enterprises have essentially the same understanding of their managerial role. Israel furnishes an excellent example because it has a mixed economy of enterprises owned and operated by private groups, by government, and by labor unions (the Histadrut). A casual observer would think that managers in these three enterprises would view their jobs differently because of their different objectives and modes of operation. In the Histadrut, for example, leadership is determined through hotly contested political elections, and positions are allocated according to votes

[5] Mason Haire, Edwin E. Ghiselli, and Lyman W. Porter, *Managerial Thinking: An International Study,* New York: John Wiley & Sons, Inc., 1966.
[6] Arvind Phatak, "Managerial Attitudes in the United States and India," *The Economic and Business Bulletin,* pp. 15–21, Philadelphia, Temple University School of Business Administration, Summer, 1969.

obtained. The leaders of private industry, however, are chosen by higher authority, as in the United States.

In spite of these differences in ownership control, management in all three enterprises is essentially the same. One study reported: "Managerial functions, attitudes and limitations are uniform to an astonishing degree among the larger private, Histadrut, and government-owned enterprises."[7] Another study of Israeli managers reached the same conclusion, reporting that the managers' role definitions were similar regardless of the ownership control of their enterprise.[8]

In conclusion, cultural differences among countries and variations in ownership control do lead to variations in managerial-role perceptions; however, higher managers substantially agree on the managerial role regardless of country or ownership control. The managerial job itself, wherever it exists, is substantially the same. This uniformity in function tends to promote similarities in perceptions by managers. For successful performance, for example, managers need to understand the nature of authority and the relationship of cost to productivity regardless of their cultural heritage.

THE MODERN MANAGERIAL ROLE

The modern managerial role has developed a well-defined set of characteristics which may be called its *role definition*. Originally this role was substantially similar to the role of ruler, deriving its powers through rights of monarchy, military control, church rank, or land ownership. Gradually it evolved in response to social values and needs until now it is a semiprofessional role requiring both training and competence. In the following discussion we focus on a social system interpretation of this role compared with a more traditional functional emphasis on activities such as planning, organizing, directing, and controlling. We refer to this role as career management.

The Modern Role of Career Management

The modern managerial role has evolved into *career management* in which management is a differentiated occupation which a person normally enters on a career basis. Career management recognizes that there is a substantial separation of ownership and management, especially in large organizations. Although a career manager may have some ownership interest in his firm by means of stock options and profit-sharing plans, he does not hold his management position on the basis of ownership. He legitimizes his power by competently performing a function which is needed and valued by owners, employees, and society alike. This condition is actually an *acceptance model of legitimacy*, meaning that the

---

[7] Milton Derber, "Plant Labor Relations in Israel," *Industrial and Labor Relations Review*, October, 1963, p. 59.
[8] Rim and Mannheim, *op. cit.*, p. 156. There were some differences, such as that 46 percent of private-business managers believe that an enterprise making larger profits is usually more efficient than other enterprises, but only 22.5 percent of government-business managers agreed.

career manager maintains the legitimacy of his role only as long as he is able to serve claimants in a satisfactory way. This relationship puts him under constant pressure to perform.

The manager of a large apartment complex was unable to satisfy the expectations of his tenants. His failure appeared to arise primarily from his inability to work with maintenance groups which kept the facilities clean, painted, and in good repair. Maintenance was so unreliable that some tenants charged discrimination. Although no discrimination existed, the complaints eventually involved public antidiscrimination groups. Finally all of these pressures forced him out of his job.

Of course, owners and even monarchs may become successful career managers, but they do so only by recognizing a separate managerial role and competently performing it for the long run.

The broad role of career management is composed of many subsidiary roles which need to be performed. Each of these roles contributes to success in the overall role. Six important ones which are involved in the relation of business to its environment are trustee, boundary mediator, system regulator, productivity catalyst, change agent, and leader.

The Role of Trustee

In terms of business's relationship with the external world, one of its most significant roles is that of trustee, as indicated by the second quotation introducing this chapter. Society commits to management its human and economic resources with the expectation that management will employ them wisely to produce more outputs than inputs. As with legal trustees, management is expected not to dissipate the resources under its care but to enhance them if at all possible. Although management may in the short run hold these resources by means of legal forms such as ownership and rights of contract, in the long run it legitimizes its custody of these social resources by being an effective trustee.

The trusteeship role was recognized early in business literature. In 1925 Robert Brookings wrote, "Management is thus coming to occupy the position of trustee . . . This change is not yet complete. It is a trend rather than an accomplished fact, but it is a very promising trend."[9] Chester Barnard, a distinguished figure in management, further clarified this role by pointing out that business actions are *representative behavior*. That which is representative is performed on behalf of others. It is done in terms of the goals and ethics of others rather than according to the performer's personal goals and ethics. For example, in a legal situation such as a trust or will, the trustee has wide latitude to apply judgment, but his judgment must be entirely divorced from his personal interest. As indicated by Barnard, the ethics of personal behavior are not identical with those of representative behavior except by chance.[10]

[9] Robert S. Brookings, *Industrial Ownership: Its Economic and Social Significance*, New York: The Macmillan Company, 1925, p. 23.
[10] Chester I. Barnard, "Elementary Conditions of Business Morals," *California Management Review*, Fall, 1958, pp. 1–13.

Regardless of how well personal ethics are defined by society, representative behavior requires a whole new set of ethical norms. A manager's decisional environment is so complex that it would be impossible to prescribe all his decisions by law. Even if this were possible, it would be undesirable because it would tie him in a straitjacket that would keep him from applying the talents which society wants from him. The result is that managers retain wide latitude to apply judgment, but they experience increasing pressures to act in a responsible manner as trustees of social investments. Since trustees act on behalf of others, many of whom are more concerned with the *quality of life* than its material productivity, *managers are becoming more accountable to society for the quality of life created by their trusteeship actions.*

The Role of Boundary Mediator

Management also performs a role of boundary mediator with all of its external claimants. Just as a fluid system in physical science has boundary conditions, so also does a dynamic organization have them. These are its points of interface with its environment, and management mediates or resolves these boundary interfaces in order to keep its organization effective. Its role is to achieve organizational objectives while supporting claimant objectives also. Managers direct an open social system, not a closed one. As indicated by the quotation introducing this chapter, a distinguishing feature of the managerial role is its system of multiple clients. Managers should expect external pressures of all types and be prepared to mediate them. Through resolving these pressures, they integrate their organization with society. Their role is largely one of mediation because they have no direct authority to order society to take—or not take—any course of action.

With the new emphasis on the social environment of business, the role of boundary mediator is increasing in significance. Company presidents and other top officers are devoting more of their time to this area, and frequently they have major staff assistants to help them. The assistants gather data, screen claims, and even help educate their manager concerning the social environment of business. A number of firms are establishing a major executive position for a vice-president of public affairs or some similar title. Because of the many claimants with which a manager must deal, he is often placed in value conflicts which he needs to resolve in order to reach a satisfactory decision.

In a large city a plant produced considerable fumes and dust. Thirty years ago the plant was located on the edge of town. Now the city has grown, and the plant is near the edge of the downtown commercial area. Pressures are building up for the plant to improve its control of fumes and dust. Figure 5–1 shows some of the value conflicts which the manager faced in this situation. Community citizens wanted a cleaner city in which to live and shop. (He and his family were citizens of the community.) The Chamber of Commerce wanted a cleaner downtown. (His firm was a member of the Chamber of Commerce.) The fumes and dust could

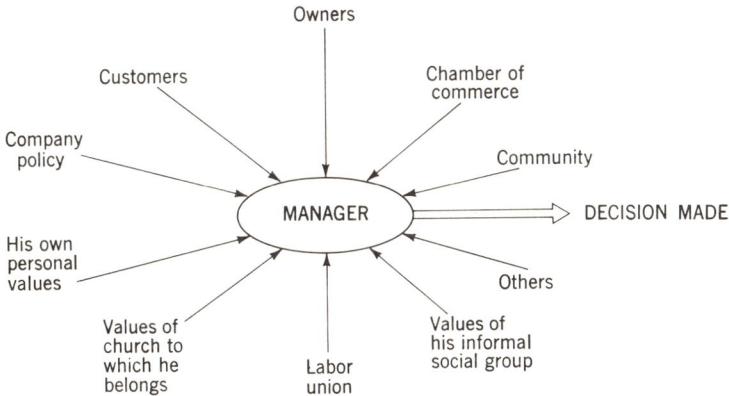

Figure 5–1 Pressures on a manager concerning an air pollution problem.

be prevented, but this would require over one million dollars of capital that might otherwise be used for stockholder benefit. (He and his children owned stock in the firm.) The cost of pollution control equipment would probably raise the cost of the firm's products about one percent. (He had personal friends who were regular purchasers of the firm's products, and he had strong feelings about inflation.) This is only a partial listing of the conflicts involved, so it is easy to see why he felt stress and conflict in trying to decide this issue. (What would you do?)

Assuming that a manager in his boundary mediator role perceives an external claim, his next step is to screen it on the basis of its validity and strength. Does it come from a group which has a genuine investment in the situation? Is the claim consistent with socially accepted customs? What is the strength of the claimants? Let us take an extreme example. If a group comes to a manager and insists that he hire no person more than ten pounds overweight because excessive weight is dangerous to health, he may sympathize with their cause and agree with their conclusion about danger to health, but he will pay little heed to their demand because it has weak rationality and is beyond the bounds of social custom. On the other hand, he may respond to a plea for hiring more handicapped persons, which would probably include a number of overweight and underweight persons.

After screening, many valid claims remain, so a manager must further resolve them through working with claimant groups both inside and outside his organization. In the long run he seeks role action which brings net outputs greater than inputs.

The Role of System Regulator

The role of system regulator is concerned with boundary mediation of subgroups *within* the firm and with their direction and control. In turn, the manager's decision may affect the subgroup's relation with its external environment. Management functions as decision maker at key junction points in the intricate social system that forms an organization. In fact, an organization may be defined as a cluster of roles having a common objective. As part of the system, management is both independent and dependent, initiating action on others and having action initiated on it. Some earlier views of management made it exclusively an independent force initiating on others, but this view lacked realism in terms of actual operating conditions. Management performs in a dynamic system relationship rather than being the static authority structure pictured on an organization chart.

An essential contradiction of decision making is that the desirable consequences of a decision are likely to be partly offset by undesirable side effects. For example, the desirable consequences of fume and dust control in the city discussed earlier could be accomplished only with the undesirable consequences of costs to owners and customers, plus perhaps an additional push toward inflation. Few decisions produce only desirable consequences for all concerned. When a manager functions in roles such as trustee, boundary mediator, and system regulator, he has to make trade-offs among the consequences in order to produce some desirable combination of them.

This trade-off of consequences is usually perceived as a satisfactory decision, rather than one which is maximal. A maximal decision wholly favors one objective or group without regard for others. For example, a manager may maximize profits. An optimal decision considers all alternatives and selects the one which is definitely best. Satisfactory decisions, on the other hand, consider a number of alternatives and select one which at least meets minimum criteria. The difference is similar to looking for the sharpest needle in a haystack and looking for a needle only sharp enough for sewing. According to March and Simon, *"Most human decision-making, whether individual or organizational, is concerned with the discovery and selection of satisfactory alternatives; only in exceptional cases is it concerned with the discovery and selection of optimal alternatives."*[11]

The Role of Productivity Catalyst

The most desirable combination of organizational consequences is that which increases the flow of outputs in relation to inputs. This is the role of productivity catalyst. Most managers in advanced nations recognize this role and are able to state it explicitly in terms such as "to make the best in quality at the lowest cost" and "more and better products for more people." This is the role which most directly expresses the business mission of "progress through productive implementation" mentioned in an earlier chapter. In the next generation's more complex society with larger organizations and a population explosion, this role of productivity catalyst becomes urgent, perhaps even essential, to sustain the larger population. "The task of the next generation is to make productive for

[11] James G. March and Herbert A. Simon, *Organizations*, New York: John Wiley & Sons, Inc., 1958, pp. 140–141. Italics in original.

Taking certain inputs & getting greatest amounts of outputs.

the individual, the community, and the society the new organized institutions of our new pluralism. And that is, above all, *management's new role*."[12]

It has been stated without great exaggeration that people in only a small part of the world understand that socioeconomic wealth can be created by productivity. In much of the rest of the globe most of the people view wealth as something to be hoarded or reallocated, so they have an entirely different—and often more negative—outlook toward work, business activities, and political power. They may have less motivation to work, view business as a selfish leech taking citizen assets, and support dictators who promise reallocation of wealth. With this attitude toward the dominant affairs of life, they find it difficult to break the bonds of low productivity and move vigorously forward.

In recent decades the principal exception among non-Western nations has been Japan, which has taken its own unique cultural heritage and successfully applied it to the industrial age. The result has been vigorous socioeconomic growth. Japan has shown that growth is derived not from a specific cultural heritage, but from social and business leadership which serves as a productivity catalyst to focus the existing heritage on productive activities.

The Role of Change Agent

In its effort to serve as a productivity catalyst in a dynamic system, management finds that it is increasingly necessary to operate as a change agent and innovator. Change is a natural condition of organizations, and managers, as the responsible directors of organizations, are continually involved with it. They initiate changes on their own behalf, apply changes required by others, and adjust to new environmental conditions.

Although management needs to motivate others to be creative, the management role itself emphasizes innovation more than creativity. Creativity deals with the generation of ideas, but innovation deals with making them work. Compared with research scientists, who emphasize creativity, managers are more concerned with innovating to bring ideas to fruition. Since creative ideas are of no usefulness until implemented, the innovative role of management becomes more important as more and better ideas are generated in modern society.

Ideas without implementers simply increase the burden of conscience on society because people know that there are better ways and are frustrated by their deficient implementation. Modern society, having generated ideas beyond our capacity to absorb them, is turning increasingly to management in order to implement them. This role of administering change is becoming so significant that some persons are venturing the thought that for this particular period of human history "possibly, the major function of management has become that of managing change."[13]

[12] Peter F. Drucker, "Management's New Role," *Harvard Business Review*, November–December, 1969, p. 54. Italics in original.
[13] Robert P. Neuschel, "Presidential Style: Updated Versions," *Business Horizons*, June, 1969, p. 23.

The Role of Leader

The leadership role has been emphasized throughout history, so it is not as new as some of the other managerial roles. Nevertheless, society expects management in all its actions to use leadership, which is defined as behavior which induces energetic, emotionally committed, cooperative followers. As has been said many times, management is not expected to perform society's operative tasks but to motivate others to do so. If better men can be attracted and motivated, then better results should be reached, other things being equal. Some of history's great business leaders recognized this role, men like Andrew Carnegie whose epitaph reads:

> Here lies a man
> Who knew how to enlist
> In his service
> Better men than himself.

Much of the leadership role is expressed by a comprehensive climate which a leader develops through sensing the needs and goals of people and relating them to organizational objectives. Men follow because they see reasons, both emotional and rational, for following. Leadership finds those reasons and makes them more appealing. It encourages average people to give above-average performance.

An Evolving Managerial Role

The managerial role in business and elsewhere is continually being redefined to gear it to new developments. The largest redefinition probably relates to the external environment and social goals, as is being discussed in this book. Social needs and goals are turning the attention of people to the social obligations of managers to work toward a high quality of life as well as toward high economic productivity. This focus requires the modern career manager to use socially "good" methods of operation toward socially "good" ends.

Since socially desirable methods and ends are not easy to achieve, the modern managerial role requires men who are intellectually capable, thoughtful, broadly trained, and professional in attitude. There is decreasing opportunity for those who are unprepared, who fail to grow, or who work mainly from their emotions, even when their emotions favor desirable social ends. The practice of management is becoming increasingly professional.

There are also other areas of role redefinition. The leadership role is being perceived as less autocratic and more participative and supportive of employee needs.[14] It is also less a matter of personality and more a matter of role behavior. Modern leaders are moving away from detailed task prescription toward goal setting which allows participants more latitude in task performance.

[14] For a presentation of this trend within a framework see Keith Davis, "Evolving Models of Organizational Behavior," *Academy of Management Journal*, March, 1968, pp. 27–38.

Similarly the role of system regulator is moving away from static emphasis on formal authority toward dynamic views of communication and decision making. The role of trustee is moving from custodianship of resources toward a responsibility to help resources grow and to use them nearer to their capacity. These are but a few of many role modifications now happening. The managerial-role definition will not remain static.

Role performance over a period of time leads to what is called the managerial mind.[15] This kind of mind is committed to results through organization. It is action-oriented and policy-oriented. It desires to seek and solve problems rather than avoid them. Tensions are used constructively toward action rather than being perceived as a psychological ill. The managerial mind learns from experience and teaches what it knows to others. It is objective and realistic in decision making, working always within an environment of change.

A Note on Managerial Values

Even though managerial and business values are discussed in a later chapter, it should be emphasized at this point that managerial-role performance is influenced by both personal and occupational values. Managers are people like the rest of us, so they are influenced by the values they hold. This rather obvious fact is often overlooked by commentators on business. They occasionally imply that business managers are single-minded individuals who cold-heartedly pursue one objective without regard for human or social values. In reality, a manager's whole value system is involved when he makes a decision. As a participant, not an observer, he experiences a personal involvement in every decision situation. The whole person decides, not a separate and abstract computer in his head. And the whole person has many ethical values, not one.

In addition, the occupational role of manager, like that of lawyer or teacher, tends to carry with it certain attitudes and values along with the knowledge and skills that are required. For example, a lawyer may believe that his role requires him to protect a guilty person even though he knows the person is guilty and will be a hazard to society if acquitted. Or, a university teacher may refuse to reveal each student's grade to other class members, believing that the grade is personal information or that the information might upset class cohesion. In a similar manner, a manager may refuse to reveal individual salaries to other managers, because he believes this information might upset managerial cohesion. Each person in the examples mentioned is acting according to perceptions of what is proper in his occupational role and acceptable to his own value system.

SUMMARY

Management is a distinct occupational role, and managers throughout the world are substantially in agreement concerning their perception of this role. The effects of different national cultures and even different forms of

[15] Charles E. Summer, Jr., "The Managerial Mind," *Harvard Business Review*, January–February, 1959, pp. 69–78; and David W. Ewing, *The Managerial Mind*, New York: The Free Press, 1964.

business ownership are surprisingly small. The role definition of career management emphasizes the following supplementary roles in relating business to its environment: trustee, boundary mediator, system regulator, productivity catalyst, change agent, and leader. Career management has a strong concern for the external environment and the quality of life as well as the economic standard of living.

The managerial role is continually being redefined to gear it to new developments. In addition, managerial decisions are always influenced by a manager's current personal and occupational values in the same way that other persons' decisions are influenced by their values.

STUDY GUIDES FOR INTERPRETATION OF THIS CHAPTER

1 Discuss why managerial role perceptions are substantially similar in spite of different cultural backgrounds or forms of business ownership.

2 If laws were proposed requiring public disclosure of all managerial salaries and all university student grades, how would you as a citizen respond to each? Why?

3 A quotation introducing this chapter states, "The managerial role, in contrast to many other professional roles, tends to be defined in terms of a system of *multiple clients.*" Discuss this statement.

4 Assume that a law is proposed—primarily because of the trustee-ship role of managers—requiring persons to be fingerprinted, screened for felony convictions, and licensed in order to serve as officers or middle managers of corporations (government incorporated organizations, profit and nonprofit). As a citizen, how would you react? Why?

PROBLEMS
TWO PROPOSALS FOR REORGANIZING BUSINESS[16]

The following proposals have been made in France for reorganizing business in order to redistribute power.

One proposal has been made by a group of Christian businessmen in Lyons. They propose that the workers establish a workers' company that is legally comparable to the regular company set up by the owners. The two companies would then enter into a contractual agreement which would be the source of all power to manage the joint assets of the two companies. The top manager would be selected by the two companies and designated in their contract. He would have full freedom to manage, but he would be ultimately responsible to both companies.

A second proposal suggests that there should be a regular board of directors whose chairman would be the top executive of the business. In addition, the top executive's activities would be reviewed by a public court consisting of members of government as well as representatives of employers, employees, shareholders, and consumers. The court would

---

[16] Adapted from P. Heymann and J. Schmidt, "French Business Probes Its *Raison d'Etre,*" *Columbia Journal of World Business,* July–August, 1967, pp. 75–76.

provide advice concerning the distribution of power in the business when cases of this type could not be resolved at lower levels. For example, a proper case for the court would be a complaint about the incompetence of a director.

1 If the first proposal were adopted in your nation in what ways would it change the role of (a) the top manager and (b) other managers? Be specific.

2 If the second proposal were adopted in your nation in what ways would it change the role of (a) the top manager and (b) other managers? Be specific.

THE LEAR JET

When William P. Lear, using mostly his own money, was engaged in a crash program to develop his highly successful business aircraft, the Lear Jet, the following events occurred.

> Lear, a short-tempered perfectionist who has frequently fired the same employee three times in one week for minor miscalculations, was breathing down everyone's neck all the time—checking, criticizing, guiding, goading, demanding—and he was finally threatened with mutiny. A delegation of employees, ready to quit, stormed into Lear's office one day and complained bitterly that he never let them do anything by themselves. "You make all the decisions," one of them said. "We can't do a thing."
>
> "That's right," Lear snapped, "but I'll make a deal with you. You guys put up half the money, and from now on I'll let you make half the decisions." End of mutiny.[17]

1 Do you agree with William Lear? In general, when the owner of a large business is also its top manager, in what ways, if any, is his managerial role changed from that of career manager?

[17] David Shaw, "What Bill Lear Wants, Bill Lear Invents," *Esquire*, September, 1969, p. 188. Used with permission.

CHAPTER 6

SOCIAL POWER AND SOCIAL RESPONSIBILITY

The responsibility of business to society in the future cannot be and will not be discharged in the same way we have been discharging it in the past.

SOL M. LINOWITZ[1]

Corporate government, like public government, needs to be subject to certain constitutional restraints.

RICHARD EELLS[2]

There is a rising public clamor for something called "social responsibility" on the part of business as well as other institutions in society. In the face of all this clamor how does a modern business manager know what to do to meet the demands of pluralistic claimants for "responsibility"? One observer says, "A businessman has no responsibility to the public except to sell at as low a price as he can." Another says, "The job of business is to make a profit, and as long as it stays within the limits of the law, it has no other responsibility." At another extreme a local activist charges, "Business materialism and unemployment are the main causes of juvenile delinquency, and business must give a job to every teen-ager in order to prevent delinquency." And a local humanist thinks that business should pay for a new hospital because, "Business can get the money, but we can't afford to raise our taxes anymore."[3]

In the face of all these claims, what guides does a manager have to assist him in making judgments concerning social responsibility? Should he avoid social involvement in his community? Should he pay attention only to the loudest claimant or to each squeaky wheel? Should he support

[1] Sol M. Linowitz, "Public Affairs: The Demanding Seventies," *Looking Ahead*, National Planning Association, May, 1966, p. 2. Italics in original.
[2] Richard Eells, "Beyond the Golden Rule," *Columbia Journal of World Business*, July–August, 1967, p. 84.
[3] Portions of this chapter are adapted from Keith Davis, "Understanding the Social Responsibility Puzzle," *Business Horizons*, Winter, 1967, pp. 45–50; and Keith Davis, "Can Business Afford to Ignore Social Responsibilities?" *California Management Review*, Spring, 1960, pp. 70–76.

only those activities in which he has a personal interest? Certainly he knows that, regardless of the claims made upon him, he cannot solve all of society's problems. If he tried to do so, he would preempt the work of other pluralistic institutions that deal specifically with social problems. Furthermore, his resources are limited; he must husband them wisely and put them to the best long-run use. But how should he respond to these different claims on his organization?

In this chapter we shall explore the development of the idea of social responsibility, including its background and the relationship of social power and responsibility. We shall examine the socioeconomic and human values that are involved with social responsibility and discuss how constitutionalism becomes the instrument for crystallizing social responsibility.

DECISION MAKING AND SOCIAL RESPONSIBILITY

During the last 100 years, business thinking and action have changed dramatically. Business practices of a century ago would not be accepted even by a backward firm today. It is academic whether business initiated these changes or whether society pushed business into them. In actuality, progress was mutual; each initiated changes on the other, assisted by other institutions in the total social system. Business could not have come as far as it has without the help of society, nor could society have developed to its present state without corresponding business progress. As the years have passed, business gradually has broadened its activities beyond its own gates into the general community, until today business shares power for economic growth, social stability, community improvements, education, and a host of other public needs.

These expanded social powers are probably greater than the narrow property rights which business had a century ago and which gave control only over property. Business holds these social powers not by legal right, but by reason of responsible and competent performance. Out of these expanded relationships the idea of social responsibility is developing as a reciprocal of evident social power.

What Is Social Responsibility?

The idea of social responsibility implies that prior to making a decision a person will consider the widest possible effects of his decision on the public interest. *Social responsibility,* therefore, refers to a person's obligation to evaluate in the decision-making process the effects of both his personal and institutional decisions and actions on the whole social system.[4] The substance of social responsibility arises from concern for the ethical consequences of one's acts as they might affect the interests of others. This idea exists in most religions and philosophies of the world. Quite frequently, however, a tendency exists to limit its application to person-to-person contacts. Social responsibility moves one large step fur-

---

[4] Although this book discusses business responsibilities, the idea of social responsibility applies to all persons and institutions.

ther by including institutional actions and their effect on the whole social system. Without this additional step, personal and institutional acts tend to be divorced. A businessman can lead a model personal life, but continue to rationalize his organization's pollution of a river because no direct personal consequence is involved. He can consider river pollution a "public problem" to be solved by public action. The idea of social responsibility, however, requires him to consider his acts in terms of a whole social system and holds him responsible for the effects of his acts anywhere in that system.

Social responsibility, therefore, broadens a person's view to the total social system. When a man's primary frame of reference is himself, he may be counted upon for antisocial behavior whenever his values conflict with those of society. If his values are limited primarily to a certain group or organization, he tends to become a partisan acting for that group. But, if he thinks in terms of a whole system, he begins to build societal values into his actions, even when they are for a certain organization. This is the essence of social responsibility.

The idea of social responsibility recognizes that each person is attached to an extended social system on which he is partly dependent; consequently, certain obligations or social responsibilities arise from this attachment. The same reasoning applies to groups and institutions. Businessmen apply social responsibility when they consider the needs and interests of others who may be affected by business actions. In so doing, they look beyond their own personal interests and also beyond their firm's narrow economic and technical interests.

While it is true that only businessmen (rather than businesses per se) make socially responsible decisions, they decide in terms of the objectives and policies of their business institution. Thus each business institution and the entire business system eventually come to stand for certain socially responsible beliefs and actions. But in the last analysis it is always the businessman who makes the decision. The business institution can only give him a cultural framework and policy guidance.

Suboptimization and Social Responsibility

When a group's values are predominately partisan without a socially responsible concern for the public interest, then from the view of the larger social system the partisan group is *suboptimizing* general social benefits. This means that the group is optimizing benefits to itself but that benefits to others are being largely neglected by its narrow view. The result is that benefits to the larger system are poorly served. The partisan group gains at the expense of others. In extreme cases, the social disequilibrium may become so intense that *all groups lose,* even the group which is seeking gain for itself alone.

An example of the costs and dangers that can result from social suboptimization is the experience of a British factory closed by a pay conflict with ten attendants of women's lavatories. The situation moved a government official to comment wryly. "One of the lavatories is working, but the factory is stopped."

When the attendants refused to clean certain women's lavatories, the company asked women employees to use other facilities available during the dispute. The women refused. They said this would be strikebreaking, so they stopped work and went home. Their absence from their work stations forced the factory to be closed, putting men off the job. In a day, the strike of attendants was settled. All employees then returned to work, but they demanded a day's pay for the day they were off the job. The company refused to pay for no work, so the employees walked out leaving the lavatory housekeepers working but a closed factory.

At this point the following organizations and interest groups had already been involved: the British government at different levels, the National Trade Union Congress, the Transport and General Workers Union at various levels, women lavatory attendants, women employees, men employees, other trade unions, management, and others. Somehow in this partisan bickering among different pluralistic groups the public need of productivity was bypassed. Britain became poorer because groups suboptimized their own interest without social responsibility toward the larger interests of all employees and customers, and the general public interest. Hence, "One of the lavatories is working, but the factory is stopped."[5]

Defining a Socially Responsible Decision

The importance of social responsibility is that it is a cultural value which may affect a businessman's decisions, along with technical, economic, and other values which he must weigh. Social responsibility is rarely the exclusive reason for a decision, but it is usually a participating influence in decision making.

A decision can be made for strictly technical reasons and by chance also be in the public interest, but this chance connection is not usually considered evidence of social responsibility. The true test of social responsibility is whether issues of public interest are considered at the time a decision is made. If so, social responsibility is involved.

A socially responsible decision does not necessarily guarantee results in the public interest. The decision may, because of poor judgment or unforeseen events, actually cause results against the public interest, but society expects the majority of socially responsible decisions to affect the public interest favorably. Actually, many business decisions start a series of developments some of which serve the public interest and some of which, considered by themselves, are against it. The discharge of an employee for cause, if the man's unemployment is considered by itself, is hardly in the public interest. The decision as a whole, however, may be in the public interest. The only realistic approach is to consider the net effect on the public interest expected from the whole decision, adding positive and negative effects.

Actions for the benefit of an organization may still be socially responsible. To require that institutional acts be only in the public interest is to

[5] "Not Even Good Enough for the Lavatory," The Economist, June 28, 1969, p. 19.

deny the pluralism of society. Centers of initiative are many, and, in order to maintain these centers, their goals must be served as well as the general welfare. But the price which public society exacts for this pluralism is that private organizational acts shall be taken with due concern for public responsibility. There is in pluralism a concurrent private freedom and public responsibility.

For example, John Doe Corporation decided to open a chain of franchised hamburger restaurants, each to be owned locally by its operators. It planned to serve a standardized menu (with some local exceptions) of good quality pure foods and to meet or exceed Grade A sanitation standards in each community. Buildings would have much more attractive design and landscaping than typical "mom-and-pop" hamburger stands. Management services, financial aids, centralized purchasing of nonperishable items, and other services would be provided to franchisees.

John Doe Corporation entered the hamburger business in order to profitably employ its capital; however, it also attempted to operate in a socially responsible manner in a number of ways. It attempted to upgrade "mom-and-pop" standards of food quality and service, thus making it possible for locally owned business to remain competitive. It gave attention to upgrading underprivileged neighborhoods, providing locations that were aesthetically attractive, providing balanced diets, upgrading sanitation, and providing franchisee participation in control. Though it acted in its own interest, it also believed it acted in the public interest in a socially responsible manner.

Actions taken by a person for his own benefit may be socially responsible if they also seek to benefit others. If we require all acts to be exclusively in the public interest, we deny the psychological fact that all men act in their own interest. Social responsibility does not try to remake man; it asks of him only that he consider the broader social system and try to act in a way which benefits others as well as himself. In this kind of social exchange both he and his neighbors should benefit. As emphasized by George C. Homans, "Not all self-interests are selfish interests."[6] A person may serve his self-needs by helping serve social needs, such as performing necessary work.

Public Interest Cannot Be Determined Exactly

Although the public interest is a useful guide for responsible decision making, there is no exact way to determine what the "public interest" is, how to measure it, or how to serve it. For these reasons socially responsible decisions will always be made in a state of imperfection and uncertainty. Consider the following situation.

In a Midwestern metropolitan area of 1 million persons a local grocery chain withdrew from its shelves all copies of one issue of a popular national magazine because they were alleged to have obscene photo-

[6] George C. Homans, "Bringing Men Back In," *American Sociological Review*, December, 1964, p. 816.

graphs. The decision was made by the company president after store managers had notified him of substantial customer complaints as soon as the magazine was placed on sale. According to the president, each store was primarily a grocery store, and magazines were strictly a supplementary business. Store policy was to maintain a family image and environment to which women could freely bring their children while shopping. Since this magazine's content for this particular week was judged not fit for family consumption according to general community standards, it was withdrawn from magazine racks. The president said the store was not on an antismut campaign and would display the next issue of the magazine for sale if it met community standards for family use.

When a local news reporter contacted the magazine's director of promotion in New York City, the director said the store action was censorship and added that people should be allowed to make their own judgments of what to buy. On the other hand, both the local mayor and the chain's majority stockholder told the reporter they agreed with the chain's action. When the state director of the Civil Liberties Union was contacted, he agreed, stating that the store had a right to sell what it pleased, especially since the magazine could be purchased elsewhere in the community.

It is evident from this case that the public interest is difficult to define. In addition, conflicts among basic values are the most difficult to resolve. Should a free press be preserved or should community standards be preserved? What were the real community standards? Was the president using the situation to justify censorship according to his own standards? Was his decision truly socially responsible, or was he allowing himself to be influenced by a few prudish dissidents in the community? In the words of one commentator, "The social responsibilities of a corporation do not demand responses to all public expectations. The public may demand too much. Its desires may be transitory. . . . The social responsibilities of a corporation, therefore, cannot be defined in terms of merely passive adaptation to the public demands on business."[7] As president of the chain store, what would you have done?

Reasons for an Expanding Emphasis on Social Responsibility

There are several reasons for society's growing emphasis on social responsibility. One is that society today is bound together in greater complexity, with each of its parts more dependent on other parts. More population, economic growth, and specialization have created an advanced social interdependence. Business, labor, government, communities, minority groups, farmers, professionals, educators, and others are closely interwoven in a complex web of social interdependence. Business layoffs or expansions of facilities, for example, have a significant effect on tax receipts, job opportunities, community development, minority opportunities, and other group interests. For the same reason—interdependence—all other groups have to be more concerned with their *social responsibilities toward business* for any actions which affect business. If they act

[7] Richard Eells, *The Corporation and the Arts,* New York: The Macmillan Company, 1967, p. 175.

with ignorance or intolerance toward business, they avoid their own social responsibilities.

A second reason is that society has more wealth and culture which it wishes to conserve. Therefore, it is less willing to risk the disruptions that might occur from irresponsible acts, such as sale of dangerous drugs, nationwide transportation strikes, or stream pollution. The climate of public opinion increasingly insists that actions by all institutions and persons must be responsible. Too much is at stake to risk irresponsibility, so responsible business action becomes necessary in order to maintain a viable institution and a favorable public image.

A third reason for interest in social responsibility is that the social sciences are giving us new knowledge about how business affects the social system beyond the company gates. Though we have always known that business affects the social system, we were not sure how, so we were not able to offer many proposals for improving its social function. We had to wait for more knowledge of the business role in society. Today we have a better understanding of the extended effects of business in society. We know that they are much more extensive than we realized earlier.

Fourth, the growing power of government looms on the sidelines waiting to add restrictive controls the moment business becomes lax in any area of responsibility. Businessmen have learned that once a government control is established, it is seldom removed even though conditions change. When freedom and initiative are lost to government, they are lost for the long run. If these are the facts, then the prudent course for business is to understand fully the limits of its power and to use that power responsibly, giving government no cause to intervene.

A fifth reason for increasing emphasis on social responsibility is that current ethical concepts are conditioning people to favor more responsible action. The businessman shares the attitudes and values of society just as he did a century ago, and he reflects today's attitudes of more responsible conduct in his actions.

Finally, and perhaps most important, ownership and control are more separated in modern society. The career manager takes the longer view over time and the broader view among claimants on the organization. The separation of owner and manager has not been required by law but has developed de facto by delegation because this arrangement worked best. But this arrangement also confuses the location of responsibility. When the owner managed, the acts of the firm proceeded from his initiative. The identity and power of the firm resided in him. In this situation the law could directly fix responsibility on him without confusion. But with the separation of ownership and management, normal legal channels of responsibility have eroded. No one is quite sure how much public responsibility managers have or through what channels it is controlled or should be controlled. To illustrate this problem, ignore legal details for the moment and assume that a corporation's owners give their stock to it so that it owns itself! How would its practices change? To whom would it be responsible, and how?

We must be cautious, however, that we do not overplay the *possible* separation of owner and manager, because there is considerable unity between

PHILOSOPHY ⟶ PROCESS ⟶ FUNCTION ⟶ END (GOAL)

| Social responsibility | Creative social decisions by business | Social action (social response) | More effective society |

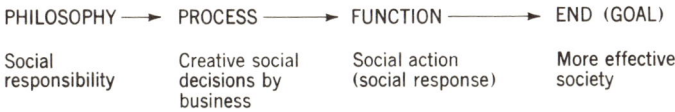

Figure 6–1 A philosophy of social responsibility provides a basis for an effective social response by business.

the two parties. The unity is evident in smaller firms. With regard to larger firms, the personal stake of stock ownership by an executive may be large, such as $1 million, even when he owns only a small proportion of the firm. Since his ownership is major to him, he behaves like an owner.

Social Responsibility and Social Response

The concept of social responsibility is merely a preliminary step toward social effectiveness of business. It is the underlying value which gives businessmen a sound basis for social action. It is the philosophy which justifies business involvement in its social community, but philosophy by itself is incomplete. It must be followed by effective social action. In the words of one observer, "Philosophy without program is shadow without substance. Perhaps one should talk, therefore, less of corporate social *responsibilities* and more of corporate social *responses.* The former is too redolent with legalisms and the notion of fixed obligations; the latter, more open, permits voluntary and creative undertakings by business on behalf of society's larger needs."[8]

If business and society get stuck on the legalisms of social responsibility, they will drift into inaction. The ultimate need is a business *response* which provides progress toward the desirable end of a more effective society. As shown in Figure 6–1, the desirable end is achieved through a sequence of philosophy, process, and function. In the area of business and society, the philosophy is social responsibility, and the process is creative decision making by business. Creative decisions lead to the function of social action by business, which produces the desirable end of a better society. Social responsibility is only the beginning of the sequence.

One fact is certain; businessmen cannot withdraw into isolation and avoid the issues of social responsibility and social response. Neither can they claim that business is amoral and exempt from considerations of responsibility. The simple fact is that business is a major social institution, and as such it is importantly involved in social values. This is to its credit—a mark of its status. If business were not importantly involved in societal value systems, this fact would be evidence that it is detached from the mainstream of society and is of little significance. But business is in the mainstream of life and, hence, in the mainstream of value. As

[8] Clarence C. Walton, "Recreating the City of Man," in *A Call to Social Action,* St. Louis, Mo.: Beta Gamma Sigma, 1968, p. 17. Italics in original. See also Dow Votaw and S. Prakash Sethi, "Do We Need A New Corporate Response to a Changing Social Environment?" *California Management Review,* Fall, 1969, pp. 3–31.

stated by one top manager: "We must sense and be responsive to the social demands of the public as well as the marketplace and recognize the social consequences of economic decision-making."[9]

The quality of life, as distinguished from traditional economic needs, has become the dominant theme of need in the United States. This means that the next great opportunity for business service is the meeting of social needs. This opportunity is comparable to the economic one which prevailed two hundred years ago. Business, if it is to remain vigorous, increasingly will turn its creative efforts toward serving social needs in a profitable manner. In the long run, provision of many traditionally "social" needs such as education and resource conservation may be a primary or line function of many businesses in the same way that manufacturing is today.

THE POWER-RESPONSIBILITY EQUATION

Social Power

Most persons agree that businessmen today have much social power. Their counsel is sought by government, and what they say and do influences their community. This type of influence is *social power*. It comes to businessmen because they are leaders, intelligent men of affairs, people with a record of accomplishing projects successfully, and managers of vast economic resources.

In the same way that physical assets are an economic resource, power is a social resource. It may be used for good or evil, and for social gain or social loss. It is subject to abuse and corruption, but it also is an agent for responsible social improvement. In a pluralistic social system it is highly dynamic, moving back and forth across the interfaces of organizations as it is redistributed by means of their social exchanges.

An example of business abuse of power, using government as an ally in this instance, is the plumbing contractor licensing board in a small community. Most of the appointees to this board are plumbing contractors. As a result of contractor dominance on the board, it rejected seven of the last eight applicants for the license required to set up a plumbing business. These rejections helped maintain favorable competitive conditions for the contractors already in business.

Most power exercised by business is functional power; that is, the power granted to business by society is roughly sufficient for business to perform the functions which society expects of it. It is power "to do," rather than power "over." The businessman deals with other persons in functional roles such as employee, customer, and vendor, not as subjects of his monolithic power. There is, consequently, much pressure from claimants to keep his power within reasonable bounds. In this instance, reasonable power is defined as that power which is necessary to perform an appropriate function.

[9] Laurence I. Wood, "Social Performance of Business," *The Economic and Business Bulletin*, p. 18. Philadelphia, Temple University School of Business Administration, September, 1964.

The power of businessmen relates to their role as businessmen. Like other persons, they are also citizens, and in their citizen role they may take a position on public issues. When they speak and act as citizens only, and those involved recognize this fact, whatever social power businessmen possess is that of citizens and is not directly attributable to business. In practice, however, it is often difficult to distinguish between these two roles, thereby further complicating the power-responsibility relationships of businessmen.

Social Responsibility Goes with Social Power

To the extent that businessmen and other groups have social power, the lessons of history suggest that social responsibility should be equated with it. Stated in the form of a general relationship, social responsibilities of businessmen arise from the amount of social power they have.

The idea that responsibility and power go hand in hand appears to be as old as civilization itself. Wherever one looks in ancient and medieval history—Palestine, Rome, Britain—men were concerned with balancing power and responsibility. Men, being somewhat less than perfect, have often failed to achieve this balance, but they have generally sought it as a necessary antecedent to justice. This idea has its origins in reason and logic. It is essentially a matter of balancing the two sides of an equation. As stated by one philosopher, "The demand of the law in a well-ordered society is that responsibility shall lie where the power of decision lies. Where that demand is met, men have a legal order; where it is not, they have only the illusion of one."[10]

The idea of balanced power and responsibility is a value supported by Protestant, Catholic, and Jewish faiths,[11] and it is also a part of business philosophy. For example, one of the rules of scientific management is that authority and responsibility should be balanced in such a way that each employee and manager is made responsible to the extent of his authority, and vice versa. Although this rule refers only to relationships within the firm, it should apply as well to the larger society outside the firm. As a matter of fact, businessmen have been strong proponents of balanced social power and responsibility in external society, particularly in their views on responsibilities of labor leaders.

Objections to a Balance of Power and Responsibility

The logic of reasonably balanced power and responsibility is often overlooked by those who discuss social responsibility. Some argue that business is business and anything that smacks of social responsibility is out of bounds. An economist contends that "few trends could so thoroughly undermine the very foundations of our free society as the acceptance by corporate officials of a social responsibility other than to make as much

[10] John F. A. Taylor, "Is the Corporation Above the Law?" *Harvard Business Review,* March–April, 1965, p. 126.
[11] John W. Clark, *Religion and Moral Standards of American Businessmen,* Cincinnati, Ohio: South-Western Publishing Company, Incorporated, 1966, especially p. 172.

money for their stockholders as possible."[12] Another author speaks of the "frightening spectacle" of a powerful business group that in the name of social responsibility "imposes its narrow ideas about a broad spectrum of unrelated noneconomic subjects on the mass of man and society."[13] He advocates a powerful democratic state to look after general welfare, leaving business to pursue its main objective of material gains within limits of everyday civility.

The objections to social responsibility are meaningful. Indeed, many dangers await as business moves into untrodden areas of social responsibility. The fallacy of these objections is that they are usually based on an economic model of pure competition in which market forces leave business theoretically without any social power and, hence, no responsibility (a balanced zero equation). This zero equation of no power and no responsibility is a proper theoretical model for pure competition, but it is theory only and is inconsistent with the power realities of modern organizations. They possess such great initiative, economic assets, and power that their actions do have social effects. In reality, therefore, the "no responsibility" doctrine assumes that business will keep some of its social power but will not worry about social responsibility.

At the other extreme, some persons would have business assume responsibilities as a sort of social godfather, looking after widows, orphans, public health, juvenile delinquency, or any other social need, simply because business has large economic resources. This position overlooks the fact that business operates in a pluralistic society, which has other institutions available to serve people in these areas. Business is one of many centers of initiative in the social system; hence, no need exists to make it a monolithic dispenser of welfare, overshadowing the state as it cares for everyone's problems. The "total responsibility" doctrine also confuses business's function of *service* to society with *servitude* to society. Workers, investors, and others participate in a business as free men—not as slaves of society. They have their own lives to live, and business is their cooperative venture for fulfilling their own needs (private needs) while serving others (public needs).

The "no responsibility" and the "total responsibility" doctrines are equally false. According to the first doctrine, business keeps its power but accepts no responsibility, thereby unbalancing the power-responsibility equation. According to the second doctrine, responsibility far exceeds power, again unbalancing the equation.

The Iron Law of Responsibility

If business social responsibilities could be avoided or reduced to insignificance, business decisions would certainly be easier. Social responsibilities are difficult to determine and apply. But what are the consequences of

[12] Milton Friedman, *Capitalism and Freedom*, Chicago: The University of Chicago Press, 1962, p. 133.
[13] Theodore Levitt, "The Dangers of Social Responsibility," *Harvard Business Review*, September–October, 1958, p. 44. See also the dangers and limitations reported in Hazel Henderson, "Should Business Tackle Society's Problems?" *Harvard Business Review*, July–August, 1968, pp. 77–85.

responsibility avoidance? If responsibility arises from power, then the two conditions tend to stay in balance over the long run, and the avoidance of social responsibility leads to gradual erosion of social power. This is the Iron Law of Responsibility: *In the long run, those who do not use power in a manner which society considers responsible will tend to lose it.* The law's application to man's institutions certainly stands confirmed by history. Though the "long run" may require decades or even centuries in some instances, society ultimately acts to reduce power when it is not used responsibly.

As it applies to business, the Iron Law of Responsibility insists that to the extent businessmen do not accept social-responsibility obligations as they arise, other groups eventually will step in to assume those responsibilities. This prediction of diluted social power is not a normative statement of what we think *should* happen. Rather, it is a prediction of what will tend to happen whenever businessmen do not keep their social responsibilities approximately equal to their social power. An early study of business social responsibilities presented this idea as follows: "And it is becoming increasingly obvious that a freedom of choice and delegation of power such as businessmen exercise would hardly be permitted to continue without some assumption of social responsibility."[14]

History supports the mutuality of power and responsibility in business. Take safe working conditions as an example. Under the protection of common law, employers during the nineteenth century gave minor attention to worker safety. Early in the twentieth century, in the face of pressure from safety and workmen's compensation laws, employers changed their attitudes to accept responsibility for job safety. Since then, very few restrictions have been imposed on business power in this area because business in general has been acting responsibly. Accident rates have been reduced dramatically until the workplace is safer than most areas away from work.

For an opposite example, consider unemployment. Business in the first quarter of this century remained callous about technological and market layoff. As a result, business lost some of its power to government, which administers unemployment compensation, and to unions, which restrict business by means of tight seniority clauses, supplemental unemployment benefits, and other means. Now business finds itself in the position of paying unemployment costs that it originally denied responsibility for but having less control than when it did not pay! Business power has drained away to bring the power-responsibility equation back into balance.

Balancing Power and Responsibility

In line with the foregoing analysis, proposals for a strictly economic function of business with no social responsibility lose some of their glamour because they mean substantial loss of business power. Historian Arnold J. Toynbee predicts this result when he speaks of business managers even-

[14] Howard R. Bowen, *Social Responsibilities of the Businessman,* New York: Harper & Row, Publishers, Incorporated, 1953, p. 4.

tually becoming part of a "new world civil service," not necessarily working for government, but working under such stability and elaborate rules from both within and without that they form a relatively powerless bureaucracy similar to the civil service.[15]

It is unlikely that businessmen will concede their social power so easily because they are men of action who will not sit quietly on the sidelines of progress. They want to be in the midst of progress, offering their innovations in all areas. It is even unlikely that society would permit businessmen to concede their power because it is coming to recognize its need for them. The more probable outcome is that society will persuade businessmen to accept more social responsibility in order to balance the power-responsibility equation. In serious situations, such as developed with trusts in the 1880s, "persuasion" will take the form of legal force on policy matters, leaving operating initiative to independent business units. The paramount point is operating initiative. If business conduct is so irresponsible that operating initiative is assumed by government boards, then the business civil service may truly develop.

It appears that both business leaders and the general public are coming to accept the idea of balanced power and responsibility. When businessmen accept the logic of this idea, their next step is learning to apply it when making decisions. Granted that there are no pat answers, they still need some guides, or else each will take off in a different direction according to his own views. At this point, the ideas already stated begin to offer operating help. If social responsibilities of businessmen need to reflect their social power, then, in a general way, in the specific operating areas where there is power, responsibility will also reside. And the amount of responsibility will approximate the amount of power. Consider the situation of two companies, each closing its plant in a different city. Company A is a major employer in a small town. It is moving its entire plant out of the community. Company B is moving its plant of the same size out of a large city, where it is one of many employers. Other things being equal, it appears that Company A needs to give more thought to social responsibilities in connection with its move because of its greater effect on its community.

Even accepting the greater responsibility of Company A, and some would not go this far, there is no measure of exactly how much more responsibility it has or of how it should adjust to its greater responsibility. Thus the equation of balanced power and responsibility serves only as a rough guide, but a real one. For example, do businessmen by their industrial engineering decisions have the power to affect workers' feelings of accomplishment and self-fulfillment on the job? If so, there is a balancing need for social responsibility. Do businessmen have power to determine the honesty of advertising? To the degree that they do, does not social responsibility also arise?

One matter of significance is that the conditions causing power are both internal and external to the firm. In the example of advertising

[15] Arnold J. Toynbee, "Thinking Ahead: Will Businessmen Be Civil Servants?" *Harvard Business Review*, September–October, 1958, pp. 23ff.

honesty, power is primarily internal, being derived from the authority structure of the firm and management's knowledge of product characteristics. In the case of Company A, much of its social power is derived from the external fact that it is the only employer in a small town. Each case is situational, requiring operating appraisal of power-responsibility relationships each time a decision is made.

External power may even arise involuntarily through no overt decision or action on the part of business. In a small town, for example, a major flood on a small river endangered one side of town. A construction company which was building a freeway nearby had the only equipment available for quick construction of levees to protect the town.

Constitutionalism

A primary way to formalize responsibility for organizational power is constitutionalism. It is the development of standards which protect society from arbitrary and unreasonable use of organizational power and establish due process for all parties involved. The words "arbitrary" and "unreasonable" are significant because any organization must have power in order to attain its objectives. Constitutionalism does not destroy power, but rather it defines conditions for responsible use of power. Its dual purpose is to channel organizational power in supportive ways and to protect private interest against unreasonable organizational power. Constitutionalism is used to balance the power-responsibility equation. Its emphasis is upon the responsibility side of the equation, primarily limiting whatever power exists. This relationship with power suggests that as more power is acquired by organizations, more attention must be given to constitutional channeling of that power.

The philosophy of constitutionalism arises from political government, but it is finding its way into other large organizations as a result of social pressures to assure that power is used justly. Selekman speaks of the "urgency of a framework of constitutionalism for the modern corporation" in order to enhance its compatibility with modern society. He recognizes the difficulties involved: "Indeed, the carrying out of social and moral responsibility in complex situations is hardly ever a tidy, roseate affair except in utopian narratives."[16]

Constitutional standards may be generated internally, as in the case of codes of ethical practice or a company judicial procedure established to resolve executive disputes. Standards more often are generated through agreement with external pressure groups, such as minority groups, community organizations, professional groups, government, and labor. The labor agreement is a constitutional document defining rights and duties of both parties. An example in another area is a manufacturing concern's informal agreement with city officials that it would use a fume-producing work process only during midday hours, when rising air currents would dissipate the offensive odors. If the process were used at night, odors

[16] Benjamin M. Selekman, *A Moral Philosophy for Management*, New York: McGraw-Hill Book Company, 1959, pp. 206, 219.

would settle in the neighborhood for hours. And in another city domestic airlines agreed that jets taking off would pass a certain landmark before turning in order not to pass over the downtown area of the complaining suburb.

An important corollary of constitutionalism is *due process,* which defines the conditions for use of power and the conditions for appeal of its excessive use. In employee relations, for example, a foreman may be unable to discharge a man directly. He can only suspend the man and recommend discharge to a higher office or a board. This procedure notifies others who may check his action, and it delays action to prevent decisions based on emotion in the heat of an argument. If an employee wishes to challenge his foreman's action, due process may permit him to have a hearing if he requests it, before discharge can be finalized. Constitutionalism thus provides procedural checks and balances on power.

SUMMARY

Social responsibility refers to a person's obligation to evaluate in the decision-making process the effects of both his personal and institutional decisions and actions on the whole social system. It broadens viewpoints to the entire social system and thus reduces the tendency of partisan groups to suboptimize general social benefits. Social responsibility is the first step in a sequence of philosophy, decisions, and actions (social response) to create a more effective society.

Business has social power. Though objections are voiced, there are valid reasons for approximately matching social responsibility with social power. In the long run, those who do not use power in a manner which society considers responsible will tend to lose it. This is the Iron Law of Responsibility. Power is especially contained by constitutionalism which provides standards to protect society from arbitrary and unreasonable use of organizational power.

STUDY GUIDES FOR INTERPRETATION OF THIS CHAPTER

1 An electric utility operates in a labor market which has an adequate supply of labor to meet its needs; however, a local community group has asked the utility to add about fifty percent to its training budget for two years in order to train members of underprivileged groups in the community. What factors would you consider in determining its decision?

2 Another utility is building a $70 million generating plant in a remote area near a coal supply. Should it spend $1 million additional to beautify and landscape its plant? What factors would you consider in deciding this issue?

3 Select an example of business social action from your local newspaper and appraise it in terms of the power-responsibility equation.

4 Interview five businessmen to learn their understanding of the term "business social responsibility." and then interpret their explanations in terms of the ideas expressed in Part One of this book.

5 Comment on the statement, "A socially responsible decision may not produce results in the public interest."

PROBLEMS
THE LSD AFFAIR

a A nationally distributed magazine in one of its issues published instructions for making LSD, a dangerous drug with which juveniles tended to experiment. At the time the issue was published it was a felony in a large number of states to make, possess, or sell this drug. The magazine's management knew of these statutes but distributed the magazine in all states.

1 Was the magazine's management socially responsible in this action? Explain.

b A local bookseller received the magazine in a state having felony laws regarding LSD. He knew of the laws and saw the instructions in the magazine. He placed the magazine on sale and sold it without any warning to buyers.

1 Was the bookseller acting in a socially responsible manner? Explain.

c In one state which had felony laws concerning LSD the governor of the state requested booksellers to withdraw the magazine from their sales racks.

1 If you were a bookseller who received this request, what would you do? Why?
2 A representative of the American Civil Liberties Union criticized the governor for interfering with freedom of the press. Appraise his actions in terms of pluralism and social responsibility.

THE EXPENSIVE PARK

In a city of about twenty thousand persons a regional manufacturer is spending over $2.5 million to convert 260 acres which it owns into a public park, including golf, swimming, and tennis. The manufacturer estimates that during the park's fifth year of operation it will reach its peak planned profit of $50,000 annually. The manufacturer's only plant is in this city, and it employs about one thousand persons. It is the town's major taxpayer; and there is already a city park, but it is smaller and of lower quality than the one the manufacturer is building.

1 Appraise management's actions in terms of social responsibility to all claimants on the organization.

PART TWO
BUSINESS IDEOLOGY

CHAPTER 7

THE DEVELOPMENT OF BUSINESS AS A SOCIAL INSTITUTION

An adequate theory of business responsibility will recognize that the present business system is an outgrowth of history and past cultural traditions. It will recognize that what we are today is, to a very large extent, a function of what we were yesterday.

WILLIAM C. FREDERICK[1]

In America the wisdom and not the man is attended to; and America is peculiarly a poor man's country. . . . They find themselves at liberty to follow what mode they like; they feel that they can venture to try experiments, and that the advantages of their discoveries are their own.

THOMAS POWNALL[2]

Social systems are products of the value systems of society, i.e., the summation of individual beliefs of members of society concerning the functions and the relationships of political, social, religious, and economic institutions which make up that society. Over time, business has nearly always been recognized as an institution of society, but it has not always played the same role or been accorded the same place in the social system. Sometimes business has played a passive role, adapting to social change as it occurred. At other times it has taken the lead in shaping social change.

In this chapter and the one following we will discuss the development of business as a social institution and consider social ideologies concerning the proper role and functions of business and businessmen. We shall not be concerned with business history per se, nor with specific dates or incidents (except perhaps a few that mark major points of change). Rather, we will focus on the evolution of business to its position of major importance in today's complex American society and the different environments in which this evolution took place.

[1] William C. Frederick, "The Growing Concern over Business Responsibility," *California Management Review*, Summer, 1960, p. 60.
[2] Thomas Pownall, *A Memorial, Most Humbly Addressed to the Sovereigns of Europe, on the Present State of Affairs Between the Old and New World* (1780), quoted in Albert Bushnell Hart (ed.), *American History Told by Contemporaries*, New York: The Macmillan Company, 1929, vol. III, p. 76.

A FRAMEWORK FOR DISCUSSION

From meager beginnings, business has matured through a series of stages until today, in America, we have a highly complex free enterprise system called capitalism. Each stage has been characterized not only by changes in ways of doing things, but by changes in ways of thinking about how things should be done and about proper relationships which should exist among various institutions in society.

Over time the shape of capitalism changes. There are different kinds of capitalism, depending on the way basic elements are modified. Our modern capitalism is the result of a series of modifications which can be identified as separate stages of development.[3] These stages can be distinguished from one another by examining the degree to which elements of capitalism are present or absent. Thus, precapitalism, while recognizing private property, did not philosophically accept profit and, in many cases, imposed severe restrictions on individual business freedom. Mercantile capitalism was characterized by the use of private property primarily for merchant and commercial activities set within a framework of strict control by strong central government. Conversely, industrial capitalism emphasized freedom of individual initiative in business, little or no interference by the state, and the predominant use of private property in industrial production. Finance capitalism implies control of private property and means of production by financial interests and absentee ownership rather than by owner-managers. And finally, state capitalism denotes regulation of business practice in the national interest and state determination of broad social policy.

BUSINESS IN ANTIQUITY

Business Emerges

No one can say at what point in history business activity first occurred. The Old Testament describes a relatively complex society based firmly upon private property, division of labor, and exchange. Manufacturing and trade were widely practiced and merchants were skilled in the use of contracts as early as 3000 B.C.

Rules and codes of conduct were formulated to govern relations between merchants and traders and also relations between merchants and governments. An excellent example of these codes is the Code of Hammurabi. Hammurabi, one of the great rulers of Babylon around 2000 B.C., promulgated a code consisting of over three hundred laws. Many of these laws were in direct support of business and not only encouraged mercantile enterprise, but also actually provided government protection in a simple form of business insurance (at no cost to the merchant). These laws

[3] Further details of ancient business heritage may be found in Meriam Beard, *A History of Business from Babylon to the Monopolists,* Ann Arbor, Mich.: The University of Michigan Press, 1962.

also contained elements not too far different from some of our own concepts of social insurance. For example:[4]

> If the brigand has not been caught, the man who has been despoiled shall recount before God what he has lost, and the city and governor in whose land and district the brigandage took place shall render back to him whatever of his was lost.
> If it was a life, the city and governor shall pay one mina of silver to his people.

Ancient Mediterranean Trading Cities

Prior to the Punic Wars (246 to 146 b.c.), most business activity occurred around the Mediterranean Sea. Philosophies concerning proper relationships among various social institutions were such that they provided a positive and favorable environment for business development in cities such as Carthage, Tyre, and Rhodes.

In these great trading cities business was accorded a high place in the scheme of things. While agriculture was recognized as an important foundation upon which cities must rest, business was generally looked upon as being more productive. Agriculture provided the necessary items for life, but business provided luxuries and items which raised standards of living. In short, business generated wealth, and wealth was desirable. Business was regarded as one of the most honorable professions, and businessmen enjoyed the highest social status.

There were three important reasons why business enjoyed a leading role in the social system of the times. First, there was no artificial class structure. Whether a man was rich or poor depended largely upon his own initiative, and it was important that the *opportunity* for wealth was open to everyone. Second, because no ruling class existed, anyone could hold public office. In reality, these offices were nearly always held by rich merchants who had time to devote to public duties. Therefore, it is reasonable to expect that public policy would favor business. Third, pre-Christian religious and business philosophies were surprisingly compatible. Temples often served as centers for local business transactions, and religious leaders often became the chief money lenders in the community (at high rates of interest).

Greek Business Environment

Influenced by the teachings of social philosophers such as Plato and Aristotle, the Grecian environment within which business operated was generally hostile toward business. Both Plato[5] and Aristotle[6] were idealists and while both admitted the necessity of commerce in the ideal state,

[4] The Code of Hammurabi (2000 b.c.). See Edward C. Bursk, Donald T. Clark, and Ralph W. Hidy, *The World of Business*, New York: Simon & Schuster, Inc., 1962, p. 9.
[5] Plato, *The Republic*, trans. by B. Jowett, Oxford: Clarendon Press, 1881, pp. 47–53.
[6] Aristotle, *Politics*, in Philip C. Newman, Arthur D. Gayer, and Milton H. Spencer (eds.), *Source Readings in Economic Thought*, New York: W. W. Norton & Company, Inc., 1954, pp. 6–14.

neither seemed willing to admit it to reality. Plato, in his *Laws* recommended such strict regulation of all commercial activities as to virtually stifle trade.[7] Aristotle, through his analysis of profit and interest, was not only instrumental in limiting commercial activity but contributed, perhaps more than any other man, to lasting negative social attitudes toward business activity. The following quotation summarizes his philosophies concerning business.[8]

> Of the two sorts of money-making one, as I have just said, is a part of household management, the other is retail trade: the former necessary and honourable, the latter a kind of exchange which is justly censured; for it is unnatural, and a mode by which men gain from one another. The most hated sort, and with the greatest reason, is usury, which makes a gain out of money itself, and not from the natural use of it.

In Greek society, the ruling class along with the military class and land owners occupied the elite positions in the social structure. Business activities were considered degrading, and anyone engaged in commerce was considered to be an inferior citizen. Merchants were not allowed to own property in the Greek city-states, nor could they hold public office, and in times of war they were pressed into military service in the lowest infantry ranks. But in spite of the hostile environment, business prospered simply because society could find no other way to solve the problem of providing for the needs and wants of citizens.

Roman Business Environment

The Roman scene was not greatly different from the Greek scene. Roman ruling classes shared Greek disdain for businessmen, and, theoretically, the highly compartmentalized social system allowed only a very low place for business as an institution. But, as was the case in Greece, social theory and the reality of social needs were not compatible. In spite of its agricultural foundation, Roman society, dedicated as it was to militarism, found it difficult to provide the necessities of life for the populace, let alone any luxury items. Roman agriculture simply could not produce enough food. But as in all societies there was a large social class willing to supply items wanted by others—for a price. Without business, the Roman Empire could not have survived. Merchants provided food for the masses, luxuries for the elite, and money for military conquests.

Besides a well-developed commercial and financial mechanism, the Roman Empire left two legacies which were to play important parts in later development of business as an institution. First was a body of law which served as a basis for later systems of law. According to Roll:[9]

> During the height of its [the Roman Empire's] power when, for a time, patricians, the new land owners, and the commercial classes lived in

---

[7] Plato, *The Laws of Plato*, trans. by E. A. Taylor, London: J. M. Dent & Sons, Ltd., Publishers, 1934, pp. 309–313.
[8] Aristotle, *op. cit.*, p. 11.
[9] Eric Roll, *A History of Economic Thought*, 3d ed., Englewood Cliffs, N.J.: Prentice-Hall, Inc., 1956, pp. 37–38.

comparative peace, there was evolved a body of laws which has had the most profound influence on later legal institutions. . . . Of more direct economic importance were the doctrines which Roman Jurists evolved for the regulation of economic relations.

Second was the Roman Catholic Church which became a major influence in shaping the social, economic, and political institutions in Europe for the next several centuries.

BUSINESS ENVIRONMENT OF THE MIDDLE AGES

The time span covered by the Middle Ages is generally agreed to be roughly from the fall of the Roman Empire in the fifth century to the middle of the fifteenth century. Certainly, the Middle Ages produced one of the most stable systems of all times, but it was a period of stagnation. The feudal system, with its nonmobile population divided into a rigid class structure, its agrarian base of large independent political units, and a powerful church which dominated not only religious but economic activities as well, did not produce an environment favorable to social change or to development of business as a social institution.

Class Structure

Well-defined class divisions were inherited from the Roman system. Division between the classes was sharp. Inequality of men on earth was recognized and accepted without question. Rights and obligations of each class were clearly defined, and every man knew what his position was in relation to that of everyone else. He knew exactly how to behave, what was expected of him, and what he could expect life to provide in the future. His world was in equilibrium. The self-sufficiency of the large land unit (the manor) along with the sedentary nature of the population produced little need for commercial activities. Traveling merchants who occasionally visited a manor were viewed with distrust.

Political Disunity

The early medieval political system was also a logical transition from the Roman system. As the Empire declined, more administrative duties fell into the landlords' hands, thus forming the basis of the manorial system. Many of the large estates became political entities unto themselves. As towns developed and became independent of landlords, they soon became self-governing. Left without a central governing body, each manor and town passed its own laws and controlled its own activities as it saw fit. The result was a political patchwork which in itself was an important deterrent to the development of commerce. A traveling merchant moving across the countryside was often subjected to tolls and taxes by every landlord whose land he crossed. Towns also extracted heavy tolls and taxes and imposed laws which favored local exchange and penalized the foreign trader.

Universality of the Church

Probably the most powerful and important institution in all medieval society was the Roman Catholic Church. More than any other force the Church shaped social philosophy toward business and defined the role of business as an institution within the social system of the times. Not only was the Church universal in the sense that it was "the one" church, but it also attempted to take responsibility for all men's actions, both spiritual and temporal. In such a role of power the Church dictated beliefs, philosophies, and actions. There were several reasons for this power.[10]

First, by the end of the eighth century, the Church was the greatest landowner in Christendom. Much of the income received from these vast landholdings was in the form of produce. While a portion of this produce was consumed in everyday operation of the estate, much had to be disposed of in commerce, thus forcing on the Church a business function.

Second, the autonomous nature of feudal political units did not provide any ties of national unity. Canon law provided the only uniform codes governing social behavior, and the Church became a great administrative body possessing widespread judicial powers in secular as well as spiritual matters.

Third, the Church obtained strength by offering a spiritual doctrine which gave meaning to men's lives. Christianity offered to thousands a framework within which they could judge their relationship with others and justify their daily activities.

Church Philosophy versus Business

Ecclesiastical hostility toward business was not an attack on trade and commerce per se. Indeed the Church itself was deeply involved in many commercial activities. One historian comments that the Church acted as ". . . a governor, a landed proprietor, a rent collector, an imposer of taxes, a material producer, an employer of labor on an enormous scale, a merchantman, a tradesman, a banker and mortgage broker, a custodian of morals, a maker of sumptuary laws, a schoolmaster, a compeller of conscience—all in one."[11] Rather, hostility was based on the belief that commercial activity turned men from the search for God by fostering self-interest and the pursuit of gain. Therefore, it was reasoned, to eliminate trade was to eliminate sin.

During the early centuries of the Middle Ages, Church dogma, which relied heavily on the philosophy of Aristotle, was generally appropriate to the static economic system of the times. But as the economic environment changed through increased trade, development of towns and trade routes, and expanding markets, Church dogma became not only unrealistic but unworkable. Neither Church nor businessmen could successfully

---

[10] For a detailed discussion of reasons for the strength of the Church see H. Pirenne, *Economic and Social History of Medieval Europe*, trans. by I. E. Clegg, New York: Harcourt, Brace & World, Inc., 1956, pp. 13ff.

[11] James Westfall Thompson, *Economic and Social History of the Middle Ages: 300–1300*, New York: Century Company, 1928, p. 648.

engage in economic activity and at the same time conform to Church dogma with its prohibitions against exchange, profit, and interest. Social demands for increased economic activities required a change in religious and social philosophy which incorporated in its value system acceptance of commercial activity and the economic institutions necessary for commercial growth.

The Protestant Revolution

Religious fetters of social theory which hampered business during the Middle Ages were virtually abandoned by the sixteenth century. The Protestant revolution of the sixteenth century further swept away Church condemnation of commercial activity.[12] Where early canonists condemned business activities as base and distinct from godly pursuits, the teachings of Protestant reformers, particularly John Calvin, encouraged business. Catholicism preached that the key to heaven lay in man's actions while on earth. Protestantism and Calvinism saw the key to heaven as being conversion as stated by Jesus Christ. That conversion led to obligations to use one's talents productively while on earth. Some measure of spiritual worth, then, was to be found in the successful pursuit of a temporal calling. Thus, Calvinism emphasized traits such as diligence, industry, thrift, and conservatism, equated spiritual worth with temporal success, and provided a religious climate which encouraged business activities based on the profit motive.

Herein lie the elements of the "individual ethic" that we, today, are prone to point to in our heritage—the belief that the individual, by diligence, thrift, wise investment, and prudent management of funds, can rise to a position of wealth. Many historians believe that one of the major underlying factors in the rise of capitalism was the change in social philosophy exemplified in the teachings of John Calvin. Heilbroner comments: "Calvinism fostered a new conception of economic life. In place of the old ideal of social and economic stability, of knowing and keeping one's 'place,' it brought respectability to an ideal of struggle, of material improvement, of economic growth."[13]

MERCANTILISM

The new conception of economic life which emerged from Calvinist philosophy paved the way for the development of business as an important institution of society. The strength of the mercantile system depended upon changing laws, customs, philosophies, and roles of social institutions. Based upon a wholly different set of underlying philosophies, mercantile policies were devoted to building strong nations through economic superiority. This was a system based upon mutual dependence between

[12] For a discussion of the Protestant revolution see Max Weber, *The Protestant Ethic and the Spirit of Capitalism* (1905), trans. by Talcott Parsons, New York: Charles Scribner's Sons, 1958.
[13] Robert L. Heilbroner, *The Making of Economic Society*, Englewood Cliffs, N.J.: Prentice-Hall, Inc., 1962, p. 55.

state and commercial interests. National good and merchant profit were considered to be two sides of the same coin. Among the more important aspects of mercantile ideology were (1) the identification of money with wealth, (2) political unification and strong government, (3) protectionism and state intervention, and (4) power. Each contributed toward a positive environment for business development.

Importance of Money

Accumulation of treasure in the form of hoards of precious metal and money was nothing new to the mercantile period. For centuries persons who had the largest hoards of money or precious metal were considered to be the wealthiest, and wealth gave the owner power—power to command goods and services.

Mercantile philosophy expanded the concept of wealth and power to the nation as a whole, and business was assigned the major role in accumulating a hoard of national treasure. National policy was designed to encourage and support business, but at the same time to regulate it. Early policy was designed to encourage business to generate an absolute flow of money into the country while preventing money from leaving the country. Because of the fallacies of storing wealth in nonproductive hoards, prohibitions against movement of gold and silver gave way to a balance-of-trade concept similar to that in effect today. The theory was simple: A country that exported more than she imported was bound to have a net inflow of money. According to mercantile philosophy, not only were exports supposed to exceed imports, but emphasis was placed on (1) importing those items of raw materials (relatively low in price) which were needed for home industry or consumption and (2) exporting finished goods (of relatively high value).

Importance of Central Government

National economic power depended upon unification of political power—a centralized political unit strong enough to impose and enforce a uniform set of commercial laws, uniform tariffs, and a uniform monetary system. To these ends merchant capitalists joined forces with rising central monarchies by financing their struggles against feudal lords and the authoritarian power of the Church. Strong central governments brought a variety of benefits to business: domestic markets were widened, movements of merchandise became safer, a uniform set of laws (based on Roman law) developed, internal communications were improved, currency was stabilized, and important commercial concessions and monopolies were often granted to merchants for political support.

Protection and State Intervention

In the early phases of the mercantile period the Crown did little more than replace the rigidities of feudalism with rigidities of nationalism. While government did encourage commercial and industrial enterprise, it did so by favoring a few at the expense of masses who were disenfranchised from economic opportunity through a rigid monopoly system. The state, theoretically, controlled all business and one could engage in a particular economic activity only by receiving a monopoly from the Crown. Discontent with this system was manifested in the Puritan revolution of the mid-seventeenth century. The whole philosophy of the mercantile system was challenged, and emphasis shifted from state *intervention* to state *protection*. Emphasis also changed from monopoly to free trade.

After the Puritan revolution, policy was directed toward making the nation as nearly independent of other nations as possible. To accomplish this task several basic concepts were stressed. First, the country was to produce all its own foodstuffs and manufactured articles. Second, the country was to control its own carrying trade (merchant shipping). Third, a colonial system was to be developed in a manner which produced raw materials and absorbed surpluses of manufactured goods.

Power

No longer was the state perceived as owning the rights to all business activity. Instead, the function of government was perceived to be one of support and control in which laws and economic policies were designed to produce national supremacy. The key to economic supremacy under mercantilism was power. Military power was necessary to obtain and hold foreign markets and to protect shipping. State power, in turn, depended upon economic activity to provide money necessary to protect commerce, enforce laws, and fight wars. Only by encouraging and at the same time regulating business activities could the nation achieve its goals.

BUSINESS ENVIRONMENT IN AMERICA

Although the American colonies were a direct product of English mercantile policy, American business was bound to develop its own unique brand of capitalism. From the start our institutions were born and matured in a capitalistic environment that was different from the mercantile capitalism of Europe. With few exceptions, the colonies themselves were founded squarely on the opportunity for private gain. Georgia was founded directly by the Crown as an experiment in growing mulberries, as well as a political effort to contain the Spanish in Florida. New York and Nova Scotia came directly under the Crown through war. All the other colonies were founded by groups of individuals stirred to action by the profit motive. Charter companies and individual proprietors were the chief agencies of settlement. The main contribution to actual colonization made by the English government was to transfer large tracts of land to private ownership for redistribution to individual farmers. These vast amounts of land, available for little effort or money, allowed the American farmer to start out as a capitalist farmer, owning his land and tools and producing for a market, as well as for himself and his family.

American craftsmen, too, started as capitalists. English industrial production remained under monopolistic authority of craft guilds which controlled production, set wages, and dictated the status of apprentices, journeymen, and masters. While the craft system of production followed immigrants to America, the guild system did not. Any craftsman possessing sufficient skill and capital could set up shop in America, free to employ his capital and take risks in any way he saw fit. Mercantile policy put severe restrictions on his ability to compete in foreign trade, but he enjoyed freedom of competition in local markets.

American merchants were also capitalists from the beginning. With the exception of those who acted as agents for large European trading companies, merchants were entrepreneurs in every sense of the word. Free from restraints of the European guild system, they traded in whatever commodities offered a profit, took title to merchandise as well as handling consignments, employed people for wages, and in many cases owned means of transportation.

Thus, whatever type of business endeavor colonists might choose in the new country, all the elements of a new kind of capitalism were present. They were free to own property and to employ that property according to individual initiative and toward any opportunity that was attractive. Of course, until the end of the Revolution, colonists were always subject to restrictions imposed by the English mercantile system, but within the system they were free to make entrepreneurial judgments, and often they moved outside the system as a matter of convenience or necessity.

Conflict of Two Systems

Colonial systems of mercantilism were based firmly upon two ideas. First was the idea that colonies should provide raw materials for industry at home and should also absorb surpluses of articles produced in the mother country. The second idea was that, in order to make the colonial system work properly, government regulation of business activity was necessary.

In retrospect it appears inevitable that, from the mercantilistic point of view, the American colonial experiment was doomed to failure. The American Colonies did not fit well into the British mercantile scheme for two reasons. First, colonization to some extent was a protest movement. Many American settlers had fled their home countries to escape governmental tyranny in business, social, political, and religious activities and beliefs, and their belief in mercantile philosophy was already weakened by the time they arrived in America. Regulation imposed by an absentee government did little to strengthen colonists' beliefs in strong central government. Laissez-faire philosophies and emphasis on the natural rights of the individual, as these ideas were reflected in the American Constitution and the Bill of Rights, were logical outgrowths of experience under British mercantile policy.

Second, British mercantilism did not work well in America because England refused to accept the Colonies as a separate economic unit, viewing them instead as an extension of British agriculture and extractive industries. Herein lay the contradictions that led to the breakdown of mercantilism. Colonies were expected to import more from England than they exported, thereby creating a balance of trade in favor of England. Moreover, balances were to be paid in gold and silver. But since the Colonies bought more than they sold, there was simply no way for them legally to obtain money necessary to pay these balances and still stay within the mercantile system.

For these reasons American business developed to a far greater extent outside the mercantile system than inside. Much of what could be produced, particularly in the Northern Colonies, was either not wanted by England or was in direct competition with British goods. Many items that were wanted by England were consumed by the Colonies themselves. Therefore, in order to survive, the Northern Colonies were forced outside the mercantile system by the very policies that were supposed to tie them closely to the mother country. The Southern Colonies produced tobacco, rice, indigo, and forest products, all of which enjoyed the protection and encouragement of the English mercantile system. But they, like their Northern neighbors, ran headlong into problems of paying their debts to England. Southern production depended heavily on availability of fresh land. When England closed Western lands to Southern plantation owners, bankruptcy or rebellion appeared to be the only alternatives.

Experiment in Freedom

The story of the American Revolution need not be recounted here. But perhaps it is appropriate to look at the economic philosophies under which the new nation started. When the Founding Fathers set about writing the Constitution, they were mindful of producing a document which would be the foundation of a strong nation and, at the same time, would provide protection against injustices inherent under types of government with which they were familiar. They had just fought a war to escape the economic tyranny of England. Armed with their own experiences and supported by the laissez-faire ideology of such men as Adam Smith,[14] it was only natural for them to conceive of the government's relation to economic activity as being supportive rather than regulatory. But freedom also brought with it a responsibility to formulate national policy concerning economic development. Limited resources and mercantile tradition favored support of agriculture and commercial activities. In spite of urging by President Washington and Alexander Hamilton,[15] manufacturing remained a relatively unimportant economic activity until well into the first half of the nineteenth century.

Preparing for Industrialization

The period between the Revolutionary and Civil Wars was one of experimentation, adjustment, growth, and development. But above all, it was a period of transition which not only shifted business emphasis from mer-

[14] Adam Smith, An Inquiry in the Nature and Causes of the Wealth of Nations (1776), New York: Modern Library, Inc., 1937, Book IV, chap. 9.
[15] Alexander Hamilton, Report on Manufacturers (1791), extracts in William McDonald (ed.), Selected Documents Illustrative of the United States, 1776–1861, New York: The Macmillan Company, 1898, pp. 111–112.

cantilism to industrialism, but also heralded sweeping social changes which were to alter the whole environment of business after the Civil War and raise serious questions concerning relationships between business and other institutions within the social system. Industrialism brought with it a concentration of economic power that threatened to move the whole social system out of equilibrium and required a rethinking of the proper roles for various social institutions.

Between 1800 and the Civil War, strong forces were at work which removed the important barriers to industrial expansion. Population increases, along with growth of cities and expanded agriculture, consolidated some markets and created new ones. Expanded transportation meant new access to raw materials and ability to deliver finished products to distant places. Improved communications meant that business could be transacted faster and easier than ever before. And the wave of inventions that appeared during these fifty years added to the base of European technology and provided the technological structure necessary for industrialization.

Political Environment

In spite of substantial increases in industrial activities during the 1840s and 1850s, political environment posed severe restrictions on full development. Depressions of 1819–1821, 1837–1843, and 1857–1858 had demonstrated to business the need for protective tariffs, a sound banking system, a cheap and nonmilitant supply of labor, and sympathetic courts. But the Southern agrarian aristocracy remained in firm control of the executive, legislative, and judicial branches of the Federal government, and they strongly opposed those things needed by business. They opposed protective tariffs, were against Federal support of railroads, turnpikes, or canals, favored state banking and cheap money, fought chartering of a Pacific railroad, opposed homesteading, and would not support a favorable immigration plan.

The election of 1860 provided the wedge. Quick to take advantage of the split in the Democratic ranks, the Republican party offered sanctuary to the abolitionists and included economic planks in the platform which offered to industrialists reforms needed for expansion. Unfortunately, Republican success in this election pushed the Southern leaders into an untenable position, one which seemingly could be resolved only by secession.

Corporate Form of Business

Perhaps more important to industrial expansion than any other single factor was the development of the corporate form of business and the general laws under which corporations were organized. Cooperative business ventures of one kind or another had been used for many years. Joint stock ventures of the seventeenth and eighteenth centuries are examples. But the total capital fund available for such ventures was limited to the private fortunes of a few individuals. However, inventions and expansion of markets stimulated the growth of business enterprise. Large amounts of capital were necessary, and these could best be raised by distributing risk and potential profit among individuals of limited financial means, as well as those with substantial resources. In addition to providing large capital funds, the corporation had the effect of making large numbers of people owners of business. Ownership in business caused thousands of people to adopt the businessman's point of view and to encourage business decisions which would yield a profit. Partly because of the recognition of economies of scale, partly as a result of changing business environment, and partly because of changes in public attitude, the corporate form of business was quite popular by midcentury. By 1850, security exchanges had been established in New York, Boston, and Philadelphia.

A New Breed of Capitalist

For the most part, the industrial capitalists of the post-Civil War period were a different group from the merchant capitalists of earlier periods. Few merchants transferred their capital into industrial development. As the shipping trade became overextended, many old merchant families moved into public works promotions, insurance, and banking.

If, then, merchants did not become capitalists, where did the class of industrialists known as the Captains of Industry originate? They came largely from independent farmers, skilled craftsmen, and small storekeepers. Eli Whitney and Cyrus McCormick came from such backgrounds. Andrew Carnegie came from a family of country weavers, John D. Rockefeller's father was a peddler, and John Gates spent his early years on a farm.

There developed, then, a group of men who were different from the Eastern merchants. They had talents which were different, and their outlooks, interests, and visions differed also. A hardy breed, they understood the potentials of the changes taking place around them; they recognized the structure and strength of the new foundations of business; and they were willing to take up the challenge.

SUMMARY

No one knows when business activity actually began, but from its humble beginnings, somewhere in antiquity, the development of business as a social institution can be traced with a reasonable degree of certainty. Phases in business maturity can be established, and environmental characteristics that either encouraged or discouraged business development can be recognized.

This chapter has summarized the role and functions assigned to business in various social systems that have existed over time. It is important to note that in every social system discussed (except colonial America) there was one social institution that held a predominant position of power. In each of these cases the dominant institution was unable fully to meet social expectations for a prolonged period of time, and, as a result, that institution was either replaced or modified. This chapter also discussed the combination of elements which together produced the environment necessary for the development of business as a major American social institution.

STUDY GUIDES FOR INTERPRETATION OF THIS CHAPTER

1 Explain the relative insignificance of business as a social institution during the Middle Ages.

2 The Protestant revolution had a major effect on business. Study the revolution developing in the Church in the latter half of the twentieth century and explain what long-run effects you think it will have on business.

3 Mercantilism was essentially a system of government intervention and regulation of business. What similarities do you see between mercantile policies and present-day government policies concerning business?

4 Explain the following statement: America, from its very inception, was bound to develop its own brand of capitalism. To what extent have environmental factors been important?

5 Contrast capitalism as it was perceived by the Founding Fathers of America with capitalism as it exists today.

CHAPTER 8

THE HERITAGE OF BUSINESS IDEOLOGY

The chief business of the American people is business.

CALVIN COOLIDGE[1]

Many a once-powerful man has learned the hard way that it is wiser to stay within the bounds of common morality than to give the public an appetite for reform.

SAUL W. GELLERMAN[2]

Not long ago a medium-sized city in the Midwest underwent a property-tax reform program. All property within the city boundaries was reappraised, but there was no adjustment in the tax rate. Every property owner, both residential and business, experienced a sharp rise in taxes. Residential property had been reassessed two years earlier and valuations had been raised to 40 percent of the current market value, but many business properties, particularly manufacturing firms in the outskirts, had not been reassessed for five years and valuations of their properties remained at 25 percent of market value at the time of assessment. With completion of the tax reform program, assessed valuation on *all* property was raised to 50 percent of the current market value. This increase, along with inflationary increases in market value, resulted in many manufacturing firms having a much larger *percentage* increase in taxes than residential owners.

The president and principal stockholder of one manufacturing firm complained bitterly and attempted in every way he could to have the assessed valuation on his firm's property lowered. The assessor's office and the tax reform committee refused. Eventually the controversy reached the local newspapers. Arguments supporting both sides appeared in editorial form and in the "letters to the editor" section. Many of the letters

---

[1] Calvin Coolidge (speech before the Society of American Newspaper Editors, June 17, 1925), quoted in the *New York Times*, Jan. 18, 1925.
[2] Saul W. Gellerman, *Motivation and Productivity*, New York: American Management Association, 1963, p. 16.

and editorials supporting the manufacturing firm came from the president himself. Those supporting the assessor's office came largely from members of the community.

Arguments supporting the president's demand for tax reductions fell generally into four categories:

My firm started here with practically nothing, and management, under my leadership, with hard work and personal sacrifice built it to what it is today.

My colleagues as well as myself were willing to take a chance by setting up our plants here. Only through good management have we survived.

Every member of this community has had an equal chance to build a successful business, but only a few have succeeded.

This tax reform program is not only inequitable, but it penalizes high performance.

Arguments supporting the tax assessor fell into three categories:

Big business takes everything out of the community and puts nothing back in.

All the businessman is interested in is high profits at everybody's expense.

Those guys that run the big plants are out for themselves and no one else.

Undoubtedly everyone in the above example who entered the controversy probably thought he was expressing a rational opinion concerning one localized incident. What is more likely is that they were expressing philosophies and ideas about business behavior in general that had grown up over long periods of time.

Recently, questions of proper relationships which should exist between business and the other parts of the social system to which it belongs, and the responsibilities of business in that system, have occupied increasing amounts of the time of business executives, government officials, theologians, and scholars. Answers to these problems do not come easily, and indeed, answers may be different at different times. But, one step toward finding workable answers is to examine the foundation of values and ideologies upon which our social system is built.

In this chapter, we shall examine industrialism as it emerged and functioned during the period after the Civil War. We shall also discuss social philosophies which supported business actions during the period and those which contributed to government regulation. Finally, we shall discuss the changing relationships between business and government which have emerged during the twentieth century.

AMERICAN INDUSTRIALIZATION: A WAY OF LIFE

By 1860, all the elements were present in the American social system which were necessary to support the sweeping social and economic changes that occurred during and following the Civil War. In many ways the Civil War and the circumstances surrounding it acted as a catalyst in the nineteenth-century transition from mercantilism to industrialism.

Techniques of mass-producing standardized items were perfected, and transportation nets were consolidated and expanded. National credit sources were expanded, and a large measure of financial stability was achieved through an improved national banking system. These, coupled with a strong technological base and the ability to concentrate capital in corporations, set the stage for industrialization.

Restructuring the Social System

The postwar years brought a whole new way of life for the American people. Because of industrialization, life became easier in many ways. But also with industrialization came an increase in business size and business power. While the first sixty years of the century had been the golden age of the small entrepreneur, the last forty were the golden age of big business, because during these years business became the most powerful group in the social system. Since most businesses were small before the war, business decisions had only limited social effects. Most businesses operated in very small closed markets, and effects of decisions were not felt outside their immediate environment. But as businesses became large after the war, effects of business decisions reached much further and had much greater social impact. Rate changes by railroads, for example, or price changes in farm machinery affected people from coast to coast.

At the same time that business was growing and gaining strength, other groups within the social system began to achieve identities of their own and become stronger. Set within the framework of the general social system, each group formed a subsystem with individual characteristics of its own and with its own culture and beliefs. Together they became the foundations of the complex pluralistic environment in which business exists today. Most of the social subsystems that rose to importance were not new. Each had stood weakly on the sidelines contributing in one way or another to business growth and power. And so long as business performance continued to satisfy the expectations of the various groups, each was content to remain passive. But when business, through misuse of power, failed to continue meeting the expectations of these groups, countervailing forces were brought to bear to modify business behavior. Among these groups were consumers, stockholders, government, and labor.

Growth of Business Power

As business size increased after the Civil War, old forms of business organizations became inadequate and unsuited to business needs. Consolidation and growth depended, in large measure, on increased use of the corporate form of business which provided large financial accumulations. With the increased economic activity that followed the war came a stiffening of competition, and because this competition was largely price competition, the winners in the struggle were invariably those firms which had sufficient financial strength to lower prices and either destroy or absorb competitors. Rate competition between railroads, for example, drove passenger fares and freight rates below costs in many cases, and in the sugar industry eighteen out of forty refineries were driven out of business by price cutting.[3] The net result of competitive warfare always seemed to be a worsening of the consumers' position. While consumers often benefited temporarily from price wars, etc., they invariably paid higher prices and accepted poorer service in the long run. As consolidations grew larger and power increased, business began to dictate what society should have, rather than responding to social values. In response to public discontent, price wars and business take-overs were usually rationalized by big business as being in the public interest. For example, when John D. Rockefeller combined his resources with several others to launch the Standard Oil Company, he gave the reason: "To stabilize the oil industry."

Finance Capitalism

As capital resources of the country became more highly concentrated in the hands of a few, a new kind of competition appeared. Rather than many small firms competing freely among themselves, the monopolists began to compete with one another, and this competitive struggle led to further consolidation of business. Size, it seemed, was the key to power, and power was the key to survival.

Most early industrial combinations were put together by men who were themselves industrialists. They were principal owners of large firms and were actively engaged in the operation of the firm. Although by modern standards they were often unscrupulous, a main objective of theirs was to produce goods and services. But, as competition became more severe and larger combinations were needed, control shifted to financial interests. For these men, production of goods and services was subordinated, in large measure, to the objective of maximizing personal fortunes. To accomplish their own personal ends, stocks were manipulated, government officials were bribed, public domain was misappropriated, and consumers were cheated and ignored. The corporate form of business was no longer adequate to support the new huge concentrations. Therefore, new forms had to be devised. Pools, trusts, and holding companies appeared, and it was against these combinations and the men who controlled them that much antitrust legislation was directed.

Misuse of Monopoly Power

Monopolies may be formed (and often are) which are not contrary to public interest and which in some cases are considered to be in the best public interest. We have, in our society today, many monopolies sanctioned by law and considered to perform certain economic functions in the best way. Public utilities are monopolies that are looked upon as being socially desirable.

[3] Harold Underwood Faulkner, *American Economic History*, New York: Harper & Brothers, 1949, p. 432.

Questions, then, concerning business concentrations during the latter part of the nineteenth century, and public reaction to them, did not revolve around the desirability of large-scale business per se. Society, as a result of industrialization, enjoyed a greater quantity and variety of goods and services than at any previous time. Rather, questions concerned the use of monopoly power. In actual practice consumers, suppliers, and competitors were all at the mercy of the monopolists. History abounds with evidence of misused monopoly power. Through economic dominance, monopolists crushed competitors by controlling prices, dictated to suppliers by the same means, and subjected consumers to high prices, poor quality, and undependable service.

With economic power came political power as well. Through bribery and coercion of public officials, business leaders exerted a tremendous influence on public policy and were usually able to manipulate it in their favor if the occasion arose, as it did frequently. Records concerning disposal of public domain to business, awarding of municipal contracts, legalizing monopoly practices, and protection from criminal acts of others all attest to the political power enjoyed by business.

BUSINESS IDEOLOGIES AND VALUE SYSTEMS

Every group within a social system develops a set of beliefs and philosophies which become both reason and justification for behavior. Like any other group, businessmen of the post-Civil War period developed a set of philosophies by which they justified their actions. Several major philosophies of the times will be reviewed here. Undoubtedly, similarities will be recognized between these nineteenth-century philosophies of businessmen's behavior and some views held by businessmen today.

Individualism, Work, and the Protestant Ethic

Several different terms have been used to describe social philosophies which stemmed from the Protestant revolution. Max Weber formalized the term *Protestant Ethic* in the title to his book, *The Protestant Ethic and the Spirit of Capitalism.* Others have used terms such as individual ethic and work ethic. Whatever name is used, these philosophies have had a profound influence on business behavior, individual behavior, and beliefs about the propriety of business and businessmen's behavior.

As indicated in the previous chapter, according to the Protestant Ethic, every man had both a spiritual and temporal calling. While man's first responsibility was to worship God and live by His laws, rewards in heaven were related to how well he fulfilled his temporal calling.

An integral part of belief in the Protestant Ethic was the concept of individualism.[4] As a philosophy it stresses man's relation to his environment. The philosophy taught that man was limited only by his own capabilities and initiative. Inherent in the philosophy were concepts of equal

[4] For a discussion of individualism as a social philosophy, see John William Ward, "The Ideal of Individualism and the Reality of Organization," in Earl F. Cheit (ed.), *The Business Establishment,* New York: John Wiley & Sons, Inc., 1964.

opportunity and individual freedom, i.e., man's freedom to pursue his own interests as he saw fit without interference from outside sources.

A second integral part of the Protestant Ethic was the belief in work. Hard work, diligence, frugality, initiative, and judgment were considered godly traits, and a man's ability to amass material wealth was a major criterion for judging success on earth. Also inherent in the work philosophy was the concept of natural talent. Every man, so the philosophy stated, was endowed by the Creator with a certain set of talents. Man not only had the right to develop and use his talents, but he had the moral obligation to utilize these God-given gifts to climb to the top.

Because of the nearly universal beliefs in the Protestant Ethic, businessmen operating after the Civil War were able to explain and justify their activities. The Protestant Ethic was a philosophy of many businessmen of all faiths, not just Protestants. But more important was the fact that the Protestant Ethic was a philosophy of society, and most nonbusiness people shared these beliefs with businessmen. While few men actually achieved great wealth, it was important to everyone to believe that opportunities for wealth were open to any individual *if only he chose to take advantage of them.* Thus, while businessmen used the Protestant Ethic to justify their actions, society used the same philosophy as a basis for accepting these same actions.

Laissez Faire and the Classical Tradition

America had, in the eighteenth century, fought a war with England over government and business relations. Difficulties resulting from government interference with American business under British mercantilism were still fresh in the minds of businessmen. It was no wonder that the men who framed the Constitution were careful to define the role of the new government in terms of laissez faire, which to them meant, "Let business alone."

Adam Smith, whose widely read book appeared in 1776, was a staunch advocate of laissez faire and provided theoretical support for this philosophy. Government, it is true, played a part in Smith's economic system, but its role was supportive. It should provide defense and justice, construct and maintain public works, and provide other essential activities that would not be carried on by private business because they could not be made to yield a profit. But Smith felt that government should not in any way become involved in workings of the market system. The greatest public good could be achieved in the Smithian system by businessmen bidding freely among themselves and by supply and demand freely adjusting to each other. The key to the whole system was freedom of competition, which assured the greatest good for the greatest numbers. The system always produced full employment, lowest operating costs, lowest prices, and economic growth.

American political and economic philosophies of the nineteenth century warmly embraced Smithian theory as an ideal model. While the model did little to describe the business system as it actually existed, it did provide a philosophical model against which to judge government and business relationships.

Social Darwinism

Approximately one hundred years ago, Charles Darwin published a most provocative book entitled *The Origin of Species,* which indirectly provided the basis for one of the most popular nineteenth-century philosophies of business behavior. In its original biological context, Darwinian theory proposed that all forms of life evolved, over time, from a few basic types and that, through a process of natural selection, only the strongest and most fit survived.

When Herbert Spencer applied the theory to society and explained social development in terms of social evolution, he gave America a new business philosophy.[5] Applying Darwinian theory to society as a whole, Spencer reasoned that if environment were not tampered with, the most able men would rise to leadership through a process of "natural selection." Nature somehow endowed only a few persons with exactly the right combination of characteristics to master their environment fully. Noninterference with the natural selection process, according to social Darwinism, would produce the greatest good for the greatest numbers by placing the most fit in positions of leadership.

Here was a philosophy ready-made for the Captains of Industry. As the nineteenth century wore to a close and society became more intolerant of business practices, business leaders championed social Darwinism as a rational justification for their position, their riches, their actions, and their power.

Philosophies of Machiavelli

Threads of Machiavellian philosophy also appeared in nineteenth-century business philosophy and continue to appear today. Niccolò Machiavelli (1469–1527) in his famous book, *The Prince,*[6] discussed the problems a prince faced in ruling his people. In his discussion, he not only identified with great clarity many problems in political administration, but also suggested what he considered appropriate solutions to the problems.

Relationships between means and ends are illustrative of Machiavellian philosophy. According to Machiavelli, means should be subordinate to ends (power of the prince); that is, a prince should take whatever measures are necessary to keep his subjects "united and obedient." Adapting this to business philosophy, it became popular to think of the businessman as feeling justified in resorting to any means to reach the end of profit. Strong arguments can be made to demonstrate that the Captains of Industry were guided by this philosophy.

The phrase "Do unto others before they do unto you" is also Machiavellian in origin. He referred to those who fared better by "overreaching

[5] Richard Hofstadter, *Social Darwinism in American Thought,* rev. ed., Boston: Beacon Press, 1955.
[6] Niccolò Machiavelli, *The Prince* (1513), Oxford: Clarendon Press, 1909.

men by their cunning" than did those who trusted to honest dealing, and he concluded that the prince should be prepared to deal with individuals at their own level and beat them at their own game. In short, one should be prepared to use unlawful means or be devious, if necessary.

While most businessmen today do not operate according to either of these philosophies, it is important to recognize that many people perceive business actions as being based on the above principles.

Pragmatism

William James[7] and John Dewey[8] added another facet to social philosophy. These philosophers viewed social progress as a process of change which could and should be controlled by men. Unlike social Darwinism, pragmatic thought viewed man's environment as a variable which could be controlled and manipulated. Experimentation with new ways of doing things would produce the greatest good for the greatest number, and the test of experimentation was: Does the new way work better than the old?

From the businessman's point of view, pragmatic thought was a mixed blessing. It encouraged industrial development and experimentation with the business system at large, and as long as results were socially profitable, businessmen received support from the rest of the social system. On the other hand, when results from business activity were viewed as socially unprofitable, the whole business system became suspect and subject to change.

THE AGE OF REFORM

Regardless of harsh criticisms which have been leveled at big business for its activities during the postwar years, those few years were truly an age of innovations that carried American society to new high standards of living. New products appeared, old products were improved and refined, new services were offered and others modified, and all this was accompanied by a general lowering of prices. Articles which before the Civil War had been luxuries now became staples in many cases. Ready-made clothing and shoes, processed foods, iron and steel implements, and machinery, to mention only a few items, were generally within the economic reach of the masses. Transportation and communication were broadened and cheapened, and innovations such as electricity and natural gas were widely available. Writing in 1889 one reporter noted over forty-five inventions, discoveries, and applications which were in wide use.[9]

In spite of tremendous strides forward in material well-being, by 1890 public dissatisfaction with big business performance was enormous. This general dissatisfaction stemmed largely from business's disregard for social and economic rights of the "little man." When business began to

[7] William James, *Essays in Pragmatism*, New York: Hafner Publishing Company, Inc., 1948.
[8] John Dewey, *Human Nature and Conduct* (1922), New York: Henry Holt and Company, Inc., 1935; and John Dewey, *The Public and Its Problems*, New York: Henry Holt and Company, Inc., 1927.
[9] *The Literary Digest* (1905), quoted in Arthur C. Bining, *The Rise of American Economic Life*, New York: Charles Scribner's Sons, 1949, p. 389.

strangle competition through huge corporations, pools, and trusts; when prices were artifically maintained; when products and services were not improved; when small stockholders lost their savings through watered stocks; when public property was freely appropriated to private use; and when labor was forcibly suppressed, a rising tide of protest appeared in spite of the predominant laissez faire philosophy. Beginning in 1870, and continuing through the early years of the twentieth century, the wave of public revolt against monopoly business practices resulted in a general reassessment of social institutions and their proper roles and functions within the social system.

Government Intervention

The first organized drive to limit and control business activity through government intervention came from consumers. Working in organized groups or through journalists they made themselves heard at the national as well as the state level, and exerted enough pressure to influence legislation against undesirable business practices. Probably the best organized action was the Granger Movement. Working through state legislatures, these groups urged enactment of laws which would prohibit greater charges for short hauls than long ones, forbid consolidation of parallel rail lines, and establish maximum rates and fares. As a result of the agrarian movement, several state laws were passed to regulate railroads, and these laws were upheld by the U. S. Supreme Court until 1886. At that time, the Court reversed itself, saying the states had no right to interfere with interstate commerce.

Continued agrarian pressure along with general public dissent resulted in the first federal legislation to regulate business. In 1887, the Interstate Commerce Act was passed. Successful evasion of the law and court decisions favorable to the railroads made the law largely ineffective in the years immediately following. However, after the turn of the century, it was strengthened by remedial legislation such as the Elkins Act of 1903, the Hepburn Act of 1906, and the Mann-Elkins Act of 1910. By 1915, the political and economic power of railroads was firmly checked. Without question, the Interstate Commerce Act was important as a major piece of restrictive legislation. But much more important from a social system's point of view is that it marked a change in social definition of the role of government and government-business relationships. No longer was the proper role of government thought to be weak, passive, and supportive. The proper role of government was thought to be one of power and regulation.

By 1890, public revolt against all monopoly practice was widespread, and the clamor for antitrust legislation was loud and sharp. As a result, the first piece of general antitrust legislation—the Sherman Act—appeared in 1890. However, the vagueness of its wording and business influence in courts produced disappointing results. Administrations under Harrison, Cleveland, and McKinley exhibited little interest or talent in enforcing the act.

Interest in business regulation and business activity was revived after the turn of the century. A group of public-spirited writers led by Ida Tarbell, Lincoln Steffens, and Upton Sinclair, who became known as the "muckrakers," dissected American business for public view in various magazines of the times. This literary movement emphasized the worst facets of government and business and revived the crusade against business.

The antitrust movement reached its peak with the passage of the Clayton Act and the Federal Trade Commission Act in 1914. Since that time, however, there seems to have been a reversal in the roles of the public and government concerning the enforcement of antitrust laws. While government interest and activity in antitrust enforcement has steadily increased since 1915, it has been observed that public concern has lessened. Hofstadter[10] suggests that the reason for this reversal in government and public roles may be that the whole antitrust issue has become so complex that it is beyond the full comprehension of the average man, with the result that only an organization of specialists in case law and economic theory can cope with the problem.

Labor Emerges

While labor will be discussed in detail in a later chapter, a few comments are appropriate here because it was during the period between the Civil War and the turn of the century that labor emerged as a major social institution. With growth in size of firms, separation of management from ownership, and increased immigration, relations between business and labor changed. No longer were personal relationships and a sense of personal responsibility possible on the part of many employers. As greater numbers of persons filled cities and became wholly dependent upon wages for their livelihood, a labor movement which had been largely weak and ineffective began to gain strength.

Emergence of the labor movement changed the shape of society and complicated the environment of business. As the labor movement grew, it added to the social system another power group with which business had to relate. Serious and widespread strikes and even violence plagued business during this period. The most extreme and spectacular examples of labor violence were the activities of the Molly Maguires.[11] The Molly Maguires were a secret group (composed mostly of coal miners) who were organized to carry out a campaign of physical violence against mine owners and mine bosses. Beatings, sabotage, and murders, as well as the strike, were their weapons. However, with the conviction and execution of their leaders for criminal acts, the organization was disbanded.

While most organized labor activity was not as violent as the activities of the Molly Maguires, labor emerged as an organized social group capable of exerting strong economic pressure against business.

[10] Richard Hofstadter, "What Happened to the Antitrust Movement?" in Cheit, op. cit., p. 151.
[11] Wayne G. Broehl, Jr., The Molly Maguires, Cambridge, Mass.: Harvard University Press, 1964.

STATE CAPITALISM EMERGES

By 1930, a marked change in relationships among social institutions was evident. The stock market crash of 1929 and the subsequent national economic collapse put American free enterprise squarely on trial for its existence. Widespread unemployment, decline of purchasing power, collapse of markets, and declining standards of living all threatened American social stability. These problems were placed squarely in the lap of American business. Business, however, was unable to respond. When it became evident that the business system, by itself, could not generate enough momentum to stimulate economic recovery, Americans began to look to other social institutions for corrective action. Government quickly took the initiative.

The New Role of Government

Until 1930 the function of government had been primarily to support the business system in its role of economic leadership and to mediate between business and society. After 1930, however, the role of government changed from judging business behavior to actual economic leadership. Putting it another way, government's role changed from judging how well business performed its social responsibilities to defining what those responsibilities should be. In a sense, after 1930, government appropriated many functions that previously had been reserved for business. According to Cochran and Miller,[12]

> Under the New Deal the federal government became a great employer of men, the greatest user of the nation's savings, the greatest underwriter of debt. The government assumed much of the risk-taking activity of private enterprise. It assumed leadership in finance and construction. Above all, it supplanted private business as the chief planner of the nation's economic life.

Individualism versus the Social Ethic

Redefinition of the functions of government and business was in large part the result of a shift in social philosophy from belief in the individual ethic to what has been called the social ethic. The term social ethic does not imply belief in socialism as a political system. Rather it describes an ever-increasing belief that the individual can no longer control his environment or be master of his destiny. Implicit in the social ethic is the belief that individuals have become so interdependant and so subordinate to various power groups in society that they are dependent on these groups for physical, social, and economic security. Putting it another way, there seems to be an increasing tendency for individuals to look to strong social groups to provide social payouts that they can no longer provide for themselves.

[12] Thomas C. Cochran and William Miller, *The Age of Enterprise*, New York: The Macmillan Company, 1942, pp. 355–356.

The New Business Environment

Within the framework of the social ethic and beginning in the thirties, government set about defining in legal terms many social responsibilities of business. Wage and hour laws, safety codes, responsibility for product safety and performance, and social security obligations imposed by government are illustrations of the new environment. Concurrently, a redefinition of power relations among other social institutions took place. For example, the Wagner Act established labor as a major power group. As a result labor was now in position to impose social restrictions on business behavior. By 1940, business found that it was no longer *the major power group* in society, but only *one power group*, whose decisions were shaped and challenged by other groups equally powerful—notably labor and government.

Increasing Joint Responsibility

During the years following World War II, additional dimensions were also added to the business environment. National problems associated with the war effort were far too complex to be solved by any one social group. Joint effort between government, labor, and business was called for. Nor has the need for cooperation between the three groups diminished. If anything, the need has become greater. The magnitude of national problems resulting from our increasingly complex industrial society will call for stronger bonds of partnership and greater understanding and mutual respect among the power groups. It seems evident that social and economic progress cannot be the result of unilateral action.

SUMMARY

The favorable environment which existed after the Civil War allowed business to emerge as the leading power group in American society. One result of the economic power of business was a tremendous increase in availability of products at ever-decreasing prices. A second and less desirable result was misuse of power by business. Use of power which produced undesirable social payouts generated widespread public dissatisfaction with the performance of business as a social institution. To justify their role and their performance, businessmen turned to a number of social ideologies. Because most Americans shared with businessmen belief in these ideologies business enjoyed general public support. But toward the close of the nineteenth century public belief in these ideologies began to diminish, and public support of business turned to outright hostility.

Public dissatisfaction with business led to a redefinition of roles of social institutions. The role of government was enlarged to include a regulatory function and a wave of legislative regulation of business followed. A further redefinition of institutional functionalism occurred during the 1930s. The inability of business to stimulate social recovery from economic collapse led government to assume many functions previously reserved for business. A third major redefinition of roles occurred with World War II. Increasing complexity of national problems of all kinds has led to a need for closer cooperation and in many cases a team approach to problem solving.

STUDY GUIDES FOR INTERPRETATION OF THIS CHAPTER

Looking back over the last hundred or so years:

1 Identify periods in which society redefined roles of social institutions. In each case, what roles were assigned to various institutions? Why did each of these redefinitions occur?

2 Can you give any evidence that businessmen today still subscribe to one or more of the ideologies mentioned in this chapter?

3 What is meant by the "social ethic"? What are the business attitudes of persons in the United States today who believe strongly in the social ethic?

4 In his book *The American Challenge*, J.-J. Servan-Schreiber refers to the "post-industrial society." Characteristics of this new society are: (1) industrial revenue may be 50 times greater than in the pre-industrial period; (2) most economic activity may have shifted from primary (agriculture) and secondary (industrial production) areas to service industries, research institutes, and nonprofit organizations; (3) private enterprise may no longer be the major source of scientific and technological development; (4) the free market may take second place to the public sector and to social services; (5) most industries will be run by cybernetics; (6) the major impetus for progress will come from education and the technological innovations it utilizes; (7) time and space will no longer be a problem in communication; (8) the gap between high and low salaries in the post-industrial society may be considerably smaller than today. (A society starts reaching the post-industrial level when per capita income reaches $4,000 per year.) Using each of the above criteria, comment regarding how close American society is today to achieving the post-industrial level.

PROBLEM
THE PORT OF NEW YORK AUTHORITY

In 1921, the states of New York and New Jersey formed the Port of New York Authority. The original reason for establishing the organization was to permit states that used New York City harbor to participate in the planning and development of that port.

Over the years the Port of New York Authority has become a major operator of transportation facilities in and around the city. It operates primarily as a public business, charging consumers mainly on the basis of services needed. It operates six interstate tunnels and bridges, four airports, two heliports, and ten marine and vehicular terminals. These operations began in 1930, when the Holland Tunnel was transferred, without cost, to the Authority. The Authority continues to charge a toll of 50 cents even though the facility has been paid for for several years. As a bistate agency, the Authority can ignore federal laws requiring that tolls be removed when cost of construction is paid.

In the 1960s, the Authority obtained approval to build huge twin 110-story skyscrapers in New York City as a World Trade Center. A 16-acre site in downtown Manhatten was obtained to accommodate the buildings. It is estimated that approximately 130,000 people can use these buildings daily.

At the same time, the Authority has avoided becoming involved in the problems of mass transit in Greater New York. This has resulted in a heated controversy over what the role and functions of the Authority should be. Critics of the Authority cite its annual income of over $100 million and its liquid reserves of nearly $700 million. Critics argue that the Authority, through its own ventures, has seriously contributed to the city's "transportation mess," and therefore should become actively involved in solving the problems. The Authority's answer is that it is not in the mass transit business. It argues further that it has an obligation to its bondholders to avoid becoming involved in chronically insolvent mass transit.

1 In what ways is the Port of New York Authority operating in the manner of (a) a private business and (b) government?

2 What are the responsibilities of the Port of New York Authority to the publics which it serves?

CHAPTER 9

BUSINESS VALUES AND CODES OF CONDUCT

In the last analysis, high ethical standards can be
achieved only through voluntary effort.
PRESIDENT JOHN F. KENNEDY[1]

Throughout society there is an intricate web of social patterns which defines how people deal with social situations. In government there are trade-offs among legislators to gain support for appropriations which benefit their particular districts; and at a wedding there is frequently a personal gift given to the church functionary who performs the ceremony. Are these practices socially "proper"?

Since business is a dominant social institution with high public visibility, its proper conduct is a matter of special social concern. Consider the following practices. Are they proper?

Regis Discount Furniture advertised in a metropolitan newspaper, "End of Month Sale: five-piece bedroom set, $399 value, special price $325." The facts were that the manufacturer's suggested retail price was $399, and Regis's advertising manager knew that the set sold for $399 in most nondiscount furniture stores. In the Regis store, however, this particular bedroom set had never sold for more than $325.

In another city a meat packer gave kickbacks to purchasing agents of clubs, hotels, and other buyers.[2] On its federal income tax return it claimed these kickbacks as a business expense, and the case finally was taken to federal court. In the court hearing, an agent of the Internal Revenue Service testified that this was such a common practice among

[1] John F. Kennedy, "A Statement on Business Ethics and a Call to Action" (statement at a meeting of the Business Ethics Advisory Council, Jan. 16, 1962), U.S. Department of Commerce, 1963, p. 9.
[2] "Kickbacks Paid," Wall Street Journal (Pacific Coast edition), Nov. 5, 1969, p. 1.

packers that the Revenue Service had adopted a standard formula for compromising claims for deductions of this type.

Whether business values are consciously established or not, they exist in the cultural heritage of civilization. Whether written or not, they do guide actions of businessmen. The question, then, is not whether to have them; rather, it is how intelligently they are established and applied. In this chapter we discuss business value systems and the managerial values that are related to them. We also examine guides to business conduct offered by others, such as professional associations. In later chapters we discuss specific applications of business values to various claimants, such as government, customers, labor, and disadvantaged persons.

AN INCREASING INTEREST IN BUSINESS VALUES

Society has a new social awareness which is encouraging it to reassess and improve its social conduct in major ways. Business will need to move with society and, hopefully, even lead it in some instances. There are many reasons for society's general reassessment of its values, and business is a part of these; however, major business reassessment was triggered by the electrical conspiracy cases initiated in 1960. On June 22 of that year, a number of electrical manufacturers were indicted in the United States District Court, Eastern District of Pennsylvania, for alleged conspiracy to fix prices and restrict competition in the sale of electrical equipment. There were subsequent convictions in this case.

In the wake of the electrical conspiracy indictments, the United States Secretary of Commerce convened in 1961 a Business Ethics Advisory Council to encourage voluntary improvement of business conduct as indicated by President John F. Kennedy's comment quoted at the beginning of this chapter. Its stated purpose was to explore "some approaches to the development of ethical guidelines that might be useful to the business community" and to encourage businessmen toward self-regulation. Strictly speaking, this council was not a group of businessmen working for self-regulation, for over half the committee consisted of educators, clergymen, and journalists. Some businessmen were on the committee. This council issued a call for better self-regulation and pointed out six areas for self-evaluation: general understanding of ethical issues, compliance with law, conflicts of interest, entertainment and gift expenses, customers and suppliers, and social responsibilities.[3]

Surveys of businessmen at this time showed that they were aware of social issues in the conduct of their businesses, and that a number of them were concerned that business practices had not kept up with social standards of conduct.

[3] Business Ethics Advisory Council, *A Statement of Business Ethics and a Call for Action*, U.S. Department of Commerce, no date; see also Theodore L. Thau, "The Business Ethics Advisory Council: An Organization for the Improvement of Ethical Performance," in Arthur S. Miller (ed.), *The Ethics of Business Enterprise*, Philadelphia: The American Academy of Political and Social Science, *The Annals*, vol. 343, September, 1962, pp. 128–141.

In 1961 an extensive survey was made of 1,531 readers of *Harvard Business Review*, 84 percent of them in management.[4] Sixty-eight percent of respondents felt there were "a few" or more unethical practices in their industry. When asked about the one practice they would most like to see eliminated, they stressed gifts and bribes, unfair pricing, and misleading advertising. When asked whether they favored a self-developed ethical code for their industry, 71 percent favored a code and only 10 percent opposed it. The benefits most expected from an ethical code were its usefulness as an aid in refusing unethical requests (87 percent) and its personal help as a clear definition of the limits of acceptable conduct (81 percent). On the negative side, 11 percent believed the code might protect inefficient firms and retard industry growth.

Other results of the survey showed that, although businessmen were alert to social responsibilities, they disagreed on what was the proper conduct in specific situations. They recognized that there were no single, clear-cut answers. Generally they rated themselves as higher in ethics than the "average businessman," and they looked to top management for leadership to improve practice.

Increasing interest in business values was shown to be worldwide when the thirteenth International Management Congress met in New York City in 1963. Several thousand delegates from more than half the nations of the world attended this triennial meeting, and one of the principal issues discussed at the congress was the ethical purpose and standards of business.[5]

Shortly thereafter a survey of 323 United States managers showed that managerial concern about ethical practice persisted.[6] Seventy-one percent thought their competitors engaged in at least a few unethical practices. (The comparable response to a slightly different question in the Harvard survey mentioned earlier was 68 percent.) Marketing managers had the lowest opinion of competitors, with 23 percent saying "frequently." Personnel men had the highest opinion of competitors, with 35 percent saying "seldom" or "never." The entire group said marketing and purchasing had the most unethical practices, and they designated pricing as the main problem area. The majority of respondents felt the public image of business practices was "not too high," and the majority also felt that more could be done to raise ethical practices. They particularly favored active discussions of business ethics among business people.

The conspiracy cases, Business Ethics Advisory Council, 1963 International Management Congress, surveys of business practice, and similar developments in the early 1960s spurred an increasing interest in business values and codes of conduct. Further interest was stimulated by

[4] Raymond C. Baumhart, "How Ethical Are Businessmen?" *Harvard Business Review*, July–August, 1961, pp. 6ff. See also the thorough analysis of this survey and others in Raymond Baumhart, *Ethics in Business*, New York: Holt, Rinehart and Winston, Inc., 1968.
[5] *Proceedings of the Thirteenth International Management Congress*, New York: Council for International Progress in Management (United States), Inc., 1963.
[6] Thomas F. Schutte, "Executives' Perceptions of Business Ethics," *Journal of Purchasing*, May, 1965, pp. 38–52.

social developments which related to business, such as concern for poverty, pollution, and urban deterioration. Businessmen around the world began to realize that business needs clear-cut social usefulness as well as economic usefulness. These events of the 1960s possibly have set the stage for major social efforts by business and other institutions in the 1970s, which may become known as the "Decade of Social Response."

MANAGERIAL VALUE SYSTEMS

Values Affect Behavior

An underlying feature of business conduct is the value systems of its people. Managerial values are particularly important because of the leading role managers play in business. Values affect behavior in several ways:[7]

1 They primarily determine what a manager (or employee) thinks is good, right, beautiful, and so on.

2 They provide norms on which he depends for guidance.

3 They determine his attitudes toward issues with which he comes into contact.

4 They influence the kinds of persons with whom he can be compatible and the kinds of social activity he can accept.

5 They largely determine the kinds of ideas he can understand and transmit without distortion.

6 They give him moral principles he can use to rationalize desired actions regardless of how realistic the actions appear to others.

Values are different for each manager, because they depend on his perception of reality. When he looks across his desk into his office, his perception of what is there will be different from that of an associate alongside him with an almost identical physical view. He may see people wasting time, while his associate sees new furniture just purchased. Similarly, he will see something different from what his associate sees when both are looking at a balance sheet. The reality which is there is identical, but each person's perception of it is not likely to be fully correct or fully complete because each situation contains ambiguous factors and unknowns. Each selects by means of perception those factors which are meaningful to him in terms of his experience, values, and capabilities. Each manager's values exist as a total system with each value rubbing against other values, amending and restraining them and, in turn, being amended and restrained. No one value independently determines behavior. As a matter of fact, studies of managers show that they generally have a fairly broad range of value interests.[8] They need this broadness, because their roles such as trustee, boundary mediator, and change agent require them to deal with many conflicting values in their daily work.

[7] Robert N. McMurry, "Conflicts in Human Values," *Harvard Business Review*, May–June, 1963, p. 131.
[8] Renato Tagiuri, "Value Orientations and the Relationship of Managers and Scientists," *Administrative Science Quarterly*, June, 1965, pp. 39–51.

Guides for Making Value Judgments

Some of the conflicting values which managers have to balance in making decisions are the following:

Technical—based on physical facts, science, and logic
Economic—based on market values determined by supply and demand
Social—based on group and institutional needs
Psychological—based on personal needs of individuals
Political—based on general welfare needs of the state
Aesthetic—based on beauty
Ethical—based on what is right
Spiritual—based on what God has revealed

This conglomerate of beliefs, standards, and ideals which a manager must somehow mediate in his decision making is called the *ethos* of the system.[9] It can be slippery as an eel, rigid as a steel girder, compartmentalized as a beehive, and fragile as a flower; but above all, it is there. It must be satisfactorily reconciled with an organization's conduct in order for the organization to remain viable.

Since managers do mediate among many claimants and value systems, there is no set of rules telling them exactly what to do in each situation. Managers are left with no choice other than to make judgments based upon whatever general ethical guides society can furnish. There is evidence of some social agreement concerning the seriousness of breaches of social conduct. In a theft, for example, research indicates that in order for one theft to be considered twice as serious as another, the amount stolen must be about sixty times as large. The act of theft is considered a breach of conduct, even if the amount is only $5; and since the breach has already been committed with the $5 theft, a person must steal much more (about $300) in order to make his deed twice as bad.[10]

With regard to business, many of our ethical guidelines arise from the following relationships.

1 Is there unfair gain to the person doing it? An example is a conflict of interest in which a manager gains through a purchase contract he makes with a firm in which he has a secret interest.

2 Is there unfair harm to others? An example is private disclosure of unfavorable financial information, which places stockholders not receiving the disclosure at a disadvantage.

3 How substantial is the unfair gain or the harm to others? For example, water pollution used to be minor. Now it is widespread and substantial, so it is considered to be much more serious. Especially in evaluating harm, two additional criteria are useful.

    a Are there offsetting gains? For example, urban renewal often harms those who must relocate their homes, but it is said that the larger community eventually will receive an offsetting gain.

[9] Clarence C. Walton, *Ethos and the Executives: Value in Managerial Decision Making,* Englewood Cliffs, N.J.: Prentice-Hall, Inc., 1969, p. 24.
[10] Walton, *op. cit.,* pp. 31–33.

b How irreversible is the harm? Traditional detergents, for example, are considered more harmful pollution than newer biodegradable ones which soon lose their polluting power.

4 Was the act a personal one, or was it representative behavior according to established practice? Discharge of an employee because of personal dislike is more serious than discharge for inadequate performance. Similarly, gain from manipulation of company stock is improper, compared with proper gain from exercising an established stock option.

5 Is there adequate due process, such as the right to appeal unjust decisions, to return faulty merchandise, and so on?

In general, it appears that society develops business conduct guidelines for two primary purposes. One purpose is to assure that knowledge and power are used in fair and responsible ways with others. Therefore, the *vulnerability of claimants* to business unfairness becomes a major basis for setting ethical guidelines on business power.[11] In a similar manner, when business is vulnerable to others, such as bad check artists, ethical guidelines are set up to protect business from their power.

A second purpose for conduct guidelines is to make business more effective as a social institution. When the foregoing ethical guidelines are compared with the criteria for an effective social institution in Chapter 2, it is evident that the ethical guidelines are ways to implement an effective social institution. The criteria in Chapter 2 for determining institutional effectiveness are an open system, a participative organization, productivity, distributive justice, and a power-responsibility balance. To illustrate the relation of these criteria to the ethical guidelines we have been discussing, let us consider the criterion of an open system. When some stockholders are unfairly harmed because they did not receive unfavorable financial information which others received, the criterion of an open system has been violated. Similarly, when there is conflict of interest resulting in unfair gain to a purchasing manager, this violates the criterion of distributive justice. Thus, society uses ethical guidelines in order to help business effectively fulfill its institutional mission.

Business Values of Managers

What values do managers hold concerning business? Managers are neither cut in the image of the early robber barons, nor are they professional people with rigid standards of conduct. Instead, they have a remarkably wide variety of viewpoints on issues, and these viewpoints become even more diverse when managers have to apply values in operating situations.

One survey presented twenty-six case situations to 103 California managers at all organizational levels.[12] Managers reported how they would

---

[11] Edgar H. Schein, "The Problem of Moral Education for the Business Manager," *Industrial Management Review*, p. 4, Massachusetts Institute of Technology, Cambridge, Mass., Fall, 1966. See also the general discussion, pp. 3–14, for comments relating to the preceding guidelines.

[12] John W. Clark, *Religion and Moral Standards of American Businessmen*, Cincinnati, Ohio: South-Western Publishing Company, Incorporated, 1966, especially p. 98.

decide each case by choosing one of four choices. Two choices gave preference to profit or personal advantage, and the other two gave preference to ethical values or social goals. Managers were substantially divided on such issues as selling speculative land, layoff of older employees compared with younger ones, and use of insider information for stock purchase.

Perhaps because the managers worked in a region with air pollution, the case with the highest agreement involved installation of a costly air filter which reduced net income of a refinery for several years. Even though no ordinance compelled this installation, 96 percent of the managers favored it. Other areas of more than ninety percent agreement were: hiding plant shutdown information from employees (91 percent rejected), use of inferior materials in an underbid contract (93 percent rejected), padding an expense account (93 percent rejected), and president performing time-consuming community activities on company time (95 percent accepted).

In the survey just mentioned, even when there was nearly uniform agreement on a social point of view, a few managers persisted with a view which tended to maximize profits. Agreement of all business managers on their social responsibilities is as unlikely as agreement of all economists, politicians, or educators on their social responsibilities. Diversity provides checks and balances.

A *Fortune* survey of chief executives of the largest corporations in the United States showed that in 1969 10 percent held a philosophy favorable to profit maximization; however, nearly all of this 10 percent reported that their firm was directly involved at that time in social programs such as training hard-core unemployed persons.[13] Apparently they saw profit and public service connected through a complex pluralistic social system. By engaging in public service they were able to maintain an environment favorable to their profitable operation. Thus, this small minority can continue to rationalize profit maximization while engaging in socially responsible activities. The remaining 90 percent already had a philosophy supporting socially responsible activities.

Managerial value systems give strong support to market freedom. Even though managers recognize the need for regulation and adapt to it once it is established, they would prefer to have the flexibility that goes with freedom. Part of this preference is the normal human desire of most persons to be free of restrictive controls; however, there is also an important philosophical foundation for placing a high value on market freedom. Managers, as well as others,[14] believe that by keeping economic decisions free and decentralized they are helping maintain political democracy and

[13] Arthur M. Louis, "The View from the Pinnacle: What Business Thinks," *Fortune,* September, 1969, p. 94. For a discussion of the conflict between profit maximization and a manager's personal ethics, see Albert Z. Carr, "Can an Executive Afford a Conscience?" *Harvard Business Review,* July–August, 1970, pp. 58–64.

[14] For example, see the comment by Walter W. Heller, former Chairman of the Council of Economic Advisers for both Presidents Kennedy and Johnson, in Dexter M. Keezer, "The Score against Capitalism," *Harvard Business Review,* September–October, 1968, p. 160.

other human freedoms. They believe that freedoms are mutually linked in a system relationship and that erosion anywhere in the system increases the probability of erosion elsewhere in the system.

The quest for market freedom is not peculiar to managers but is a general cultural phenomenon. Almost all groups seek autonomy, even though—like business—they are subject to controls. Educators seek academic freedom for their group so that ideas instead of products can be freely traded. Laborers want to be free to make whatever demands they wish without wage and other governmental controls. Minorities want freedom to operate in their own interests. All are brothers in their search for operating freedom, and all can philosophically justify it as a contribution to the public interest.

Four Primary Claimant Groups

Surveys, managerial speeches, and other data indicate that business managers essentially see themselves as serving many claimants, trying to provide each with some quality of output larger than inputs. Most typically they classify their claimants into four groups: investors, employees, customers, and society (including government). Values supporting benefits to these four groups usually apply to both private and public organizations, and many managers have shown the capacity to move from one to the other and perform effectively without modifying their value system about these areas of benefit. For example, a government office must satisfy its citizen customers by producing services just as much as a private factory must satisfy customers by producing goods. Personnel services of the two institutions are even more similar. Likewise, the government office must in the long run provide an output for citizen investors, or else it will not receive adequate operating appropriations, or capital for expansion. It is true that measurement of investor return is slower and more indirect in public organizations, but it is there. Government offices do close and charities do go out of business when they inadequately use the resources society has invested in them.

Management's tendency to classify claimants in terms of investors, employees, customers, and society was clearly shown by a survey of 152 chief executives and finance executives.[15] The executives were asked to rank their responsibilities to four claimants; and since the focus of the study was financial, creditors were on the list instead of customers. Many executives detected this "oversight" and gave such a hearty write-in vote for customers that they ranked third! Further, there was no difference in the average rank order given by the chief executives and the finance executives, even though it might be assumed that the finance managers would give more emphasis to creditors. The average rank order of the five groups was as follows: stockholders, employees, customers, creditors, and society. In ranking society last, a number of executives voluntarily added that, in their opinion, service to other claimants is effective service to society as a whole.

[15] Arthur W. Lorig, "Where Do Corporate Responsibilities Lie?" *Business Horizons*, Spring, 1967, pp. 51–54.

BUSINESS CODES OF CONDUCT

All businesses must meet certain standards of law and minimum cultural standards. All are further influenced by the general cultural milieu of their time. But in spite of these tendencies toward uniform conduct, there are important differences among businesses. Each has its own personality, as each human being does. These organizational differences are reflected in company codes of conduct, and they do produce different results.

Models of Business Conduct

As a guide to understanding different types of business conduct, Walton classifies six models of conduct.[16]

1 The austere model. It gives almost exclusive emphasis to ownership interests and profit objectives.

2 The household model. Following the concept of an extended family, this model emphasizes employee jobs, benefits, and paternalism.

3 The vendor model. In this model, consumer interests, tastes, and rights dominate the organization.

4 The investment model. This model focuses on the organization as an entity and thus on long-term profits and survival. In the name of enlightened self-interest it gives some recognition to social investments along with economic ones.

5 The civic model. Its slogan is corporate citizenship. It goes beyond imposed obligations, accepts social responsibility, and makes a positive commitment to social needs.

6 The artistic model. This model encourages the organization to become a creative instrument serving the cause of an advanced civilization with a better quality of life. The organization's people perform in the manner of artists, building some of their own creative ideas into the institution's actions, leading it toward new contributions not originally contemplated.

The six models may be thought of as points on a continuum from low to high social responsibility. Regardless of the model sought by an organization, one of its most important jobs is to establish and blend its values together so that they become a consistent, effective system that is known and accepted by claimants. The system must be strong enough to withstand challenges by partisan pressure groups, but flexible enough to move with a changing society. Establishing and maintaining an organizational value system is a difficult management task.

Written Codes of Conduct

Business conduct standards are expressed in meetings, bulletins, company magazines, employee statements, policy manuals, and countless other ways. Many organizations also have a written code of conduct or

[16] Clarence C. Walton, *Corporate Social Responsibilities,* Belmont, Calif.: Wadsworth Publishing Company, Inc., 1967, pp. 122–141.

creed which establishes the general value system that the firm tries to apply. Written creeds are developed in order to define organizational purpose, establish a uniform ethical climate within the organization, and provide guides for consistent decision making.

Written creeds are especially important for large organizations, branch units, and franchisers. These types of organizations tend to have complex structures, difficult lines of communication, and regional, national, or even international images which they are trying to project. Retail franchisers usually find that systemwide standards are necessary because clients expect a uniform quality of service. Consider, for example, the rapid growth of Kentucky Fried Chicken based on a uniform product and Holiday Inns based on a dependable standard of service.

Figure 9–1 presents a short, traditional code of conduct for a metal stamping company. It is evident that the statement is an ideal to be sought, rather than a daily operating guide. In fact, if the word "profit" is amended to read something like "additional capital for growth," this code could apply to nonprofit organizations, governmental units, and community-service groups. All of them compete with regard to ideas, resources, and/or services, and they want the services which they offer to be "equal to or better than that of any competitor." They also believe they are in a vocation which serves society.

Considering creeds as a whole, one weakness is that they are sometimes stated for their public relations value and not really made an actuality within the company. One of the greatest limitations of creeds is that those who prepare them assume that the meaning and feeling shared at the time they are written can be transferred to others by distributing a document for others to read. This is not so. Conduct codes are too complex and full of values to be conveyed in a few written words. For this reason, businesses use participation in planning a code in order to build more understanding and commitment to it. In addition, reevaluations in which there is wide participation will help maintain standards. Equal in importance with participation is the necessity for higher managers to support the code by example, because the standards they set will tend to be the ones others use, regardless of what the written statement says.

Specific areas of conduct are illustrated by the following discussion of conflict of interest and business gifts. Other areas are examined in subsequent chapters in connection with the subject to which they apply.

Conflict of Interest

A conflict of interest arises when an employee, either management or nonmanagement, has an interest in a transaction or is a party to a transaction that is so substantial that it reasonably might affect his independent judgment in his acts for the business. Both purchasing and sales are special areas of sensitivity, but the situation could exist anywhere.

One area of conflict of interest is substantial financial investment in a supplier, customer, or distributor. Usually it is acceptable to hold a small percentage of stock in a publicly owned supplier, especially when it is

In the conduct of our business, day by day, our chief thought may well be directed to the acceptance of our due responsibilities and to the fulfillment of our varied duties in the hope that their accomplishment shall have helped to raise, in some measure, the level of human ideals and achievement. And to this end, it may prove helpful to us to hold before us these principles:

- That we consider our vocation worthy as affording us distinct opportunity to serve society.
- That we desire to improve ourselves, increase our efficiency, and enlarge our service, that by so doing we shall measure up to the highest standards of worthwhile ambition.
- That the ambition to succeed is worth while, but that we desire no success that is not founded on the highest justice and morality.
- That the exchange of our product, our service, and our ideas for profit, is legitimate and ethical, provided that all parties in the exchange are benefited thereby.
- That we believe that no success is legitimate or ethical which is secured by taking unfair advantage of certain opportunities which may be questionable.
- That we should so conduct our business that we may approach a perfect service, equal to or better than that of any competitor, and when we are in doubt, that we should give an added service beyond the strict measure of debt or obligation.
- That we believe in the universality of the Golden Rule— "All things whatsoever ye would that men should do unto you, do ye even so unto them"—and that so believing, its application to our daily endeavor shall prove helpful to us and of benefit to society.

Figure 9–1   Code of conduct of a metal stamping company. Source: Sorrell M. Mathes and G. Clark Thompson, "Ensuring Ethical Conduct in Business," *The Conference Board Record,* December, 1964, p. 18. Reproduced with permission.

listed on a public stock exchange. The amount of ownership permitted varies. In one company it is 10 percent of outstanding stock; in another it is one-tenth of 1 percent. Another criterion is the percentage of the employee's total investment funds involved in this one investment. Some companies require key executives and purchasing agents to disclose outside business interests. One company's standard reads as follows: "Any member of management who has assumed, or is about to assume, a financial or other outside business relationship that might involve a conflict of interest must immediately inform his supervisor of the circumstances involved."

Another area of conflict of interest is the use of privileged information or one's official position to make transactions for personal gain. An example is the purchase or sale of real estate whose value might be affected by company activities.

In its totality, conflict of interest is difficult to control because of its many variations and dependence on personal interpretation. For these reasons, the most effective approach is self-discipline by ethically oriented individuals; however, management needs to provide a basic code to encourage uniform action and to provide follow-up to assure that a few unprincipled persons do not pull down the whole level of ethical practice. In the last analysis, a company's conduct can never be better than its people.

Business Gifts and Entertainment

Related to conflict of interest are business gifts, particularly those which are of more than nominal value and might influence a business decision of the person receiving it. Nominal value is, of course, difficult to define, and there are many situational and cultural variables which must be interpreted to determine appropriateness of a gift. Consider the following situation.

Walker Wright made an $70 business transaction with the Jones Company, using the services of a Jones employee named Baxter. Wright usually dealt with Baxter in his transactions with the Jones Company; so, when he completed his $70 transaction, he left Baxter a cash gift of $10 which he hoped would influence Baxter to continue his good service.

In this situation was Wright trying to influence Baxter? Yes, he was. Was the gift nominal? That depends on interpretation, but we still need more cultural and situational information before we can determine the ethical appropriateness of the gift. For example, if the Jones Company is an office supply company and Wright is the office manager of a small five-person office, what would be your answer? What would your answer be if Wright were a sales manager taking four clients to dinner at his favorite restaurant and leaving a tip for the waiter, Baxter? In this instance the tip is an established way of trying to influence good service, and it is even included by the employer in computing appropriate wages for his waiters.

In determining appropriateness of a gift, factors such as the following need to be evaluated: value of gift, purpose of gift, the circumstances in which it occurred (for example, more leniency at the Christmas season and for store openings), influence sensitivity of the recipient (such as a purchasing agent), and general cultural practices (i.e., accepted business practice). In application of these criteria, for example, an advertising item of nominal value with the donor's name imprinted thereon, such as a mechanical pencil or an appointment calendar, is usually an acceptable gift. It has low value, has a purpose which is an accepted business practice (advertising), and is given under open circumstances (name imprinted thereon).

In an effort to keep gifts within reasonable bounds most firms have guides restricting employee acceptance of gifts. Some are informally communicated, while others are quite specific, such as no gifts of more than $10 value, received not oftener than annually.

Entertainment of customers and suppliers is usually defined separately from gifts. Entertainment is an accepted business practice and is much more liberally interpreted because it is a social situation in which business affairs are conducted. One company informally distinguishes entertainment from gifts as follows: "If you can eat it or drink it on the spot, it's entertainment." Applying this definition and the $10 gift rule just mentioned, a business dinner costing $15 at an expensive club is permitted entertainment, but the gift of a $15 ham is prohibited. Entertainment is generally controlled through expense-account policies and rules.

CONDUCT GUIDES OFFERED BY OTHERS

The conduct of a business is influenced strongly by external organizations which interact with it. These organizations may be classified as professional associations, public advisory groups, and business associations.

Professional Associations

As occupational groups professionalize, they tend to develop codes of conduct which support fairness, full disclosure, independent decisions free of influence, and other actions in the public interest. These codes govern the conduct of their members in business and thereby determine minimum standards of conduct in their jobs. The codes also spill over into surrounding functions and eventually become adopted by the whole business. The standards for buying and selling sponsored by the National Association of Purchasing Management, for example, surely encouraged the growth of companywide policies on gift giving and acceptance.

Professional codes normally apply to professional conduct of a person both as an employee and as a businessman seeking consulting contracts or managing a firm providing professional services. Thus, an architectural firm and an engineering consulting firm are governed by codes of their profession. For example, the code of the American Society of Civil Engineers states that the civil engineer "shall not create obligation on prospective clients or employers through extravagant entertainment, gifts, or similar expenditures," and "He shall not engage in 'fee splitting' or other distribution of fees for other than services performed and in proportion to the value of such services."[17] In this manner business conduct is governed directly, as well as indirectly, by codes of professional associations.

Advertising is another occupation where professional standards are developing. This occupation has perhaps greater public visibility than any other business group. The Advertising Code of American Business was endorsed by the American Association of Advertising Agencies in 1964. It deals specifically with a number of advertising practices in an effort to

[17] Guide to Professional Practice under the Code of Ethics, New York: American Society of Civil Engineers, 1964.

encourage advertising truth, responsibility, public decency, bona fide offers, guarantees, and fair-price claims. This code represents a strong move toward social responsibility on the part of the advertising profession.

It appears that codes of ethics established by occupational groups, especially professional groups, are an excellent way to develop higher standards of business conduct. Even though the influence of these codes is mostly indirect, it is powerful because it brings the weight of professional opinion on business. Since professional codes are developed democratically by those who must live by them, they earn strong commitment from members. Their image is favorable because they are a means to achieve status and public recognition for an occupation. Originating with many groups, these codes offer avenues for experimentation and variety in the search for better standards of conduct. They can work their way piece by piece into organizational life, proving their value as they go.

A major advantage of professional codes is their democratic gradualism. Reformers would have businesses suddenly change into ethical models by edict from the president, but conversions of this type seldom stick. The democratic gradualism represented by professional codes tends to be more lasting. These codes are not substitutes for internal codes within each organization, but they are an important adjunct to them. In a number of cases they serve to stimulate a business to develop better internal codes.

Codes Offered by Advisory Groups

Public advisory groups also offer to business a variety of codes which they want it to adopt.

Examples are foundations, religious action groups, and minority groups. There is a significant difference between professional and advisory groups. The professional groups are self-generating a code for their own self-control, both in business and out of it. They seek to raise their standards. Advisory groups, on the other hand, offer to raise the standards of others. They say to business: "This is the way we think you ought to live if you want to live better." Usually they do not offer evidence that they follow these standards in their own organizations, and frequently their views represent special pleading for a certain philosophy.

The fact that advice arises externally does not make it improper or unwise. Much that is offered to business is useful, and businessmen would do well to heed it, but it is of a different quality than professional codes. It lacks the reality that being on the inside can bring. It lacks the personal commitment that self-generated standards for one's self can bring. Sometimes it has the taint of the ivory tower because it comes from the "sayers," not the "doers." And the sayers may be the last to adopt the code themselves, usually because they feel their situation is different. A foundation, for example, may object to economic layoffs, but when its own income drops, it makes layoffs, which it wants private business not to do. Or a social-action group which discovers a disloyal employee may dismiss him or drive him away, even though it does not want "business" to do so in a similar situation.

Business Associations

There are hundreds of business associations representing specific groups such as florists, retail druggists, and soft drink bottlers. These groups are primarily operating to promote their own interests, but in doing this they often find it necessary to set ethical standards for dealing with consumers and others. A primary reason for these standards is to control unscrupulous members and to maintain a public image for services fairly and reasonably rendered.

Florists, for example, in order to join an association for telegraphic delivery of flowers from one city to another must agree to inspections to assure that flowers ordered from a distant city have been delivered. Without inspections it would be relatively easy and "safe" for a florist to substitute flowers of lesser quality in a funeral bouquet and pocket the difference. The inspection discourages potential dishonesty and maintains a public image of dependability by expelling offenders. The individual florist is under pressure to maintain high standards, because if he is expelled from the organization, he cannot participate in this additional source of business.

One business group which has achieved national prominence for its recommendations, especially regarding business policy for social action, is the Committee for Economic Development (CED). It is a select group of about two hundred business leaders, including some educators. It is nonprofit, nonpartisan, and nonpolitical. Its reports and recommendations represent carefully developed, balanced viewpoints oriented toward general public benefit rather than partisan needs of business.

The CED represents primarily a *managerial ideology*, the kind found among career managers in larger businesses. "It argues that management is a trustee who serves the interest of all groups, taking account of more than just the concern of his own stockholders for profits."[18]

SUMMARY

There is a growing interest in business values because of business's dominant position in society. Surveys show that most businessmen are aware of value issues, believe that there are some unethical practices in business, and want to improve standards of conduct. Since businessmen mediate among many claimants and value systems, they must make frequent value judgments. Codes of conduct give them useful guides for making proper judgments. Two social purposes of business conduct guidelines are to assure a balance of responsibility with power and to help business more effectively fulfill its institutional mission.

Professional associations, public advisory groups, and business associations help business establish and maintain effective codes. Professional codes of conduct are especially effective because they focus on the public interest, are self-generated, develop gradually, earn strong psycho-

[18] R. Joseph Monsen, Jr., and Mark W. Cannon, *The Makers of Public Policy*, New York: McGraw-Hill Book Company, 1965, p. 47.

logical commitment from members, and maintain indirect as well as direct influence on business.

STUDY GUIDES FOR INTERPRETATION OF THIS CHAPTER

1 Following is a statement from a corporate annual report. "We consider it important that people are free to express themselves in their work and, more importantly, to feel the full impact of their ideas upon their company and their community. Motivated people with 'running room' not only adapt to change but also create it."[19] Which of Walton's six models of business conduct does this statement best fit, and why?

2 It is said that professional codes are especially effective in improving business standards. Why? How many of the reasons given apply also to codes developed by business associations?

3 You are president of a bank which is building a new branch in a middle-class neighborhood. Indicate ways in which the following value systems may apply to your decisions about this new branch: technical, economic, psychological, political, and aesthetic.

4 Comment on President John F. Kennedy's statement quoted at the beginning of this chapter, "In the last analysis, high ethical standards can be achieved only through voluntary effort."

5 Discuss pro and con the conduct of Regis Discount Furniture and the meat packer mentioned at the beginning of this chapter.

PROBLEMS

THE MEDICAL GIFTS

For years it has been the practice of pharmaceutical companies to aid students in medical schools with medical gifts, such as plastic models of human organs and samples of company drug products. This practice occurred with the knowledge and implied approval of medical schools which sometimes cooperated in distributing the gifts. The practice originated with two purposes in mind: (1) to provide informational advertising of company products, and (2) to aid students in the arduous and expensive task of completing medical school.

Recently the Blazer Corporation sent samples of some of its popular drug products to seniors at Eastern Medical School. The wholesale value of each sample kit was about $50. Shortly thereafter an organized group of twenty-four students returned the samples, protesting that the donor was trying to buy their loyalty. The students released their letter to news media and received favorable national publicity for their action.

1 In the role of marketing manager, what response, if any, would you make to the students, and why?

[19] Boise Cascade Corporation, *Annual Report*, 1968, p. 26.

2 In the same role, what response, if any, would you make within the firm, and why? Is it possible for conditions to change, making a formerly accepted practice now unacceptable? In this case what pertinent conditions have changed?

3 The Blazer Corporation also gives three student scholarships to Eastern Medical School. The scholarships bear the Blazer name. Their annual cost is nine times the cost of the drugs sent to Eastern seniors. Further, the cost of medical scholarships given by Blazer to all schools is five times the cost of drugs given to all schools and their students. Should the company reconsider its scholarship policy, and why?

THE ADVERTISING EPISODE

The advertisement of a food company showed an animated cartoon of a bandit making a holdup to secure the advertised food product because he craved it so greatly. The scene then shifted to regular photography of a household where a family member was enthusiastically sneaking a bite of the advertised food, and this person was also labeled a bandit. The entire theme was comical.

The cartoon bandit was a person who appeared to be Mexican-American, and the household bandit appeared to be an Anglo-American. In one state a representative of the Mexican-American Anti-defamation Committee approached the program director of a television station and asked him to discontinue showing the commercial because it portrayed Mexican-Americans as thieves.

The advertising code of this station contained the following statement: "Taste and Decency: Advertising shall be free of statements, illustrations, or implications which are offensive to good taste or public decency." The population proportion of Mexican-Americans living within the viewing area covered by this station was approximately 15 percent.

1 As program director, what factors would you consider in your response to the protest? What action would you finally take, and why?

CHAPTER 10

THE INDIVIDUAL AND THE ORGANIZATION

Oneness, they say, creates harmony. But with oneness, flabbiness and decay may also come.
WILLIAM G. SCOTT[1]

*It is our hypothesis that the incongruence between
the individual and the organization can provide the
basis for a continued challenge which, as it is fulfilled, will help man to enhance his own growth and
to develop organizations that will be viable and
effective.*
CHRIS ARGYRIS[2]

In this chapter we discuss the role of an individual as a *person* in his
relationships with organizations. In this role he is a separate *human
being* with inherent dignity, integrity, independence, and rights of privacy.
Even though an individual is an employee within a company, he is still a
person; and *in this role he is an outsider beyond the company gates.* He
is a part of the environment of business. The focus of this chapter, therefore, is upon the individual as a human being and how this humanness
affects his social transactions with business. Both business and the individual need ideological and operating guides to make their relationship
effective. We discuss claims of the individual on the organization, the
organization-man thesis, legitimacy of organizational influence, and rights
of privacy. We conclude with a brief statement of individual responsibilities to the organization.

Consider the following situations. In the first one, is the repairman
seeking to serve his personal interests in a way which conflicts with obligations that arise from social transactions he has made with his employer? In the second situation, is the organization improperly invading
the privacy of four individuals?

[1] William G. Scott, *The Social Ethic in Management Literature*, Georgia State College of
Business Administration, Studies in Business and Economics, no. 4, Atlanta, Ga., 1959,
p. 98.
[2] Chris Argyris, *Integrating the Individual and the Organization*, New York: John Wiley
& Sons, Inc., 1964, p. 7. Italics in original.

John Jones, one of seventeen television repairmen working for Mather Electronics, was called to a residence to repair a television set. He repaired the set and presented the bill, but he also did something else. He called the owner aside, gave him a business card bearing his name and home telephone number, and stated in a confidential tone, "Next time something goes wrong, call me at home. I'll come out in the evening and do the job for less than my company charges." In this manner, John earned added income that was nearly fifty percent of what his employer paid him.

During the same week the wholesale supplier of television parts to Mather Electronics gave each of its four shipping clerks their quarterly polygraph test to determine if they were handling orders honestly. Two years earlier the supplier had a 20 percent inventory loss in one year as a result of a theft conspiracy by all four shipping clerks. It replaced them with carefully screened clerks who agreed as a condition of employment to have a quarterly polygraph test restricted only to queries about on-the-job theft.

CLAIMS OF THE INDIVIDUAL ON THE ORGANIZATION

In order to understand the relationship of an individual person with an organization, it is necessary to examine in a general way what individuals expect from organizations. These generalizations normally apply whether the individual is a customer, neighbor in the community, stockholder, or some other person. As with most generalizations, there are exceptions.

Normally, an individual claims three basic payoffs or benefits in his social transaction with an organization. None of them can be provided in the absolute, but a measure of each is necessary to maintain a viable relationship. The more of each benefit that can be gained, other things being equal, the more successful the relationship will be for a person. The three claims are:

Improvement—the psychological purpose of an individual's relationship with an organization
Independence—the individual price required for cooperation
Justice—the social standard for relating to an organization

Improvement

Improvement is the basic reason a person chooses to become a client of an organization. For his role investment he expects a payoff which brings him closer to his goals. If there is no payoff, he will cease his relationship if he is free to do so. Improvement is expressed in terms of the rewards he receives such as opportunity, money, recognition, and personal development. Improvement has become so much of a normal expectation that one business leader believes the development of people should be a major social purpose of business, equal in significance with good products and profit (which are themselves a type of improvement for customers and owners respectively).[3]

[3] Henry G. Pearson, "A New Co-aim for Business," *MSU Business Topics*, Spring, 1968, pp. 51–56.

Just as clients expect improvement from business, so do other claimants. Community citizens expect business to help build a better community. Looking even more broadly, people throughout the world expect business to improve both the material goods and the quality of life. For example, infant mortality is decreased through new drugs, hospitalization programs for employees, and so on. Learning is improved through better books and teaching aids. As explained by the chairman of the board of one of the world's largest oil companies: "Every problem we face, whether of economics or technology or whatever it may be, is truly significant only as it bears on our great underlying concern: the fullest development of the potential which is hidden in every human being."[4]

B. Independence

Independence is the basic demand that a person makes of any organization in return for his cooperation. He does not give all of himself. He reserves something for his own initiative, self-determination, and privacy. In interacting with the organization he insists on some freedom of action. He seeks organizational practices which give him more independence. This is a part of his cultural heritage as well as his natural drive as a human being. This was the situation with the television repairman mentioned at the beginning of this chapter. He felt that his time off the job was his own, even if it placed him in competition with his employer. However, did he overstep the bounds of his social contract with his employer when he solicited business from his employer's customers on his employer's time?

C. Justice

Justice is the standard of treatment which a man expects from an organization in order to continue his relationship with it. Justice makes group life tolerable. It is based on fairness, reason, and prudence in organizational acts. It gives substance and meaning to human dignity because it protects the person in his dealings with the group. Justice means compliance with the spirit of a relationship as well as the letter of it. Justice is what holds an organization together in voluntary cooperation. If a man has a measure of independence plus improvement in the direction of his goals but suffers injustice, he will withdraw his cooperation and seek to place his role investments elsewhere.

The justice which a person typically seeks from organizations is *distributive justice* concerning "the feelings of rightness or wrongness in the balance between environmental rewards and social investments. . . . Individual rewards, when compared with the rewards received by other group members, should be proportional to social investment."[5] Education, for example, is considered to be a social investment. When an employee uses it in his job, he expects appropriate rewards. In general, if investments

---

[4] M. J. Rathbone, *The Businessman and the Problems of Progress,* New York: Standard Oil Company (New Jersey), 1963, p. 15.
[5] Abraham Zaleznik and David Moment, *The Dynamics of Interpersonal Behavior,* New York: John Wiley & Sons, Inc., 1964, pp. 330, 400.

and rewards are not in agreement, people feel that the situation lacks justice. To them it is not fair. They express unhappiness, they complain, and they withhold their cooperation.

Justice is a social comparison with others; therefore, a change in what others receive can cause a person to feel injustice just as much as a change in what he receives. Assume that a business partner feels he has a satisfactory situation in a partnership. He then discovers when he examines yearly expense accounts that two other partners have been entertaining business clients more often and much more expensively than he has. If in his mind he can find no "rational" reason for the difference, he may feel that the situation is unjust, even though he did not feel so until this moment.

Justice has a historical basis. A person feels that there should be some relationship between what he has contributed in the past and received in the past, and what he is contributing and receiving now. A physician, for example, makes major internship investments with low financial rewards; therefore, he expects justice to provide him with quick financial rewards when he finally reaches his productive years. His is a delayed payoff in relation to investment. A different situation is that of a construction superintendent who has had high pay and status in the past and who expects the same on his present assignment, even though his contribution on this job is not quite as great as usual because the job is a small one. The just organization relates each person's investments to benefits, both in relation to history and in relation to the investments and benefits of others.

THE ORGANIZATION-MAN THESIS

The Basic Thesis

The underlying idea of the organization man is conformity by the individual to the organization in a way which threatens his claim for independence. This contest between man and organization is as old as organized society. Man has a drive for freedom and self-actualization, while the organization needs coordination and control to unify effort toward objectives. Modern interest in this struggle against conformity was stimulated by publication of *The Organization Man* by William H. Whyte, Jr., in 1956. The book quickly became a best seller. Whyte stated that a new social ethic had developed to rationalize the organization's demands for wholehearted dedication and loyalty. He wrote:

> By social ethic I mean that contemporary body of thought that makes morally legitimate the pressures of society against the individual. Its major propositions are three: a belief in the group as the source of creativity; a belief in "belongingness" as the ultimate need of the individual; and a belief in the application of science to achieve the belongingness. . . . Essentially, it is a utopian faith. . . . It is quite reminiscent of the beliefs of utopian communities of the 1840s.[6]

[6] William H. Whyte, Jr., *The Organization Man*, New York: Simon & Schuster, Inc., 1956, p. 7.

The social ethic according to Whyte is an ideology provided by intellectuals, not by the organization. As a result of broad acceptance of this ideology, people are "imprisoned in brotherhood." They "belong" to the organization. They are the ones "who have left home, spiritually as well as physically, to take the vows of organization life"; however, the fault is not in the organization itself but "in our worship of it."

Whyte perceived the individual as cared for and kept by organizations, and he strongly opposed personality testing, bureaucracy, and conformity. He even offered an appendix on "How to Cheat on Personality Tests." To Whyte, man's answer to the social ethic should be to fight the organization, but not self-destructively.

Whyte's organization-man thesis was supported by publication in the following year of Chris Argyris's *Personality and Organization,* which dealt particularly with psychological problems of work, such as alienation, frustration, and suppression of self-actualization.

The basic philosophy in Argyris's own words is as follows:[7]

> An analysis of the basic properties of relatively mature human beings and formal organization leads to the conclusion that there is an inherent incongruency between the self-actualization of the two. This basic incongruency creates a situation of conflict, frustration, and failure for the participants. . . .

When the ideas of the organization man are applied to the whole society, the result is a *beehive model* of society in which the total system perfects itself as the individual becomes steadily less significant.[8] Large organization overwhelms the individual until society becomes like a hive of bees in which there is little individuality. Even the queen bee is no exception, because she is a functional slave to the system like all the other bees.

Interpreting the Organization Man

There is an element of truth in the organization-man thesis. Individual and organizational goals are different, but this is only one side of the story. People and organizations have strong *mutual interests* in their relationship. People need organizations. Without organizations, many modern social goals would be impossible to accomplish. Organizations make available resources and opportunities which an individual operating alone could not have. They also satisfy many of his higher-order needs and provide psychological support for him.[9] There is no ultimate conflict which either the individual or the organization must win. Rather, there is the constant need to reappraise organizations so that they can be improved in order to serve the individual better.

[7] Chris Argyris, *Personality and Organization: The Conflict between the System and the Individual,* New York: Harper & Row, Publishers, Incorporated, 1957, p. 175.
[8] John W. Gardner, "Toward a Self-renewing Society," *Time,* Apr. 11, 1969, pp. 40–41.
[9] Harry Levinson, "Reciprocation: The Relationship between Man and Organization," *Administrative Science Quarterly,* March, 1965, p. 378. See also research reported in William P. Sexton, "Organizational and Individual Needs: A Conflict?" *Personnel Journal,* June, 1967, pp. 337–343.

The differences which remain are not necessarily undesirable. An individual develops through challenge; consequently, some differences can be psychologically and socially healthful. This is the manner in which democratic elections produce a more effective society. In other words, differences which are constructively directed can enhance individual growth and develop more effective organizations, as Argyris explains in one of the quotations introducing this chapter.

Is Business a Special Source of Conformity?

The organization-man thesis is occasionally interpreted as an attack on business as a special cause of conformity compared with other organizations; however, there is little evidence that conformity is a hallmark of business culture. Business has no special problem, compared with the military, government, or even the slum street gang. The issue of the organization man is a universal one applying to all organizations and cultures. Whyte says: "This conflict is certainly not a peculiarly American development," and he adds with a flourish:

> Blood brother to the business trainee off to join Du Pont is the seminary student who will end up in the church hierarchy, the doctor headed for the corporate clinic, the physics Ph.D. in a government laboratory, the intellectual on the foundation-sponsored team project, the engineering graduate in the huge drafting room at Lockheed, the young apprentice in a Wall Street law factory.[10]

Limited research agrees with Whyte that business is not a special source of conformity. Perhaps it goes even further and suggests that business gives above-average emphasis to nonconformity. It is, for example, popularly considered that university professors are a prime example of a nonconforming group; therefore, they make a good group to compare with business executives. One study administered a psychological test on conformity to these two groups and found that the businessmen were no more conforming than the professors. (And both were found to be less conforming than college students!) The study did find a wide range of conformity among both businessmen and professors; so if one wanted to find examples of conformity in business he could find many.[11]

Another study examined whether the reward structure in business tended to support conformity.[12] Contrary to popular writing and opinion, the study found that those managers who scored lower in conformity were given higher ratings by their superiors.

Whyte did express concern that the business schools compared with other branches of the university were developing organization men for businesses of the future. If business is a conforming institution, we might

---

[10] Whyte, op. cit., p. 3.
[11] John B. Miner, "Conformity among University Professors and Business Executives," Administrative Science Quarterly, June, 1962, pp. 96–109, reporting on 44 executives and 41 professors. The study found older persons less conforming; so if a business had predominantly younger persons in it, it might have a higher conformity index.
[12] Edwin A. Fleishman and David R. Peters, "Interpersonal Values, Leadership Attitudes, and Managerial 'Success,' " Personnel Psychology, Summer, 1962, pp. 127–143, covering thirty-nine managers in four soap manufacturing branches.

expect that business schools would have a similar emphasis. The evidence just presented, however, shows that business is not especially conforming. A study in the late 1960s suggests the same conclusion regarding business schools. This study covered personnel directors in business, using the questions which Whyte originally used to distinguish an organization man from an individualist. When these respondents were classified according to their college majors, the business majors were less organization-man-oriented than any other group. Humanities majors were the most organization-man-oriented. The researchers concluded that, in general, "the trend is consistent: practicality of the curriculum appears to be *negatively* correlated with preference for the organization man."[13]

The Individual in a Large Organization

It is sometimes thought that big organizations are at the root of the organization-man problem. It is assumed that if we could splinter organizations into small pieces, thereby diffusing authority, harmony would again prevail. With smaller organizations, man would be proportionately stronger, and power would be equalized. However, some analysts believe that big organizations diffuse power through decentralization in a manner which more than offsets centralization of certain functions. One observer comments: "The result of bigness is actually a diffusion of the decision-making and decision-influencing process far beyond the wildest dreams of those worshippers at the shrine of Louis Brandeis, who wanted to keep power diffused by keeping the units of society small."[14]

A survey of 1,916 managers reported that more organization men were in smaller companies.[15] They gave less emphasis to forcefulness, imagination, and independence, but more emphasis to caution and tact. In addition, emphasis on conformity came not from the executive suite but from lower management in these companies.

Considering the organization-man issue as a whole, it does not appear to be a special problem of business. To assure that individuals get maximum values from organizations which make minimum infringements on their freedoms is, however, an issue for genuine long-range social concern. These ideas are further developed in the next two sections. Primary emphasis is given to the employee because of his close relationship with the organization, but the ideas discussed apply in a general way to individuals in any relationship with an organization.

LEGITIMACY OF ORGANIZATIONAL INFLUENCE ON EMPLOYEES

To What Does One Conform?

The organization is one of many influences to which an individual conforms. Conformity implies a dependence on the norms of others without

---

[13] Robert C. Leonard and Reta D. Artz, "Structural Sources of Organization Man Ideology," *Human Organization*, Summer, 1969, p. 113. Italics in original.
[14] Harlan Cleveland, "Dinosaurs and Personal Freedom," *Saturday Review*, Feb. 28, 1959, p. 12.
[15] "Tracking Conformity to Its Business Lair," *Business Week*, Feb. 27, 1965, p. 74.

independent thinking. To develop this point it is necessary to recognize the different groups to which one conforms. First, there is a pseudo-conformity by which one conforms to the technology. That is, when the pot boils, take it off the fire; or when the batch in the furnace is ready, take it out. Some so-called conformity in industry is actually a response to the technology; but this is not true conformity because it does not involve the norms of others. Furthermore, this "conformity" is the same in or out of an organization.

Looking at genuine conformity to group norms at work, there are three groups to which one conforms. One of these is the organization itself. Another is the informal work group, and the last is the external community. It is evident that the last two represent conformity *in* the organization instead of conformity *to* the organization. The organization does not impose these last two norms; they are simply there because the organization operates in a social system rather than a vacuum. Excluding the two norms just mentioned, what is the extent and legitimacy of the organization's influence?

A Model for Legitimate Areas of Organizational Influence

Every organization develops certain policies and requirements for performance. If the organization and an individual define the boundaries of legitimate influence differently, then organizational conflict is likely to develop. This conflict can be sufficient to interfere with accomplishment of organizational purpose. If, for example, an employee believes that it is legitimate for management to control how much time he talks with his wife on the telephone while at work, he may dislike management interference with his freedom on this matter, but he is unlikely to develop serious conflict with management about it. If, however, he believes that talking with his wife on the telephone is his own private right, then this issue may become a center of conflict with management.

This same type of reasoning applies to any claimant with which the organization deals. As long as there is agreement on the legitimacy of influence among the parties involved, they should be satisfied with the power balance in their relationship.

Limited research shows that there is reasonable cultural agreement concerning areas where organizational influence on employees is considered legitimate. Studies have covered labor leaders, managers in management-development courses, university students in three areas of the nation, and managers in companies. The studies used the Schein-Ott legitimacy questionnaire which covers fifty-five areas of organizational influence ranging from highly job-related ones (such as employee working hours) to highly personal ones (such as the church an employee attends). The studies report general agreement on areas of legitimacy among all four groups, with high rank-order correlations for the fifty-five items ranging from .88 to .98. Managers gave somewhat more support to legitimacy than labor leaders, with students ranking in the middle; however, the important point is the general agreement among all groups. Items of high legitimacy were those which involved job performance and the work

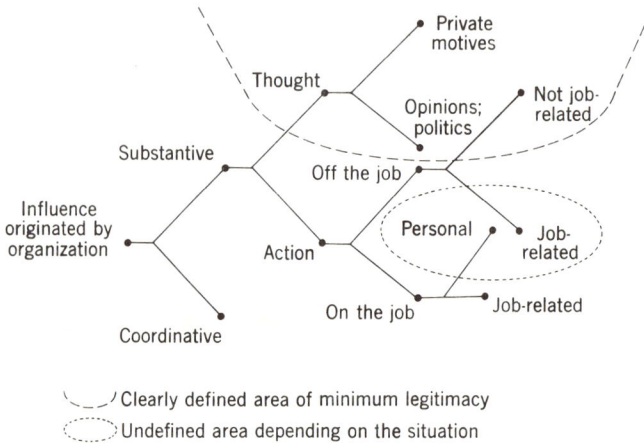

Figure 10–1   Projected chart of legitimacy of organizational influence with employees.

environment. Moderate legitimacy related to off-the-job conduct which might affect organizational interests, and low legitimacy concerned private acts and beliefs.[16]

Figure 10–1 presents a system of legitimacy which reflects both research and experience. The higher an item is in the system, the more probability there is that employees and the community will question management influence on that item. The system shows that routine coordinative requirements are the most readily accepted. We are all acquainted with the traffic light, which does require a sort of conformity, but its purpose is to coordinate the free flow of traffic. The same reasoning applies to justify certain hours for a department store to be open, which in turn limits the choice sales clerks have for hours of work.

Substantive items relate more directly to job choices by management, such as the quality of work required. Legitimacy tends to become less accepted, however, as an act's connection with the job becomes more hazy. An example is the type of clothing worn to work. In some instances this is clearly job-connected for safety or public relations reasons, but in other instances it is unrelated to the job. As a further example, all groups surveyed showed low legitimacy concerning whether the employee wears a beard.

Off-the-job Conduct

For off-the-job conduct, the organization can exert influence by means of educational programs, hobby groups, and communications, but what about its right to use disciplinary power to enforce its desires? We can

[16] Edgar H. Schein and J. Steven Ott, "The Legitimacy of Organizational Influence," *American Journal of Sociology*, May, 1962, pp. 682–689; and Keith Davis, "Attitudes toward the Legitimacy of Management Efforts to Influence Employees," *Academy of Management Journal*, June, 1968, pp. 153–162.

begin with the premise that it cannot use its disciplinary power to regulate employee conduct off the job; however, the line of separation is difficult to draw. What about a petroleum employee living on a company pumping site and on twenty-four-hour call? But even when an employee has departed company property and is not on call, the boundaries of employer interest are still not fixed. Consider the angry employee who waited until his foreman stepped outside the company gate and then struck him several times in the presence of other employees. In cases of this type, arbitrators consistently uphold company disciplinary action because the action is job-related. In the United States at least, the organization's jurisdictional line is clearly functional, related to the total job system and not the property line.

One study of sixty-six arbitration awards found a number of ways in which off-the-job conduct could be involved in disciplinary action.[17] In addition to job-related fighting, conduct which damages organizational reputation or business interests is subject to discipline. This factor has been significant in public-service employment such as bus driving and news editing where employee reputation is likely to affect customer acceptance. In other instances, off-the-job conduct may show that the employee is unfit for his present responsibility. In one case a plant guard pulled a gun in an after-hours fight, and this action was held to indicate lack of judgment in the use of firearms. Another example is alcoholism which makes an individual unfit for a hazardous job.

D. Trade Secrets

An area of both legal and ethical difficulty is the maintenance of a firm's trade secrets in a mobile society in which professional employees frequently move to a better job with another company. The basic issue with trade secrets is twofold. The organization certainly has a right to protect its trade secrets and other proprietary data which it may have spent much time and effort in developing. On the other hand, the individual is a free person who has rights to seek employment wherever he wishes and to try to make the best possible use of his abilities wherever he can do so. He is free of the master-servant relationship.

In serious cases a firm may go to court to protect its trade secrets. An example is an employee who steals and sells secret documents not ordinarily accessible to him. In normal relationships, however, the better approach is to develop procedures mutually agreeable to both parties. Some firms set up part-time consulting arrangements following employment, but these are available only if the employee does not work for a competitor during this period. Others provide stock options which the employee forfeits if he leaves the company. For example, do you consider the following option program to be a fair one?

An electronics company had a stock option plan available to key professional employees in exchange for their agreement that they would not "be

[17] Arthur M. Sussman, "Work Disputes versus Private Life: An Analysis of Arbitration Cases," *ILR Research*, vol. 10, no. 1, pp. 3–12, Ithaca, N.Y., Cornell University, New York State School of Industrial and Labor Relations, 1964.

directly or indirectly engaged in, . . . or have any material investment or any other material interest in, any business that is competitive with the business of the Company" for a period of one year after leaving the company. Exceptions were made in the case of merger and other special situations.

IV. RIGHTS OF PRIVACY

Figure 10–1 shows that areas of least legitimacy are private thoughts, opinions, and motives. Privacy in this context refers to the individual's private person or psyche more than to his private (noncompany) activities. Employees, customers, and others believe that their religious, political, and social beliefs are part of their own inner self and should not be subject to snooping or analysis as a requirement for getting or keeping a job. The same view applies to personal conversations and to certain personal locations such as company restrooms and private homes. Exceptions are permitted grudgingly only when a job involvement is clearly proved, and burden of proof is on the company. For example, it might be appropriate to know that a bank teller is deeply in debt to his bookie or that an applicant for a national credit card has twice been convicted for stealing and using credit cards. On the other hand, does the credit card company really need to know the applicant's grandmother's maiden name and the kind of car he drives?

A. The Polygraph

The polygraph is one instrument whose legitimacy is often questioned, and some states have outlawed its use in employment situations. We have learned that conscience usually causes physiological changes when a person tells a significant lie. Based on this information, the polygraph (lie detector) was developed. Business claims ample reasons for using the polygraph in special situations because its losses from pilferage are several billion dollars annually.[18] Losses of this size have to be passed on to the customer, along with the extra expense of protective efforts; so business claims it is in the public interest to use the polygraph in certain situations.

In decentralized retail operations, such as drive-in grocery stores, business states that polygraph tests permit it to abolish various audits and controls that would otherwise be oppressive. This arrangement gives the employee more freedom from surveillance and leaves him free to work in whatever manner is most productive to him. Similar reasoning applies to other positions of trust.

Regardless of need for the polygraph, its intrusion upon the individual's psyche is evident. In addition, it is sometimes claimed that polygraph tests are improperly extended from theft investigation to drinking

---

[18] The loss during the 1967–68 fiscal year was estimated to be $3 billion. See "Senate Tracks Business Thieves," *Business Week*, May 31, 1969, p. 100.

habits, marital life, political beliefs, and other nonjob subjects. Even when the polygraph is used only concerning theft, employees tend to resent it because they consider their conscience personal and they object to "being judged by a machine" over which they have no control. They especially object to having to prove themselves innocent, that is, take a test routinely even when no theft has been discovered or no evidence points to them as a thief. They object less to a specific test about a specific known theft of major proportions. In this situation they may welcome a test to take the pressure of suspicion off them.

Personality Tests

Equally at issue is the use and abuse of personality tests. Workers respond fairly well to tests of skill, but when their psyche is invaded by tests they are understandably rebellious. When one executive was asked in a test whether he was ever bothered with a feeling that someone was following him, he answered in derision: "No, I got rid of him before I came into the building to take the test!" Some psychologists admit that personality testing invades privacy, but they contend that an employer has a large investment in an employee, which justifies invasion of privacy, but only for information directly bearing on job performance. One psychologist states: "Tests in professional hands are perhaps the safest and certainly the least public invasion of privacy."[19]

Even if the psychologist handles his work perfectly, management is likely to require a report from him, and he has no control over how management may later misuse confidential data in his report. In one instance, for example, test files were available to any personnel clerk, and some clerks tended to pry into these files more than their jobs justified.

Another danger is that personality tests may produce a standardized work group because the tests overemphasize conformity and fitting into the group. The creative individualist is likely to fail because he *is* different; hence, a firm may test itself into conformity and stagnation. Furthermore, are we really testing what we want to know? Every man has primitive, uncivilized drives as far as can be determined. The crucial question is: How well does he handle them? With most normal people we learn this easily enough by observing their conduct, not by exploring their psyche.

An additional difficulty is that personality tests can be faked by an employee to give results that he thinks the employer desires, making their effective use even more difficult. The test result is then a fiction, rather than a genuine reflection of the employee's personality. Over the years many studies by competent social scientists have proved that a wide selection of personality tests can be faked.[20]

---

[19] Roger Ricklefs, "How Companies Are Using Psychological Tests," *Wall Street Journal,* Feb. 9, 1965, quoted in *Management Review,* April, 1965, pp. 46–47. For a more detailed discussion on personality testing as an invasion of privacy, see Alan F. Westin, *Privacy and Freedom,* New York: Atheneum Publishers, 1967.
[20] Several studies reporting that different personality tests can be faked are reported in Marvin D. Dunnette and others, "A Study of Faking Behavior on a Forced-choice Self-description Checklist," *Personnel Psychology,* Spring, 1962, pp. 13–24.

Taken as a whole the history of personality tests in employment raises serious questions of social responsibility. Legislation may be expected to correct abuses, just as occurred with polygraph tests, unless improvements are made. Perhaps an employee bill of rights may be necessary to guarantee the right of private motives, as distinguished from acts. One writer comments: "If the corporation assumes responsibility for raising 'mature individuals' (whatever that means) . . . it assumes a power and responsibility over private folly and uniqueness that goes beyond that demanded by even the family, the church, or the university."[21]

Sensitivity Training

Sensitivity training is a group training method which may be rather routine, or it may employ intense, emotional group sessions which lay bare a person's psyche to the group. When it does so, it is an invasion of privacy; however, as with personality tests, the invasion is often justified because it is conducted by professional psychologists and is secondary to a more important purpose. In this instance the purpose is sensitivity to the feelings of other people. Some individuals especially object if sensitivity training is required. Usually an employee is allowed to volunteer, but it is difficult to mark the fine line between genuine voluntary choice and coercive pressure to "volunteer." If sensitivity training becomes the route to special status and favors and if people who lack it are bypassed for promotion, they are being coerced to submit to what they perceive is an invasion of privacy.[22]

Medical Examinations

Even though medical examinations may invade privacy, the relationship of physician and patient is such a private and privileged one that medical tests of employees are usually permitted. In addition, the health and safety of the patient, as well as others, may be involved; so there is good cause for medical examinations. Normally a manager may require an employee to take a medical examination to determine either physical or emotional fitness to continue work. Some other situations, however, are more sticky. Should a package delivery firm, if it suspects a driver is under the influence of alcohol, be permitted to require a medical test to determine alcohol content in the blood? In this case both employee and public safety are involved; but some employees object to blood tests and others will say this is an invasion of their privacy. What other alternatives might be used to deal with this problem?

Surveillance Devices

Surveillance devices are especially used to observe shoplifting, which is estimated to cost business from one to three billion dollars annually. A

---

[21] George S. Odiorne, "Management's Motivation Muddle," *Michigan Business Review*, March, 1965, p. 31.
[22] A study by Robert J. House confirms the view that required sensitivity training is an invasion of privacy. See Robert J. House, " 'T-group' Training: Some Important Considerations for the Practicing Manager," *NYPMA Bulletin*, pp. 4–9, New York, New York Personnel Management Association, May, 1965.

simple device is the curved mirror which is seen in some retail stores. Another is a camera mounted on a wall or ceiling. There are also more sophisticated electronic devices. Since the shopper is in a public place, these devices normally are not considered an invasion of privacy as long as they are used for the purposes intended and especially if their existence is indicated by a posted notice. Similar reasoning applies to secret surveillance of public places to provide evidence of illegal behavior. For example, in the following situation could the robber properly claim his privacy was invaded?

A statewide banking system installed hidden cameras which could be secretly activated during bank robberies. When the bank had pictures of the robbers in four unsolved robberies, it published close-ups of them in newspaper advertisements throughout the state. The next day one of the men pictured walked into a police station and gave himself up, saying that after seeing his picture in the paper he felt he could not hide any longer!

f. Confidential Records

In addition to psychological records mentioned earlier, confidential information is often kept by credit bureaus and firms extending credit to customers. When information such as his annual income is supplied by an individual, the argument is that this is his voluntary act and that the information is functionally necessary in determining credit risk. However, business needs to take great care to keep this information protected from prying eyes. In addition, if negative information comes from other sources and is significant enough to damage a person's credit rating, the individual insists upon the right to challenge the information's accuracy or significance. This is simple due process which protects an individual from being unfairly victimized by the system. It is an example of the basic human claim for *justice* mentioned earlier.

G. Invasion of the Privacy of One's Home

It has been said that a man's home is his own private castle, and an area of increasing irritation at home is the large amount of unsolicited "junk mail" received from business. Computer tapes have made inexpensive the addressing of this kind of mail, so its quantity is increasing. An authority on privacy comments that "as long as I have the right to throw junk mail in the wastebasket, I think my liberty is pretty well protected."[23] Nevertheless, complaints persist on the basis that the recipient's private time is consumed in processing the unwanted mail to separate it from other mail.

There are also special situations where privacy is more directly threatened. For example, if unsolicited credit cards are mailed and a person unknowingly tosses them into his wastebasket, they may be used by others and ruin the recipient's credit rating. The same reasoning applies when they are stolen from his mailbox. For this reason the Nixon Admin-

---

[23] Alan Westin, quoted in "Squeezing Even More out of Tax Returns," *Business Week*, Dec. 6, 1969, p. 69.

istration in 1969 requested a law to prohibit mailing of unsolicited credit cards in order to guard consumers from "unwarranted invasion" of their privacy.[24]

Unsolicited obscene mail definitely may invade the psyche, shock the recipient, and cause emotional upset; so a federal law permits the recipient to file a form which requires the sender to remove the individual's name from his mailing list. According to this law which was upheld unanimously by the Supreme Court in 1970, the obscenity of any piece of mail may be determined by the recipient. For example, a householder who was tired of junk mail objected to department store advertising on the basis that it showed girdles and lingerie. The Post Office Department agreed that the law allows an individual choice on this matter without relation to generally accepted community standards.

Judging Infringements on Privacy

There are many situational variations, some of which probably constitute infringements on privacy while others do not. Four tests may be applied to help determine the degree of privacy invasion. First, does the device invade the psyche, such as polygraphs and personality tests? Second, is the device unnecessarily secret? Companies are regularly using television cameras for various types of controls, but these are work observations that are not secret, so an employee has some opportunity to know whether he is being watched and, if he desires, to challenge the instrument. A third test is whether the activity or instrument serves a purpose which is predominantly in the public interest (such as observation of shoplifters), with any invasion of privacy being incidental and secondary. Fourth, is a private act or location being observed? According to this criterion, hidden cameras or microphones in locker rooms have been condemned.

Sometimes novel questions of privacy arise. Women employees in a major English company persuaded management to remove from their restroom a loudspeaker on the regular paging system. This was not a case of snooping. They simply claimed that they were shocked to hear a man's voice in their restroom, and they demanded privacy therefrom!

Indeed, privacy is a worldwide issue. As industrialization advances along with the technology of snooping, business must increasingly seek responsible behavior measured by criteria of the type we have been discussing.

RESPONSIBILITIES OF THE INDIVIDUAL TO THE ORGANIZATION

The relationship of an individual to an organization is typically a mutual social transaction, and mutual responsibilities arise out of that relationship. This mutual relationship deteriorates if either party fails to act

[24] Joseph D. Hutnyan, "Nixon Aide Asks Mail Ban on All Unsolicited Cards," *American Banker*, Sept. 11, 1969, p. 1.

responsibly toward the needs of the other. An advanced civilization in which individuals have relative freedom is built upon responsible action by its individuals as well as by its organizations. For example, individual theft from the organization is just as irresponsible as organizational theft from the individual.

The polygraph provides a useful illustration of the mutual responsibilities of individuals and organizations in a complex system. There would be no use for the polygraph if it were not discovering breaches in conduct which the individual's *own conscience* recognizes. In fact, it is rarely used with groups such as professional accountants whose high standards of integrity and responsibility make it unnecessary. All individuals could destroy the usefulness of the polygraph by similar conduct. In other words, the roots of the polygraph problem lie in individual conduct and not in the device itself. We deal with only half the problem when we condemn the polygraph without also condemning the conduct which makes it useful. Theft was the original action which made a counteraction by the organization appropriate. This reasoning does not justify organizational use of the polygraph, but it does recognize from the point of view of the whole social system the mutual responsibility that exists for its use.

A word which comprehensively reflects the mutual responsibilities of individual and organization to each other is *integrity*. The idea of integrity applies in two separate meanings of the word. First, each party in the social transaction needs to *respect the integrity* of the other, which means to accept the other's individuality and social function. Second, each party needs to *practice integrity* in its relationships with the other. Integrity in this context implies that each party acts in an open, responsible way, without deception and shallowness. If both parties respond with integrity, they will be able to develop greater benefits in relation to inputs, and society will be able to relax many social controls put upon them.

SUMMARY

The contest between man and his organizations is as old as history, and this condition challenges business to develop systems of accepted legitimacy which serve the needs of both. Three claims which the individual makes on business are improvement, independence, and justice.

The organization-man thesis, although it is sometimes overplayed, suggests vigilance to assure that organizations serve social needs with minimum intrusion on individual freedom and privacy. Some areas which raise issues of rights of privacy are the polygraph, personality tests, sensitivity training, medical examinations, surveillance, handling confidential records, and unsolicited mail to one's residence.

The social transaction between the individual and the organization typically creates mutual responsibilities. When these are discharged with integrity, mutual benefits should predominate. In the final analysis, we do know that organizations can be used to free individuals as well as to confine them. For example, the more sophisticated structure of republican government freed men from autocratic rule by kings.

STUDY GUIDES FOR INTERPRETATION OF THIS CHAPTER

1 AB Sales, Inc., employs ten women at telephones all day long calling household numbers listed in the telephone directory to offer a sales pitch for a household appliance. Several persons have complained to the Chamber of Commerce that this is an invasion of their privacy. Give your own analysis concerning whether this is an invasion of privacy.

2 Mabel Tyro, speaking for a group of sales clerks at Martin Department Store in a middle-class shopping center, says that women clerks should be permitted to wear slacks because it is sometimes drafty near doors and clerks have to stoop and bend to reach merchandise under counters. Store manager Mark Gomberg says that the requirement that women sales clerks wear dresses is necessary to provide the proper store image and sales climate. Comment.

3 Read literature on personality tests. Then (a) discuss specifically how they invade privacy, and (b) comment on whether a test of this type could be given without invading individual privacy.

4 (a) Examine union newspapers or booklets and comment on the manner in which they do, or do not, discuss responsibilities of the individual employee to the organization.

(b) Use the same procedure with regard to consumer publications and their discussion of consumer responsibilities to the organization from which they make purchases.

PROBLEMS

THE FORBIDDEN MERGER

August Bern was president and chief executive officer of a large, merger-minded conglomerate in which he had an insignificant ownership interest. The firm had sales of over $100 million and was listed on the New York Stock Exchange. In this firm the chairman of the board of directors headed a committee of board members which initiated and appraised merger possibilities. This committee operated independently of the president until merger negotiations advanced to a serious stage. Recently a member of the merger committee mentioned in a board meeting that the committee was considering merger with a tobacco company. When the president heard this he said that he was a member of a religion which forbids use of tobacco and that he would not be associated with a firm which sold it. He threatened to resign if the merger was consummated.

1 Appraise the legitimacy of individual and organizational interests in this situation.

2 In the role of chairman of the board, what response would you make, if any?

THE SMOKING BAN

A representative of an antismoking group proposed to airlines that they ban all smoking on passenger flights. He acknowledged that they voluntarily ban smoking during takeoff and landing as a safety measure, but noted that they still allow each passenger to use "his own conflagration kit" during flight. He said that smoking could cause a flash fire under certain conditions; consequently, it is a safety hazard to all passengers and a psychological threat to those individuals who realize the fire danger from smoking.

1 In the role of president of a regional airline how would you respond when the letter making this request is brought to your attention?

THE HOLDEN TRANSIT COMPANY

Holden Transit Company provided bus service for a large metropolitan area with a population of over two million persons. It accepted advertising for "car cards" which were placed in display panels immediately above bus windows inside the bus. Advertising was also accepted for the outside of the bus. One advertiser approached the company with a request to furnish each bus with tape casettes which would announce advertising messages intermittently. The company accepted several installations on an experimental basis.

When the casettes were installed on the buses, large numbers of bus users protested that the announcements were an invasion of their privacy as passengers. When they were asked to explain why they objected to the voice announcements but not the car cards, they replied that they could choose whether to read the car cards but the voice announcements distracted them and interfered with what they were doing, such as reading, thinking, or talking to a friend. Some threatened legal action if the tapes were not removed.

1 Analyze this situation in terms of invasion of privacy. As company president, after thorough study of this situation, what action would you take and why?

PART THREE
BUSINESS AND ITS PUBLICS

CHAPTER 11

BUSINESS AND THE NATIONAL INTEREST

One thing is certain, I believe: that no modern, dynamic society can operate at all if either industry or government is to be straitjacketed by outmoded concepts concerning size and scope. What is wanted is more understanding of the needs of both; not less.

ROGER M. BLOUGH[1]

We are in an economy which more and more is being politically directed and ordered.

LOUIS T. RADER[2]

Jack Smith grew up outside a small town in a forest country of the northern United States. Like most of his friends, he attended public schools. At the outbreak of World War II, Jack entered the Army and served four years. Upon discharge, he enrolled in the state university and received his degree with support from the federal government's GI Bill of Rights.

After graduation, he moved to the Rocky Mountains and obtained a job with a lumber company. Shortly thereafter he married and bought a home with a federal Veterans Administration guaranteed mortgage. Jack was smart and capable. He advanced rapidly with his company and was able to save money. With the help of a federal Small Business Administration loan, he built a sawmill and entered business on his own. He was, at the same time, the successful bidder in a timber sale held by the United States Forest Service.

Because Jack was a veteran, he received priority in bidding on some land which the United States Bureau of Land Management was selling at public auction. He was successful in obtaining a small parcel of land and built a modest home on it. His retired parents soon moved into the house, where they lived comfortably with the aid of their Social Security checks.

---

[1] Roger M. Blough, "The Real Revolutionaries" (address before the Whirlpool Corporation Management Club, Benton Harbor, Mich., Sept. 15, 1963), New York: United States Steel Corporation, 1963, p. 15.
[2] Louis T. Rader, "Will Management Be Automated by 1975?" *Management Science*, July, 1968, p. 721.

As Jack became more firmly established in business, he became more interested in local and state development. Under a federal program, he was instrumental in having his town declared a recreation area, which made it eligible to receive federal funds to develop recreation. A park and swimming pool were built. He was also active in getting the government to build a large dam and irrigation project close to town. He was appointed to the State Planning Commission and was elected to the State Chamber of Commerce.

One day Jack wrote to his congressman: "I urge you to do everything in your power to curb increasing governmental give-away programs. Government's willingness to enter virtually every phase of private and business life is rapidly destroying the American heritage of individualism. In addition, the high taxes which businessmen must pay to support these programs are rapidly destroying the profit motive and sapping the vitality of the business system. I demand that you exert all effort to preserve free competition and our laissez faire tradition."

To illustrate a different point of view toward government-business relationships, consider the case of Bill Jones. Bill was born and grew up in a medium-sized Eastern town in which there were two major employers. One of the major employers was a large privately owned manufacturing company. In addition to being a major source of employment for local townspeople, the company was also the major taxpayer in the community. The other major employer was a large government installation, and because it was a government installation, it paid no taxes at all.

Bill's father owned and operated a successful medium-sized business in the community. While he was by no means rich, Bill's father had ample financial resources to educate his son outside the public school system. Bill received his early education in a parochial school, and during his high school years, he attended a private boys' school.

Bill's father believed strongly in business involvement in community affairs. He not only gave generously of his own time but also encouraged employees at all levels in his company to become involved in important community projects. His company usually contributed relatively large sums of money to these projects.

After finishing high school, Bill entered the armed forces. During Bill's absence, his father retired and lived comfortably from investments and annuities which he had accumulated during his business career.

Bill applied for and received a four-year college scholarship from the Ford Foundation. He attended a private university where he majored in sociology.

After graduation Bill accepted a job with the government as a sociologist. He now often makes speeches on the immorality of business and the failure of the private sector to meet needs of society. He urges more involvement by the government in the operation of the economic system.

Both Jack Smith and Bill Jones follow idealistic concepts. Smith follows an idealistic concept of laissez faire which is far removed from modern reality. He wants the benefits of government without its interference. Jones follows an idealistic concept of the social ethic and of bureaucracy and monolithic central planning. Neither view is wrong. What is important is that both business and government, and their representatives, agree on what kind of socioeconomic system we should have. Continued disagreement will result in continued conflict.

THE LAISSEZ FAIRE TRADITION: A FICTION?

Like Jack Smith and Bill Jones, thousands of businessmen and government officials today are deeply concerned about government-business relationships. Also, like these two men, most of these same people enjoy a vast variety of benefits which stem directly from the free enterprise system and from government participation in the system.

A Dual Ideology

John R. Bunting has pointed out that most businessmen are victims of dual economic ideology.[3] They are, according to Bunting, happily inconsistent, arguing on the one hand for a pure form of free enterprise and decrying unrestrained competition on the other. To illustrate, he contrasts two speeches given before a convention of businessmen. In the first speech a businessman thoroughly denounced "price chiselers" and accused them of "leading us back to cutthroat competition." "The only way to ensure profits," the speaker continued, "is to stick together, keep prices high, and maybe push them higher." Bunting, then a Federal Reserve officer, followed with a speech entitled "Free Markets and the Federal Reserve System." In his speech, Bunting explained ". . . how the Federal Reserve, by its decision to stop pegging government bonds, had helped to start a trend back to free-market principles." Although the speeches contradicted each other, the audience made no distinction. They agreed with both speakers.

Businessmen do appear to have a schizophrenic philosophy toward the roles of business and government in the national economy. The reason businessmen seem to be inconsistent is that modern business philosophies are a blend of those portions of classical and modern economic models which best fit their needs. When a businessman says he believes in the free enterprise system and laissez faire, he does not mean that he accepts Adam Smith's laissez faire and pure competition. He is talking about something else. How a businessman feels about a particular act of government depends on how it affects him. For example, many New York businessmen who believe in free enterprise opposed the efforts of a large New York store to sell nationally labeled whiskeys at a price below that set by the state liquor control agency. Apparently their own financial interests and other values in the situation took precedence over the value of free competition.

Modern Concepts of Competition and Laissez Faire

While businessmen, over time, have professed a belief in perfect competition and laissez faire, they have recognized, to an increasing degree,

[3] John R. Bunting, *The Hidden Face of Free Enterprise: The Strange Economics of the American Businessman*, New York: McGraw-Hill Book Company, 1964.

that these economic models simply do not fit the realities of today's economic system.

Businessmen today have modified these theories to fit their needs. For the modern businessman, pursuit of self-interest means securing and holding a competitive advantage. Laissez faire means to him minimum interference with *his* pursuit of self-interest and maximum support of *his* endeavors. The modern businessman often views the problem emotionally, so that when he advocates cuts in government spending, he often means in all areas or regions except his own. Or when he encourages free trade and cutting tariffs, he usually means in all areas except his own. For example, when a recent decision to close a number of military establishments in various parts of the country was announced, floods of letters poured into Washington from businessmen in the affected areas protesting the closing of *their* installation.

Business efforts of the type described are not necessarily wrong. On the contrary, they add strength and vitality to the economic system. What is important is that both business and government, as two major agents of society, agree upon what kind of system is best. Businessmen's thinking, reflected in their speeches and actions, appears to affirm their belief in monopolistic competition and their rejection of a pure laissez faire philosophy. On the other hand, government's actions often appear to emphasize a belief in a weakly modified form of pure competition. What is needed by each is an understanding of the other's basic philosophy. Failure to understand and respect the other's point of view will result in continued conflict.

The focus of this chapter is on the general roles of government and business in the American free enterprise system. More and more, business is becoming involved in what have traditionally been considered nonbusiness problems of society. While problems such as air and water pollution, urban decay, and disadvantaged citizens are touched upon briefly in this chapter, they will be more fully discussed in later chapters. In the following section we discuss the growing concern in the business community regarding the business image and the growing role of business in coping with social problems. Then we proceed to various relations between government and business. Finally we discuss the roles of business and businessmen in politics and the separate and joint responsibilities of each for a strong national economy.

THE BUSINESS IMAGE

Businessmen's concern over public views of business is nothing new. Indeed, businessmen have been fighting against an unfavorable public image for hundreds of years. People have distrusted the business system to one degree or another since the earliest forms of business emerged. But people throughout the world and over time seem simultaneously to have held two opposing views of business. Since business has been the prime mover in economic development over the centuries, people have looked favorably upon economic results generated by business. Job opportunities, investment opportunities, and a constant flow of new and improved products have led a majority of people to accept and encourage business growth. On the other hand, a deep and persisting fear remains that too much economic power has been concentrated in big business. This fear is reflected in periodic waves of restrictive public policy directed toward the business system.

A Socially Unstable Image

In America, the public attitude toward business has been remarkably inconsistent, vacillating between support and encouragement of business growth and attacks on concentrations of economic power. These attitudes are, in turn, reflected in ever-changing public policy toward business, which has left businessmen unsure of their economic behavior. Public attitudes toward business seem to be a function of national emergencies. Figure 11–1 shows the relationship, over time, between public confidence in and public suspicion of the American business system. During periods of national emergencies, such as war, when national security depended upon performance of America's productive powers, public confidence in business has always been high. National need for production has been accompanied by reductions in restrictive policies and emphasis on policies which favored business integration and increased capital accumulations.

On the other hand, during periods of national crisis resulting from internal economic and social disorders, when national well-being depended, as it did during the depression of the 1930s, on something other than America's technological and production abilities, business seemed either unable or unwilling to respond. The result was a wave of legislation which restricted and modified business activities.

Today's Challenge

In the 1970s the United States faces numerous serious social problems of major proportions. Urban congestion, ghetto poverty, education of disadvantaged citizens, transportation deficiencies, and air and water pollu-

Figure 11–1 Historical relationships between public confidence in business and government restrictions on business.

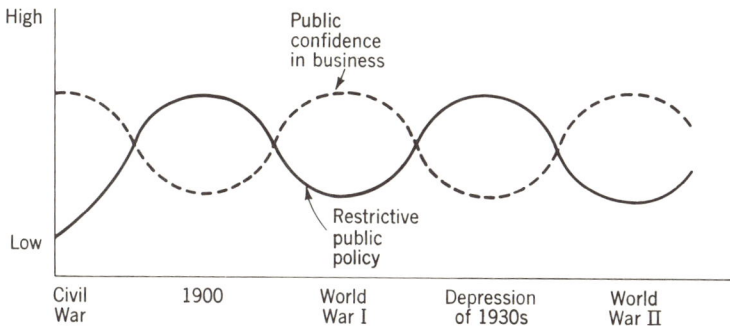

tion are some of the major issues. In a variety of ways and from a variety of sources, business is under attack for either contributing to the problems or for failing to devote enough effort toward solutions.

Businessmen are keenly aware of the demands being made upon them by society and are struggling not only to enhance the image of business as a socially responsible institution, but also to find answers to the question of how to accomplish best the tasks ahead. In increasing numbers, business leaders are accepting the challenge of social problems. Henry Ford II, in a speech before the National Association of Purchasing Agents, said:[4]

> Those who are more fortunate, including the leaders of the business world, have a duty to their country and themselves to join the war on poverty, on discrimination, on ignorance, on unemployment. As long as these evils persist, our society will be diminished by crime and violence and demagoguery.

The question bothering most business leaders today is not whether business should participate in solutions to social problems, but how and to what extent.

Many individual businesses have exerted considerable effort to enhance their image through involvement in social problems. Economic education has been emphasized and encouraged in recent years. Support of community projects and activities has stressed corporate citizenship. Some companies have met head-on the problems of employing and training hard-core unemployed. On a broader scale, the American Management Association has established a summer camp dedicated to showing high school boys what makes business tick. A group of successful New York executives organized an Interracial Council for Business. By contributing their talents in the form of free consulting services to black businessmen, they see an opportunity to take a positive part in the civil rights movement. On a national scale, the National Alliance of Businessmen has been formed to work on social problems.

But efforts of this type have only scratched the surface. Many business leaders have concluded that the problems are so large and so complex that no single social institution working alone can solve them. Instead, many are becoming increasingly convinced that only a partnership between the major institutions of American society—particularly government and business—can achieve national social and economic objectives.

HOW MUCH GOVERNMENT?

From the time the Constitution was written and signed, government has been active in one way or another in American business. The Constitution itself provides for certain government interventions in the business system. It specifically gives Congress the power to tax, to regulate commerce, to establish a mail system, to grant patents, and to provide for a

[4] Quoted in Raymon H. Mulford, "Pluralism Redefined," *Saturday Review*, Jan. 13, 1968, p. 33.

common defense. In the history of America, there has never been a question (as many people would like to believe) of *whether* there would be government participation in business. Rather the questions have always been, and will continue to be: *How much* and *what kind* of government participation is appropriate?

Traditionally, business has been given major responsibilities for national well-being. Until the latter part of the nineteenth century, business bore these responsibilities practically alone. But experience gained during this period shows the undesirability of what Mund calls the "law of the jungle."[5] The results of unbridled pursuit of self-interest in a no-rules, no-holds-barred sort of competitive game were the misuses of monopoly power discussed earlier in this book. Clearly, this was not the best way to achieve maximum social well-being. It was evident to society that rules were desirable and that a referee was needed to enforce the rules. Society empowered government to perform these functions.

Big Business and Big Government

Government intervention in business affairs has not stemmed the growth of business, as was prophesied by nineteenth-century proponents of laissez faire. Business has continued to grow. But as business has grown, so has government. The federal government is the biggest spender, the biggest employer, the biggest property owner, the biggest tenant, the biggest insurer, the biggest lender, the biggest borrower, and the biggest customer in the free world.[6] It is also true that government exercises powers which many consider to be violations of individual liberties. Indeed, as one businessman observed: "The federal government is a partner in every business in the country. For most of us . . . it has been a majority partner."[7]

There are today many who feel that in trying to escape the "law of the jungle," society has gone too far in the other direction, and they point to the undesirability of the "law of the jail."[8] They condemn increasing authoritarian control by government with its restrictions and regulations. They contend that excessive government involvement in the private sector of our economy has a demoralizing effect which invites evasions of laws, destroys the American innovative spirit, crushes the profit motive, and therefore dilutes the strength and vitality of the economy. Many among this group cry for a return to the good old days of laissez faire.

Both business and government have grown tremendously, and they will continue to grow. Utopian pleas to return to the "good old days" will do little to develop proper business-government relationships. Rather, managers' jobs today are dependent upon finding ways to live and work with government. Both government and business are striving for the same

[5] Vernon A. Mund, *Government and Business*, 3d ed., New York: Harper & Row, Publishers, Incorporated, 1960, p. 520.
[6] Lammot du Pont Copeland, "It Takes Two to Make a Partnership Work" (speech before the New York Chamber of Commerce, Feb. 10, 1964), p. 5.
[7] *Ibid.*, p. 4.
[8] Mund, *op. cit.*, p. 520.

objective of greater social well-being. Businessmen need to overcome any remaining views of government as an enemy bent on destroying them. Similarly, society (through the eyes of government) needs to stop looking at business as a hostile force bent on destroying society's well-being. Strong economic growth will be hampered as long as these attitudes prevail. Roger Blough expressed the relationship nicely when he said:[9]

> Blind opposition [by business] to governmental growth and to the enlargement of government power can, I believe, be as disastrous to the progress of this economic revolution as the failure to guard our freedoms with discerning vigilance. The idea that government must be the natural and irreconcilable enemy of the individual and his enterprises is—it seems to me—as anachronistic in this day and age as the outworn Marxist doctrine of eternal enmity between owner and employee.

The Concept of Functionalism

In a modern, complex society, there is plenty for everyone to do. Obviously, some jobs which are necessary to society's well-being can best be done by government. Equally obvious is the fact that other jobs can best be performed by business. This is the concept of *functionalism*, which holds that functions desirable for social well-being should be performed by the institutions which can do them most efficiently. National defense, reclamation, and policing activities appear to be functionally appropriate jobs for government. On the other hand, product planning, product decisions, actual production, and market innovation appear to be appropriate business functions.

In simple societies, division and assignment of social functions usually appear to be uncomplicated matters, with functions relatively well-defined and clearly delegated to one institution. But as societies advance economically and socially they also become more complex, and the concept of functionalism becomes less easy to apply. Not only are social problems more difficult to define because they are more complex, but lines of responsibility become blurred as well, and questions of who can do things best are hotly debated. Jobs which were once considered to be the domain of government are now, in certain instances, being shifted to private business. For example, a substantial amount of training of hard-core unemployed is being done by private business. Courtney C. Brown, Dean of the Columbia University Graduate School of Business, has commented that: "More of the methods of business are getting into government and more of the purposes of government are getting into business."[10]

The Vital Partnership

As our society becomes more complex and as social problems become more severe, there is an increasing business recognition of the need for

[9] Blough, op. cit., p. 15.
[10] Courtney C. Brown, "The Fading of an Ideology," in Robert W. Miller (ed.), The Creative Interface, Washington: The American University, 1968, p. 39.

joint action by business and government, which former Secretary of Commerce John T. Connor has called the vital partnership.[11]

In late 1968, a symposium was held in which ten members of the Committee for Economic Development (CED) were asked to present their views on how corporations can help solve some of the social and economic problems facing America today. All agreed that American business must become more involved in social problems. The consensus of opinion was "that the corporation as such should identify those social problems on which its particular resources and skills can be most effectively brought to bear, and make these virtually as much a part of its business objectives as traditional commercial activities."[12]

Business leaders who participated in the symposium not only recommended a strong commitment by business to social problems, but also advocated a strong partnership with government. The conclusions were "that business and government must develop the same kind of effective partnership in social problem-solving that has hitherto only been achieved in major wartime emergencies."[13]

The Role of Government

While there is increasing agreement that a partnership between business and government is desirable, no one seems entirely sure what the role of each partner should be. There appears to be a general feeling among the business community that the proper role of government is rule maker and referee and that it should not, at the same time, attempt also to be a player. According to Peter Drucker,[14] the proper role of government is to formulate social objectives so that they can become opportunities for other institutions to serve society. Except for a few instances, government's role is not "to do," because it is generally an inefficient performer. The reason why other institutions may accomplish many social functions better than government is that a government, by design, is a protective institution rather than a performing and creative institution. Active business executives also support the same idea. The chairman of the board of one company commented: "Government must lead. But it cannot be the sole problem solver. Its role is to define problems, articulate desired results, organize, directly and indirectly, the whole potential of the society, in a coordinated effort to remake the society and save it from destroying itself."[15]

The Role of Business

While businessmen seem relatively clear about the proper role of government, they are less sure how to proceed in their commitment to social

[11] John T. Connor, "The Vital Partnership," in Robert W. Miller, op. cit., p. 3.
[12] Emilio G. Collado, "Toward a More Productive Dialogue," Saturday Review, Jan. 13, 1968, p. 62.
[13] Ibid.
[14] Peter F. Drucker, The Age of Discontinuity: Guidelines to Our Changing Society, New York: Harper & Row, Publishers, Incorporated, 1968, pp. 225, 242.
[15] Irwin Miller, "Business Has a War to Win," Harvard Business Review, March–April 1969, p. 8.

problem solving. Business has been cooperating with government in a number of ways. Several large companies, for example, have loaned executives to the antipoverty program. A number of companies have volunteered to operate one or more centers for the Job Corps and have become deeply involved in training hard-core unemployed. But these activities, while successful in their own areas, have had minimal impact on the overall problems.

Most business leaders continue to accept the need for social actions such as support to education, support of nondiscriminative hiring, donation of money and executive skills to community projects, and related activities. But they also feel that the profit motive is the real key to bringing corporate resources to bear on social problems. Few, if any, corporations could for long periods of time afford to channel large portions of their resources toward solutions of any problems, social or economic, without being paid for their expenditures. Many feel, to one degree or another, that business is making a social contribution by performing its economic functions effectively and efficiently. And this view is supported by at least one eminent social scientist. Theodore V. Purcell says, "I argue that management has a social responsibility to make a profit."[16]

Only by making a profit, it is argued, can business maintain and increase the assets which are so necessary for solving the immense social problems facing America today. Experience has shown that money, by itself, has had little effect toward solutions of problems such as urban decay, pollution, transportation, hard-core unemployment, and poverty. Most businessmen and many government leaders believe that these problems can be solved only by bringing to bear the research and development expertise of business along with its organizational and productive resources. In this new partnership there is a growing agreement that business must be the doer while government formulates objectives and provides support.

BUSINESS IN POLITICS

In recent years questions about the proper role of business in politics have been widely discussed, and many reasons both for and against corporate involvement in politics have been advanced. For example, in justifying corporate political involvement, Edwin M. Epstein comments, "Corporate political involvement enhances the quality of pluralism and provides an additional safeguard against the authoritarian potential of a mass society."[17]

Arnold Maremont, on the other hand, states:[18]

It is my conviction that business ought, for its own good, *to stay out* of politics.

[16] Theodore V. Purcell, "Work Psychology and Business Values: A Triad Theory of Work Motivation," *Personnel Psychology,* Autumn, 1967, p. 246.
[17] Edwin M. Epstein, *The Corporation in American Politics,* Englewood Cliffs, N.J.: Prentice-Hall, Inc., 1969, p. 285.
[18] Arnold H. Maremont, "The Dangers of Corporate Activity in Politics," *Business Topics,* Winter, 1960, p. 7. Italics in original.

I favor the widest possible participation in politics on an *individual* basis, for when it becomes the province of the elite few, our system is in danger. It is when corporations begin running political classes, conducting political schools, and urging that their executives enter the political arena to expound the corporation viewpoint that I become deeply fearful of the consequences.

Business has, to one degree or another, been involved in political activities since the founding of America, and there is every reason to believe that it will continue to be involved.

Corrupt Practices Act

Political activity by business has also been a matter of public concern since at least the beginning of this century.[19] The Tillman Act of 1907 prohibited contributions by business to campaign funds involving election to federal offices. The first objective of this law was to destroy business influence over elections; the second was to protect stockholders from use of corporate funds for political purposes to which they had not given their assent. Later the Corrupt Practices Act of 1925 broadened this concept (this later became Section 610 of the U. S. Criminal Code), and the Labor-Management Relations Act of 1947 (Section 304) extended the prohibition to labor. Today both business and labor are by law prohibited from making donations to political campaigns from company or union funds. Thus, society specifically defines proper political action for business and labor in at least one area.

Need for Business Involvement

Most businessmen, at least those who direct large business units, feel that there is an increasing need for business involvement, and that business can and should influence government wherever appropriate. David J. Galligan, in his post as Director of the Citizenship Responsibility Program of the New Jersey State Chamber of Commerce, summarizes the feeling for increased involvement as follows:[20]

What is happening in today's business-government relationship is not something new in our political process but rather an accelerated and genuine interest on the part of business concerning developments that portend great changes in our free enterprise system.

The question most businessmen are grappling with is not *whether* business should be in politics, but rather *how and to what extent* it should be involved. Most responsible businessmen view political involvement as part of corporate citizenship; i.e., because business is one of the major social institutions, it has an obligation to become involved in the political

[19] For a discussion of legislation prohibiting business and labor contributions to political campaigns see Edwin M. Epstein, *Corporations, Contributions, and Political Campaigns: Federal Regulations in Perspective,* Berkeley, Calif.: University of California Institute of Governmental Studies, 1968.
[20] David J. Galligan, *Politics and the Businessman,* New York: Pitman Publishing Corporation, 1964, p. 3.

process which directs and controls forces for social well-being. Others view political involvement as a necessary matter of self-interest. Still others think that business should be in politics to balance the power of other social institutions. For example, some feel that since labor is in politics *as labor,* business should also be in politics *as business* to balance the equation. Otherwise, labor's political power may become dominant, thereby destroying pluralism. All of these views are valid. The important point is that business is a major social institution and its viewpoints are needed on major issues *where it is qualified,* just as its efforts are needed on social problems *where it is qualified.*

What Are Proper Political Activities for Business?

It is becoming increasingly clear that businessmen need to become more concerned with governmental processes. Because of the growing complexity of government-business relationships, businessmen can ill afford to stand silent. Just as business needs the support of government to do its job, so also government needs participation by businessmen in formulating public policy.[21] It needs advice and information from business leaders in making policy decisions, and this is true at local and state levels as well as at the federal level. But yet the nagging question remains: For the business firm, what kinds of political actions are proper?

In the light of public attitudes toward this problem as expressed by the Tillman Act, the Corrupt Practices Act, and later the Labor-Management Relations Act of 1947, a good rule of thumb is that *business should support issues—not candidates.* This rule of thumb is in keeping with the underlying purpose of corrupt practices legislation, that is, to protect the freedom of the individual's vote and at the same time to prevent an organization from misappropriating funds which were entrusted to it for purposes other than political.

A 1964 survey of businessmen's attitudes about political activity showed an increased interest in and enthusiasm for more political activity by business.[22] Figure 11–2 indicates that executives participating in the survey believed that business should further increase political activity. It is interesting to note that the four activities in which the largest percentages of companies were involved concerned issues rather than candidates.

Figure 11–3 indicates the type of political activities executives think appropriate for business to engage in. Providing government officials with businessmen's views on selected political issues leads the list. The function of communicating the business point of view on issues is often considered to be one of the foremost social roles of business leaders.[23] Business leaders, because of their knowledge and experience, are qualified to make judgments about business-related issues in the same way a

[21] Marion B. Folsom, *Executive Decision Making: In Business and Government,* New York: McGraw-Hill Book Company, 1962, pp. 134–137.
[22] Stephen A. Greyser, "Business and Politics, 1964," *Harvard Business Review,* September–October 1964, pp. 22ff.
[23] Harold Brayman, *Corporate Management in a World of Politics,* New York: McGraw-Hill Book Company, 1967, pp. 108–109.

"IN WHICH OF THE FOLLOWING ACTIVITIES DOES/SHOULD YOUR COMPANY ENGAGE?"*	1959 DOES	1964 DOES	1964 SHOULD
Urge employees to register and vote	70%	68%	73%
Belong to organizations designed to make the political climate more favorable to business	44	50	59
Participate actively in formulating trade association policy on government issues	25	48	55
Belong to organizations designed to improve the efficiency of government operations	36	40	64
Encourage employees to participate actively in campaigns	21	31	47
Urge executives to serve as elected officials in the city where plant is located	16	29	45
Take stands on specific political issues	22	24	39
Encourage campaign contributions by employees	15	21	31
Allow candidates to come into the plant and meet employees	14	21	29
Invite elected officials to meet with the management group	13	21	46
Have top managers make talks on important issues	14	20	38
Employ specialists to deal with elected officials	13	20	20
Carry articles on current public issues in the company paper	15	19	37
Give employees time off to work on campaigns	12	14	20
Perform services for politicians	12	12	9
Invite elected officials to talk to employee groups	6	12	35
Consider political activity in recommendations for promotions	3	5	7

* Question did not include "should" in 1959.

Figure 11–2   Opinions on Company Political Activities. Source: Stephen A. Greyser, "Business and Politics, 1964," Harvard Business Review, September–October, 1964, table 3, p. 177. Reproduced with permission.

medical doctor is qualified to make judgments about issues concerning medicine.

Views concerning the propriety of some other activities listed in Figure 11–3 indicate either the respondents' ignorance of the law or their confusion of actions taken as individuals and actions taken as agents of business. Clearly company contributions to candidates' political campaigns are illegal, yet 52 percent viewed this activity as proper. It may well be that these respondents were ignorant of the law because it has not been well publicized nor has it been widely enforced. The Wall Street Journal reports that only two cases had been tried under the Act between 1907 and 1969.[24] For example, one Los Angeles businessman was asked

[24] Jerry Landauer, "Delinquent Donors: U.S. Starts Enforcing Laws Barring Political Gifts by Firms, Unions," Wall Street Journal (Pacific Coast edition), Nov. 21, 1969, p. 1.

	1964	1959
Company X offers cash to those politicians who will take it	7%	5%
Company X's representative writes a legislator to explain the firm's position on pending legislation	98	96
Company X invites campaigning politicians into the plant	56	54
Company X hires legislators as consultants	14	14
Company X gives executives time off to work on a campaign	64	71
Company X makes available a few jobs which selected legislator can give to constituents	3	5
Company X's president endorses a candidate in a newspaper advertisement	55	52
Company X provides legal and other specialized services to politicians	13	15
Company X's representatives take legislators to lunch on company funds	57	60
Company X gives presents or vacation trips to legislators	1	2
Company X contributes to candidate's political campaigns*	52	—

* This statement was not included in 1959.

Figure 11–3   Percentage of Respondents Rating Selected Company Political Activities as "Proper." Source: Stephen A. Greyser, "Business and Politics, 1964," *Harvard Business Review,* September–October, 1964, table 4, p. 177. Reproduced with permission.

for a political donation while attending a political cocktail party. Rather than writing a personal check, he innocently instructed one of his company officials to send a company check for the amount promised. Five years later, much to his surprise, he was indicted, found guilty of violating the Corrupt Practices Act, and fined.[25]

Other activities which respondents favored bring up the difference between the propriety of certain actions when a person is acting as an individual and when he is acting as an agent for a business. No one would argue with the propriety of a company president endorsing a candidate for political office so long as it is clear that he is acting as an individual. Individuals can and should endorse any candidate they choose. But when a company president or any company officer uses his title or his company name in publicly endorsing a candidate in a paid political advertisement, this is a questionable use of company position and borders on violation of the Corrupt Practices Act. It may give some persons the impression that the company—not the individual—has endorsed the candidate. While there is nothing illegal about such action, it appears inconsistent with the philosophy of corrupt practices legislation. The same reasoning applies also to union officers because the Corrupt Practices Act applies equally to them.

[25] *Ibid.*

Businessmen in Politics

Because of the special talents which business leaders have, they are often called upon to assume either political posts or leadership of a government project on a temporary basis.

Research showed that "Businessmen accepted almost 180 appointments at the level of assistant Secretary or higher in the 18 years from the beginning of President Truman's second administration in 1949 to January 1967."[26] Most of these jobs were in the Department of Defense, the Treasury Department, the Commerce Department, and the Post Office. Half of President Nixon's Cabinet have held responsible positions in the business or financial community. In addition to responsible positions at the national levels, businessmen often accept political jobs at local and state levels. The important point here is that, by political involvement, businessmen are often in an excellent position to influence government policy in the same way that leaders of other pluralistic groups are able to do.

While some businessmen do attain public offices, companies often resist having their executives and/or employees become active participants in party politics for three main reasons. First, employees in a corporation who rise to high places in a political party or who campaign for political office while still in the employment of the company are likely to generate public criticism of the company itself. Even though the individual and the company may be unselfishly motivated, skeptics are likely to consider such a person a "tool of business" with special interests and, therefore, a poor public servant.

Second, from a personal standpoint, many individuals may not be willing to make the necessary sacrifices. Movement into public office from private employment often demands that the individual face a substantial financial loss.

Third, loss of a key individual from the organization may impose serious hardships on a company's operations. A policy of leaves of absence for political activity creates an even greater dilemma. Few businesses can operate effectively if they are unsure, from election to election, which employees will remain and how many will return.

Whatever the method used, both business and government need each other's help. The strength and growth of the national economy depend upon cooperation, and as society grows more complex, the need for cooperation and understanding will become more important and demanding.

RESPONSIBILITY FOR A STRONG ECONOMY

Since the industrial revolution, business has been viewed by most people as the prime mover of the American economic system. Society depends upon business to produce an ever-increasing flow of goods, jobs, and investment opportunities. Business has not always lived up to these

[26] Alan H. Schechter, "Businessmen as Government Policy-Makers," *Columbia Journal of World Business*, May–June 1968, p. 67.

expectations. During the prolonged depression which followed the stock market crash of 1929, there was a diminishing public confidence in the ability of the business system alone to maintain a strong and viable economy. There was a growing belief that government should share with business responsibilities for national economic well-being. In 1936, Arthur Burns stated that "all efforts to deal with unsatisfactoriness of the outcome of the present organization of industry lead in the end to the acceptance by the state, in some form or other, of responsibility for participating in the exercise of economic power."[27] John Maynard Keynes also expressed doubts that a free enterprise market system could maintain full employment without assistance from government spending.[28]

In the years since 1936 the observations of both of these men have come true. But conditions and environment of the 1930s favored looking at social institutions as separate and only remotely related entities with each having separate and unrelated social goals. These views provided society with a relatively simple "either-or" approach to responsibilities: *Either* business finds ways of moving the economy out of depression, *or* government will have to do the job.

In the complex society of today a philosophy of "either-or" is no longer sufficient. The assigning to one institution of single responsibility for national well-being is a thing of the past. Problems of national economic strength and other associated problems have become so complex that acceptance of a concept of joint responsibility is vital. There is mounting evidence that, whether various social institutions know it or not and whether they like it or not, a vital partnership has been formed. We appear to be in an era which will require increasing cooperation between the many institutions that make up our pluralistic economy, an era in which the strength of one depends on the strengths of the others.

Many businessmen, economists, educators, union leaders, and government officials have recognized this partnership. J.-J. Servan-Schreiber attributes America's economic superiority in the international scene to the partnership of business, government, and university education and research.[29] John Kenneth Galbraith also discusses a close relationship among social institutions.[30]

The challenge to each partner in maintaining a strong economy appears to be to perform in the most effective manner possible those functions for which each is best suited. Economic success continues to be the most important contribution of business, that is, providing goods and services, jobs and wages, and technical expertise to solve social problems. Government's greatest contribution will come from setting social objectives and maintaining appropriate government policies which will provide the positive climate in which business can perform.

[27] Arthur J. Burns, *The Decline of Competition: A Study of the Evolution of American Industry,* New York: McGraw-Hill Book Company, 1936, p. 29.
[28] John Maynard Keynes, *The General Theory of Employment, Interest and Money,* New York: Harcourt, Brace and Company, Inc., 1936, pp. 30–31, 378.
[29] J.-J. Servan-Schreiber, *The American Challenge,* New York: Avon, 1969, p. 53. Translated from the original French, *Le Défi américain,* Paris: Editions Denoel, 1967.
[30] John Kenneth Galbraith, *The New Industrial State,* New York: The New American Library of World Literature, Inc., 1967.

SUMMARY

Several times in the history of America, society has redefined roles of social institutions and relationships among these institutions. Universality and growing intensity of social problems are causing another redefinition of roles and relations.

There is a growing belief that social problems cannot be solved by any single social institution. Rather, solutions will come only by institutions working together in partnership, each performing those functions which it is best equipped to perform. Government, by its very nature, should formulate social objectives. Business, on the other hand, should apply its management, technological, and research capabilities to achievement of social objectives.

As society becomes more complex, it seems clear that national economic performance depends on both a strong government sector and a strong business sector. If complex social and economic problems are to be met and solved, greater trust, understanding, and cooperation will be needed between business and government as well as other social institutions.

STUDY GUIDES FOR INTERPRETATION OF THIS CHAPTER

1 Using as criteria selected activities listed in Figures 11–2 and 11–3, interview businessmen in your community to learn their beliefs concerning appropriate political activities for businessmen.

2 The issue of whether or not postal service in the United States should be transferred to private business has been hotly debated. What arguments for and against this action can you present?

3 What is meant by the term "vital partnership"? What evidence can you present that such a partnership is being formed?

4 Compile arguments both pro and con on the question: Should businessmen be active in politics: (a) as individual businessmen? (b) as representatives of business firms?

5 Select from newspapers or magazines an example of political action by business, and evaluate it in terms of propriety.

PROBLEMS
SERVICE VERSUS PROFIT?

The following views were expressed at a national symposium marking the 25th Anniversary of the Committee for Economic Development.[31]

> The principal reason industry is ready and eager to work on social problems is that these areas offer great opportunity for growth and

[31] Donald C. Burnham, "Partners in Pragmatism," *Saturday Review*, Jan. 13, 1968, p. 60. Reproduced with permission.

profit, as well as for the betterment of our society. Our motives—as they should be in our system of free enterprise—are economic as well as social. The second reason business and industry are eager to attack social problems is that only in this way will such problems be solved. Most of these problems will yield only to research and development by engineers and scientists who are technically equipped to deal with them. Only through research and development can industry provide the greater productivity needed, for example, to solve the problems of the urban ghetto or the underdeveloped nation. Here is perhaps the greatest social problem of all. The world problem is not underdeveloped countries; it is underproductive people. Only by teaching these people how to produce more and by providing the required tools can we improve their standard of living. That job can best be done by the industrial engineer whose business is improving productivity.

1 Are these views compatible with what society thinks the social responsibility of business should be?

WHAT'S IN A NAME?

During a recent political campaign a newspaper advertisement appeared which endorsed certain candidates for the office of President and Vice-President of the United States. The advertisement was placed and paid for by an organization of businessmen. It told why the organization felt that the two men were the best candidates and also solicited financial contributions to support the organization. Although the advertisment was signed by the executive director of the organization, there also appeared at the bottom of the advertisement a list of the names of approximately one hundred business leaders. Nearly all of these men were presidents or board chairmen of the country's leading businesses. Each man was identified by his corporate title and his company's name. The following sentence appeared at the extreme bottom of the advertisement: "Partial list of founding members. Corporate affiliations are for identification only."

1 Does the inclusion of titles and company names, along with the names of individual founding members, constitute endorsement of candidates for political office by the various companies?
2 Does the disclaimer statement at the bottom of the advertisement relieve the company from charges of endorsing candidates?

THE HAMMERMILL PAPER COMPANY

The advertisement accompanying this problem is one of a series from an advertising campaign by Hammermill Paper Company. Other advertisements which appeared during 1969 discuss issues such as poverty and welfare, voting age, citizen safety on the streets, and privacy for citizens. The format and text of all the advertisements are quite similar.

Is a college education still a luxury, or has it become a necessity that should be tax deductible?

A prerequisite for employment? A "union" card? A modern-day work permit? Is this what a college degree has come to mean in today's complex and technically-oriented working world?

A great many people think so. And they feel obligated to provide their children with this "necessity." Yet with the cost of a college education soaring to nearly $4000 a year, most people need some kind of help to handle it. One proposal is to make college costs an income tax deduction, like any other professional expense.

But others argue that going to college is a luxury. An option for those who can afford it; unnecessary for those who can't. They feel that an income tax deduction certainly won't solve the college-cost problem; will be, at best, an after-the-fact alleviation of expense in favor of a small minority. Everybody's taxes help support public colleges and universities and make them available to all. And many people feel that's enough.

The point is, what do you think? It's not your job to come up with the final answer to this issue — but it's important that you come out with your opinion about it. And make your opinion known. In writing. To your Congressman, so he can weigh what you think when he votes on legislation.

We hope you'll write your Congressman on Hammermill Bond — world's best-known letterhead paper. But whether you write on Hammermill Bond or not . . . write. A paper-thin voice is a powerful persuader. Hammermill Paper Company, Erie, Pa., maker of 33 fine printing and business papers.

HAMMERMILL BOND.

Hammermill urges you to write your Congressman.

Figure 11–4 A company advertisement focuses on a social issue. Reproduced with permission of the Hammermill Paper Company.

1 To what extent is the company politically involved by such a campaign?

2 Do you feel that the company is supporting one side or the other of this social issue? Why?

CHAPTER 12

ISSUES OF GOVERNMENT REGULATION AND INFLUENCE

Americans have always had to balance their love of bigness and efficiency against their fear of power and their regard for individualism and competition.

RICHARD HOFSTADTER[1]

The countervailing power hypothesis, according to which big government serves as a check on big business and big labor, is dead.

SAMUEL RICHARDSON REID[2]

"New York: December 27, 1993

The United States of America, Inc. (USA), the Solar System's largest multidiverseconglomerategrowth corporation, has announced plans to acquire European Common Nations, Ltd. (Europe), a large holding company that controls all of the land and manufacturing operation in what was once known as Western Europe. If the merger goes through, it will be the largest in history—far surpassing the merger two years ago between USA, Inc. and Canada, Ltd., in which USA bought Canada through an exchange of securities valued at 463 billion dollars."[3]

This quotation carries to extremes the possible ultimate end in merger activity, this end being control of the entire universe by a few unimaginably large and powerful organizations. And to project a bit further, the author goes on in the article to point out that the regulating agency, "the Interplanetary Trade Commission," had been ineffective in controlling the "oligopolistic tendencies of corporations."

While the above example is fictitious, it does illustrate a phenomenon which is causing considerable concern both to society and to business.

[1] Richard Hofstadter, "What Happened to the Antitrust Movement?" in Earl F. Cheit (ed.), *The Business Establishment,* New York: John Wiley & Sons, Inc., 1964, p. 131.
[2] Samuel Richardson Reid, *Mergers, Managers, and the Economy,* New York: McGraw-Hill Book Company, 1968, p. 6.
[3] Bernard J. Zahren, "Merger Madness," *The MBA,* January, 1970, p. 54.

This chapter is concerned with government influence on business decisions and business activity. The first part of the chapter will be concerned with direct statutory regulation, including the reasons for it and the effectiveness of it. The second part of the chapter will be concerned with more subtle indirect government pressures and influence on business.

I. REGULATORY RELATIONS

Beginning with the Sherman Act, businessmen increasingly have been subjected to regulation and policing by government agencies. Economic profits normally are made by producing more and better goods and services. But unfortunately for society, more profit can sometimes be made (at least in the short run) by producing inferior goods, by misusing business power, and by misleading or deceiving customers. In order to curb social evils and ensure maximum social payoffs, society has seen fit to impose controls and restrictions on a variety of business activities.

Most people, including businessmen themselves, agree that some regulation of business practice is desirable. Partly because of a genuine recognition of public need and partly to avoid unrealistic regulatory action, businessmen often join public authorities in formulating regulations.

For example, a plant manager of a large Eastern company recognized the appearance of a strong, local demand for legislation on air and water pollution which would affect a large and highly concentrated manufacturing area. Instead of waiting for legislators to draft and introduce bills, he and his associates, with the help of their engineers and technicians, drafted what they considered an effective bill. It solved the problem and yet was a regulation they "could live with." The proposal was enacted into law to the satisfaction of all concerned.

A more complex cooperative approach to workable regulations is seen in the modification of the New York City building code. During the 1960s city government, building experts, builders, and trade unions all participated in developing a code which produced cost savings and innovation in building. Basically the code substituted performance requirements for those requiring specific materials, thus clearing the way for the city to deal better with urban problems such as low-cost housing.

In many other areas businessmen feel that regulations hamper their effectiveness and act as a damper on their ability to move the economy into high gear. These criticisms are true to some degree, but society has felt it necessary to establish rules. And as the economy becomes more complex, businessmen and government will need to work more closely than ever before and with greater understanding and appreciation of each other's needs. If business is to have rules and regulations which it can live by and which will encourage it to perform its economic task, it needs to take a more active part in the developing and modifying of regulations.

ANTITRUST POLICY

Background of Antitrust Policy

The avowed purpose of antitrust legislation has always been to preserve competition. To appreciate society's concern with bigness, one needs to examine the attitudes, economic philosophies, and emotional involvement surrounding the changes which took place during the closing years of the nineteenth century.

From colonial times until after the Civil War, America was largely a nation of farmers and small town entrepreneurs. All in all, the American economic system fit fairly well the economic model of perfect competition. Most businessmen competed on reasonably even terms within small closed markets, and government stood weakly by, performing its assigned limited functions. Belief that perfect competition was right and natural became a national philosophy as experiences under British rule combined with the inherent characteristics of business and markets and economic theory of the times. Nearly every person grew up believing in the classical economic model, complete with its requirements of smallness, large numbers, and diffusions of power.

Social Concern over Business Concentration

After the Civil War, the economic system underwent such drastic and rapid change that most men of the times were ill-equipped either theoretically or emotionally to cope with the new environment. Looking at the social results of business mergers in the late 1800s, it is little wonder that men of the times forecast gloomy consequences if mergers and concentrations were not carefully controlled.

A major concern of society at the turn of the century was the question of where business concentration would lead if left unchecked. In light of experience, it seemed reasonable that, unless the merger trend was stopped through exercise of government control, great corporations might continue to absorb one another until there existed one great syndicate of giant businesses which, if unchallenged, could control the whole country.

Another social concern that led to antitrust legislation was the belief that monopoly hindered the progress of industry. Concentration, it was felt, always led to monopoly, and monopoly always inhibited technological progress.

And finally, society was concerned with ideas of consumer protection. It had been observed that when business firms combined to form a monopoly, the quality of products and services often deteriorated rapidly.

In retrospect, we can observe that these things did not happen. Even though mergers have continued in ever-increasing numbers, business has not become monolithic. The tremendous technological affluence which we enjoy today has come as a result of large firms with large accumulations of capital—not from small business. There are more small businesses today than ever before. However, large size has enabled many firms to make positive contributions to consumer welfare through economies of scale.

Objectives of Antitrust

The objectives of antitrust legislation, at least as the policy was originally conceived, were threefold: (1) economic, (2) political, and (3) social. From the economic viewpoint, antitrust was an attempt to cling to the belief in the economic model of perfect competition. From the political viewpoint it stemmed from a reluctant choice to allocate to government more power over business. It seemed that the only way to check the powers of business was to increase the power of government. And from a social viewpoint antitrust was a result of a continuing belief in the Protestant Ethic.

Contemporary public policy continues to reflect a lingering belief in the philosophy of perfect competition, and in the Protestant Ethic. These lingering beliefs have resulted in antitrust policies which appear in many cases to be incompatible with the real world. Probably in no other area of regulation have businessmen encountered more confusion and frustration. The vagueness of the laws themselves and judicial inconsistencies in enforcement have left businessmen uncertain as to what they can do. It has become increasingly difficult for businessmen to conform to legal requirements and at the same time perform their economic functions as they perceive them. One observer has commented:[4]

> There can be no doubt of a need for a philosophical reappraisal of our attitudes and our legislation in the field of competition.
> It would seem that having accepted the economists' definition of perfect competition and finding it unattainable, we have lost all confidence in the ability of competition to do its work.

Herein lies a social challenge to both business and government. Most businessmen agree that some form of regulation is needed to control unscrupulous business practices. The challenge is in reexamining where the public good lies and what kinds of regulation will contribute most to that public good. The problem seems to lie in trying to apply postulates left over from an earlier era to a dynamic period of rapid change—rather like driving a Model T Ford in the Indianapolis 500.

Effects of Antitrust Legislation

If, indeed, a major objective of antitrust legislation has been to limit size of business firms as a way of protecting competition, it has not been effective. Whatever else it may have done to preserve and promote competition, antitrust legislation has neither stopped mergers nor reduced the size of firms.

Mergers have occurred in waves, and each wave has been larger than the previous one. But, until recently, there has been little corresponding increase in attempts to curb business consolidation through exercising antitrust legislation. Furthermore, increases in numbers of mergers have

[4] Courtney C. Brown, "The Fading of an Ideology," in Robert W. Miller (ed.), The Creative Interface, Washington: The American University, 1968, p. 44.

occurred during periods of economic prosperity. All of this suggests that society wants the economic benefits which result from large-size firms, but at the same time wants to guard against too much concentration of power by imposing restrictions and checks on business. This also suggests that government actions to enforce antitrust legislation or to "go easy" possibly may have reflected fluctuating pressures on government from other pluralistic groups indirectly seeking to restrain business.

From a social point of view the result of antitrust legislation has been to limit business consolidation to magnitudes which were socially acceptable at various times. From the businessman's point of view the result has been to crowd his life with uncertainties.

The biggest problem most businessmen have today in living within the antitrust laws is not so much that the laws regulate business. The real problems revolve around the ambiguity of the laws themselves and of government enforcement policies which result in confusion for the businessman. One company president expressed the problem as follows:[5]

> I fail to understand the rationale of the federal government, particularly the Federal Trade Commission. On the one hand, if U.S. industry is to be attacked under the guise of the Sherman Act, the FTC, and so on, wholly on the basis of bigness, then I think there is something illogically wrong. On the other hand, I completely agree and support the government in its contentions that any combinations which create restraint of trade, or develop trade practices which are unfavorable or unfair procedures, should be regulated. But to attack a merger movement or combination in the form of bigness and bigness alone is not, in my opinion, fair.

The Businessman's Dilemma

At the center of businessmen's confusion are the antimerger policies of the government. It has been observed that the ". . . most important . . . antitrust development from the viewpoint of managerial decision making is the tightening up of the prohibitions against corporate mergers and acquisitions."[6] In 1950, the Celler-Kefauver amendment to Section 7 of the Clayton Act made it clear that mergers would be illegal if they substantially lessened competition or created a monopoly. The rules which were laid down stated that: (1) companies who are major competitors cannot merger under any circumstances; (2) companies cannot merge if, as a result, they would control 30 percent of the market; and (3) if one company is already a giant, it cannot acquire another, no matter how small the share of the market is.

Considerable controversy exists over whether or not antitrust laws, as they are currently being administered, really do strengthen competition. The Justice Department's policy of "grow from within, not by merger,"

[5] Frank Peterson, "Planning the Premerger Pattern," in G. Scott Hutchison (ed.), *The Business of Acquisitions and Mergers*, New York: Presidents Publishing House, Inc., 1968, p. 53.
[6] Jesse W. Markham, "Antitrust Trends and New Constraints," *Harvard Business Review*, May–June, 1963, p. 85.

has been attacked as lessening competition rather than strengthening it. As a result of the Justice Department's blocking the merger of Mack Trucks, Incorporated, with Chrysler Corporation, one Mack official commented that "the Justice Department attitude itself tends to lessen competition, since it leaves small companies no way to grow and diversify in an industry dominated by giant corporations who themselves originally took the merger route. Ironically, the department is helping the giants by stopping mergers that would make others stronger."[7]

To add to the confusion, policies of government agencies other than those responsible for enforcing antitrust seem to encourage companies to take the rapid path to expansion through merger.

One case resulted from the Armed Services' policy of evaluating companies who bid on government production contracts in terms of existing production facilities and financial strength indicated by working capital. Because it was strong in research engineering, one company was awarded a research and development contract. As a result of this contract, the company developed and designed a new piece of equipment which needed to be produced in volume. When the same company bid on the subsequent production contract its bid was not accepted because "it was not big enough."[8]

Officials responsible for antitrust enforcement also face other difficulties which add to the confusion of businessmen. Officials seem to be considering the social as well as economic ramifications of their decisions. For example, objections to a merger between electrical appliance maker Landers, Frary, and Clark with General Electric were later withdrawn. The apparent reason for blocking the merger was that General Electric is so large that acquiring even a small competitor would violate the Clayton Act. However, two senators, learning that Landers, Frary, and Clark plants in their states might shut down, thereby causing unemployment, asked officials to reconsider the decision. The decision was reversed and the merger approved, ". . . apparently on the theory that antitrust enforcement should consider other dimensions as well as competition."[9]

Businessmen increasingly are making demands for clarification and rewriting of antitrust laws. And enforcement agencies are responding to some degree. One observer commented:[10]

The major innovation during the 1967–68 period was the emergence of guidelines or formal statements by the enforcement agencies concerning their merger policies. . . . During the year, also, the Federal Trade Commission published summaries of its advisory opinions on

[7] "If You're Big, Grow from Within," *Business Week*, Aug. 8, 1964, p. 26.

[8] Myles L. Mace and George G. Montgomery, Jr., *Management Problems of Corporate Acquisition*, Boston: Harvard University, Graduate School of Business Administration, Division of Research, 1962, pp. 11–12.

[9] "Antitrusters Drop Fight on G.E. Deal as Senators Fear Closing of Plants," *Business Week*, Apr. 17, 1965, p. 36.

[10] Betty Bock, *Mergers and Markets: 7, An Economic Analysis of Developments in 1967–1968 under the Merger Act of 1950*, New York: National Industrial Conference Board, Inc., Studies in Business Economics, no. 105, p. 3.

proposed mergers where individual companies had requested an advance opinion.

The Rise of Conglomerates

Most consolidation of business before 1950, and many that have occurred since, have been of the conventional forms of horizontal (one steel mill acquiring another) or vertical (a cement company acquiring a ready-mix concrete company) mergers. However, since 1950, the conglomerate form of merger between companies neither in the same market nor in a vertical relationship with one another has far surpassed other forms in popularity. In 1968 there were 4,462 mergers. Of the approximately 200 mergers in that year which involved companies with assets over $10 million, about 170 qualified as some form of conglomerate.[11]

Because conglomerates combine different kinds of business rather than similar or related businesses, they are not easily brought within the control of current antitrust legislation. Nevertheless, the growth in business concentration is reawakening social fears of business power. The result is increased attention to conglomerates by both enforcement agencies and law makers.

In trying to make social evaluations of modern conglomerates, arguments for and against them are much the same as they have been since before the Sherman Act. Society fears the concentration of power in one social institution will upset social equilibrium among pluralistic groups and destroy our pluralistic system. This philosophy is illustrated by the comments of the government's antitrust chief in his reaction to a prediction that within ten years everyone will be working for 200 top companies. He commented: "Personally, I take a very dim view of that possibility. I think the Republicans want to see opportunities left open to people."[12]

Counter arguments stress the idea that national well-being depends on the best allocation and use of resources and that conglomerates can best perform this function. One business leader comments:[13]

Everyone benefits from the takeover, including the public. It should be obvious that our national prosperity depends upon the maximum use of our existing resources and of our capital. National *policy* should direct funds into the hands of those who can and will invest them in a way to create the most productivity. If takeover accelerates this process and benefits stockholders, too, then who should protest?

While most people are in favor of maximizing social well-being, just how conglomerates contribute to such well-being is not entirely clear to many. Those who support conglomerates answer the question in a number of ways. Conglomerates contend that they contribute substantially to the economy by helping their subsidiaries grow internally. The key, according to one author,[14] lies in the ability of very large firms to supply capital and

[11] "McLarin Wades into Merger Tide," *Business Week*, Mar. 22, 1969, p. 42.
[12] *Ibid.*
[13] Bruce D. Henderson, President, The Boston Consulting Group, Boston, Mass., in a letter "To Clients and Friends." (no date)
[14] David N. Judelson, "The Role of the Conglomerate Corporation in Today's Economy," *Financial Executive*, September, 1968, p. 21.

highly specialized management talents that smaller companies cannot supply for themselves. By providing these resources, conglomerates help other companies become more competitive. For example, Profexray, a small manufacturer of X-ray equipment, grew sevenfold after Litton Industries acquired it and made it competitive in its market. And, ITT helped Avis effectively challenge Hertz in the car rental field.[15]

Another answer is that conglomerates provide economic stability. Because of diversification, conglomerates can absorb economic setbacks in one area while moving ahead in others, thus smoothing out cyclical variations.

Conglomerates also contribute to social well-being through the ability to coordinate the activities of subordinates. While conglomerates are made up of firms from different industries, these firms often have complementary technology which can quickly and efficiently be directed toward solutions of economic and social problems.

Conglomerates also have the flexibility to capitalize on growth opportunities. Overall national economic growth depends, to a substantial degree, on recognizing and developing individual growth opportunities. Because of the very nature of conglomerates, they can move quickly in making decisions and committing capital to growth opportunities.

The conglomerate form of business is not uniquely American. Other countries have similar forms of business consolidation, and these provide some evidence that large business concentrations do contribute to economic strength and viability. Japan, for example, is second only to the U.S. in economic strength. Yet, in Japan, there are business consolidations, known as *zaibatsu,* which dwarf even the largest U.S. conglomerate. It is reported that:[16]

> The four largest zaibatsu account for about 20% of Japan's gross national product. Combining industrial, commercial, and financial concerns, they make their U.S. counterparts look like small potatoes. The famous Mitsubishi is king of the clan, accounting for 7% of the gross national product. An American conglomerate comparable to Mitsubishi would rake in about $63 billion in business each year. On 1967 figures, this hypothetical American zaibatsu would combine General Motors, General Electric, US Steel, Du Pont, Anaconda, Celanese, Eastman Kodak, Mobil, and International Paper in the industrial group. In commerce and finance it would combine Prudential Insurance, Sears Roebuck, First National City Bank of New York, and American Export Lines.

For Japan, at least, economic concentrations of power have not been deterring forces in national development. The exact opposite seems to be the case. Along these lines it has been observed that:[17]

> This misconception [about conglomerates] is also indicative of a basic myopia on the part of both government and business regarding their mutual relationship. Their existing views of each other's roles appear

[15] *Ibid.*
[16] "Zaibatsu," *Growth Stock Outlook,* Chevy Chase, Md.: Apr. 15, 1969, p. 1.
[17] Henderson, *op. cit.,* p. 2.

to be quite obsolete. The government is exercising its very great power with rather limited insight and using assumptions that are no longer valid. Conversely, business on the whole is relying on largely outdated concepts and standards of measurement in managing its resources, and thus is failing to optimize its performance—and hence its contribution to the common good.

GOVERNMENT INFLUENCE IN THE BUSINESS WORLD

In the previous section we have discussed business regulation through antitrust legislation. As we have seen, antitrust legislation is concerned with controlling the size and power of business. Businessmen also must live with a myriad of other regulatory laws which directly prescribe and limit day-by-day activity. Some of these will be discussed in later chapters. In addition to these laws which directly affect business activity, there are many laws which indirectly affect business.

As significant as these direct and indirect laws are to businessmen, perhaps equally significant is the influence government exerts on business through various roles it performs in the economy, such as the business role of customer. One by-product of this role which has caused major concern is the military-industrial complex.

The Military-Industrial Complex

On January 17, 1961, in his farewell address to the nation President Dwight D. Eisenhower used a phrase which was to become one of the most quoted statements made by recent presidents. This phrase was a reference to "the military-industrial complex." He commented as follows:

> In the councils of Government we must guard against the acquisition of unwarranted influence, whether sought or unsought, by the military-industrial complex. The potential for the disastrous rise of misplaced power exists and will persist.
>
> We must never let the weight of this combination endanger our liberties or democratic processes. We should take nothing for granted. Only an alert and knowledgeable citizenry can compel the proper meshing of the huge industrial and military machinery of defense with our peaceful methods and goals, so that security and liberty may prosper together.

Interpreting the Military-Industrial Complex

In popular usage the military-industrial complex has developed two meanings. One meaning is that there is a group of high-technology companies of large economic size which work in close cooperation with the Department of Defense to design and produce military weapons. These firms depend primarily on military contracts for their sales. They have on their payrolls many retired military officers who help maintain close liaison with the Department of Defense; therefore, they constitute a closed power group bent on heavy military spending.

A second meaning is that the Defense Department through its massive military spending leads to business dependency reaching even to a small clothing store in a town near a military base. Similarly, the prosperity of communities depends on large military contracts awarded to business in their areas, so military spending and location of military installations become political issues.[18] This whole economic-military relationship creates an unhealthy power bloc always pressing for more military spending. President Eisenhower appeared to have this meaning in mind, because in his speech he commented, "The total influence—economic, political, even spiritual—is felt in every city, every statehouse, every office of the Federal Government."

Discussion of the military-industrial complex frequently becomes the proverbial can of worms, because it is intricately related to many emotional and social issues. It is a convenient whipping boy for those opposed to war, those opposing a particular war, isolationists opposed to foreign involvement, those objecting to weapons designed to harm others compared with surveillance equipment, those opposed to business profit of any type, and others. The military-industrial complex also suffers from cost overages and poor performance and is subject to political pressures, but there is no evidence that these characteristics are worse in defense than in other large government programs such as highway construction and social programs. Our discussion is primarily limited to the two stated definitions, since they most directly affect business.

Firms Which Are Primarily Defense-oriented

The first definition related to large firms which are primarily defense-oriented and work in close cooperation with the Department of Defense. Companies of this type do exist, but their number is small. The Department of Defense releases annual statistics on its one hundred top contractors (including in 1967 two universities), and sales data are available for eighty-two of them. These data show that in 1967 only seventeen of the eighty-two firms received as much as 50 percent of their sales from defense contracts. Of the top ten contractors only four had defense sales of 50 percent or more, and two had defense sales of only 5 percent or less.[19]

These data show that at least two-thirds of the top hundred defense contractors do not depend primarily on defense business. The remaining defense-oriented firms often do work closely with the Department of Defense, but they hardly constitute a large economic power bloc, compared with the combined power of all other businesses or even all other direct competitors for the defense budget. The power which they do

[18] For example, see the discussion of San Diego in Bill Sluis and George Grimsrud, "Defense-oriented City Strives to Ease Impact of Pentagon Cutbacks," *Wall Street Journal* (Pacific Coast edition), Nov. 28, 1969, pp. 1, 15.

[19] A. E. Lieberman, "Updating Impressions of the Military-Industry Complex," *California Management Review*, Summer, 1969, pp. 51–62. Although defense contractors also receive defense-related subcontracts from other firms, the contractors also subcontract some of their work, so these offsetting actions do not appear to alter the basic proportions discussed.

possess arises more from their maintenance of a large pool of scientific manpower than any other reason. Because of their substantial resources, they are the ones to which the Defense Department is likely to turn for performance of large projects. This is as true among the universities as it is among businesses.[20] The large, capable ones secure the prime contracts.

It can be argued that the firms with less than 50 percent of defense sales derive most of their profit from this part of their business; hence, they unduly profit from defense business and bring social pressure for defense activity. In earlier decades there was considerable evidence to support charges of high defense profits, but tighter controls by the Dpartment of Defense have changed this situation. Data for the 1960s show that defense profits are lower than profits on civilian business. The lower profit applies both to return on equity capital and return on total capital invested. If there is a profit-oriented military-industrial conspiracy, as is sometimes emotionally charged, "Conspirators should expect to be rewarded more favorably than that."[21]

Defense business is a boom-and-bust, high-and-low, unstable type of work which upsets employment and prevents long-range planning. This instability coupled with low profit is causing major defense contractors to diversify as fast as possible into civilian business so that military work will not dominate their business. In an advanced technological society, reasonably stable economic and social conditions are most conducive to profitability. They provide an environment which permits business to do the long-range planning for capital use, marketing, and pricing that is essential for profit success. For this reason the stock market tends to rise when there is news of peace and to decline when there are unsettling threats of war.

The dangers of power among defense-oriented contractors can best be evaluated in terms of proposed alternatives. One alternative is to reduce further the seventeen identified companies among the top one hundred. This can be done, but it poses some risks because large military projects require giant firms with substantial pools of talent. Another approach is for the government to produce its own military materials. This was more frequently attempted in the past, for example, in government shipyards and arsenals, but it proved less efficient. In addition, this approach would increase military concentration and power, further reducing the pluralistic balance which now prevails.[22] In view of the alternatives, the most prudent course of action seems to be the present pluralistic system which uses different institutions while checking and controlling them carefully to assure that there are no undue profits or power.

[20] Peter Drucker observes that it makes more sense to speak of the military-university complex because many universities are increasingly dependent on military support. See Peter F. Drucker, The Age of Discontinuity: Guidelines to Our Changing Society, New York: Harper & Row Publishers, Incorporated, 1968, p. 177.
[21] Lieberman, op. cit., pp. 54, 55, 59.
[22] One other alternative is to stop major defense activities entirely. This is a political decision for which it has been difficult to build popular support.

Large Military Spending and Business Dependency

The second meaning of a military-industrial complex refers to the size and pervasiveness of military expenditures. Over half of these expenditures are direct business contracts, and even military wages find their way into the business system through local businesses where military personnel live. This viewpoint is directly related to ideas of pluralism. It is rooted in the philosophy that any large power bloc endangers pluralistic balance within the system. It may become so powerful that it is self-sustaining and not subject to adequate checks and balances. In times of changing social needs, it may divert to its own use resources which are sought for higher social priorities.

Arguments relating to the second definition concern pluralism, military-economic power, and social priorities. Those who discuss the dangers of the military-industrial complex in these terms do not imply conspiracy; "There is no more of a conspiracy here than in numerous other matters where legitimate lobbies influence public policy makers, or where conflicts of interest affect decisions of the legislative and executive arms of government."[23] Neither is there a charge of unilateral military control. As stated in a report by forty-five antiwar congressmen, "It is not the uniformed military which has created the present situation, but the civilian leadership and the institutions they have created to centralize and expand the performance of national security functions."[24]

How large is the military-industrial complex? It is the nation's largest employer. In 1969 it was estimated that one of every nine jobs was defense-related, including military personnel, civilian employees of the Defense Department, and private business employees in defense jobs. The defense budget was a hefty 10 percent of the gross national product.[25] It consumed over 40 percent of every federal tax dollar.

Economic effects of defense activities are definitely substantial; however, they do not portray a growing complex when compared with recent history. President Eisenhower made his speech in a relatively peaceful year, but military expenditures in that year consumed more of the federal tax dollar than they did in 1969, which was a period of undeclared war. In other words, other government spending increased more than defense spending; other priorities were winning the pluralistic battle for government funds. Similarly, although the defense budget was 10 percent of the gross national product in 1969, this was no higher than in a time of relative peace a decade earlier. Defense expenditures rose only in proportion to the gross national product.

In view of the trends mentioned, what is the basis for growing public concern about the military-industrial complex? The reason is that at the

[23] Jack Raymond, "Growing Threat of Our Military-Industrial Complex," *Harvard Business Review*, May–June, 1968, p. 64. See also John Kenneth Galbraith, *How to Control the Military*, New York: New American Library of World Literature, Inc., 1969, pp. 26–41.
[24] "Remarkable Document," *Arizona Republic*, June 15, 1969, p. 6.
[25] "Whether for Good or Ill, The Military's Impact on Nation Is Pervasive," *Wall Street Journal* (Pacific Coast edition), Apr. 28, 1969, pp. 1, 11.

time of this writing the Defense Department controlled the largest portion of the federal budget, but was engaged in an activity of low public priority, so other power groups were using public pressures to chip away at its funds in order to get more resources to serve social needs which they considered of greater priority. They, too, are legitimate claimants on public funds to serve the priorities they think important. This is normal operation of a pluralistic system.

Barring unusual military developments, it appears that some other priorities will gain dominance. For example, one estimate predicts that as early as 1975 the Department of Transportation budget will equal the defense budget, and the Housing and Urban Development budget will be twice as large.[26] Predictions often fail to materialize, but if this one does it will be appropriate at that time to become concerned about the urban-industrial complex or the city-federal complex! In a pluralistic society we need to keep in mind President Eisenhower's admonition, "We should take nothing for granted."

Influence through Indirect Laws

Government, in addition to influencing allocation of resources and business activity through direct laws and through the military-industrial complex, exerts substantial influence through laws which affect business only indirectly. These laws do not directly impose specific activities on business, but make government support and assistance dependent upon certain conditions or actions which business must follow. Putting it another way, government sometimes achieves its desired results by threatening to withhold rewards or benefits unless certain conditions are met.

These benefits which can be given or withheld are usually in the form of monetary contributions, awarding of government contracts, licensing, or the like. Some of these kinds of legislation directly affect business, while others are directed toward states in the hopes that state government will require certain minimum standards of performance. For example, the Bacon-Davis Act prevents awarding government contracts for construction, alteration, or repair of public works to any firm that does not pay wage rates equal to those established by the Secretary of Labor. Similarly, the federal government may refuse to provide funds for highway construction unless vehicles using the highways comply with certain regulations. Another example is the refusal of the Federal Aviation Authority to license private aircraft which do not meet certain safety standards.

Indirect laws are justified in the same way other laws are—that is, in the interest of social well-being. Businessmen, on the other hand, sometimes look at them as somewhat backhanded ways of doing things which could not have been done by straightforward means. Oftentimes businessmen are so far removed from the source that they have little or no knowledge of the law until it is an accomplished fact. Or, because these laws are passed as riders on major laws, they are obscure to businessmen.

[26] "Livelihoods of Many Hinge on Development of New Military Gear," *Wall Street Journal* (Pacific Coast edition), June 6, 1969, p. 23.

Whatever the reason, businessmen often feel that they are subject to regulation about which they have had no *opportunity* to voice opinions.

Other Roles of Government

Today, government in one way or another is involved in virtually every phase of business life. In addition to its regulatory function, government relates to business in a variety of ways. It plays various roles in the social system and therefore affects businessmen in various ways. Government acts as a customer, as a competitor, as a supplier, as a partner, and as a financier. While each of these roles is important, only the roles of consumer and competitor will be discussed here.

Government has always depended upon business to furnish a variety of goods and services needed to accomplish its function. In 1790 government spent $14 million. As America has grown and the economy has become more complex, government expenditures have steadily increased. In 1914 total government expenditures were $735 million, and by 1945 they had climbed to over $12.5 billion. In 1964, however, government spent more than that (about $17 billion) for research and development alone. It is expected that in 1970 expenditures for education and other social programs will total nearly $24 billion. The 1970 budget calls for approximately $200 billion. This is more than was spent by all presidents from Washington through the first two terms of Franklin Roosevelt, a period of 153 years.

Government purchases an almost incomprehensible array of goods and services. Disregarding military and defense spending, purchases range from paper clips to space capsules, and from adding machines to huge electric generators. Government also buys services and skills of thousands of people who perform the tremendous variety of activities it is engaged in.

Government purchases of goods and services have become a substantial factor in national economic health. Some industries and firms are almost wholly dependent on government for survival, and others depend heavily on government to purchase a major portion of their production. This dependent relationship of business firms on government creates conflicting responsibilities for government. On the one hand, government cannot support programs or continue to purchase goods and services which are not needed. On the other hand, substantial withdrawal of government purchases from captive suppliers may cause undesirable economic adjustments. There are other dangers of a broader nature inherent in selling to government. Government, in its role as a buyer, has had tremendous influence on business policies. Its purchasing power is sufficient to allow it to dictate terms of purchase, and as a result, management decision and control have been narrowed. So great has been the influence of government that many companies have found it necessary to modify policies in the areas of pricing, products, marketing, financing, and labor.

From a social point of view it seems desirable to encourage captive businesses to limit their dependence on government purchases to a reasonable proportion of total business. To accomplish this, these firms may find it necessary either to expand or to diversify, or both. In order to allow these firms to become economically and socially stable, government may find it necessary to reevaluate its stand on mergers and conglomerates.

Government also engages in a variety of activities that compete directly with private business. Businessmen feel (and so does much of society) that the government should not operate enterprises such as tin smelters, auto repair shops, paint production facilities, shipyards, or air and water transportation. Over the years government has, at one time or another, engaged in each of these activities. Experience has shown, however, that government operation of activities such as these has, in general, proved to be inefficient.

Government also competes with private business in a number of other ways. Through agencies such as the Small Business Administration, the Commodities Credit Corporation, and others, it loans money in competition with conventional lending agencies. Power produced by the Tennessee Valley Authority competes with privately produced power. And the Veterans Administration insures lives. In other areas, the government operates the largest single employment agency, competes with printers, makes false teeth, and provides a wide variety of consulting services which compete with private consulting firms.

In an attempt to help ease competitive pressures on private business, the Bureau of the Budget set out to revise the guidelines on when and how the government can provide products and services for its own use. While the order provides many conditions under which government may provide its own goods and services, it does spell out in detail a specific procedure that a federal agency must conform to in order to enter into any industrial or commercial activity. One businessman commented: "It may be that the most help we get from the new order will come in keeping the government from starting new things, rather than getting it out of old things it's already doing."[27]

SUMMARY

Since the Civil War society has been concerned with the increasing size of business firms and with the economic and social power which accompanies size. In an attempt to control business growth and to limit business power, society enacted a series of laws to prohibit mergers. These laws have been relatively ineffective. The number of mergers has continued to increase over time. With the increasing popularity of corporate conglomerates, the size of firms continues to grow. The issue before society is how to achieve maximum social well-being. Postulates and assumptions which are at the base of antitrust legislation appear to be inappropriate to today's dynamic pluralistic economy.

[27] "Uncle Sam, Inc., Drive to Cut Rivalry by U.S. with Business Makes Little Headway," *The Wall Street Journal* (Pacific Coast edition), Apr. 27, 1965.

Government also attempts to control the activities of business through direct and indirect laws, as well as through influence. Of major concern is the military-industrial complex because the defense budget is currently around 10 percent of the gross national product.

Important, too, is the influence government exerts through its various relations with business. Government acts as a consumer, a supplier, a competitor, and a financier, and in each of these roles has an effect on business decisions.

STUDY GUIDES FOR INTERPRETATION OF THIS CHAPTER

1 Study recent antitrust cases brought either by the Justice Department or the Federal Trade Commission. To what extent, if any, do the cases reflect the economic philosophy of perfect competition?

2 One author has made the following statement: "We can no longer be lulled into the belief that the exercise of private economic power will be held within reasonable bounds by the Federal government. At the moment we can only hope that those capable of wielding economic power will be prudent and charitable."[28] What evidence can you present to justify or repudiate this statement?

3 There is considerable argument today concerning the social desirability of conglomerates. Take a position either for or against conglomerates and compile a list of reasons to support your arguments.

4 From newspapers or periodicals find estimates of the amounts of money that will be needed in the future to overcome social problems such as urban decay or pollution. How do these figures compare with current defense spending? Do you see in these figures a danger of a future urban-industrial complex or something similar?

5 Using your hometown as a model, list as many examples as you can of ways in which government (at all levels) influences business.

PROBLEM
THE GREEN ACRES FUNERAL HOME

For several years Samuel J. Brown and his son operated the Green Acres Funeral Home in a Texas town of less than eight thousand persons. As part of its services, the funeral home operated the only ambulance service within a radius of 25 miles. In addition to attending to heart attack and accident victims and other emergencies, the ambulances were used routinely to move patients to and from rural communities where no hospitals existed to the hospitals and nursing homes in the cities. The service was licensed by the state.

The newest ambulance owned by Mr. Brown was fitted with the latest equipment, but the older vehicles had little or no special equipment. A

[28] Reid, *op. cit.*, p. 6.

few of the drivers and attendants were specially trained, but most were students from the local college. The specially trained personnel and the specially fitted ambulance were reserved for emergency calls.

The federal government passed legislation regarding standards for ambulance service. This legislation required that (1) ambulances must provide oxygen and resuscitation equipment and (2) the attendant to the patient must have passed advanced Red Cross instruction. The funeral home was informed by the Social Security Administration that unless its ambulance service met these requirements Medicare payments for transporting the elderly would be withheld. The federal government also notified the state that federal funds for highway construction would not be forthcoming unless all ambulances using public highways met the standards. The state passed legislation similar to federal legislation and notified Mr. Brown that unless all his vehicles met the standards, his license would not be renewed.

Because of the cost involved in meeting these requirements and the difficulty in maintaining a qualified work force, Mr. Brown discontinued the ambulance service; consequently, persons in this community and adjoining small towns had no ambulance service.

1 To what extent did or did not federal legislation serve social well-being?

CHAPTER 13

OWNERSHIP CLAIMS ON BUSINESS

Now that public expectations are exploding in all directions, we can no longer regard profit and service to society as separate and competing goals, even in the short run.

HENRY FORD II[1]

Management responsibilities to shareholders should be defined with reference to shareholders' legitimate expectations, a reflection of goals of passive investors rather than those of co-owners in business enterprise.

DAVID B. WEAVER[2]

During a series of regular meetings, the executive committee of a large American manufacturing firm was considering whether or not the company should attempt to penetrate a particular foreign market. Research indicated a rich potential, and all the executives agreed that the company had the technical competence and the marketing capabilities to make a successful market penetration. A new dimension was added to the question when it was learned that if the company were to be allowed to enter the new market, it would have to pay graft to a functionary of the foreign government concerned.

Some executives argued that the company should not pay graft under any conditions, even if it meant losing the market. Others argued that the risk of losing a highly profitable market jeopardized stockholders' interests, and that paying graft was a necessary cost of doing business.

Peter Drucker, in *The Practice of Management*, tells us that the first duty of business is to survive.[3] And to survive, it must operate at a profit. One hundred or so years ago there was little question that the sole function of profit was to provide reward for entrepreneurial risk. Today, in our

---

[1] Henry Ford II, "Business, the Environment and the Quality of Life," (speech delivered before The Harvard Business School Public Affairs Forum, Boston, Mass., Dec. 2, 1969), p. 6.
[2] David B. Weaver, "The Corporation and the Shareholder," in Arthur S. Miller (ed.), *The Ethics of Business Enterprise*, Philadelphia: The American Academy of Political and Social Science, *The Annals*, Vol. 343, September, 1962, p. 84.
[3] Peter F. Drucker, *The Practice of Management*, New York: Harper and Row, Publishers, Incorporated, 1954, p. 46.

complex pluralistic society, many groups make strong demands on business which tend to dilute profits. Each group, including stockholders, feels that it has a vested interest in business firms, and each, in its own way, tries to maximize satisfactions of its demands.

Partly because of increased size of business and partly because of increased strengths of social groups, relationships between managers and owners have changed during the last 100 years. As indicated by the second quotation at the beginning of this chapter, stockholders in widely held corporations, for the most part, perceive themselves as passive investors rather than co-owners of a business. Under these conditions, traditional control and decision making by stockholders breaks down and becomes unrealistic, thus placing on professional managers (who may or may not also be stockholders) the responsibility of making choices between alternative demands of claimant groups. And to make managers' jobs more complicated, they also must make decisions concerning present versus future demands of these same groups.

In this chapter we discuss conflicts between owners and managers occasioned by changing relationships between the two groups, legal responsibilities of management to stockholders, and finally the "management-trusteeship" concept of management responsibility to stockholders.

MANAGEMENT-OWNER RELATIONSHIPS

In every business there are two separate and distinct functions which must be performed if the business is to have life and survive. These have nothing to do with the traditional organizational functions of marketing, production, and finance. They are more basic than the organizational functions. They are the function of ownership and the function of management.

Every business must have a supply of money with which to acquire production resources in quantities necessary to achieve business objectives. Businesses are owned by those who provide the necessary capital. In the ultimate sense, then, the sole function of ownership is to provide capital. Owners expect to be rewarded through business profits. Management, on the other hand, is charged with the responsibility of operating the business and ensuring its survival. Questions of how a business should be operated, for whose benefit it is operated, and the purpose of a business in our society have often led to conflict between owners and managers because their points of view are different.

Conflict of Viewpoints

Separation of functions and conflict of viewpoints between ownership and management exist regardless of whether the business is organized as a single proprietorship, a partnership, a corporation, or a government business. Where owners and managers are the same person, as in a proprietorship, a partnership, or a small, closely held corporation, owner-managers play two roles which are in conflict with each other. But the very fact that owners and managers are the same person aids in resolving conflicts. In publicly held corporations conflict is more severe because owners and managers are two separate groups.

What are the responsibilities of managers to owners? Answers to this question depend on whether one takes the managers' viewpoint or the owners' viewpoint. Owners perceive management's responsibilities to be the operation of the business in a way that (1) provides the largest possible return on their investment and (2) causes the value of their ownership shares to appreciate. Both emphasize the concept of maximum profits. Both emphasize priority of ownership demands upon the firm.

There is an increasing tendency for managers to view their responsibilities as being primarily to the firm, rather than to owners. They perceive themselves to be responsible (1) for economic survival of the firm; (2) for perpetuating the firm through product innovation, management development, market expansion, and other means; and (3) for balancing the demands of all groups upon the firm in such a way that these demands do not hinder achievement of the firm's objectives. This viewpoint emphasizes optimization of profits within various constraints imposed by pluralistic groups. It emphasizes satisfactory rather than maximum profits. It emphasizes the idea of a "socially profitable business" and considers owners to be one group among many. Concerning their specific responsibilities to owners, managers today often express the belief that "what is good for the business is good for the owner."

The Functions of Profit

The heart of owner-manager conflict lies in arriving at a common definition of profit. Differences of opinion arise over what items should be deducted from gross revenue to arrive at a profit figure. What are the unavoidable costs of doing business? What are "legitimate" expenditures of company funds? Speaking from the managerial point of view, Drucker observes that profit serves three purposes:[4]

It measures the net effectiveness and soundness of a business's efforts.

It is the "risk premium" that covers the costs of staying in business.

Finally, profit ensures the supply of future capital for innovation and expansion.

To Drucker, "costs of staying in business" cover a wide range of expenditures including (in addition to the usually accepted costs) contributions to a variety of social costs. He summarizes by saying:[5]

None of these three functions of profit has anything to do with the economist's maximization of profit. All the three are indeed minimum concepts—the "minimum" of profit needed for the survival and pros-

[4] *Ibid.*, pp. 76–77.
[5] *Ibid.*, p. 77.

perity of the enterprise. A profitability objective therefore measures not the maximum profit the business can produce, but the minimum it must produce.

Profit Maximization versus Security Maximization

Most managers learned long ago that emphasis on short-run profit maximization is a shortsighted approach to operating a business. Businessmen today speak of long-run profit maximization and acknowledge their obligation to "make a dollar for the owner." But even the concept of long-run profit maximization is unsatisfactory. Businessmen today do not maximize profits (as the classical economists defined maximization) in the long run.[6] Rather, they maximize security and survival. For example, one business leader commented: "You make too much profit and you're vulnerable to critical inquiry."[7]

Managers have learned that they cannot ignore demands made upon business by various groups such as consumers, labor, and suppliers. Emphasis on profits (short run or long run) at the expense of one of these groups (either by individual firms or by the business system as a whole) has always resulted in pressures that threatened survival. Regarding the problems of survival and profits which business faces, Henry Ford II commented:[8]

> The company that sacrifices more and more short-run profit to keep up with constantly rising public expectations will soon find itself with no long run to worry about. On the other hand, the company that seeks to conserve its profit by minimizing its response to changing expectations will soon find itself in conflict with all the publics on which its profits depend.

Few, if any, managers today focus on absolute maximization of profits. Whether they like it or not, managers are required to consider in their everyday decisions forces which dilute profits that might be forthcoming if these forces did not exist. Legal requirements on business operations, labor market pressures, the public visibility of business, and public expectations of business performance are some of the forces with which managers must be concerned when making decisions.

Examples of firms maximizing security and survival rather than absolute profits can easily be found.

Two engineers who became dissatisfied with working for a large firm resigned and started their own company. The new company planned to develop and manufacture scientific breathing equipment which could be used in underwater work, in space exploration, and in hospitals. Partly in order to attract highly qualified personnel and partly to discourage unionization, the company established wage rates well above the union scale.

[6] Robert N. Anthony, "The Trouble with Profit Maximization," *Harvard Business Review*, November–December, 1960, pp. 126–134.
[7] Philip B. Hoffmann, "Calculated Generosity," *Forbes*, Aug. 1, 1969, p. 23.
[8] Ford, *loc. cit.*

Another illustration is that of a large forest products company that established a paper manufacturing mill outside a small town near the heart of a large forest area. After the mill was built, it was discovered that soil engineering work done on the problem of disposal of waste from manufacturing processes had been incomplete. There appeared to be a remote chance that waste from the plant could filter through the soil and contaminate the ground water, thus endangering domestic water supplies several miles away. Even though the chance of such contamination was slight, the company spent large sums of money to rebuild its waste disposal facilities.

Managers in the above examples were, by their decisions and actions, maximizing security and survival by making expenditures that would prevent certain groups from exerting pressures that would restrict the firm in attaining its objectives.

OWNERSHIP AND POLICY FORMULATION

Unity of Ownership and Control

Conflict between owners' views and managers' views is most apparent in the area of financial policy. Owners, in their role as owners, of course, favor financial policies that will provide the most return on their investment. They favor policies which emphasize that business should be run for the benefit of the owners. Expenditures which may reduce the amount available for distribution to owners at the end of the year are often questioned. This kind of policy implies strong resistance from other groups. Managers, in their role as managers, favor policies which emphasize the idea that business should be run for the benefit of a large group of claimants. Expenditures which may reduce the profit picture at the end of the year but which enhance survival of the firm appear quite justifiable in the managers' eyes. The job of today's manager is to formulate financial policy that will resolve the owner-manager conflict.

In single proprietorships and partnerships, the management problem of balancing demands of owners with those of other groups is less severe than in the corporate form of business. But even in proprietorships and partnerships, managers must guard against the temptation to emphasize short-run profits at the expense of long-run survival and long-run profits. In his role as an owner, it is difficult for the manager not to give priority to his economic payoff *as an owner* and subordinate claims of other groups to ownership demands. For example, expenditures for plant beautification are often weighed heavily against projected year-end profits, or there may be a temptation to use needed working capital to pay traditional dividends.

Separation of Ownership and Control

Stockholders as a separate group—aside from, and external to, the actual business—are a relatively new development in American business. Prior to 1900, the majority of corporate securities in existence were held in large concentrations by only a few individuals. The objective of holding stock, for these people, was ownership and control. As nineteenth-century firms expanded into today's industrial giants, new issues of stock were dispersed over a wider range of buyers. Many old stock concentrations were broken up and spread over a greater number of people through inheritance or sale on the market. As stock ownership became more diversified and as greater numbers of people held smaller amounts of stock, their reasons for holding stock changed. Few small shareholders today equate their ownership with corporate control. Rather, they view themselves as investors and are primarily concerned with returns on investment, not control.

As David Weaver points out, "the distinction is one of attitude,"[9] but this is an important distinction. As corporations have matured and grown in size and wealth, there has been an increasing separation of management and ownership and the growth of a professional management group. Dispersion of shareholdings has diluted or destroyed internal ownership control on management decision making and transferred the power of decision to the management group, who may or may not hold stock in the corporation.[10] Owners of large corporations (with the exception of those stockholders who are also corporate officers) do not make decisions. Rather, the small stockholder, in his role as an investor, depends upon professional managers to make corporate decisions.[11] Stockholders, at least in the large and socially powerful corporations, have been removed from decision-making roles and emerge as an external force exerting pressures on professional managers.

WHO ARE STOCKHOLDERS?

Individual Investors

After World War I, the public at large became significant holders of corporate stock. Today, over twenty million people have direct ownership in our great corporations. That is, they own stock of one or more companies. People from practically every occupational group own stock. Professional people, farmers, teachers, workers at all organizational levels, merchants, public-service workers, and housewives represent a few groups that own stock.

As owners have increasingly changed from active participants in business to absentee owners who view themselves primarily as investors, relationships between owners and professional managers have also changed. The approach to corporate financial policy varies considerably between these two groups. Managers use different yardsticks from those which

[9] Weaver, op. cit., p. 90.
[10] For a complete discussion of this thesis, see Adolph A. Berle, Jr., and Gardiner C. Means, The Modern Corporation and Private Property, New York: The Macmillan Company, 1932.
[11] Discussions of implications of growth of professional management groups are presented in Adolph A. Berle, Jr., Power without Property, New York: Harcourt, Brace, & World, Inc., 1959; and Edward S. Mason, The Corporation in Modern Society, Cambridge, Mass.: Harvard University Press, 1959.

TYPES OF DECISIONS	MANAGEMENT'S YARDSTICKS	STOCKHOLDER'S YARDSTICKS	SAMPLE AREAS OF POSSIBLE CONFLICT
Measuring financial performance	Anticipated changes in specific cash flows in the foreseeable future—amount, certainty, and timing	Anticipated changes in property values as measured by trends in earning per share (E.P.S.) and dividends	Ranking of investment alternatives; depreciation policy; stock options; acquisition of subsidiaries
Investment proposals	Internal rate of return which existing management is capable of achieving— as indicated by past performance	External as well as internal investment opportunity rates, including competing business organizations of comparable risk	The cutoff rate on acceptable investment opportunities and amounts committed to perpetuate existing investments
Sources of funds	Preference for (a) retained earnings, (b) long-term debt, and (c) new common stock—in that order	Preference likely to be for (a) debt, (b) retained earnings, and (c) new common stock —in that order	The extent of use of these sources in financing growth
Assumption of voluntary risk	Risk standard in terms of preserving the individual corporate entity and management's goals	Risk standard in terms of a portfolio of investments over many companies	Diversification of products and markets; debt/equity proportions

Figure 13–1 Different yardsticks used by management and stockholders. Source: Gordon Donaldson, "Financial Goals: Management vs. Stockholders," *Harvard Business Review*, May–June, 1963, p. 121. Reproduced with permission.

stockholders use to measure financial performance. Figure 13–1 illustrates different approaches by managers and stockholders concerning four types of financial decisions. Management yardsticks emphasize security, while stockholder yardsticks emphasize priority of stockholder claims.

Institutional Investors

During the 1960s the growth of institutional investors was phenomenal. This means that ownership in large corporations is being expanded further. In addition to the more than twenty million people who have direct ownership in corporations, additional millions have indirect ownership through purchasing shares of institutions such as banks, savings and loan associations, pension funds, insurance companies, investment companies, and university endowments.

What this means for professional managers is that while ownership is being spread wider, control is becoming more concentrated. For the most part, individual holdings of stock in any one company have been small, and the individual, *as an individual investor,* had little inclination to interfere with the management of the firm. But with purchases of large blocks of stock by institutional buyers, comes potential power to influence substantially management decisions and the securities market in general.

Institutional investors have now grown to such size that serious questions are being raised concerning their power and their responsibilities in exercising that power. The two main fears are that these institutions (1) may exercise irresponsible (from a social point of view) influence upon the corporations in which they hold substantial interests, and (2) that as their holdings grow larger, they may no longer be able to sell their stock without endangering the interests of other stockholders or without having an adverse effect on the market generally.

Most institutions have not exercised their growing power. Rather, they have been content to sell when dissatisfied with management. However, it has been observed that a few institutions "figure they can manage the assets of the company better than the management, and they don't hesitate to let that be known."[12]

WHAT DO STOCKHOLDERS OWN?

It is commonly accepted that stockholders "own" the company in which they hold stock. But what do they really own? Do they own property? Do they own certain rights which are attached to private property? Or do they own merely pieces of paper whose value is determined in the stock markets? One author explains it this way: "A share is just what the word implies, a fractional interest in a whole of undefined size—not a claim for any fixed amount payable at any stated time."[13] However, answers to these and similar questions depend on whether one approaches them from a legal viewpoint or the viewpoint of what seems to be reality.

Stockholders do not own property in the sense in which we usually think of property ownership. That is, they do not have title to company property, nor can they control its use in the same way that a single proprietor can control his property. Property is owned by the corporation, not by the stockholder, and corporate management determines how corporate property will be used. Since stockholders do not own company property, they can control its use only to the extent that they can influence corporate policy and management decisions. Therefore, the small stockholder who owns only a few shares has little influence by himself.

[12] Charles N. Stabler, "Takeover Strategy: How a Securities Firm and a Few Institutions Can Influence a Merger," *Wall Street Journal* (Midwest edition), Jan. 26, 1970, p. 1.
[13] Weaver, *op. cit.,* p. 85.

From another point of view, since the small stockholder does not have a specific claim against the corporation for any fixed amount, he is likely to look to the market to determine the value of his ownership share. From this viewpoint he is likely to perceive that he owns merely certificates that derive their value from the marketplace. Inability of the small stockholder to influence corporate policy encourages him to take this point of view and focus on his role as an investor. From this viewpoint he loses identity with the corporation and often becomes apathetic.

For the reasons given, stockholders generally have become a weak and passive group, dependent for their fortunes or misfortunes upon decisions of professional managers. To protect this group from managerial indiscretion or irresponsibility, certain rights have been established for stockholders.

LEGAL RIGHTS OF STOCKHOLDERS

While the law grants wide latitude of decision and action to corporate officers, it does not relieve them of their fiduciary responsibilities. However, the law does not define exactly what the corporate responsibilities should be nor to whom the corporation is ultimately accountable.

Specific rights of stockholders are established by law. Legally, stockholders can influence corporate policy through the voting mechanism or, if necessary, by challenging actions of corporate officers in the courts. Stockholders have the following legal rights (and these vary somewhat among states):

1. To share in the profits of the enterprise—*if dividends are declared by directors*
2. To elect directors
3. To receive annual reports of company earnings
4. To inspect the corporate books
5. To hold directors responsible for their acts—by lawsuit if they want to go that far
6. To vote on mergers, consolidations, changes in the charter, and bylaws
7. To dispose of ownership certificates

Even though stockholder rights are clearly established, it is difficult for small stockholders to exercise these rights except in a perfunctory manner. If stockholders are dissatisfied with management actions, they have three alternatives. First, they may replace corporate officers by voting the old regime out and new officers in. Second, they may sue corporate officers for misuse of power. Third, they may sell their stock.

Stockholders' Meetings

Annual stockholders' meetings are held by law for the purpose of discussing corporate business, and to offer an opportunity to shareholders to approve or disapprove of management. Approval is generally expressed by reelecting incumbent directors and disapproval may be shown by replacing present directors with new ones. Where corporations are small and local in nature or where they are closely held, annual meetings work reasonably well. It is relatively easy to assemble a majority of stockholders, and corporate business is considered and acted upon personally by at least a majority of stockholders. But for the large, publicly held corporation with thousands of stockholders, annual meetings are not so satisfactory. The number and wide geographical dispersion of stockholders have altered the character of annual meetings. Typically, only a small portion of stockholders attend.

Even if they were so disposed, few small stockholders are equipped financially to initiate and wage a fight for control with existing management. To unseat present management requires gathering enough voting power by proxy to outvote the incumbents. In proxy fights, the odds for success are heavily weighted in favor of incumbent management. It is not easy to stir a group of apathetic stockholders to join the opposition. Lack of knowledge concerning issues typically leads small, uninterested stockholders to cast their lot on the side of management. Financially, too, present management has the upper hand. It may, and typically does, use both corporate personnel and corporate funds to gather proxies which it may vote in its own support. Financial competence necessary to overcome these odds does not lie with the small stockholder.

Large institutional investors, on the other hand, are a different story. These institutions are in a position to bring their voting power to bear on corporate management. While these institutions have typically been reluctant to exercise their power, occasionally they have voted their large holdings of stock against managements. It appears that in our society a new social institution is emerging which may act as a check and balance on business decisions. But an interesting question arises: Who will provide the checks and balances to the power of these institutions?

Stockholder Suits

Just as it is difficult for small stockholders to engage in proxy fights, so is there little to encourage them to engage in stockholders' suits. Certainly, under law, dissatisfied stockholders may sue the corporation, but this right has been substantially diluted by limitations placed on instituting this kind of suit. Attempts to prevent harassment through the courts and to ensure pursuit of genuine complaints have led to serious impairment of small stockholders' rights to bring suit. In New York, for example, a stockholder-plaintiff who brings suit must own 5 percent of the shares, or if he does not he must be joined by others whose combined holdings equal or exceed 5 percent. In addition, the combined shares must have a market value in excess of $50,000. If the plaintiff does not own or control stock in the required amount and value, he may still be allowed to sue, but he must post sufficient security to cover litigation costs of defendants if he is unsuccessful in his suit. Many other states have similar statutes.

In spite of the difficulties involved, the number of stockholder (derivative) suits has increased. Many corporate lawyers believe that few stockholders' suits are initiated by unhappy stockholders. One attorney commented that "many of them . . . are suits initiated together with proxy battles for control. In others, the stockholders stand to gain so little that it is scarcely worthwhile for them to bring suit, but the attorney's fees are large."[14] For example, one suit brought on behalf of a stockholder who owned twenty-five shares netted the owner $50 and brought a fee of $800,000 for the attorney.[15] In other cases the stockholder does not receive any direct cash benefit. Cash benefits recovered from corporate officers often go to the corporation. All that most stockholders can expect is an unknown increase in future dividends, and they are not assured of that.

But in spite of comments and examples such as those just mentioned, the number of stockholder suits continues to increase. In the past most stockholder suits were brought under state laws and the central issue was dishonesty. Generally, if a stockholder was to be successful, he had to prove that the defendant deliberately intended to deceive him. Today, more and more stockholder suits are being brought in the federal courts under the Securities Act of 1933 and the Securities and Exchange Act of 1934. Under these laws no security is required of stockholders, nor is it necessary to prove dishonesty. The law may be violated just by carelessness. One lawyer commented:[16]

> All day when he [the businessman] deals with customers or competitors it's *caveat emptor*—let the buyer beware. But the law doesn't allow him to deal with his shareholders that way.

The Texas Gulf Sulphur Case

Government is becoming increasingly concerned with stockholders' inability to protect their own interests. Where stockholders cannot protect their own interests, the government through the Securities and Exchange Commission (SEC) and other agencies may do the job for them. The SEC has, for a number of years, had authority to protect stockholders from "inside dealings," that is, the ability of corporate officers to profit from inside knowledge that is not yet public. Among other cases, the SEC in its civil suit against the Texas Gulf Sulphur Company is setting precedent which may well open the doors for a tremendous increase in stockholder suits.

The Texas Gulf Sulphur case dates back to 1965 when the SEC charged that a group of company directors, officers, and employees violated the disclosure section of the Securities and Exchange Act of 1934 by purchasing stock in the company while withholding information about a rich ore strike the company had made.

In 1963, test drillings by Texas Gulf Sulphur Company indicated a rich

---

[14] "Gadflies Who Put the Bite on Business," *Business Week*, Oct. 14, 1967, p. 126.
[15] *Ibid.*, p. 124.
[16] Quoted in "The Law: Trouble for the Top," *Forbes*, Sept. 1, 1968, p. 23.

ore body near Timmins, Ontario.[17] On April 12, 1964, the company attempted to play down rumors by describing the Timmins property as "a prospect." But four days later, a second press release called the Timmins property "a major discovery." In what the judge described as the first application of a "due diligence test" . . . the first press release was found "to have been misleading to the reasonable investor using due care, and since the framers did not exercise due diligence in its issuance, TGS violated security laws."[18]

The insiders were directed by the court to pay into a special court-administered account all the profits they had made by trading on inside information. They were also ordered to repay profits made by outside people whom they had tipped. This account is to be used to settle stockholder suits brought by those who were led into selling their Texas Gulf Sulphur stock on the basis of the press release.

This case appears to say that corporate directors, officers, and key employees are insiders, and that they may not profit, or help others to profit, from knowledge about the company which is not public. It further seems to say that an outsider, if he is temporarily employed, becomes an insider. If these rulings are strictly enforced, it could mean that a corporate official or key employee, a legal counsel, a representative of an accounting firm, or a member of an outside firm doing contract work may be in jeopardy every time he discusses the company or releases information to the press.

The case appears to raise many difficult questions for businessmen. When can one buy or sell securities in his own company? How much information must he disclose to stockholders about the company's plans and outlook? Answers to these questions will probably not come easily, and the chances are that courts will become increasingly sympathetic with stockholders.

While this trend will no doubt have many effects on businesses and businessmen in the future, two phenomena are already apparent. First is the reluctance of highly qualified "outsiders" to serve as directors. Many feel that the risks involved simply are not worth the return. Second is the tremendous growth in liability insurance which insures corporate officers against personal loss from stockholder suits that allege carelessness (not dishonesty). Many major companies feel they cannot be without such protection for their officers, and the company generally pays all or a large portion of the premiums, thus reducing the amount of profit available to stockholders.

MANAGEMENT TRUSTEESHIP

The point has been made, very convincingly at times, that American stockholders are virtually at the mercy of professional managers.[19] Cor-

---

[17] For a review of the Texas Gulf Sulphur case and court remedies see "Texas Gulf Ruled to Lack Diligence in Minerals Case," *Wall Street Journal* (Midwest edition), Feb. 9, 1970, p. 1.

[18] *Ibid.*

[19] J. A. Livingston, *The American Stockholder*, Philadelphia: J. B. Lippincott Company, 1958, p. 44.

porate law seems to support this position. According to legal rules of thumb, "Directors are said to owe loyalty not to stockholders, as such, but only to the corporation. . . ."[20] This leaves unanswered the important and interesting question: To whom is the corporation accountable? Large corporations carry great power with their size. The results of their actions are widely felt, not only by stockholders but also by many other pluralistic groups.

Relationship of Stockholders and Professional Managers

Today, corporate directors and officers are generally considered to stand in a fiduciary relationship not only to stockholders but also to society as a whole. In establishing corporation policy, officers are increasingly guided by the philosophy of "what is good for the corporation is good for the stockholders." Courts seem to uphold this philosophy.

A basic case establishing this philosophy is *A. P. Smith Manufacturing Company v. Barlow.*[21] On July 21, 1951, the directors of A. P. Smith Manufacturing Company, wishing to exercise what they considered to be corporate public responsibility, donated $1,500 to Princeton University. Certain stockholders challenged management's right to dispose of corporate funds in this manner on the grounds that it was a misappropriation of corporate money and was, in fact, an *ultra vires* act. The stockholders contended that the directors of a corporation had no power to use corporate funds for any purpose other than those set forth in the corporate charter.

Through its president, the company argued that it considered the contribution to be a sound business investment. By contributing to educational institutions, it was argued, corporations were assuring a supply of properly trained people for future employment. It was further argued that the public expects corporations to support such institutions and that by doing so they gain goodwill in the community. Several highly respected business leaders supported this position by their testimony. The chairman of the board of Standard Oil testified that it was good business to accept "obligations of citizenship in the social community," and a former chairman of U.S. Steel commented that such expenditures were necessary for a company ". . . in protecting the long range interests of stockholders, its employees, and its customers."

Both the trial court and the appellate court upheld the corporation and its directors and agreed that "anything that tends to promote with the public a company's good will is a reasonable measure toward the corporate objective of earning a profit." The United States Supreme Court dismissed the case for lack of a Federal question.

[20] Jacob Weissman, *Law in a Business Society,* Englewood Cliffs, N.J.: Prentice-Hall, Inc., 1964, p. 39.
[21] 13 N.J. 145, 98 A.2d 481 (1953). Appeal to the New Jersey Supreme Court found in 26 N.J. Super. 106, 97 A.2d 186 (1953). Appeal to the United States Supreme Court found in 346 U.S. 861 (1953). A complete review of this case may be found in D. R. Forbush et al., *Management's Relationships with Its Publics,* Evanston, Ill.: Northwestern University Press, 1960.

The Trusteeship Concept

With the growth of large corporations has come growing support of the "management-trusteeship" concept. This view deemphasizes management's primary identification with ownership and emphasizes the social-responsibility concept. It recognizes that business, in modern society, has responsibilities to many pluralistic groups. It is a concept of plural trusteeship. Under this concept, ownership interest must take its place alongside vested interests of other social groups. Management, then, becomes an arbitrator in balancing conflicting interests of all groups.[22] In the final analysis, business is accountable to society, not to any one social group.

The trusteeship concept, however, is not universally accepted as being the correct approach to management-stockholder relations. Those opposed to the concept[23] see it as establishing managers in authoritarian roles whereby they apportion shares of corporate income according to their own personal value systems. Shares are dictated on the basis of personal morals and ethics, rather than according to economic concepts of returns to factors of production. It is argued that acceptance of the trusteeship concept alters the nature and purpose of corporate enterprise and undermines the foundations of private property.

Even the most ardent proponents of management trusteeship would not contend that management has no responsibility to stockholders. On the contrary, it has very real and definable responsibilities. As Eells and Walton have stated, "It is one thing to say that the risk-bearing stockholder has little function; it is quite another to say that he deserves little respect."[24] It is generally conceded that management is obligated to preserve and protect the interests of stockholders—to operate the company in a way that does not waste corporate resources and thus endanger or threaten stockholder investment. Management decisions that result in large losses for the company always make management competence suspect, in the eyes of both stockholders and society in general. Ford Motor Company's debacle with their Edsel and General Dynamics' fiasco with the Convair 880 and 990 are cases in point. Unsound management practices endangered stockholders' interest as well as public interest in both cases.

The Edsel Case

Within the four years and seven months from the time the Edsel program was started until it was discontinued, Ford spent some 350 million dollars on the new Edsel project.[25] Why was the venture a failure? It is difficult if not impossible to focus the blame at any one point. A combination of sev-

[22] Berle and Means, op. cit., p. 356.
[23] Among those opposed to the management-trusteeship concept are David McCord Wright, Theodore Levitt, and others.
[24] Richard Eells and Clarence C. Walton, Conceptual Foundations of Business, Homewood, Ill.: Richard D. Irwin, Inc., 1961, p. 151.
[25] John Brooks, The Fate of the Edsel and Other Business Adventures, New York: Harper & Row, Publishers, Incorporated, 1963.

eral factors is probably the real answer. Poor timing has been suggested as a major reason. The Edsel, a medium-priced, medium-sized car, was offered at the precise time that compact cars were becoming popular. Second, motivational research used to design the car did not provide the right kind of information. Third, the intense preintroduction advertising based upon suspense and mystery had the public so worked up that they expected a radical dream car. When the car proved to be fairly traditional, disappointment turned to resentment. Fourth, the car was introduced at the beginning of the 1957–1958 recession. Fifth, the design, while not wholly traditional, was not sufficiently different to motivate people to buy. Sixth, it has been suggested that the name Edsel conveyed the wrong image to the public. Last, heavy mechanical failure among the first cars along with considerable unfavorable press coverage destroyed public confidence.

While some of the above circumstances such as the 1957–1958 recession were difficult to forecast, others could have been avoided. In actual fact, the results were not as catastrophic for the company or its stockholders as might be imagined. Strength of the other Ford divisions allowed the corporation to absorb the huge losses. But potential dividends were lost, and market prices of stocks tumbled. Those stockholders who held their stock survived, but those who lost confidence and sold lost heavily.

The Convair Case

Even more severe were General Dynamics Corporation's losses through Convair Division's attempt to enter the market for commercial jet aircraft.[26] General Dynamics lost $490 million on its jet program. In effect it lost 90 percent of its assets on one venture. Again a number of managerial errors combined in an exponential progression to result in the debacle. Poor cost analysis, unsound pricing, wrong forecasting of market needs and market potential, underestimating competition, and poor contract negotiation all contributed to the staggering losses. Death of a strong autocratic president who closely controlled the far-flung divisions left a gap in top management with no strong replacement. Lack of information and control at the corporate level occasioned by a highly decentralized organization let danger signals go unheeded. All these errors pointed General Dynamics squarely for the bankruptcy courts. Only putting strong controls into the hands of an executive committee of seven directors and imposition of severe financial restrictions by the banks has saved the corporation.

In retrospect, one senior vice-president of the company summed up by saying: "It's a grave question in my mind as to whether General Dynamics had the right to risk this kind of money belonging to the stockholders for the potential profit you could get out of it. All management has to take a certain risk for big gains. But I don't think it's right to risk so much for so small a gain."[27]

[26] Richard Austin Smith, "How a Great Corporation Got Out of Control," 2 parts, *Fortune*, January, 1962, and February, 1962.
[27] *Ibid.*, February, 1962, p. 187.

NONPROFIT AND GOVERNMENT BUSINESSES

So far in this chapter, we have discussed business in a narrow sense. We have limited our discussion to private enterprises, but there are many other kinds of businesses, and people invest in them in various ways.

In Chapter 1 we said that we were going to use the term "business" to include more than private enterprises. In our broad use of the term we include all economic and commercial activities of organizations such as opera companies, philanthropic organizations, government agencies, and others. All these organizations engage in business activities in one way or another.

Nonprofit businesses depend on resource inputs just as profit-oriented businesses do. People invest in nonprofit organizations in a variety of ways. They contribute time, talent, effort, financial support, and other inputs necessary for the business to function. Like investors in private enterprises, they depend on management to use these resource inputs wisely and to give the payoffs these investors seek. For example, the large symphony orchestra association or the large civic theater association is supported financially by contributions and ticket sales. Others invest time and talent. But the investors have little to say about how the resources are used. These decisions are made by a professional manager who is hired by the investors, and they depend on him to provide culture and a better community, which are their payoffs.

The same applies to many government activities. For example, national parks are purchased or developed with tax funds and hence are "owned" by citizens. But ownership does not carry control with it. Only in a remote way do citizens control the way national parks are run. They depend upon managers to run the parks for their benefit. And the "owners" pay fees for their use just as a nonowner (noncitizen) does. Or consider a municipally owned sewage disposal plant bought by citizen investment. Citizens, or investors, depend on professional managers to run the plant and, except through occasional elections, have little direct control.

Ownership in nonprofit and government institutions is somewhat different from ownership in private enterprises. Owners do not own title to property. They do not even own certificates which they can sell in the market. Ownership in these institutions is really only an "investorship." Investors enjoy the right to use the benefits of their investment, but when they leave the area covered by the investment (for example, a city) they have no marketable shares to cash in.

In other words, the investor-manager separation prevails everywhere, not just in private enterprise, and the responsibility of managers to investors is the same whether we are talking about a private enterprise, a nonprofit enterprise, or a government enterprise. Managers are trustees for all the groups which make claims against the enterprise. Opera companies and national parks must bargain with labor, deal with suppliers, anticipate consumer demand, provide investor returns, and relate to other groups in much the same way as do other enterprises. And they must depend upon managers to fulfill these responsibilities.

SUMMARY

Conflicts sometimes arise between owners and managers because owners feel that businesses should be operated in a way that will provide maximum returns on invested capital. Managers, on the other hand, feel that they must balance the demands of owners with demands of other claimants, thus maximizing security and survival of the firm.

As stock ownership has become widely dispersed among large numbers of individuals, motives for owning stock have changed. Small stockholders see themselves only as investors. They have emerged as an absentee-owner group exerting pressures on a group of professional managers for social and economic payoffs.

With increased separation of management from ownership has come an increased acceptance of the management-trusteeship concept. Because results of business decisions are so widely felt, not only by stockholders but by other groups as well, management is increasingly considered to stand in a fiduciary relationship not only to stockholders but also to the rest of society. Increasingly, there has been an acceptance of the philosophy "what is good for society is good for the stockholder." Increasingly, management has come to view stockholders as one of several groups whose demands of the firm must all be properly balanced. Stockholders have the right to demand that management properly safeguard their investment in the enterprise, but so do other social groups.

STUDY GUIDES FOR INTERPRETATION OF THIS CHAPTER

1 From various sources at your command, gather all the facts you can about a stockholder suit and present the case to your class for discussion.

2 It has been observed that in modern society it is a mistake to think about pursuit of profit and pursuit of social values as separate and competing business goals. Develop two sets of arguments: one to support this statement, and one to repudiate it.

3 Does the management-trusteeship concept apply to nonprofit and government enterprises as well as to private enterprises? Select a nonprofit or government enterprise in your community and analyze it in terms of its responsibilities.

4 Find out all you can about institutional investors. What is your assessment of the power of these institutions to influence management decisions? Do you view this power as good or bad? Why? Do you think it is necessary to regulate these institutions in any way? Why or why not? If you think it is desirable to regulate institutional investors, how should they be regulated?

PROBLEMS

THE BLUE LAKE CHEMICAL COMPANY

The Blue Lake Chemical Company is located in a major Midwest city on one of the Great Lakes. The plant discharged its industrial waste into the city sewer system, which emptied into the lake. The company was charged by conservationists with contributing to the pollution of the lake and was asked to allocate $1 million to clean up its part of the problem. Analysis showed that only 6 percent of the pollutants were contributed by the chemical plant. The other 94 percent came from general use of the city sewer.

The question of whether or not to allocate the money was discussed in several meetings of the board of directors. In considering the question the following points were made:

1. Even if the company did spend $1 million, the largest part of the problem would still exist.
2. The public would not be able to see much improvement.
3. Expenditures of this sum would not increase future earnings.
4. Immediate earnings per share would be decreased, thus reducing the amount available to distribute to stockholders.
5. Failure to act would probably not result in widespread public reaction against the company.
6. People were becoming increasingly alarmed and aroused about injury to swimming and fishing areas.
7. If pollution is to be stopped, someone has to take the lead.

1 If the board of directors decided *not* to allocate the money, how can the decision be justified?
2 If the board decides to allocate the money, how should the company proceed?

THE SOCIALLY SIGNIFICANT STOCK

One evening, a small group of young businessmen were discussing social problems and the relations of business to those problems. They agreed that because of its managerial and technical expertise, private enterprise should take the lead. They also argued that maximum profits and maximum social good rarely go together. The question then became how can private enterprise make a maximum contribution to the solution of social problems and at the same time provide a satisfactory return to ownership.

A new kind of company was suggested, a company whose objectives would be the solution of social problems. But how could the company be financed? It was suggested that there were many people, particularly among the more affluent investors, who would invest in a company of this type. These people might be willing to trade off some economic gain for social gain and to accept a modest financial return if they could be assured of maximum social returns. The young businessmen reasoned that there are numbers of people who are willing to support financially a cause in which they believe, and used as an example to support their point the tremendous sale of low-yield war bonds during World War II.

1 Do you believe that a company of this type might be successful? Why?

2 Do you believe that a company of this type could be financed in this way?

THE PACIFIC COAST COMPANY

In an interim statement, the Pacific Coast Company declared an unaudited profit after taxes of slightly over $900,000 for the first three quarters of the year. The company's annual report, which was audited by a national accounting firm, showed a loss for the year of about three and one-third million dollars. A number of stockholder suits followed. Among them was a suit against the national accounting firm. The shareholders contended that the national accounting firm, even though it had not audited the interim report, had sufficient information to know the figures were incorrect.

1 Should the accounting firm have made a public announcement that the interim statement was incorrect? Should it have advised the Pacific Coast Company to amend its statement?
2 What other courses of action might have been open to the accounting firm?

CHAPTER 14
BUSINESS AND ITS CUSTOMERS

Modern civilization is dependent for its existence absolutely upon the proper functioning of the industrial and business system.

HENRY L. GANTT[1]

Consumers are turning more and more to their government for protection. They have to.

BESS MYERSON GRANT[2]

In a major Eastern city, the board of directors of a large corporation was holding its usual monthly meeting. Outside, the street was jammed by a large and noisy crowd of demonstrators. Many of the demonstrators carried signs which read, "Don't buy the XYZ product," "The XYZ product is no good," and "You'll be sorry." They were also chanting anticompany and antiproduct slogans. In short, they were protesting against quality of products and services provided by the company.

Elsewhere in the country, the National Commission on Product Safety urged eleven major television set makers to recall over one hundred color models to check for potential fire hazards. The Government commission reported that sets sold by six of the companies exceeded industry averages of 0.120 fire and smoke incidents per 1000 color sets sold.[3]

In another city, the State Attorney General announced that an order filed in Superior Court gives the state's residents the right to cancel orders for books purchased as a result of misrepresentation by salesmen, and to have their money refunded.[4]

On a major highway an automobile broke away from the truck which was towing it and crashed into an oncoming car. Both occupants of the

[1] Henry L. Gantt, *Organizing for Work*, New York: Harcourt, Brace and Company, Inc., 1919, p. 3.
[2] Bess Myerson Grant, "Protecting the Consumer: An Interview with Bess Myerson Grant," *The MBA*, March, 1970, p. 29.
[3] "Product Safety Board Urges 11 TV Makers to Recall 122 Models," *Wall Street Journal* (Midwest edition), Jan. 27, 1970, p. 25.
[4] "Consumers Win Rights in Landmark Order Filed in Spokane against Grolier Inc. Unit," *Wall Street Journal* (Midwest edition), Jan. 29, 1970, p. 6.

oncoming car were severely injured. In a suit against the automobile manufacturer, the injured parties claimed that the accident was the result of defective design of the front bumper tow bracket on the runaway car. The jury agreed, and the plaintiffs received a large monetary award.

While the incidents mentioned above are not directly related to each other, they are all part of a growing movement in which consumers, sometimes with the help of government and sometimes without, are increasingly making demands on business to improve quality and reliability of products and make buying decisions easier. In this chapter we will discuss business and customer relationships and the ever increasing responsibilities of business to interpret consumer wants, to provide dependable products, to help customers make intelligent choices of products, and to assume risks of product failure.

BUSINESS-CONSUMER RELATIONSHIPS

In the eighteenth and early nineteenth centuries the United States was primarily an agrarian nation with relatively simple needs and wants. The bulk of its population lived in rural areas. Those who lived on farms produced a substantial portion of the goods they consumed. Even many of those who lived in cities and towns produced domestically much of what they wore, ate, and used. Businesses were small for the most part. Merchants dealt mostly in either luxury goods or basic items which could not easily be produced at home. Manufacturers, likewise, concentrated their efforts on basic items which were difficult, if not impossible, to manufacture at home. Crude iron, gunpowder, and firearms, for example, found a ready market. Similarly, luxury items (for the times) such as china, silverware and pewter ware, and high-quality clothing found a market among the wealthy. And because technology was relatively unadvanced, most products were fairly easy to judge for quality. For the same reason, products were simple to use, and repairs were uncomplicated. For the most part, then, consumer reliance on business was limited.

As the nation became increasingly industrialized, as raw materials changed character and finished products became more complicated, and as urban concentration grew, consumer dependence on business also increased. New products appeared, and old products became more refined and more complex. And the United States, more and more, became a nation of specialists dependent in turn on other specialists for the assortment of goods and services necessary to live in an increasingly complex economy. Rather than each citizen being a rugged individualist, independent and capable of providing for his own needs, citizens today both individually and collectively are highly dependent upon others for their well-being. The typical individual no longer grows or preserves his own food, makes his clothing, provides his own transportation, or makes his own tools. Nor does he attempt to make or build the hundreds of other items that go into making his life pleasant. The consumer today depends upon hundreds of businesses to satisfy his needs and wants. Dependency is one side of a coin. The other side is responsibility. Since citizens as consumers are dependent upon business to satisfy their needs, business must have responsibilities to consumers.

II. THE CONSUMER MISSION OF BUSINESS

The first quotation at the beginning of this chapter expresses the idea that business is the key subsystem in our modern society. While this may not be true in the strictest sense, the economic well-being of modern industrial society depends heavily on the proper functioning of business. But businessmen should never be viewed as the leading group in society because there are many groups, all interacting with one another. On the other hand, businessmen do "play a central organizing role in a private-enterprise economy."[5] But what is this central role that business plays?

Paul Samuelson points out that every society must answer three fundamental questions:[6]

1. What commodities shall be produced and in what quantities?
2. How shall goods be produced?
3. For whom shall goods be produced?

A. Business Decisions

In the free world, businessmen play a key role in answering the questions above. On the basis of their interpretation of consumer wants, they decide what commodities should be produced and in what quantities. And they bear the risk of wrong decisions. A decision to produce a radically different automobile model may be unprofitable for both the company and society if society rejects this type of model. Businessmen also decide how goods shall be produced. They decide how factors of production shall be combined and choose the best production process so that products and services may be produced at the lowest cost and thereby offered to consumers at the lowest price. Decisions concerning for whom goods will be produced are also made by businessmen. Decisions to produce high-quality and high-priced articles limit the number of consumers who can obtain the commodity. Businessmen, then, have a strong voice in determining the variety, quantity, and quality of goods and services that people depend upon for their comfort and well-being. In 1923, Oliver Sheldon summed up these ideas by saying:[7]

> Industry exists to provide the commodities and services which are necessary for the good life of the community, in whatever volume they are required. These commodities and services must be furnished at the lowest prices compatible with an adequate standard of quality, and

---

[5] George L. Bach, *Economics: An Introduction to Analysis and Policy*, 5th ed., Englewood Cliffs, N.J., Prentice-Hall, Inc., 1966, p. 4.
[6] Paul A. Samuelson, *Economics*, 8th ed., New York: McGraw-Hill Book Company, 1970, p. 15.
[7] Oliver Sheldon, *The Philosophy of Management*, London: Sir Isaac Pitman & Sons, Ltd., 1923, chap. 8, reprinted in Harwood F. Merrill (ed.), *Classics in Management*, New York: American Management Association, 1960, p. 300.

distributed in such a way as directly or indirectly to promote the highest ends of the community.

3. Consumers as Advisers

In a planned economy such as Russia's, answers to the basic economic questions of what commodities to produce, how they shall be produced, and for whom they shall be produced are provided by a central planning agency. Russian businessmen are relieved of much responsibility to consumers. But businessmen in a free economy need to be consumer-oriented. They can best accomplish the mission of business as outlined by Sheldon and answer the questions posed by Samuelson by obtaining guidance from consumers.

Businessmen in free economies have no place to turn for answers except to consumers, who hold a veto power over business decisions. Businessmen can determine how best to serve society only by reviewing consumer votes in the market, that is, by noting what consumers buy or do not buy. Willingness to buy, in turn, depends upon how well products satisfy consumer needs. And customer satisfaction and loyalty are readily translated into profits for the company.

Dissatisfied consumers, on the other hand, often undergo a strange transformation and become anticustomers.[8] Rather than passively boycotting a product or a firm, dissatisfied customers often try to influence potential customers not to buy. Consider an extreme case.

Ed Smith purchased a new model automobile from the Jones Automobile Agency. Unfortunately, it was one of the occasional automobiles which seemed to have an unending series of defects. Dissatisfied with the car and with the treatment received from the dealer, Ed Jones finally painted the car a bright yellow and parked it prominently in his front yard. Across the side of the car he had lettered in prominent black letters the following announcement: "THIS IS A LEMON. PURCHASED FROM THE JONES AUTOMOBILE AGENCY."

Obviously, not all businesses serve the same consumer groups. Some businesses, such as General Dynamics or Motorola's aerospace division, concentrate on government agencies as their customers. Others, such as Fisher Body, produce for the automobile industry. Still others, such as General Mills, produce items for general public consumption. Many companies produce for a variety of markets. But whatever consumer group a business concentrates on, whatever market it tries to claim, it must first look to consumers for survival and vitality. As Peter Drucker tells us: "There is only one valid definition of business purpose: *to create a customer.*" And later he expands his idea by saying: "Because it is its purpose to create a customer, any business enterprise has two—and only these two—basic functions: marketing and innovation. They are the entrepreneurial functions."[9]

[8] William G. Kaye, "Take in a New Partner—The Consumer," *Nation's Business,* February, 1970, p. 54.
[9] Peter F. Drucker, *The Practice of Management,* New York: Harper & Row, Publishers, Incorporated, 1954, p. 37.

But, if business is to fulfill its purpose, it needs to be sensitive and responsive to the desires and requirements of those whom it claims to serve, that is, consumers.

III. THE SYSTEM CONCEPT OF BUSINESS

From a functional standpoint it has been traditional to view marketing departments as being responsible only for activities concerned with the movement of goods and services from producers to consumers.[10] Marketing and production were seen as two separate and unrelated activities. But this view fails to recognize that production and marketing are both part of the same entrepreneurial function of satisfying consumer needs. To properly discharge its responsibilities to consumers, business needs to recognize and build upon the interdependence among all functional specialties. The business enterprise is a total system whose basic purpose is to satisfy consumer wants.

A. Difficulties with a System Concept

There are two reasons why it has been difficult for businessmen to integrate marketing and production activities. First is a general misinterpretation of the economist's term "production." Production, to the economist, means creation of form, time, place, and possession utilities. In economic theory, the production process includes all activities necessary to create a product *and put it into consumers' hands.* Economic theory clearly recognizes the necessity for a system approach in defining business purpose. But practitioners—businessmen themselves—have historically viewed production as being concerned only with creation of form utility. A typical attitude was that the sales department should sell whatever was produced in the plant.

Today, many businessmen are shifting emphasis away from production per se and focusing upon responsibilities to consumers. No longer is the preceding definition of marketing sufficient. Phelps and Westing suggest: "It needs extension backward toward product planning and forward toward responsibility for the product subsequent to sales."[11]

B. Consumer Orientation

The second reason it has been difficult for businessmen to view the enterprise as a total system is the historical view of selling as a base and ignoble activity. In early chapters we discussed how social attitudes toward commercial activities were shaped by Aristotle's teaching and by Christian dogma. Although business activity in general has lost much of its social stigma, selling, as a specialized activity, has been slower to

[10] "Report of the Definitions Committee," *Journal of Marketing*, October, 1948, pp. 202–217.
[11] D. Maynard Phelps and J. Howard Westing, *Marketing Management*, rev. ed., Homewood, Ill.: Richard D. Irwin, Inc., 1960, pp. 1–2.

attain full respectability. Fifty or so years ago, marketing and selling were viewed as synonymous, and because selling lacked respectability, the entire marketing function was generally deemphasized. Because seventy-five or one hundred years ago consumers were so starved for factory-made goods, whose shortage was sometimes aided by monopoly in many industries, it was relatively easy to dispose of any commodities that provided reasonable satisfaction of consumer needs. Production decisions could be made with only the broadest concern for consumer preferences because consumers were presented with a narrow range of choices. A philosophy of *producer sovereignty* rather than *consumer sovereignty* was popular among businessmen. The philosophy of producer sovereignty embodied the idea that producers knew better than consumers what products would best satisfy consumer needs. Therefore, producers frequently made unilateral decisions about what, how, and for whom goods should be produced.

But as monopoly power of producers diminished and was replaced by monopolistic competition, the philosophy of producer sovereignty became inappropriate. As ranges of choice among products increase and competition for consumer votes becomes keener, it is increasingly important that producers turn to the consumer himself for production decisions. This means finding out what customers want before goods are produced, rather than producing and waiting for consumers to apply their veto power or accept the product. In this way producers can best exercise their responsibility to provide goods at the lowest possible price consistent with adequate quality. Wrong decisions are expensive and add to the total costs of operating a firm. Losses in one period must be recovered in the next if the firm is to survive in the competitive environment in which it finds itself.

The primary responsibility which business has to consumers is to identify their needs and wants. Only after needs and wants are known can a producer hope to find ways of satisfying them, but their identification is a major task in itself. Often consumers cannot define their own needs and wants because they do not recognize that these desires change over time. In order to do a better job, Boyd and Levy suggest that production decisions be made in terms of *consumption systems*, that is, "the way a purchaser of a product performs the total task of whatever it is that he or she is trying to accomplish when using the product—not baking a cake, but preparing a meal."[12]

IV. BUSINESS AS AN INSTRUMENT OF CHANGE

Business is a major instrument of change in our society. Remembering that we are including the business side of nonprofit organizations and government agencies in our definition of business, it is evident that business is the major instrument of change.

---

[12] Harper W. Boyd, Jr., and Sidney J. Levy, "New Dimension in Consumer Analysis," *Harvard Business Review*, November–December, 1963, p. 130.

Expectations for Change

Because we live in a capitalistic economic system, we have grown used to change. Indeed, we have come to expect it, for capitalism itself is an evolutionary process. Competitive forces at work within our capitalistic economy center around finding better ways of performing the consumer mission of business, that is, providing more and better goods and services for consumers at lower prices. In short, we expect the economic system under which we live to provide a rising standard of living, and "the fundamental impulse that sets and keeps the capitalistic engine in motion comes from the new consumers' goods."[13]

Business as an Agent

As the agent of consumers, business has the responsibility of producing a never-ending flow of new and different goods and services, thereby contributing to increased consumer well-being. Consumers, then, have delegated to business certain responsibilities for their well-being, and increasing consumer well-being depends upon change. When a consumer thinks of improvements in his standard of living, he usually thinks of new products that have become available. But business responsibility for innovation goes much further and includes not only improvements in form utility but also improvements in time, place, and possession utilities. Whether a company produces goods or services makes little difference. Responsibilities remain the same.

Responsibility for Innovation

How can business enterprises provide the kinds of goods and services demanded by consumers? How can business enterprises know what consumers want or need? The answer seems simple: Ask them. But in reality the answer is more complex. Consumers rarely know what kinds of products will best satisfy their needs. But they can and do define the need itself.

A few years ago women could not have told du Pont that they wanted nylon stockings. But they could and did express their need for stockings which were as sheer as silk but which were more durable, held their shape better, and were easier to launder. Once the need was identified, a product could be developed that would satisfy the need.

Similarly, a few years ago not many home insurance buyers could define "comprehensive homeowners' policies" as we know them today, but they recognized the convenience of combining their insurable risks and dealing with just one company.

The companies that pioneered nylons and homeowners' policies were consumer-oriented. They were sensitive to the needs of the consumers *from the consumer point of view.* Examples of product innovation which

[13] Joseph A. Schumpeter, *Capitalism, Socialism, and Democracy,* New York: Harper & Row, Publishers, Incorporated, 1942, quoted in Edwin Mansfield (ed.), *Monopoly Power and Economic Performance,* New York: W. W. Norton & Company, Inc., 1964, p. 30.

has satisfactorily met consumer needs are numberless. Garbage disposals, television, electric garage doors, new techniques in vascular and heart surgery, computers, nuclear energy, new metal alloys, jet engines, plastics, and automobile and equipment leasing are a few examples of product research and innovation.

Innovation responsibilities go much further than just product research. These responsibilities today extend to broader questions of what society considers to be the quality of life and which products and services support that quality of life. As environmental problems become more severe, business may well find it necessary to accept increasing responsibility to provide an array of goods and services entirely different from that offered today.

In order better to exercise innovative responsibility, businessmen have learned to encourage and develop upward communications from consumers. They are beginning to listen to customer complaints and to encourage customer suggestions, and more research is being done to identify consumer needs. Only when consumer needs are understood can business properly exercise its innovative responsibility—its responsibility to be creative in the consumer interest.

THE CONSUMER MOVEMENT

Considerable difference of opinion exists concerning whether or not business has lived up to its social mandate of providing proper quantities of goods and services at the lowest price compatible with adequate quality. Many consumers feel that business has not lived up to its responsibilities, and the increasing number and size of organized consumer groups stand as testimony to this belief. For example:

> Representatives of 60 national and state consumer groups met in Washington for two days . . . to found the Consumer Federation of America. Its aim: to give consumers a single influential voice—a full time national lobby.[14]

While there have been attempts by consumer groups to exert pressure directly against business, these activities have had limited success. Most consumer groups are concentrating on efforts to initiate new consumer protection legislation. And government at all levels is becoming increasingly responsive to consumers' voices. This response by government has taken the form of new consumer protection laws such as the Federal Consumer Credit Protection Act of 1969 (also known as The Truth-in-Lending Act) and the Consumer Protection Act passed in New York City.

There seems to be little question that consumer dissatisfaction is growing. The New York City Department of Consumer Affairs reported an increase of 86 percent in consumer complaints in one year.[15] And a California deputy attorney general reported an annual 27,000 protests against

[14] "Consumers Try to Organize," *Business Week*, Nov. 11, 1967, p. 56.
[15] Grant, *op. cit.*, p. 27.

faulty auto repair.[16] While there are many complaints against product performance, complaints against services of all types seem to be a major contributor to consumer frustrations. The following case is illustrative of the increasing number of stories about consumer frustrations that appear in the news media.

Mrs. L. Hugh Hutchinson, wife of a retired Air Force colonel, ordered a self-cleaning oven for her new Atlanta town house. Workmen jammed the oven into a wall opening that had been cut for a smaller appliance, thereby bending the oven out of shape. They removed it and more carefully installed another that turned out to have a defective thermostat. A repairman pulled out the thermostat and broke it. He summoned a colleague, who arrived with a new thermostat that was 15 inches too short. The two procured yet another thermostat, spent an afternoon trying to install it, and after much hammering and knocking reduced the oven to what Mrs. Hutchinson calls "a basket case—literally. They carried it out in 14 pieces in a basket."[17]

We are not suggesting that the experience of Mrs. Hutchinson represents typical performance of American business. Far from it. There are thousands of businesses providing products and services which are far superior to any that have been offered in the past. The Commissioner of the New York City Department of Consumer Affairs commented that "we have found that there are as many consumers who come to us with complaints which are irresponsible and without basis in documentation as there are fraudulent merchants."[18] The important point is that consumers are becoming more critical and are demanding more from business than ever before. It is also important to note that stories such as the experience of Mrs. Hutchinson are more and more frequently finding their way into print, thus making consumer dissatisfaction more visible.

In a broader sense, consumers are also becoming more knowledgeable and more aware of product safety and the effects of products and services on their individual and collective well-being. Led by men like Ralph Nader, John Banzhaf, and others, society is increasing its demands on business for greater responsibility to consumers. And as social concern over the myriad of environmental problems grows, it is likely that demands for more responsibility to consumers will be directed toward both business and government.

VI. RESPONSIBILITY FOR PRODUCT INFORMATION

Understanding consumer needs and producing goods and service to satisfy those needs do not complete business's responsibility to consumers. Business has additional responsibilities to produce goods and services which contribute to the health and safety of consumers and to provide

[16] America the Inefficient," *Time*, Mar. 23, 1970, p. 74.
[17] *Ibid.*, reprinted by permission from *Time*, The Weekly Newsmagazine; Copyright Time, Inc., 1970, Mar. 23, 1970, p. 73.
[18] Grant, *op. cit.*, p. 29.

adequate and truthful information so that consumers can make intelligent buying decisions.

Product Information and Consumer Well-being

It seems clear that business should offer to consumers only products and services which enhance their health and safety when properly used. This assumption implies, on the part of producers, adequate engineering, research, and testing of products before they are offered to consumers. But high costs of these activities have sometimes tempted manufacturers to offer products that were not fully proven. And also, unforeseen consequences of product use sometimes emerge after products have been put on the market.

In order to help protect consumers against substandard goods, Congress in 1938 passed the Food, Drug and Cosmetic Act. This Act prohibits movement in interstate commerce of adulterated and mislabeled foods, drugs, and cosmetics. It is also the law which controls what information may or may not appear on labels and packages. The Food, Drug and Cosmetic Act has provided consumers with two basic services. It has established minimum standards of quality and safety, and it has assured full disclosure of ingredients contained in manufactured foods, drugs, and cosmetics.

The law also established the Food and Drug Administration, whose duty it is to keep a watchful eye on labeling practices and acceptability of products for human consumption. This organization can, if it is not satisfied, require removal from the market of products which are unfit for human use or of even questionable fitness for use.

Some mislabeling is done intentionally, just as some products are produced with low standards. But often developments occur unexpectedly.

In 1969 it was found that cyclamates (artificial flavoring used in diet soft drinks and other diet foods) when administered to rats in certain ways produced cancer. The Food and Drug Administration issued an order withdrawing from the market any food or drink containing cyclamates. However, because of the large amount of cyclamates necessary to produce cancer in rats and because of the medical requirements of diabetics and others for cyclamates, the ban was modified and eased.

Business often responds quickly and voluntarily when an ingredient used in manufacturing consumer products becomes suspect or is proven dangerous.

During 1969, for example, the use of a popular food flavor enhancer named monosodium glutamate was questioned by the Food and Drug Administration. Research indicated that the chemical caused brain damage in infant mice when fed *in large doses*. As a result, the three largest producers of baby food voluntarily announced that they would discontinue the use of the chemical until further research proved it safe for use, even though there was no evidence that the small amount in baby food could possibly cause damage.

Society is becoming increasingly alarmed over the safety of consumer products other than foods, drugs, and cosmetics. The U. S. Public Health Service estimates that there are about twenty million injuries and eighteen thousand deaths in and around homes each year. To help raise safety standards of consumer products Congress in 1968 created the National Commission on Product Safety. The purpose of the Commission is to investigate hazards of household appliances. To obtain changes in products found to be unsafe, the Commission may use either persuasion or compulsion. As a result of its recommendations the Federal Housing Administration has agreed to require shatterproof glass in sliding glass doors and glass panels.

The chairman of the Commission has reported little need for compulsion. Most businessmen seem quite willing to make changes. The chairman has commented that "we've discovered that it isn't too difficult to initiate changes."[19] So far most changes have been made by producers quickly and voluntarily after defects were called to their attention.

B. Responsibility for Truthfulness

In addition to assurance that products are appropriate for human consumption, consumers need a variety of information about products if they are to make buying decisions. Business is the organization best able to provide this information, and information about products is best accomplished through advertising.

There has been, over the years, considerable controversy over both the economic justification and the legitimacy of advertising. It has been argued that advertising is economically undesirable because it serves no economic purpose. Further criticism also centers around truthfulness.

While criticisms of economic waste are still occasionally directed against advertising, they seem to occur less frequently and with less intensity than they did a few years ago. This may well reflect a more sophisticated understanding which accepts advertising as both socially and economically desirable.

Before production becomes economically meaningful, ownership of goods must be transferred to consumers. But before consumers can or will consume, they must know that the product exists, how it will satisfy their needs, and how they can obtain it. Some product information reaches consumers by word of mouth. But word-of-mouth communication has limited usefulness in modern society. For one thing, it is usually slow. For another, it is most effective in limited local markets. For rapid dissemination of product information over wide areas, advertising through mass media is much more effective.

More severe and persistent than questions of economic justification are criticisms of untruthfulness in advertising—misleading statements, half-truths, and failure to disclose full information about products. In order to provide some standards against which to judge the propriety of advertis-

[19] Ronald G. Shafer, "Household Hazards: A New Agency Strives to Make Life Safer in and around Home," *Wall Street Journal* (Pacific Coast edition), May 12, 1969, p. 1.

ing claims, Congress in 1938 passed the Wheeler-Lee Act. The Wheeler-Lee Act empowers the Federal Trade Commission to prevent the use of false and misleading advertising of goods moving in interstate commerce. The law covers not only specific representations about products, but also the extent to which material facts are *not* revealed.

Responsibilities of business to provide full and truthful information are clear. Consumers are fully dependent upon producers for product knowledge. Therefore, to fulfill adequately its responsibilities in its trading exchange with customers, business needs to provide as much truthful information as possible. Consumers seek confidence that the product will do what is claimed for it.

Not all businessmen have seen fit to assume their responsibility for advertising accuracy. Nor is this situation peculiar to the present. Much advertising of a generation or two ago would be distasteful if repeated today. Consider some of the early advertising claims of one prominent company. In reviewing early U. S. Borax Company advertising, one observer commented:[20]

> There is little doubt as to how the sophisticated customer of today would react to the optimistic selling pitch of one of the company's first advertising booklets: 20 Mule Team Borax was recommended as an aid to digestion; to keep milk sweet; as a complexion aid ("Don't wash your face in ordinary lake water"); to remove dandruff; and for the bath ("Use half a pound of powdered borax to the ordinary family bath of twelve gallons of water"). . . . And as a final fillip, Borax, claimed the advertisement, was also "excellent for washing carriages" and useful in curing epilepsy and bunions.

While there are few advertisers today who could make such broad claims for their products, many current advertising practices are frowned upon. It is not so much the blatant untruths that cause the trouble as the half-truths and the subtle deceptions. Untruths are relatively easy to detect and control. Subtle misrepresentations and deceptions are much more difficult to control because they are subject to debate.

The Federal Trade Commission, for example, charged that some photographs advertising a soup were misleading because the company and its advertising agency placed clear glass marbles in the soup to support vegetables and other solid ingredients. The Federal Trade Commission said the photographs exaggerated the amount of solid material actually present.

The company responded that no extra food ingredients had been added. But since the solid ingredients tended to sink to the bottom they needed to be supported so they could be seen in a picture.[21]

What way do you suggest for fairly representing the amount of solids in a soup?

[20] Velma A. Adams, "Why the Old Products Last," *Dun's Review and Modern Industry,* April, 1965, p. 112.
[21] Ronald G. Shafer, "Campbell in the Soup Again over Past Use of Marbles in its Ads," *Wall Street Journal* (Midwest edition), Feb. 5, 1970, p. 1.

On another front the Federal Trade Commission warned tire manufacturers against making advertising claims implying their tires can be safely used on speeding cars.

The Federal Trade Commission objected to the following claims on the grounds that they may be deceptive concerning tire safety.
"Built low and wide like a racing tire. Tested at 130 m.p.h."
"All new, wide tire made especially for the young crowd and today's high performance cars."
"Certified safe at 100 m.p.h., so you're sure you're safe at 60, 70, or 80."
"Stamina so great we safely tested them at 130 m.p.h."
The Federal Trade Commission said such advertisements may be deceptive because the speed tests don't disclose how the tires will perform at such speeds under all road conditions encountered under normal driving at various states of the life of tires.[22]

What is your opinion of the deceptiveness of these advertisements?
Closely related to truth in advertising has been the so-called "truth-in-packaging" and "truth-in-pricing" area. Because of the practice of some producers to package their products in odd units, it has been claimed that it is difficult and sometimes impossible for consumers to know how much a product really costs. Practices such as packaging a product in odd numbers of ounces or giving measures of liquids in fluid ounces are claimed to be confusing to consumers.
To help overcome this problem, the City of New York established a regulation requiring retailers to price by the pound, ounce, or other common unit of measure six different classes of merchandise. In other areas retailers voluntarily moved toward developing a workable system of unit pricing.
Another area in which it had been deemed necessary to impose legislation has been the area of consumer credit. The "truth-in-lending" law established the type and amount of financial information to be given to customers. Basically the law requires that all financial charges be clearly stated and that the true annual rate of interest be given to the customer.

c. Need for Legislation

Passing legislation does not solve the problem. In one way it only complicates the situation, because legislation encourages businessmen to focus on legal boundaries of advertising behavior rather than on ethical considerations. In considering this question one author polled New York City managers in seventeen different industries. He reported:[23]

In personal interviews, time after time these executives told me, "It's for Legal to decide," when they were asked whether there were any

[22] "FTC to Challenge Ads It Says Misrepresent Tire Safety Factors," *Wall Street Journal* (Pacific Coast edition), June 4, 1969, p. 1. For a philosophical discussion of embellishment and deception in advertising, see Theodore Levitt, "The Morality (?) of Advertising," *Harvard Business Review*, July–August, 1970, pp. 84–92.
[23] Tom M. Hopkinson, "New Battleground: Consumer Interest," *Harvard Business Review*, September–October, 1964, pp. 98–99.

special ethical, moral, or public relations considerations in those particular marketing areas heavily concerned with "consumer interest." Only 3 out of 31 executives could see any such relationship.

We are not suggesting that the Food, Drug, and Cosmetic Act and the Wheeler-Lee Act be repealed, nor are we questioning the usefulness of these acts. We are suggesting that legislation is not enough. This fact is evidenced by increasing demands for more power to be vested in the Federal Trade Commission and by proposals of additional legislation to control advertising.

There will always be needs for legislation, but there should be a minimum of legislation, not a maximum. What is needed is not a flood of new legislation but a new kind of thinking among businessmen. President Lyndon B. Johnson emphasized this idea in his remarks announcing the establishment of top-level consumer representation in the White House. He said: "The remedy for errors of taste, poor judgment and disorder in our economic life is not to be found in the legislatures or the courts but in the leadership of those who care." The entire problem, the President said, is "a matter for corporations and organizations dedicated to the public interest."[24] This thinking does not focus on legal boundaries of advertising but rather is sensitive to consumer demands and complaints. A straightforward approach to evaluating advertising decisions concerning consumer interest has been suggested by Hopkinson.[25] He suggests that businessmen evaluate a decision in terms of questions such as:

Is this fair?
Is this ethical?
Would I like to be treated in this way?
What would my wife think about the labeling on this package?
Do I want my children to watch this kind of T.V. program?

VII. RESPONSIBILITY FOR PRODUCT PERFORMANCE

Consumers expect products to perform in the way producers claim they will. Advancing technology makes consumers increasingly dependent on producers for full and accurate product information. Most products are no longer simple, familiar to consumers, or easy to inspect. Rather, they have become so complex and technical that consumers in most cases are no longer competent to judge either their quality or their operating characteristics. This lessening of consumer ability to judge products places responsibility for product performance more squarely than ever before on the shoulders of producers. Consumers have no place else to go. They must depend heavily upon producers' information when they make buying decisions.

Concern over problems of fraudulent claims for products and shoddy merchandise has plagued consumers for generations. Aristotle (384–322 B.C.) was concerned with the problems of value of exchange.[26] St. Thomas

[24] *New York Times*, Feb. 6, 1964, quoted in Hopkinson, *op. cit.*, pp. 97–98.
[25] Hopkinson, *op. cit.*, p. 102.
[26] Aristotle, *Politics*, quoted in Arthur Eli Monroe, *Early Economic Thought*, Cambridge, Mass.: Harvard University Press, 1951, pp. 13–22.

Aquinas (1225–1274) in his *Summa Theologica* showed considerable concern over selling defective merchandise.[27] Both English and American common law are full of product liability cases. But until the last few years, producers have been relatively successful in minimizing their responsibility for product performance. Most producers of consumer products could limit product liability by very narrow express warranties and specific statements disclaiming responsibility for anything other than defective parts. Most producers could also avoid responsibility if a product was purchased from someone other than the producer himself on the grounds that no direct contractual relationship existed. The legal term for this direct contractual relation is *privity*. And furthermore, if a producer were to be held liable, negligence on his part had to be proved.

Warranty

Because buyers today are so heavily dependent upon producers' information in their buying decisions, problems of misleading information, fraudulent information, implied safety of use, and shoddy merchandise are receiving more attention than ever before. And the defenses mentioned above are becoming much weaker. Consumer complaints, pressures in the courts, and a general change in social philosophy have combined to make businessmen more sensitive to problems of product liability.

Heavy pressures from courts have emphasized business responsibility in the area of warranties. Recent decisions have stressed the point that since producers have done everything they can through advertising to convince consumers that their products are suitable and safe for a specific use, they must be liable for product performance.

In a landmark case Mr. Claus Henningsen purchased a new automobile which he and his wife drove around town for several days.[28] Then, when driving out of town, the steering mechanism failed, and Mrs. Henningsen crashed into a highway sign and then into a brick wall. She sustained injuries and the car was a total loss. Mr. Henningsen went to court. The automobile company claimed that Mr. Henningsen had signed a disclaimer when he bought the car and this limited the liability of the company to replacement of defective parts. The court held that the company could not avoid its legal responsibility to make automobiles good enough to serve the purpose for which they were intended.

Contractual Relationship

In our relatively uncomplicated society of the early 1800s a large proportion of items were purchased by users directly from the producers of those items. Under these conditions, the lack-of-contractual-relationship defense against improper product performance probably made a great deal of sense. But as the distance between user and producer widened

---

[27] St. Thomas Aquinas, *Summa Theologica*, quoted in Monroe, *op. cit.*, pp. 56–62.
[28] *Henningsen v. Bloomfield Motors, Inc., and Chrysler Corporation*, 32 N.J. 358, 161 A.2d 69 (Supreme Court of New Jersey, 1960).

and as products passed through longer and more complex channels of distribution, the strength of this defense has been dissipated through court decisions. The landmark decision was rendered in 1916.[29]

Mr. MacPherson purchased a new Buick automobile from a local dealer. Shortly thereafter defective wooden spokes in a wheel collapsed, and Mr. MacPherson was injured as a result. He sued Buick. The company claimed that MacPherson had purchased the car from a dealer and not from Buick and therefore Buick had no obligation to him. The judge ruled that Buick had been negligent because the wheel had not been inspected before it was put on the car. He further ruled that Buick was responsible for defects resulting from negligence, regardless of how many middle men were in between.

C. Doctrine of Strict Liability in Tort

Tort is the law of personal injury. Courts are increasingly taking the position that manufacturers are responsible for injuries resulting from use of their products.

Mr. Greenman, after reading promotional material and watching demonstrations of a Shopsmith combination power tool, expressed to his wife his desire to have one for his home workshop. She purchased one of the tools and gave it to him as a gift. Two years later he purchased a lathe attachment for the basic tool. While using the lathe attachment, the wooden block upon which he was working flew out of the machine and seriously injured him. He sued Yuba Power Products, the manufacturer, and he was able to prove certain screws in the machine were inadequate to hold the parts together. The California Supreme Court ruled that issues of negligence or breech of warranty were not relevant. The Court held that: "A manufacturer is strictly liable in tort when an article he places on the market, knowing it will be used without inspection, proves to have a defect that causes injury to a human being."[30]

D. Broadening Liability for Product Performance

Social philosophy, reflected in court decisions, seems to be demanding that manufacturers assume an increasing burden of liability for injuries sustained from use of their products. Expansion of the concepts governing product liability has been incorporated into uniform-commercial-code laws by twenty-eight states. The uniform code holds that "a manufacturer is open to suit by anyone using his products who claims injury, even if the claimant is not the original buyer."[31] Manufacturers are being held liable for an increasing variety of injuries, both physical and financial. Manufacturers are being held liable for loss of value of a product due to improper manufacturing, for failure of products to perform according to

[29] *MacPherson v. Buick Motor Company,* 217 N.Y. 382, 111 N.E. 1050 (Court of Appeals of New York, 1916).
[30] *Greenman v. Yuba Power Products, Inc.,* 59 Cal. 2d 57, 27 Cal. Reptr. 697, 377 P.2d 897 (Supreme Court of California, 1963).
[31] Consumers Sue for Defective Products," *Consumer Bulletin,* November, 1964, p. 43.

advertising claims, and for negligent product design. And liability is beginning to extend beyond the manufacturer to his suppliers, to his advertising agency, to his outside accounting firm, and to others who stand in close relation to him and upon whom consumers depend to make buying decisions.

RESPONSIBILITY FOR SERVICE

Because many products are so complex, consumers also depend more heavily on producers to provide service in case of product failure. Few consumers today can repair their own refrigerator, washing machine, lawn mower, or automobile. As products become more complex and technical, producers have an increasing responsibility to provide parts and service. Manufacturers of farm machinery and automobiles have long recognized their responsibility in this area and have maintained marketwide service organizations and local inventories of parts.

Businesses are liberalizing their policies on repair of faulty products, cash refunds, and exchanges of unsatisfactory products. There is an increasing trend to formalize and strengthen warranties. Most electrical appliances now carry with them express warranties for one year. Not many years ago the usual warranty on a refrigerator was three months; now a five-year warranty is normal. The Federal Housing Authority requirement of a one-year guarantee by builders on houses to be sold under FHA mortgages has set a precedent for general contractors. Chrysler Corporation pioneered in the automotive field with liberalized guarantees. In the retail field, Sears, Roebuck led the way with their unconditional money-back guarantee. Much of Sears's success has been attributed to consumer confidence built in this way.

While many manufacturers cannot afford to maintain large service organizations, this does not relieve them of responsibility for service. Most reputable manufacturers have recognized this responsibility and have accepted it by maintaining stocks of parts, authorizing and training private service enterprises to service their products, and/or standing ready to repair items at their factories.

RESPONSIBILITY FOR SELF-REGULATION

Under ideal conditions the business system would be a self-regulating system in regard to consumer responsibilities, particularly for product information and performance. Ideally, every firm should recognize its responsibilities to consumers and willingly exercise these responsibilities to its fullest ability. But this is a utopian approach which has little meaning in the real world. Because business behavior in the area of product information and performance revolves heavily around ethics, it is difficult to obtain general agreement on proper ethical behavior. There are differences of opinion between consumers and producers concerning what is proper behavior.

Earlier chapters of this book emphasized the idea that if a social institution does not serve society in a manner which provides suitable social payoffs, society will replace or modify that institution. Society, then, ultimately controls various institutions by setting standards of product information and performance. Business has little choice but to accept and conform to these standards. However, it does have two choices of how to conform. It may voluntarily regulate its own performance, or it may submit to forced regulation by society through legislation.

Business has not always taken the initiative in establishing high ethical performance standards for product safety and product information. This lack of leadership has encouraged minimum legal standards, such as those set by the Food, Drug, and Cosmetic Act and the Wheeler-Lee Act. On the other hand, much effort has been devoted by individual firms and by entire industries to encourage high ethical behavior.

Basically, there are three reasons why business tries to regulate and police its own activities. The first and most often proposed reason is to avoid government action. This reason reflects defensive thinking on the part of businessmen and focuses on minimum compliance with society's standards. It emphasizes legal performance boundaries beyond which business cannot go without interference. Review of relations between the Federal Trade Commission and the cigarette industry over the years suggests that efforts toward self-regulation on the part of the industry have been largely efforts to avoid restrictive legislation.

The second reason for self-regulation is to achieve status. In an attempt to "professionalize" an industry, businessmen sometimes submit themselves to self-administered policing under government procedures. For example, in many states contractors must be registered and licensed before they can operate. Contractors themselves often are quite active in establishing criteria for both registry and licensing and in formulating criteria for withdrawal of registry or license.

A third reason for self-regulation is a growing belief on the part of both industries and individual firms that "what is good for society is good for business." This belief is reflected in the authority given to some trade associations and in company codes of ethics. Rather than focusing on minimum performance, firms that hold this belief often choose to exceed society's standards.

Historically, fear of government interference and regulation has been the prime force motivating business toward more responsible behavior. Businessmen for the most part have taken a defensive position based upon the concept that any action not specifically declared illegal is legal and therefore appropriate. But judging actions solely on the basis of legality is not enough. Since legislation reflects public displeasure with actions, it defines only minimal conditions, leaving to business the responsibility to go beyond legislation. The prime responsibility of business to consumers is to understand and predict how it can best serve consumers, to view itself as existing for consumers—not the other way around.

IMPACT AND IMPLICATIONS OF CONSUMERISM

Whatever else may be said about the consumer movement, it is difficult to deny that it has become a formidable force within the environment of business. Consumerism has become a real and powerful challenge to business. One businessman expressed the relationship between consumers and business as follows:[32]

> Reduced to its absolute essentials, consumerism challenges business to do better . . . and if this is not done, consumerism could pose a serious challenge to the core of private enterprise: the profit system itself.

Consumers are rapidly emerging as an important and powerful institution capable of making their collective voice heard. Dissatisfied with shoddy products and service, concerned with environmental issues, and impatient with the response of business, consumers are demanding more from business than ever before.

Indeed, the challenge to business to "do better" seems clear. If it is to meet the challenges of the consumer movement, business needs to emphasize the philosophy of "let the seller beware," and discard whatever remains of the philosophy, "let the buyer beware." But how can business meet the challenges imposed by consumers? One step forward is to listen more to consumers themselves. This will require more and better market research, both before and after a product or service is put on the market. Safety audits of products currently being produced are another step forward. More and better product design effort and closer attention to manufacturing processes, including greater emphasis on quality control, will help business go far in meeting the challenge. And finally, more and better communication with customers concerning products and their use will contribute most toward improved busines-consumer relations.

SUMMARY

Consumers are beginning to emerge as a powerful pluralistic social institution. As the nation has become industrialized, as products have become more complex, and distances between consumer and producer have increased, consumers are forced to depend on producers more than ever before for product reliability and for truthful product information upon which to base purchasing decisions.

Business has not always responded well to consumers' needs and wants. As a result there has been an increasing amount of restrictive legislation. Courts, too, have become progressively more strict in requiring producers to assume responsibility for product failure. All in all the consumer movement poses a challenge for business: a challenge to become more consumer-oriented, and a challenge to "do better."

[32] Aaron S. Yohalem, quoted in "Consumerism Labeled Industry's Challenge at New AMA Briefing," *Management News*, American Management Association, January, 1970, p. 2.

STUDY GUIDES FOR INTERPRETATION OF THIS CHAPTER

1 Select two advertisements for consumer goods from newspapers, magazines, or television. Evaluate and compare them in terms of how well they provide reliable information which would help consumers make buying decisions.

2 How and to what extent can business depend on consumers to advise in production decisions? Do such activities add unnecessarily to costs?

3 Find out all you can about government consumer protection programs. Evaluate the following statement:

The purpose of government consumer protection programs is "to help honest and conscientious businessmen by discouraging their dishonest and careless competitors."[33]

4 From interviews with insurance company representatives, lawyers, and others, find several examples of court cases concerning producer liability for product performance. To what extent do you or do you not agree with the decisions of the court? Why?

PROBLEMS
THE NEW RULE

A federal government agency proposed rules that would require food stores to have available all advertised items and to sell them at advertised prices. The proposed rules came as a result of consumer complaints. The agency said that its investigators found considerable evidence that items advertised as "specials" in newspapers either were not available, or had not been marked down to advertised prices.

The evidence was gathered as a result of two surveys made by the agency. One survey covered 137 stores operated by ten chains. The other survey covered 154 stores operated by nine different chains. The first survey showed that 11 percent of the items advertised as specials were not available in the 137 stores. The survey also revealed that substantially more "special" items were unavailable in low-income areas than in high-income areas.

About 9 percent of the advertised items were marked with prices higher than those advertised. And at the stores of several chains 10 percent or more of the items were mispriced.

The proposed rules would require any food retailer to have advertised specials readily available to customers in quantities sufficient to meet reasonably anticipated demands, and at or below the prices advertised. Under the proposed rules, companies cited by the agency for alleged violations would have the burden of proof that the rules were inapplicable to them or that the alleged violation did not occur.

[33] President Richard M. Nixon, quoted in *Washington Report*, Washington, D.C., National Restaurant Association, Nov. 10, 1969, p. 2.

The agency announced that it will have a hearing on the proposal and interested parties are invited to present their views.

1 You are a major official of a large grocery chain and the president (your manager) has asked you to attend the hearing and present the company's views. What stand will you take toward the proposal, and how will you present your case.

THE NEW RUG

Mr. Abel Smith purchased an expensive rug which had been manufactured by a well-known rug producer. After being on the floor in Smith's home for a short time, the rug developed a strange line. Smith telephoned the dealer who told him that rugs of that kind sometimes developed strange markings after they were put on the floor, but that it was a temporary condition. Smith was assured that the line would disappear with wear. As time went on not only did the line not disappear, but others appeared.

Finally Smith decided to take legal action. Since the retailer had gone out of business, Smith asked the manufacturer to replace the carpet.

1 Regardless of legal liabilities in this situation, what responsibilities does the manufacturer have to Smith? Explain.

2 What responsibilities does Smith have in this situation? Explain.

CHAPTER 15

BUSINESS AND LABOR

New relationships are in the making today among business, government and labor in America. All three of these great centers of decisions in our economy face a set of unfamiliar and potentially dangerous forces which won't spare the slow-witted or the fainthearted.

M. J. RATHBONE[1]

A [labor] movement born as a voice of dissent has become a mainstay of the status quo in a period when even the staidest institutions . . . have felt obliged to take a critical look at all their most cherished percepts and scrap those made obsolete by changing technology and mores.

A. H. RASKIN[2]

As suggested by the first introductory quotation, organized labor has become a major power group in our pluralistic society. In discussing national economic problems, organized labor is usually accorded a place beside business and government. Seldom are problems of productivity or economic growth discussed without considering the roles, contributions, and relationships of these three social institutions.

In large part, growth of union power has been based upon social considerations. Society has been willing to confer power on organized labor because it felt unions needed power to promote the welfare of working people—a responsibility which society perceived had not been met by business alone.

The second introductory quotation suggests that organized labor is now in the most critical period of its development. Many feel that labor has largely achieved its objectives of improving wages, hours, and working conditions, and must now concentrate on social responsibilities which are commensurate with its size and power. Others feel that the original objectives remain but have changed form. But few would contest the fact that organized labor has become a potent economic and social power in the environment of business.

[1] M. J. Rathbone, chairman of the board and chief executive officer (retired), Standard Oil Company (New Jersey). "Three Men in a Boat" (speech before the Harvard Business School Club of Washington, D.C., Nov. 28, 1962), p. 1.
[2] A. H. Raskin, "The Labor Movement Must Start Moving," *Harvard Business Review*, January–February, 1970, p. 110.

Much criticism leveled at labor today revolves around the concept of balanced power and responsibility. While business is held economically and socially responsible for its decisions and actions, it is often argued that labor is not. As social and economic problems become more complex, labor, like business and government, will need to broaden its vision and look at itself as a partner rather than an antagonist of the other two.

In this chapter we will discuss the evolution of the business-labor relationship during which the objectives and policies of contemporary unionism were formulated. We will also discuss the changing growth patterns of the labor movement, the need for a changing labor philosophy, the challenges which a changing economy pose for business and labor, collective bargaining, and labor as a political force.

THE EVOLVING BUSINESS-LABOR RELATIONSHIP

It has been said that there is little new in the labor movement. Certainly labor unions are nothing new. Indeed they have been an integral part of American national development. Activities of workers, organized for a specific purpose, date back to at least 1636 when a group of fishermen appealed to authorities to help collect unpaid wages. In 1768, journeymen tailors in New York struck for higher wages. Ten years later printers in the same city struck for the same reason.

Government Intervention

Government intervention, too, is no stranger to relations between business and labor. High demand for skilled labor coupled with severe labor shortages led the government of Massachusetts in 1633 to attempt wage controls through legislation.

Union Concepts

In spite of the instability of worker organization, unions had by 1830 introduced most concepts common in today's business-labor relationships. Collective bargaining was in use by 1800. In 1799, employers and the Philadelphia Journeymen Cordwainers negotiated a compromise of a wage dispute. Strike benefits, too, received the attention of early unions. As early as 1786, Philadelphia printers pledged money to support journeymen who lost their jobs by refusing to accept wage cuts, and, in 1805, the New York Shoemakers established a permanent strike fund. Demands for and attempts to maintain closed shops were also relatively common by 1830. One observer commented that "a charge that appears in almost all of the labor conspiracy trials is that trade societies sought to compel all craftsmen to affiliate."[3]

[3] Philip Taft, Organized Labor in American History, New York: Harper & Row, Publishers, Incorporated, 1964, p. 8. The conspiracy trials were the result of applying the English common-law doctrine of "criminal conspiracy" to strike activities of labor organizations.

Social Reform

In the decades between the panic of 1837 and the Civil War, labor as a social institution moved in two separate directions. Some labor organizations continued to pursue the objectives of improving the lot of working men through economic pressures on individual employers. In large part, however, labor turned to intellectuals for leadership and became involved in issues of social change or in utopian socialist schemes. One historian commented that "many union members looked to utopian experiments of the day for their economic salvation and became supporters and members of cooperative colonies established by the followers of the British industrialist and dreamer, Robert Owen, the French Utopian Socialists, etc."[4] Another observed: "When the foundation for labor's bargaining power was lost, many workers became more interested in the more ambitious projects to restructure the entire organization of the economy. The intention was not to secure a 'fair day's pay for a fair day's work' within a labor market, but rather to eliminate the labor market."[5] In retrospect, those unions which refused to waver from principles of business unionism remained strong and viable. Those who became involved in social reform disappeared.

The Public Visibility of Labor

As business became more active during the latter part of the nineteenth century, so did labor. The thirty years from 1870 to 1900 were a period of labor violence in which the public became aware of the seriousness of the labor problem. As the labor movement grew in size and power, its public visibility increased. It has been observed:[6]

> Heretofore the labour question had forced itself upon the attention of the public merely for brief moments and then invariably in a catastrophic setting. . . . Since then the labour question has held the public stage practically without interruption, though the interest it has aroused has of necessity fluctuated.

Just as society had become distrustful of an unrestrained business system, it began to look upon labor also as an institution which needed restraint, even though its social objectives were admirable. Public concern over demonstrations of union economic power, along with the willingness of courts to support business in disputes with labor, kept business in a dominant power position during the late 1800s and early 1900s.

[4] Harry W. Laidler, "A Brief Labor History," *Current History*, July, 1954, p. 2.
[5] Paul E. Sultan, *Labor Economics*, New York: Holt, Rinehart and Winston, Inc., 1957, p. 102.
[6] John R. Commons and associates, *History of Labour in the United States*, New York: The Macmillan Company, 1918, vol. II, part 2, pp. 527–528.

The Foundations of Contemporary Unionism

Despite public concern over union activities during the closing years of the nineteenth century, it was precisely during this period that the foundations of contemporary unionism were laid.

Experiments in social reform had all failed. So, too, had the experiment of the Noble Order of the Knights of Labor which was based on the concept of one organization for all working men regardless of skill or profession. Armed with the experience of the past, Samuel Gompers and other leaders of the American Federation of Labor (AFL) formulated objectives and policies which were based firmly on the concept of business unionism, that is, economic concepts rather than political or social concepts. Simply stated, the objectives of the AFL were "more and better"— more union security, higher wages, and better hours and working conditions.

The basic policies formulated to reach the objectives were also clear and uncomplicated. First, the AFL was organized exclusively on a craft basis. Second, national unions which belonged to the AFL were guaranteed "trade autonomy," which meant that decision making was to rest with the national union and not with the AFL. Third, the national unions were guaranteed exclusive jurisdiction over their particular craft or occupation, thus creating for the national union a labor monopoly.

The objectives were to be achieved through emphasizing collective bargaining. But when collective bargaining failed to produce the desired results, economic pressures were to be applied.

Economic Depression and Social Gains

Throughout the first one-third of the twentieth century, public opinion was generally against organized labor. Certainly the courts favored business. But with the Great Depression of the 1930s came a massive change in public opinion. Failure of business to generate economic recovery, declining public confidence in business, mass unemployment, and declining wage levels all contributed to a changing environment of business-labor relations.

With the passage of the Wagner Act in 1935, the environment of business as it is affected by labor relations was changed. Heretofore, bargaining relations between business and labor had existed in an informal atmosphere in which business was free to negotiate or not negotiate with labor as it saw fit and as the economic powers of one or the other prevailed. The Wagner Act forced business to recognize labor organizations and bargain collectively with them. In addition, it did much more than that. By the passage of the Wagner Act, American society officially recognized American labor as a major social institution and conveyed upon it by legal decree powers commensurate with its social position.

Balance of Power Reevaluated

Supported by public opinion and government sympathies, labor made substantial progress prior to World War II, thus creating a new environment for business. And business, persuaded by law and social pressure, was learning to adjust to this social change. After the war, however, the environment changed. Labor reformulated Samuel Gomper's objectives of "more and better" and pressed for economic gains on virtually every front. Vigorous and militant actions by labor led to serious questions concerning its power and responsibilities. McGuire comments on social attitudes toward labor as follows:[7]

> The end of World War II produced an environment which was completely different from that which existed in 1940. During the war American business had redeemed itself through its productive effort. Franklin D. Roosevelt, the great champion of organized labor, was dead. Many labor leaders had acted capriciously during the war and in the immediate postwar years. People were tired of conflict. They were opposed to strikes, which came with mounting frequency in 1946. They were prosperous and wanted to be able to purchase goods immediately, and they couldn't understand why labor held up production. Labor obviously was no longer the underdog it had been in the 1930s; now the public considered it arrogant and dictatorial—almost un-American.

In many cases it was obvious that unions had misused the power granted them under the Wagner Act. Unions often resorted to practices which a few years before they had labeled unfair in the hands of management. People became concerned that the Wagner Act had "loaded the dice" too heavily in favor of labor. They became concerned that society had conveyed to labor great social and economic powers without exacting equal responsibility or accountability.

The Labor-Management Relations Act (Taft-Hartley) of 1947 and the Labor-Management Reporting and Disclosure Act (Landrum-Griffin) of 1959 were attempts to reverse the pendulum of power and bring the power relations of business and labor nearer to equality.

UNION GROWTH PATTERNS

Growth in Numbers

An integral part of the philosophy of the American labor movement has always been that there is strength in numbers. Growth, then, is an important key to union success, but growth has been disappointing to labor leaders in recent years. After a spectacular growth in membership between 1936 and 1944, membership continued to increase, but at a much more modest rate than before. By 1956, membership (excluding Canada) had reached 17.5 million. But between 1957 and 1961 labor lost over a million members. The loss has been recovered and membership in 1970 stood at approximately 18 million.

[7] Joseph W. McGuire, *Business and Society*, New York: McGraw-Hill Book Company, 1963, p. 117.

Growth as a Proportion of the Labor Force

But a more discouraging fact for organized labor is that union membership has continued to decline as a proportion of the total labor force. Among workers in nonagricultural establishments, where most members are found and where organizing efforts are greatest, the proportion fell from 33.4 percent in 1955 to 27.9 percent in 1968.[8]

There are two reasons why union growth has slowed, and both are important to business. First, expansion in employment has largely occurred in service-oriented occupations—not in the traditional manufacturing occupations which have been the stronghold for union membership. Over half of all workers in the United States are engaged in furnishing services of one kind or another, and labor force projections indicate that the proportion will increase. These occupations have been slow to respond to union organizing efforts.

Second, the increase in numbers of professional, semi-professional, and white-collar workers has been much greater than the increase in blue-collar workers. The increase in white-collar employment has come first from the expansion of service jobs and second from the creation of different jobs in manufacturing resulting from increased technology.

A New Organizational Model

What do these shifts in the composition of economic activity and of the labor force mean for business? Two things seem inevitable. One trend that is developing is increasing militance among professionals, semi-professionals, and workers in service-oriented jobs. Unrest and militancy among these groups may well add another dimension to the labor scene. No one seems to have found the correct formula for organizing white-collar workers, although unions have had partial success with these groups and continue to do so. More important is the recent trend of professional organizations that are not unions to act like unions and to use union weapons. One observer of the labor scene suggests:[9]

> There is an uneasy feeling in some union circles that perhaps the organizational model for white-collar workers, like the organizational model for professional and scientific workers, may not be a *union* model at all, but one that more closely resembles a professional association, like the National Education Association, The American Association of University Professors, or the Nurses Association.
>
> The recent activities of some of the professional groups—nurses, teachers, even physicians—suggests that they may adopt union tactics and union strategies without becoming unions.

[8] Telephone interview, Harry P. Cohany, Chief, Division of Industrial Relations, Bureau of Labor Statistics, U. S. Department of Labor, Washington, D. C., June 5, 1970 (1968 data are latest available).
[9] Merten Estey, *The Unions: Structure, Development, and Management*, New York: Harcourt, Brace & World, Inc., 1967, p. 118.

The Challenge for Business

These trends mean that business will need to relate to organized groups of workers, both union and nonunion, on a variety of new fronts. These trends also mean new challenges for business on the productivity front. Technological change has increased productivity in production industries, and new technologies have enabled a constant or decreasing number of employees to produce more goods. On the whole, little has been done to apply new technology to service industries, although there are notable exceptions. Production of services, in general, remains labor intensive. As workers in the service industries press for higher wages, more fringe benefits, shorter hours, and so forth, business will be challenged to find ways to increase productivity in order to keep prices within reasonable bounds. This problem will be especially challenging where personal services are involved. Areas such as education, government, recreation, and lodging and restaurant businesses will be particularly hard pressed to respond to the challenge.

LABOR PHILOSOPHY AND THE CHANGING ECONOMY

Successful unionism in America in the past has emphasized a "bread and butter" or business approach to union activity. Long experience taught union leaders that little was to be gained by attempts at social reform through political activity. Based on a philosophy of "more and better" and on concepts of business unionism which stressed improvements in wages, hours, and working conditions, labor has made significant gains. The eight-hour day and forty-hour week are common. In some cases labor has been successful in reducing the length of the workweek even further.

Standards of living for American workers are at the highest level in history, and social barriers between blue-collar and white-collar workers are rapidly disappearing. Additionally, the climate of violent warfare between business and labor is rapidly disappearing. To be sure, the public is often painfully aware of conflicts between labor and business, but it fails to consider that approximately ninety-eight percent of labor contracts are negotiated by business and labor peaceably. It is the other two percent that reach public notice.

In view of the economic gains which unions have made for their members, it has been suggested that the labor movement has largely fulfilled its objectives as stated by Samuel Gompers and that its objectives need to be reevaluated in the light of contemporary national social and economic problems. Another point of view suggests that traditional objectives are still the base upon which the labor movement must stand, but that stronger supplemental objectives must be developed.

Need for Change

There is little doubt that the business-labor environment is changing. Demands for increased wages still remain prominent in contract negotiations today, but they are being overshadowed by security issues such as retirement, seniority, job security, negotiated unemployment benefits, and guaranteed hours.[10] However, as unions gain economic and social power, they increasingly find themselves confronted with problems of a much broader nature than heretofore.

Statements have been made by many writers (Paul Jacobs, Sidney Lens, Solomon Barkin, Paul Sultan, and others) that labor is in the middle of a crisis of survival. The main theme advanced by these authors is that the entire labor movement is in danger because it has failed and continues to fail to adjust to new problems and new challenges which confront it. Labor leaders themselves recognize and admit the dilemma they find themselves in today. A survey of thirty-eight union presidents and forty-seven union staff officers indicated that many of them are aware of this crisis and concerned about it.[11] They perceive their main problems to be technology, unemployment, unfriendly legislation, weakness of union structure, increased management power, and unsympathetic public opinion. To these have been added a variety of other problems, such as rank-and-file dissent, civil rights, inflation, and foreign competition.

Quantity or Quality?

The dilemma facing labor today is one of philosophy and ideology, which may well occasion a shift from business unionism to social unionism. Traditionally labor philosophy has been based on considerations of quantity. Increasingly there is need for philosophical revisions which include issues of quality.[12]

Problems facing labor today no longer lend themselves to solution by earlier union methods. Under concepts of business unionism the three major problems of wages, hours, and working conditions were largely autonomous problems which did not necessarily have any relation to one another. They were solved on the basis of individual bargaining between one firm and one local union, and results had little impact elsewhere in the economy. Problems facing unions today are no longer isolated and mutually exclusive. Rather, they are dependent one upon the other and will need to be solved as a series of simultaneous equations. No longer are unions involved with questions which affect only one employer and one local, but with problems whose solutions have significant and widespread impact on the American economy. To complicate the unions' dilemma, the problems confronting labor are also, for the most part, the same problems which are confronting business. They do not lend themselves to solution by militant action and unilateral demands. They are broad social problems of national scope whose solutions depend upon

[10] Millard E. Stone, "Emerging Concepts in Labor Relations," *Personnel*, March–April, 1965, p. 37.
[11] Edward T. Townsend, "Is There a Crisis in the American Trade-union Movement? Yes," in Solomon Barkin and Albert A. Blum (eds.), *The Crisis in the American Trade-union Movement*, Philadelphia: The American Academy of Political and Social Science, *The Annals*, Vol. 350, November, 1963, pp. 16–24.
[12] Albert A. Blum, "Union Prospects and Programs for the 1970's," *Monthly Labor Review*, March, 1970, p. 37.

cooperation between the major social institutions of business, labor, and government.

A different point of view stresses that "unions are not in business to solve the problems of society."[13] Rather unions are in business to meet the needs of members. But even this point of view concedes that needs of workers have moved from those that are entirely quantity-oriented to needs that are substantially qualitative, such as health, leisure, child care, and housing.

Need for New Direction

The new posture of unions, if there is to be one, will not be easily attained. Rather than discard all the old goals and objectives, as some would have unions do, it seems more realistic that they retain them but pursue them within limits set by broader social considerations. At the same time unions need to formulate other objectives and pursue them within the framework of the extensive social responsibilities which they have.

CHALLENGES OF CHANGE

Labor's Image

Union use of tactics and practices which had been declared unlawful for management under the Wagner Act contradicted the public's sense of fair play. Legislative hearings and investigations which exposed corruption and Communist activity within the union movement have also added to public distrust of unions. Furthermore, unions' occasional disregard of leadership control and even of court orders has contributed to a deteriorating image.

High-level labor leaders are becoming increasingly concerned over labor's image and are attempting to do something about it. One major strategy is to get labor representatives, along with business and professional representatives, on committees dealing with overall community problems. There is concerted effort to participate actively in problems dealing with civil rights, medical care, child welfare, urban renewal, education, alcoholism, and drug addiction. The objective is to portray union members and leaders as conscientious citizens, concerned with progress of the entire community and not just with their own selfish demands.

Other top leaders attempt to improve organized labor's image by working to prevent unwise local strike activity. But because they lack direct control over locals, this is not always effective. For example:

Imprudent use of strike power by a local teamsters' union in a large Eastern city drew stiff legal penalties for the union and its leaders. The walkout caused a shortage of food and other products and idled some ten thousand other workers in the city. It ended only after a judge found the

[13] Peter Henle, "Comment on Union Prospects and Programs," *Monthly Labor Review*, March, 1970, p. 38.

local guilty of contempt of court for violating an injunction he had issued earlier barring the strike.

Similarly, the strike of federal postal workers in 1970 did little to bolster public confidence in the responsibility of labor. In violation of a federal anti-strike law covering government employees and with disregard for urging by national leaders that they return to work, postal workers remained off the job, demanding pay increases. These actions created a national emergency so severe that federal troops were assigned to postal duties in several major post offices.

Such disregard for the law contributes to labor's image of arrogance and irresponsibility. Declarations by union leaders in high office that the national union did not sanction the strike do little to improve the image. Similarly, incidents of election rigging have further contributed to the image of corruptness.

Labor's image is the key to many of its other problems. Changing its image will not be easy. Change will come only with demonstrations of responsibility. Instead of being an antagonistic element in the environment of business, it needs to show a spirit of willing cooperation and joint participation in solving common problems. There will always be differences in the viewpoints of business and labor. But as President Lyndon Johnson suggested: "It is possible to disagree without being disagreeable." This phrase is the key to a successful pluralistic society and is at the heart of mature business-labor relations.

Union Organization and Structure

Another problem is union structure. Traditional union structure is no longer adequate in a rapidly changing economy which increasingly depends for its existence on technology and knowledge. Emphasis today needs to be on doing new things—new skills, new knowledge, and new jobs—rather than on doing things the way they used to be done. Craft-union structure with high degrees of "trade autonomy" and "exclusive jurisdiction" is rapidly becoming obsolete, even though unions are slow to meet this challenge. Peter Drucker observed that:[14]

> The craft is obsolete. It is the wrong way to acquire skill. We can no longer afford apprenticeship, either economically or educationally. Skill, to be productive today—in fact, to be "skill" today—has to be based on systematic knowledge. But even if craft skills were still the right skills, craft organization of work would be the wrong organization.

Increasingly in today's modern plants, workers need to be generalists, capable of performing several operations, or at least several parts of the same operation. Because of new technology, jobs are being enlarged and changed, and many workers in today's automated plants need a number of high order skills and the ability to move freely among them. A manager

[14] Peter F. Drucker, *The Age of Discontinuity: Guidelines to Our Changing Society*, New York, Harper & Row, Publishers, Incorporated, 1968, p. 59.

of a Southwestern oil refinery explained his company's requirements this way:[15]

> When we pick a man to do a repair job, we expect him to do it *all*. There's no calling back for an electrician or a plumber while the carpenter sits on his tool box. Not any more.

Craft union preoccupation with protecting job security through maintaining obsolete "jurisdictions" and limiting access to trades through apprenticeship rules has presented many barriers to technical innovation and productivity.

Industrial unions face similar problems of job security. Organized to provide for needs of unskilled workers, some industrial unions have watched their ranks dwindle as mechanization and automation have replaced many unskilled jobs. For example, approximately 125,000 miners now produce more coal than 500,000 did at the end of World War II. Many unskilled workers have not been able to learn new skills or to increase their skills to enable them to perform at higher skill levels. At the same time unions have found it difficult in many cases to attract new-style technicians, craftsmen, and maintenance men.

Upward attrition through job improvement has often been viewed by labor as a deliberate effort by business to weaken unions. Perhaps such charges are justified in some cases, but inability or refusal to modify union structure appears to be the main difficulty. Whatever the case, union frustration often leads to conflict.

Civil Rights

The civil rights problem is a multidimensional problem which affects practically every segment of our pluralistic society, and both business and labor have experienced some difficulties in adjusting to demands of civil rights groups. In 1964 labor was instrumental in having the equal employment opportunity requirement clause included in the Civil Rights Act. Labor viewed the Act as a way of getting some of their local unions to comply with the Federation's own ban on discriminatory membership policies. But even the passage of the Civil Rights Act has not solved labor's problems. Discrimination against membership for members of minority groups has been, and continues to be, particularly troublesome in the highly paid and highly skilled unions. Discriminating unions have been challenged by civil rights groups and particularly by the government. For example:

The Justice Department brought charges of race discrimination against a plumbers' and pipe-fitters' local in Indiana and a steam-fitters' union in California. The suit charged that there were no black persons among the 3,000 members of the steam-fitters' local or among the 400 members of the plumbers' and pipe-fitters' local. Furthermore there were no blacks in either apprenticeship program.

[15] "The Blue Collar Elite," *Dun's Review and Modern Industry*, March, 1964, Special Supplement, p. 122.

On the other hand, labor has made some substantial efforts to help disadvantaged citizens through membership in unions. Organizational activities also have been increasingly successful among low-paid workers in the service industries. Labor, too, in a number of cases has cooperated with business in attempting to find answers to the difficult social problem of recruiting and training hard-core unemployed. But the greatest social challenge to labor is in opening up highly skilled and highly paid jobs to members of minority groups.

TOWARD MORE RESPONSIBLE BARGAINING

Each year businessmen and their employees lose millions of dollars in profits and wages because of work stoppages resulting from labor disputes. Each year society suffers inconvenience and hardship because of these same labor disputes. And each year charges of failure to exercise social responsibility are directed against both labor and business. There will probably always be disagreements between employees and employers because they perceive things from different points of view. Most people accept these disagreements as being natural and healthy in a pluralistic society. It is not the disagreements that are objected to, but the social and economic results of the method by which disputes are settled.

A growing realization that business and labor have much in common has led to an increased awareness by both sides that they have a joint role in the national interest. Strikes today can lead to heavy economic losses for both parties, as well as for the nation, and often bring government into the bargaining process. Few in either management or labor welcome an increased government role in labor relations. This recognition of joint responsibility had led to a search for ways of promoting industrial peace.

Most companies and unions have learned to bargain responsibly. One factor which has contributed to greater labor peace is the realization that bargaining is a day-to-day process, rather than a once-a-year controversy. Negotiations are given more time, and communications between labor and management are much improved. For example:

One large pharmaceutical manufacturer signed a three-year contract with its union-represented employees more than five months before the old contract expired.[16] The reasons given by a company spokesman were ". . . to avoid having to pay for a possible strike, which is very costly, and [it] enables us to pass along savings in the form of a better contract for our workers."

Another factor contributing to more responsible bargaining is that bargaining has become largely professional. The fact that the same men face one another across the bargaining table on many different occasions has led to mutual respect and understanding. Although professionalism is

---

[16] "Squibb Beach-Nut Unit Signs Labor Contract Five Months Early," *Wall Street Journal* (Midwest edition), Nov. 19, 1969, p. 12.

open to some criticism, it has caused better preparation for bargaining, which in turn has led to more responsible action by both sides.

A third factor which has added to industrial peace is that many managements and unions have learned to live together and have found that it is possible to resolve differences without resorting to the economic pressures of a work stoppage. A variety of plans are being formulated which guarantee no strikes or lockouts.

The Kaiser Steel–United Steelworkers plan, started in 1959, was a pioneer in assuring immunity to strikes. In an agreement between management and employees a set of mutually agreeable guarantees were worked out. Management guaranteed to match, without participating in negotiations, any gains that other unions won from "Big Steel." In return the union guaranteed not to strike.

More recently building trades unions agreed with Procter and Gamble and Anheuser-Busch not to strike or otherwise interrupt work on proposed new industrial construction. Disturbed by the possibility that the new plants might be built in another location, St. Louis building trade unions pledged not to strike. The pledge bound the unions to work out peacefully, and before the contracts were let, all jurisdictional problems. It also bound them to handle preassembled equipment.

Not only does the latter kind of agreement go far toward establishing industrial peace, but it also accepts technological innovation and enables a contractor to estimate precisely what his labor costs will be.

There has been a constant search for a formula which will protect the public from the consequences of work stoppages and at the same time preserve the collective bargaining system. And although many ideas have been advanced, no single workable solution has been found. Legislation has been passed which allows the government to participate in settling labor disputes that result in a national emergency. Neither business nor labor is happy with these procedures. There are those who favor compulsory arbitration, but the disadvantages seem to outweigh the advantages. And suggestions have been made that representatives from either government or the public be included in the bargaining process. None of these approaches has met with sufficiently wide approval to make it workable.

One interesting approach to the social problem of work stoppage is the semi-strike in which the public is not injured as a result of disagreement between employees and employers.

In 1960 the Miami Transit Company and its bus drivers experimented in what may have been the first semi-strike.[17] The city buses continued to run even though the drivers were on strike. The two parties agreed that:

1. The public would receive free bus service.
2. The "striking" drivers were to receive no pay and were not to accept any tips.
3. The Miami Transit Company, the employer, would supply the fuel and maintenance required for the buses.

[17] David B. McCalmont, "The Semi-Strike," *Industrial and Labor Relations Review*, January, 1962, p. 191.

Under the agreement, the public was spared loss and inconvenience while the opposing parties to the dispute remained under heavy economic pressure to resolve their differences.

While substantial progress has been made in labor-management relations over the past few years, there is still room for improvement. As mature social institutions, both labor and business have inherited broad social responsibilities whether they want them or not. By subordinating their self-interests to broader social interests and by learning to work together, they will produce the social payoffs expected by a free enterprise society.

LABOR'S PRESSURES ON BUSINESS THROUGH POLITICAL ACTION

Labor philosophy toward political action was well stated in an editorial which appeared in the August, 1908, issue of the *American Federationist.*[18]

> We now call upon the workers of our common country to Stand faithfully by our Friends, Oppose and defeat our enemies, whether they be Candidates for President, For Congress or the other offices, whether Executive, legislative, or judicial.

This philosophy stressed lobbying and the use of labor votes to tip the election balance in favor of friendly candidates. It also stressed avoidance of partisan politics.

Today labor is in a position to influence election results through contributions of money, organization, and votes to favored candidates. What is important is that labor is in politics *as labor* and therefore acts as a countervailing force to political action by business.

Money

The Corrupt Practices Act (discussed earlier) applies to labor just as it does to business. The Act prohibits contribution of dues money of union members to candidates for political office. But voluntary contributions by union members to the AFL-CIO Committee on Political Education (COPE) may be freely used for political purposes. In addition the law does not prohibit the use of dues money for educational purposes such as newspaper, radio, and television advertising directed toward public issues. Thus labor can indirectly back candidates who favor these same issues. In addition, the time and effort of full-time union officials may be devoted to political activity.

On balance, direct monetary contributions to political campaigns by labor are probably considerably less than contributions made by all businessmen. And it is tempting to businessmen to become complacent in this knowledge. What is important to businessmen is that while the num-

[18] Quoted in Mollie Ray Carroll, *Labor and Politics*, Boston: Houghton Mifflin Company, 1923, p. 173. (Capitalization is from quoted source)

ber of union members who refuse to contribute to COPE *when asked* is negligible, *the number of members who are never asked is enormous.*[19]

Organization

Every political campaign needs a large organization of campaign workers to organize and conduct meetings, to distribute campaign literature, to solicit and collect campaign contributions, to increase voter registration, and to ensure that people get to the polls and vote. Organized labor provides a massive pool of potential campaign workers. Thus a favored candidate has at his disposal a potential campaign organization that pro-business candidates are hard pressed to match.

Votes

Is there, in fact, such a phenomenon as a "labor vote"? There is little or no evidence that unions control a large bloc of votes that can be allocated to one party or one candidate. Union members, for the most part, continue to vote their own personal convictions at the polls. But at the same time, votes of union members do become important. Labor has traditionally favored the Democratic party and Democratic candidates. Unions can and do encourage more workers to vote—and to vote Democratic more often than not. Thus the number of union members voting or not voting may have an effect on which party or candidate receives a majority of votes.

What Does the Future Hold?

It seems clear that a labor party will not appear on the American scene in the foreseeable future. It seems equally clear that labor is committed to a policy of organized political action. George Meany, president of the AFL-CIO, stated this policy well when he said:[20]

> The gains labor has made at the collective bargaining table are threatened in the legislative halls of Congress and the State Legislatures. To meet that challenge, effective political activity has of necessity become a vital part of effective trade unionism.

This policy statement, like much collective bargaining activity, seems to be directed toward maintaining the status quo or in applying pressures on business to do something. If labor is to fully live up to its position of a major social institution it will need to revise its policy and mobilize its potential political power toward solutions of problems of a much broader social nature than union security, wages, and working conditions.

[19] Charles H. Rehmus, "Labor in American Politics," in William Haber (ed.), *Labor in a Changing America,* New York: Basic Books, Inc., Publishers, 1966, p. 262.
[20] George Meany, *How to Win: A Handbook for Political Education,* Washington, D.C.: AFL-CIO Committee on Political Education, undated, p. v.

SUMMARY

Traditionally, labor has been an aggressive and militant factor in the environment of business, demanding (and getting) improvements in wages, hours, and working conditions. But as labor has gained strength, many persons have come to believe that it is on the threshold of an expanded role in society. In its new role, labor will need to assume its share of responsibility for national well-being.

To succeed in its new role, labor will need to reassess its philosophy and its structure in terms of the social system of which it is part. Just as businessmen, in many cases, have found it necessary to subordinate their self-interest to national interest, so must labor do the same if a creative interface is to be maintained. There seems to be increasing willingness on the part of both business and labor to solve their problems peacefully within the framework of each other's needs. And both seem increasingly willing to view their problems within the context of national well-being.

STUDY GUIDES FOR INTERPRETATION OF THIS CHAPTER

1 Consult local union leaders in your community to determine the extent of union involvement in finding solutions to community problems. Examples of problems might be school dropouts, poverty, or slum clearance and rehabilitation of cities.

2 From recent newspapers and magazines select and present to your study group an illustration of cooperative effort between business and labor to work out solutions to mutual problems.

3 Discuss the issue of coalition bargaining. Compile a list of advantages and disadvantages of coalition bargaining (a) for unions, (b) for business, and (c) for society.

4 Select for investigation one national labor organization. To what extent is that organization involved in political activity (1) locally, (2) statewide, and (3) nationally?

PROBLEMS
THE SEMI-STRIKE[21]

The Universal Company had a history of moderately successful labor relations. Most contracts had been negotiated without work stoppages, but there had been some strikes. A few of the strikes had been long and costly for all concerned. As the time approached to sign a new contract, it became apparent that several basic issues could not be resolved and that a strike would result.

The following plan was suggested to the company and the union as an alternative to the traditional strike. It was proposed that production and sales be continued just as though no strike had been called. The plan

[21] Adapted from a program outlined in David B. McCalmont, "The Semi-Strike," *Industrial and Labor Relations Review*, January, 1962, p. 192.

called for "striking" workers to forgo one-half their normal wages. A group composed of representatives of management, labor, and the public would determine what the reduction in net earnings for the company would be if a regular strike were to be called, and the company would forgo one-half of this amount until the issues were settled and a new contract was signed.

The plan would be implemented as follows: At the end of each week the company would pay each worker one-half of what he would normally earn. The company would also write one check equal to one half the wages of all workers. At the same time the company would write another check equal to one-half the profits that would have been lost if a strike had been in effect. Both of these checks would then be given to the local school board or the community fund or some other civic organization.

1 What advantages and disadvantages do you see for the different investment groups in this situation?

THE NEW PLANT

The Green Manufacturing Company completed plans for the construction of a new $10 million plant to be located in a Midwestern city on the shore of one of the Great Lakes. New Town Construction Company was the successful bidder on the project, and contracts for construction were signed.

When it became public knowledge that the new plant would discharge large quantities of oil and sludge into the lake, one union in the city declared that its members had voted unanimously to refuse to work on the new plant.

1 What would you do if you were the president of the Green Manufacturing Company?

2 What would you do if you were the president of the New Town Construction Company?

3 Appraise the union action from the point of view of different investment groups affected.

PART FOUR

BUSINESS AND THE COMMUNITY

CHAPTER 16

BUSINESS INVOLVEMENT
IN COMMUNITY ACTIVITIES

Business leadership is more than leadership in business; it entails community responsibilities, often of a high order and expensive to a company.

RICHARD EELLS[1]

One thing seems clear, the corporation cannot occupy the publicly accepted leadership roles of our business-oriented culture in the local community and wash its hands of the responsibility that occupation implies.

NORTON E. LONG[2]

The community discussed in this chapter is an organization's area of local business influence. It often includes more than one political community, for political boundaries do not necessarily follow economic and social boundaries. A major company in a metropolitan area might have as its community the central city and nine satellite cities. Another company might be located in a rural area having three surrounding cities as its community. A public utility has a separate community for each of the local economic areas it serves. In all cases both company and community have a mutual dependence which is significant economically and socially. The following situations show how this mutual relationship is expressed in practice.

Residents in one city prepared to go before the city council to prohibit factory trucks from using streets in a nearby residential neighborhood as a regular thoroughfare. Plant officials responded by rerouting the trucks.

In another city during a coal strike the principal factory supplied two carloads of coal to the local hospital, even though the factory supply of coal was very short. During the same strike a factory manager in another city rejected a civic organization's plea for coal for a recreation hall. He

[1] Richard Eells, "Beyond the Golden Rule," *Columbia Journal of World Business*, July–August, 1967, p. 87.
[2] Norton E. Long, "The Corporation and the Local Community," in Arthur S. Miller (ed.), *The Ethics of Business Enterprise*, Philadelphia: The American Academy of Political and Social Science, *The Annals*, vol. 343, September, 1962, p. 127.

silenced requests with the comment: "Which is more important, to assure work for several thousand men or to continue a recreation program?"

During a local recession in another city, a corporation found it necessary to lay off several hundred women assemblers. After consultation with local leaders, it made an exception to its regular policy of layoff by seniority. Women who proved they were the sole breadwinner in a family were not laid off, regardless of seniority.

Since this chapter is the introductory chapter in a part containing five chapters on "Business and the Community," discussion will be limited to general business involvement with the community. Subsequent chapters will discuss specific areas of involvement such as urban issues and pollution. Following a general introduction covering community relations, this chapter will discuss three ways in which business affects the community. These are involvement of businessmen in civic affairs, business giving, and regular business practice in the community.

COMMUNITY RELATIONS

The involvement of business with the community is called *community relations*. Two characteristics distinguish modern community relations from those 100 years ago. One is *urbanization*. Migration from rural areas to urban centers has changed community life and created new stresses for business and community. This is a worldwide trend, and there is no evidence that it will soon stop. Each census shows a greater proportion of population living in metropolitan areas (central city and suburbs).

The second characteristic is *greater system interdependence* of business and community. Urbanization is a partial cause of interdependence, but so is technology, for it requires communities to become much larger in order to maintain self-sufficiency. Ancient communities could be self-sufficient with a farm and a few artisans. But a modern industrial community needs a college nearby to support lifelong learning, recreational facilities, public utilities, specialized service facilities, urban transportation, capital sources, and a host of other services. Business depends on these services in greater variety than ever before. Just as a rocket can fail because of some tiny malfunction, so can a community experience difficulty because of indirect effects of some isolated event. There is no escaping general community interdependence today. Business cannot remain detached from the community.

Small and Large Businesses Compared

Another feature of community relations, substantially unchanged over the years, is that small companies are vitally involved in setting general community standards. The conduct of home builders, used-car salesmen, and retail proprietors is a significant influence on the business image in a community, regardless of what United States Steel Corporation does at the national level. If these small businessmen let downtown go to seed, take advantage of their customers, and oppose civic improvement, the community climate will be poor. If they take an opposite approach, the climate is likely to be good, regardless of what industrial giants decide to do nationally.

We can speak of the small businessmen as Lincoln spoke of the common people: "God must have loved them because he made so many of them." Approximately ninety-five percent of all business firms have less than twenty employees. Even more startling is the fact that the number of small business firms is increasing faster than the general population. The number of firms per 1,000 persons in the United States increased between 1900 and 1960. A total of 1.6 million firms in 1900 provided twenty-one firms per 1,000 persons. In 1960, 4.7 million firms provided twenty-six firms per 1,000 persons.[3]

In a community there are so many small businessmen that diverse viewpoints may be expected. This fact sometimes stymies unified effort for civic improvement. It is difficult to get them all going in the same direction. But most of all, because they control individually their business practice, their personal ethics are much more involved than is the case with managers in large firms. The large organization makes decisions based on policy, but the small one usually decides according to the proprietor's personal views. As explained by one author: "The family farmer can and will cheat where the vast corporate farmer will not. Altruism is a scarce good, and [large] corporations may help society economize on its use."[4]

On the other hand, the large business has its negative aspects also. Though its business practice may be more consistent, its community interest is frequently more detached. There are two reasons for this detachment. First, the larger firm's sales area usually extends far beyond the community, even though its only office is in the community. In contrast, the small retail or service business depends on the community as its primary market.

Another reason that community detachment develops in large firms is that many of them have decentralized branches. The result is that the firms have an interest in many communities rather than one. Although they have many operational locations, they have only one headquarters where top management can be directly contacted for major support of community projects.[5] Managers in the branches come and go as they move through the promotion ladder of the total organization. It is difficult for them to have the same interest in the community that a small retail proprietor has because their relationship to the community is different. Therefore, their decisions have to be based more on policy than on per-

[3] A. D. H. Kaplan, *Big Enterprise in a Competitive System*, rev. ed., Washington, D.C.: The Brookings Institution, 1964, pp. 62–72.
[4] Paul A. Samuelson, "Personal Freedoms and Economic Freedoms in the Mixed Economy," in Earl F. Cheit (ed.), *The Business Establishment*, New York: John Wiley & Sons, Inc., 1964, p. 207.
[5] Warner reports that two-thirds of the headquarters of the 700 largest corporations are located in the ten largest metropolitan centers. W. Lloyd Warner, *The Corporation in the Emergent American Society*, New York: Harper & Row, Publishers, Incorporated, 1962, p. 27.

sonal interest, and that policy is centrally determined, often without recognition of the peculiar needs of a certain community. This condition places heavy responsibilities on central headquarters to give local managers broad leeway to make community-related decisions. Even when these decisions seem to be exceeding the bounds of policy, there may be justifiable local reasons for them.

Headquarters policies emphasize branch economic performance, usually giving minimum attention to social performance. Branch managers act accordingly, often trying to squeeze out a few more dollars of economic performance while depleting human and community social assets. To avoid this unfortunate tendency, headquarters management has a responsibility to include in its branch appraisal process some measures of social effectiveness and community role. Unless these measures are genuinely valued by headquarters, branch management will be tempted to give them little attention.

Community relations difficulties which branch managements face are shown in a survey of community leaders in three cities.[6] The community leaders were asked whether they thought branch managements were more interested or less interested in the community than local businesses. In each city the majority thought that branch managements were *less* interested in the community as follows:

Far Western city	95%
Eastern city	79%
Midwestern city	57%

However, the study did show that a branch plant could be recognized as an outstanding community citizen if its management was willing to make the effort. In one city, when community leaders were asked to identify businesses which were outstanding community citizens, one branch rated high, but two others rated low as follows:

Branch of large automobile producer	64%
Branch of a heavy equipment manufacturer	14%
Branch of a large electrical equipment manufacturer	7%

This information suggests that branches operate under a handicap compared with local businesses, so they probably have to make a greater effort than local businesses in order to be recognized as an outstanding community citizen.

The decentralized firm has special responsibilities for dealing with community rumor about its operations. Since some of its decisions are made in headquarters, the local operation is a natural subject for rumors, such as "leaving the community" or "won't help," every time a local problem arises.

[6] Opinion Research Corporation, *Community Relations* (*Executive Summary*), April, 1966, p. 6–7.

Following World War II, for example, automobiles were in short supply. Rumors started near an Eastern seaboard branch of an automobile manufacturer that it was withholding automobiles to create an artificial shortage. The rumor was based on the fact that several thousand cars were stored in fields near the branch assembly plant. When the corporation learned of the rumor, it issued news releases explaining that these cars were designed for export, had steering wheels on the wrong side, and were awaiting shipping space. The rumor soon subsided.

Offsetting the personal detachment which branch executives may have is the fact that they do represent additional resources brought to a community from outside. They also can call upon headquarters for specialists to aid in civic planning. They can even call for economic support in special cases, beyond what a local business might be expected to contribute. They bring to communities a high quality of leadership which may be in short supply in depressed localities. Perhaps more important they bring a steady stream of new leaders with fresh ideas. The branch managers have broad experience and a viewpoint far beyond local provincialism. They can expand community horizons and help a community adjust to changing world conditions.

The net balance of all these competing advantages and disadvantages appears to be favorable. Communities usually seek the help of branch executives and use them effectively. The possibility of transfer during a term of civic service is usually ignored. After all, small businessmen leave communities too.

The Pittsburgh Experience

An early example of business initiative in a major community development was the Pittsburgh Renaissance.[7] Located in a soft-coal area and having much heavy industry, Pittsburgh, Pennsylvania, has always been smoky and dirty. As early as 1840 Charles Dickens called it "hell with the lid off." Even in the 1940s lights sometimes had to be burned at midday because of the pall of smoke that obscured the city. The city came out of World War II with a bleak outlook. It had smoke, dirt, and few civic improvements. Urban blight had overcome its downtown Golden Triangle. Vigorous younger people were beginning to move elsewhere.

In this depressing situation, a group of business leaders formed the Allegheny Conference on Community Development to initiate a bold improvement program. Their first effort was smoke control because the smoke was destroying beauty and lowering morale in the community. In determining to control smoke, businessmen were in effect deciding to control *themselves* as well as homeowners with soft-coal heating systems. Working closely with local government, they overcame vigorous opposition from homeowners, politicians, and those within their own ranks. Through

[7] Edward C. Bursk, "Your Company and Your Community: The Lesson of Pittsburgh," in Dan H. Fenn, Jr. (ed.), *Business Responsibility in Action*, New York: McGraw-Hill Book Company, 1960, pp. 29–54.

smoke-control ordinances and voluntary effort, smoke was eventually reduced 90 percent.

With this victory the group tackled the Golden Triangle to convert it from a slum to a community showcase. One large improvement required nine major companies to sign twenty-year leases for space before ground could be broken. Since only the top executive in a firm could make this kind of decision, Pittsburgh was fortunate to have home offices of a number of major corporations. There was also opposition to the Golden Triangle project. Legal battles about some improvements were carried eventually to the United States Supreme Court. Finally, however, the Golden Triangle was rebuilt into a beautiful area. Although the primary objective of the Allegheny Conference was economic rejuvenation, cultural improvements followed once the morale of the city was restored. The conclusion from the Pittsburgh experience is that business-government-citizen cooperation can restore blighted communities. In Pittsburgh the initiative came from business; in other cities initiative might arise elsewhere.

Community Responsibilities to Business

In the business-community relationship we cannot ignore the responsibility of community to business. If citizens, labor, and government abuse business or take advantage of it, then cooperation for improvement becomes more difficult. As stated by one businessman: "It's difficult to cooperate with a community which discriminates by taxing business property at one rate and other property at a cheaper rate." A retailer added: "Business should be friendly and courteous, but what about the customers? Some are so suspicious and irritable that no one likes to serve them." A manager of a used-car firm spoke up: "You should see the 'lemons' the customers trade to me without revealing defects. I could sue some of them for fraud, but what would that do to my business?" A grocery store proprietor added: "I accidentally caught one of my regular customers putting butter in a margarine box in order to cheat me of a few pennies." If a business relationship is to be viable, then mutual responsibilities are required.

BUSINESSMEN IN CIVIC AFFAIRS

In a pluralistic society, multiallegiant man has interests in many organizations. The businessman is no exception. Two of his allegiances are to his business and to his community. It is difficult to generalize about either allegiance because there are perhaps as many varieties as there are businessmen. Some businessmen were born and reared in their community. Others moved to their community when they graduated from college. Others may be transients merely seeking to make a "fast buck" and move on. Still others are young corporate experts more interested in their profession than in their community or company.

As with all pluralism, conflicts of allegiance sometimes develop. As a representative of the corporation, the businessman must be detached and objective about community demands. But as a family man and a member of social groups within the community, he is also intimately tied to community affairs. As described by a political scientist: "The corporate manager, like many other powerholders in history, is asked to serve two masters—the corporation and the local community. The service is difficult." Also the manager is an "implicit servant of the national and general economy," further dividing his responsibilities.[8]

Community Activities

Managers do not seem to shirk participation in civic affairs simply because conflict of allegiance may arise. Used to resolving conflict in organizational affairs, they feel at home in a similar civic environment. Nearly every museum board, development committee, or other civic group has business managers well represented among its members.

One survey of 129 top managers reported that 80 percent played a responsible role in civic affairs. Nearly all of them used company facilities such as business machines and secretarial service in their civic work, and they permitted their employees to do likewise. For 44 percent of the executives, public service was time-consuming enough to intrude on the time they devoted to their businesses. Others admitted that their civic work intruded on their family life. Regardless of time intrusion, they continued their civic services because they believed it is a responsibility of good citizenship. Many of those whose businesses sold primarily to the local market also believed that public service improved their business.[9]

Another survey covered members of a management-oriented professional group in one city. Most of these men were middle managers. *All respondents* reported some involvement in community service work both during their regular working day and after work hours. The most involvement was in civic groups (such as a Rotary Club), service groups (such as Boy Scouts of America), and charitable groups (both religious and nonreligious). Moderate involvement was in cultural activities, and minimum involvement was in political-governmental activities.[10]

Reasons for Community Involvement of Managers

Many managers become involved in community service because their company encourages them to do so, but the research just mentioned suggests that managers also have strong personal drives to serve their community. As human beings they have the normal altruistic drives which most other people have. They also relate to their families, desiring the community to be a better place for them to live.

Perhaps a more complex reason for community service work is that its satisfactions are of a different psychological nature from those derived in employment. The reward is more immediate than the indirect feeling of service derived from productive work as an employee. Also the reward

[8] Long, *op. cit.*, p. 127.
[9] "Top Management and Public Service Activities: A Survey," *Management Review*, December, 1964, pp. 45–47.
[10] Keith Davis and Frank H. Besnette, "Management's Obligation to Public Service Activities," *Advanced Management Journal*, April, 1969, pp. 33–39.

more directly relates to one's immediate neighbors, instead of an unknown and distant consumer public. Furthermore, in public service work, the person gives his time and talent without direct "cost" to the organization served. He does receive "compensation" in the form of personal satisfactions, as all persons in public service must do in order to be motivated to participate, but his compensation is of an intangible nature which does not require a major "give up" from the organization. His "costless" reward means that he can feel he has unselfishly given, whereas in employment he knows he is a direct cost to his employer and must render services at least equal to his cost in order for his employer to break even in the exchange. There is, therefore, a feeling of less risk of loss in public service work; that is, less chance that one will contribute less than his cost and thus create a net social loss. This low-risk and high-reward relationship in public service work is undoubtedly one of the reasons many people are turning to it as an outlet for their excess time and energy.

Community Involvement Can Be Rewarding to Business

There is also the probability that community involvement will bring benefits to the business itself. There are, of course, the usual worries that active community participation will cause a business to lose customers when it is associated with a project which certain customers oppose. This does occur, but wise community leadership can also gain customers and goodwill. Limited research suggests that the key to community relations success is genuine *involvement,* as distinguished from more traditional approaches such as making charitable contributions and being a good employer. These more traditional activities are now expected from any business, so the business which wants outstanding recognition will need to become directly involved in current issues such as pollution, education, transportation, and crime. The outstanding company makes a commitment to improving the quality of life in the community.

Opinion Research Corporation surveys show that both the general public and community leaders rate a company outstanding primarily because of its participation in local affairs. "Participation" means business leadership, expertise, and cooperation in solving problems, not passive financial aid. In two cities the main reasons for rating a company outstanding were as follows:

	COMMUNITY LEADERS (EASTERN CITY)	GENERAL PUBLIC (SOUTHERN CITY)
Participation in local affairs	67%	48%
Financial contributions	41%	23%
Good employee relations	20%	5%

In both surveys "participation in local affairs" was mentioned more times than the next two reasons combined.[11]

[11] Al Vogel, "Urban Crisis: New Focus for Community Relations," *Public Relations Journal,* September, 1967, pp. 12–13.

Another study covering ninety-seven small businesses reported that those "organizations whose managers are actively involved in community affairs are also those that are most profitable for the owner." This correlation of community participation and profit was significant to the .01 degree of confidence.[12]

Community Power Structure

In their activities businessmen become part of the community power structure. Power is not in the man himself, but flows from the role he plays in the social system. It is dynamic and cannot be viewed apart from the community itself. If a businessman moves to another community, he is in a new system, and his power does not transfer. In fact, within the community the power structure varies with the problem being considered.

In a New York town having about six thousand persons, five major community decisions were studied. Thirty-six leaders were involved, but twenty-two of them participated in only one of the five decisions. Only eight leaders were involved in two decisions; only four were involved in three decisions; only two were involved in four decisions; and no leader was involved in all five decisions. Businessmen's participation depended on the subject being considered. Flood control and the municipal building were determined by political leaders, and specialists determined the school bond issue. Decisions on the new hospital and new industry were dominated by businessmen.[13]

Evidence supports the general conclusion that there is no standard power structure in communities. Power varies depending on hundreds of factors, such as community history, degree of industrialization, and type of problem being considered. Businessmen do participate in the total power structure, but not necessarily in every major civic decision. Usually businessmen are influential, and they also may dominate. Some investigators believe that businessmen frequently dominate decisions. On the other hand, one investigator concluded that politicians actually initiated policy choices and that businessmen merely rubber-stamped them after decisions were made.[14]

Of special interest is the manner in which labor leaders view the community activities of businessmen. A study of Lansing, Michigan, an industrial city, showed that labor leaders felt that businessmen dominated community decision making as a whole. However, when labor leaders named the ten persons they thought most influential in the community, they named only four businessmen. Only one of these, a newspaper pub-

[12] Frank Friedlander and Hal Pickle, "Components of Effectiveness in Small Organizations," Administrative Science Quarterly, September, 1968, pp. 289–304.
[13] Robert Presthus, Men at the Top: A Study in Community Power, Fair Lawn, N.J.: Oxford University Press, 1964, pp. 92–100. Somewhat similar results are reported in Endsley Terrence Jones, "The Businessman and Small City Problems: What They're Doing, Not Doing, and Why," Michigan Business Review, November, 1968, pp. 18–23.
[14] Charles M. Bonjean and David M. Olson, "Community Leadership: Directions of Research," Administrative Science Quarterly, December, 1964, pp. 278–300. This article provides an excellent summary of the literature. Comparative studies cited in the article show that two Mexican cities and one British city were less influenced by businessmen than were ten United States cities.

lisher, was in the top five; therefore, the labor leaders' selections did not support their general conclusion of business domination. Others in the top five were the mayor, a Catholic bishop, the superintendent of public schools, and the president of the Labor Council. Labor leaders generally but not wholly supported the idea that businessmen are ". . . interested, hard-working citizens who act openly and responsibly for the good of the community."[15]

Viewed as a whole, businessmen are men of power and status in the United States, but they are not an exclusive group dominating community decisions. They tend to be extroverted leaders willing to enter into affairs of the community, especially where business interests are involved. Effects have been both negative and positive. There has been interference and occasional autocratic control. On the other hand, communities have in this way gained the assistance of some of society's most competent leaders.

BUSINESS GIVING

Specific areas of giving, such as gifts to education and art, are discussed in the appropriate functional chapters. This section focuses on the general concept of business giving in the community. Since 1936 the federal government, through its income tax law, has encouraged corporate giving for educational, charitable, scientific, and religious purposes. Corporations are allowed to deduct contributions which do not exceed 5 percent of their taxable income.[16] If this deduction were not allowed, corporations would have to pay taxes and then give gifts from the residue of net income, thus requiring them to earn about $2 in order to have $1 to give away.

Average corporate giving exceeds 1 percent of net income before taxes. A number of businesses, especially larger ones, have established foundations to handle their contributions. This approach permits them to administer their giving program more uniformly and objectively. It also provides a central group which handles all requests. This procedure is usually not used for minor local contributions in order to avoid red tape and permit some local autonomy.

Reasons for Business Giving

There are several rationalizations to support business giving. Business giving is frequently justified as an *investment* which benefits the business in the long run by improving the community, its labor force, the climate for business, or other conditions affecting a particular business. A gift to a hospital building fund is rationalized in this way because it should create better health in the community. Gifts for education are viewed as

[15] William H. Form and Warren L. Sauer, "Labor and Community Influentials: A Comparative Study of Participation and Imagery," *Industrial and Labor Relations Review,* October, 1963, pp. 18–19.
[16] Gifts given by business partnerships or proprietorships are governed by individual income tax laws.

improving the labor market or expanding the economy, thereby increasing a firm's potential market.

Another basis for giving gifts is to consider routine local ones as an *operating expense of doing business*. Gifts of this type are often thought to provide public relations or advertising returns and are treated like any other public relations expense. Examples are gifts of money to a local charity or literature to a high school.

Both the investment and the expense philosophies are directly related to business objectives. Some of these gifts can be rationalized as supporting profit in the long run, if not in the short run. Others, such as general aid to education outside the plant community, have no direct connection with profit, but they are relevant indirectly because they affect the general economic and social climate of business.

A third philosophy assumes that a corporation is a citizen of the community as a person is, except that it has greater resources than most citizens. As a citizen it has a duty to support *philanthropy* without regard to its self-interest in the same way that a private person does. This approach can open a Pandora's Box of giving. Unless it is governed by carefully formed policies, it may bind the corporation to support requests without careful screening simply because it has no policy reason to say "no." Since the corporation has money in the bank and philanthropy is one of the noblest qualities of civilized man, how can it refuse its needy brother? This kind of reasoning can lead to imprudent waste of funds in the trusteeship of management and thus be irresponsible action rather than a display of responsibility. A number of observers consider this philosophy dangerous for a corporation;[17] yet, it undoubtedly is a philosophy which influences business giving. As we have said before, businessmen are human and are likely to act that way. They do feel concern for their community and are partly motivated by philanthropic ideals.

Another assumption is that some corporate gifts take on the characteristics of *taxes*. Since it is the prevailing opinion that corporations should be good citizens, helpful neighbors, and human institutions, the community comes close to imposing some types of gift giving on the corporation as a kind of informal taxation. The gifts are a cost of doing business. They are given to retain public approval for the business.

Regardless of whether gifts are viewed as an investment, an expense, a philanthropy, or a tax, most of their costs are probably passed on to consumers, because giving in the long run becomes a cost of doing business. If this view is valid, then the fifth reason is that business is acting partly as agent and *trustee* for the community, receiving funds and distributing them according to community needs.

Policies for Giving

Any business which makes contributions needs a carefully thought-out policy for its actions. If a business lacks a carefully developed policy,

[17] A strong statement of the dangers is given by Richard Eells, "Corporate Giving: Theory and Policy," *California Management Review*, Fall, 1958, pp. 37–46.

there is danger that an aggressive minority of gift seekers will get most of the available funds, leaving an unbalanced company gift program and an unbalanced community.

Most firms concentrate their giving in selected areas in order to make an impact with a substantial gift, rather than spreading their resources thinly. Furthermore, there are several areas where businesses either do not give or exercise great care in giving. Law prohibits political contributions. Companies usually do not give to religious groups, because they believe religion is an individual choice for owners, employees, and others. (They may, however, give to religious-oriented groups such as the Salvation Army or to community projects with religious groups among their sponsors.) Some firms avoid gifts to groups with limited membership such as veterans' organizations and fraternal societies. Others confine their giving to their market territory or the community where their facilities are located. Each firm's policies are different, based upon its own perceptions of needs and social responsibilities.

Business giving has become an integral part of modern society. In a pluralistic society, giving is an effective way to support other free institutions such as private education and local charity. Without this support, the local initiative and voluntary action which characterize communities might collapse. This situation would surely endanger pluralism and lead to concentrations of power which might in turn threaten free business institutions.

BUSINESS PRACTICES IN COMMUNITIES

Business practice has direct, significant effects on the community. These are not the effects of giving gifts or of volunteering time, but are the result of the way business conducts itself in the ordinary course of operations. Does business, for example, cause stream and air pollution? Are its plants an aesthetic asset or a blight? Do its policies encourage unfair competition and business conflict?

Community Influence of Large Firms

It is evident that the day-to-day activities of many different firms help establish a climate of friendliness, distrust, or other characteristics in a community, but dominance by one or two large firms can have even greater effects. In this instance the success of a community is inevitably tied to that of its major business firm. When the business employs skilled and professional workers, the community has better-educated citizens, higher-quality homes and shopping centers, and a richer residential tax base. However, the situation is reversed when most of the employees are unskilled. In this case the social cleavage between management and workers, and between rich and poor in the community, may be more severe.

In a similar manner, if the business prospers economically, the community usually prospers, but the reverse can also occur. When Studebaker ceased making automobiles in South Bend, Indiana, that community was set back economically for years. This situation was recognized by management, which worked closely with the community to encourage other companies to move into the sprawling Studebaker plant in order to maintain employment. In the long run, the adjustment actually was desirable because South Bend became less dependent on one business.

Although dominant firms can hurt a community by leaving it or letting it deteriorate, these same firms can help in many ways. Their staff consultants and economic resources are especially helpful with community projects that are business-related, such as a downtown improvement study. Usually these efforts are justified under an investment philosophy because they promise long-run business benefits along with community improvement. Even in the days of rampant business individualism business investments of this type were made, such as in the following example.

In the early 1900s, Birmingham, Alabama, was menaced by serious health problems. Malaria, typhoid fever, and other diseases were prevalent because of unsanitary community conditions. This city was the site of a United States Steel subsidiary, Tennessee Coal and Iron Company, whose productivity was lowered by illness. Tennessee Coal and Iron organized a health department and hired a prominent specialist in the offending diseases from the Panama Canal Zone. In its first year of operation the health department spent $750,000 for draining swamps and improving sanitary facilities. This amount was thirty times the total health budget of the *entire state* of Alabama.[18]

Large business indirectly helps local communities by solving nationwide problems in which there is local involvement. Figure 16–1 shows the company announcement of an electronic breakthrough in controlling obscene telephone calls. This problem had caused much emotional suffering, invaded privacy of the home, and frustrated local citizen and police efforts to control it. Local and federal laws had failed to produce results, but a company research effort and equipment installation did get results. Furthermore, results were accomplished in a way which retained privacy of normal telephone conversations.

Easy-open beverage cans provide an example of group cooperation to deal with community problems caused by misuse of business by-products. Shortly after these cans were introduced, many communities discovered that the ring-pulls were being used as counterfeit coins in parking meters. Since parking meters could not be economically modified, municipalities appealed to can manufacturers, and the two groups worked together with parking meter manufacturers to design new ring pulls which would not work in parking meters.

Large Business in Small Communities

Whenever large companies operate in suburban communities or small towns, they play a substantial role in community life. Early in industrial

---

[18] Roger M. Blough, *Golden Anniversary*, New York: United States Steel Corporation, 1957, p. 14.

A warning to people who make obscene phone calls.

You're sick. Not clever, but sick.

Because the calls you make aren't jokes. They're crimes. By local law and now, by Federal law.

Congress has just recently passed a bill that can fine you and send you to prison for 6 months if you're caught and convicted.

And you will be. Because now the odds are on our side, not yours.

We can say that because as General Telephone—the second largest telephone operating company in the country—we know what's being done about you.

Although we don't have it throughout our entire system yet, today's special telephone equipment can not only trace back and identify your phone from the receiving party's end; it can also identify any number you call from your end.

And don't think you can beat it by keeping your call short, either.

Because it can also prevent you from disconnecting. As long as the party you call doesn't hang up, the line will remain open. No matter what you do.

And while they keep the line open, they can make another call. To us.

Then there's the work being done on the voice print—an electronic picture of the human voice.

If yours is taken, it's as good as getting your fingerprints. That's how distinctive your voice is. No matter how good you are at disguising it.

And if all that isn't enough to stop you, remember this the next time you get the urge to call:

We haven't told you everything.

General Telephone & Electronics

Figure 16–1 Company announcement of a useful device for protecting privacy of the home. Source: *Life,* May 23, 1969, p. 24. Used with permission.

history many of these communities became virtual company towns, with the employer owning retail stores, the water system, and other public services. Historians have presented the difficulties with this kind of community. Primarily pluralism does not develop, and control becomes monolithic. There is dissatisfaction of all parties involved, regardless of their good intentions. Modern companies face the same need for a complete community that their ancestors did, but they are taking a more sophisticated approach toward getting it. Usually they initiate long-range planning and coordinate it with public authorities, but they leave development to others. They own and control nothing in the community but their plant. Nevertheless, citizen concern about influence and dominance remains.

In 1964, a giant paper firm which had a lumber mill in a town of less than three thousand people decided to build an adjoining $35 million paper mill. The new mill added several hundred workers and changed the community in a number of ways. New community construction included a motel where visiting headquarters managers could stay, a shopping center, and a 200-lot real estate subdivision. Since paper mill work was new in the area, the company brought in twenty-five management men from company mills in the South. Other workers came from elsewhere, so it became easier to buy regional foods such as okra and grits in stores. The community's mix of religious faiths changed, and new power alignments developed. The paper mill required a new group of skilled workers who earned more than lumber mill workers, so bickering arose about the lumber workers being "poor second cousins."

Most citizens agreed that the company brought new resources and leadership to the community, plus much more economic stability. However, there was uneasiness about the town's dependence on a company with headquarters far away in New York. Meanwhile company management carefully tried to avoid interfering in community affairs in order to prevent a charge of "company town" or company control. Some persons felt the firm should take a more active part in community affairs, but others preferred the existing situation.[19]

Self-policing by Community Business

In direct transactions with customers a fraudulent operator, "con man," or gyp may quickly harm the community image of business. There may also be honest misunderstandings about transactions in which mediation will help. An effective organization for meeting these needs is the local Better Business Bureau.

Better Business Bureaus are nonprofit, public-service organizations created by private business for self-regulation. There are Better Business Bureaus in most metropolitan areas of the United States. There are also Bureaus in Mexico, Canada, and other nations, indicating a gradual international expansion of self-regulation. In the words of President John F. Kennedy:[20]

> By serving the public as a clearing house of factual information about business practices affecting the consumer, the Better Business Bureaus throughout the country effectively express the business community's sense of responsibility for high ethical standards and integrity, in trade practices and business-consumer relations.

The unique and effective idea of Better Business Bureaus is that they reach the customer directly, receiving his complaints and inquiries. There is no charge and no disclosure of names. This approach gives customers confidence that business genuinely seeks fair business practice and will

[19] William McAllister, "International Paper Co. Brings Wealth, Strains to Small Oregon Town," *Wall Street Journal*, Oct. 9, 1968, pp. 1, 19.
[20] *Facts You Should Know about Your Better Business Bureau*, New York: Better Business Bureau, Educational Division, undated, p. 16. Other data presented are from this pamphlet and other publications of the National Association of Better Business Bureaus.

aid customers in exposing rackets and gyps. The bureaus are well used, as shown by the fact that they receive several million inquiries annually. They investigate inquiries or complaints and make factual reports to the inquirer. They also bring any illegal action to the attention of law-enforcement groups. When an unfair or misleading practice is encountered, they try to discourage it, even using paid newspaper advertising to warn the public.

The Better Business Bureau approach to self-regulation does not stop all shady business practice, but it has been effective in discouraging practices of this type, and it should continue to expand internationally. It is one more step toward the maturity of business in working with the community.

SUMMARY

The community is an organization's area of local influence, rather than the political unit in which an organization is located. As a possessor of community social power, a business cannot remain aloof from its community responsibilities. Small and large businesses, local and national, all affect their communities, but in different ways. Businessmen are an active group in the community power structure, but are not necessarily the leading power group. Businessmen primarily affect their community through active involvement in civic affairs, business gifts, and business practice in the community.

STUDY GUIDES FOR INTERPRETATION OF THIS CHAPTER

1 In a complex world of big business and frequent mergers, how do you explain the increase in number of firms per 1,000 persons from twenty-one in 1900 to twenty-six in 1960?

2 Discuss from a stockholder's point of view the different philosophies for business giving. Then give your discussion from a community citizen's point of view.

3 One of the two accountants in your small business has asked for a two-hour lunch period once a week so that he can join and attend a Rotary Club. What would be your response and why?

4 Dustin Tower, a plumbing wholesaler in a town of 100,000 persons, claims that the community is giving all its efforts to attracting new large businesses headquartered elsewhere. He wants effort redirected to attract regional and small businesses "which would keep their profits here and would have more growth potential." He wants to organize a group to accomplish this objective. As a small businessman how would you respond to his idea?

5 Have you ever used a Better Business Bureau? Survey a sample of citizens and offer your opinion of how effective Better Business Bureaus are.

PROBLEMS
GIVING TO THE UNITED FUND

The president of a large local firm employing thousands of workers had a major responsibility in the industrial division of the community's annual United Fund charity campaign. During the campaign he sent a memorandum to each employee through company mail. The letter pointed out that last year employees of a major competitor in town gave an average donation of $1.00 monthly, which was nearly twice as large as his firm's employees gave. He concluded his letter with the following statement:

> We never have, in this corporation, demanded a gift from any employee, and I hope we never shall. However, I personally shall be greatly disappointed if our employees cannot afford an average gift of $1 per month to help alleviate some of the human suffering that exists in this community we all call home.

Upon receipt of the letter a number of employees complained that it was improper use of company power to coerce employee giving in order to make the company's community record look good.

1 Comment on the letter and the employee response mentioned.

THE GENTLEMEN'S AGREEMENT

In an Eastern state only one of its sixty-seven counties levied a property tax against industrial machinery. In order to place all counties on an equal footing for securing new industry, the state legislature in 1957 repealed the tax. To make the adjustment easier the legislature reduced the tax 20 percent annually for the following five years. County and municipal officials said that public schools and other services would be disastrously affected because this tax provided about fifty percent of their revenue. They pleaded for help from major corporate taxpayers in the county. Finally corporate officials made a gentleman's agreement that they would continue paying taxes on all existing machinery, but not new machinery, even though it was clearly understood that they were not legally liable for further taxes beyond five years on existing machinery. As stated by the president of one of the nation's top 100 firms, his company recognized ". . . that the sudden withdrawal of these very large revenues would cause a financial crisis for the taxpayers, the councils, and school districts."

About a decade later, in 1967, a stockholder filed suit for $29 million against one of the companies and its directors alleging that they had illegally paid that amount in accordance with the gentlemen's agreement. A Chancery Court then issued an order seizing all shares of company stock held by sixteen directors named in the suit. If this case did succeed, many other companies would be subject to suits for tens of millions of dollars. The plants of a large number of these firms served national markets rather than local ones.[21]

1 Bypassing legal issues, thoroughly appraise in terms of social responsibility and pluralism the management decision represented by the gentlemen's agreement.

2 Discuss which philosophy of business giving probably dominated management thinking in this case.

[21] *Public Affairs Review,* Jan. 23, 1968, pp. 2–3.

CHAPTER 17

THE URBAN COMMUNITY AND
LESS-ADVANTAGED CITIZENS

What is certain is that in the way we conceive of
our cities, and meet their challenges, we are determining for better or worse the next chapter of
man's adventure on this planet.

AUGUST HECKSCHER[1]

But many of us feel that business and businessmen, more than any element outside of government itself, hold the key to solving our great urban
problems.

MAX M. FISHER[2]

Businessmen throughout the corporate community are becoming more
and more convinced that they should play a role in helping to solve the
urban crisis which includes physical problems of the cities as well as
problems concerning less-advantaged citizens. But many are uncertain as
to what that role should be or how extensively involved business should
become.

One businessman argued that business efforts should be confined to one-
time, short-term efforts directed exclusively toward the solution of a specifically identified problem. Business should, for example, make a one-
time maximum effort to solve the ghetto problem.

Another businessman said that while business contributions to solving
city problems inevitably reduce profits in the short run, these same
contributions will increase profits in the long run. Indeed, such contributions now may ensure that there is a profit system in the future.

Still another businessman observed that being involved in urban problems was good for his company because it brought him in contact with
people he might not otherwise meet and thereby gave him the opportunity
to sell more of his company's product.

[1] August Heckscher, "The City: Work of Art and Technology," in Brian J. L. Berry and
Jack Meltzer (eds.), Goals for Urban America, Englewood Cliffs, N.J.: Prentice-Hall,
Inc., 1967, p. 21.
[2] Max M. Fisher, "Managing for Progress in the 70's: The Urban Crisis," Transacta:
Michigan State University Business Alumni Magazine, Winter, 1970, p. 7.

All of the above observations are probably correct *from the limited point of view* of those making them. The problem is that these men probably all perceived the proper role of business to be philanthropic. But business has much more to offer and much more to contribute than money.

Some others believe that the proper way to solve urban problems is to turn the whole thing over to business and let it define the problems, set the objectives, and implement the solutions.

But this view is as unrealistic as the opposite extreme mentioned above. One critic of business commented that:[3] "Satisfying social needs and making money are two distinct and often antagonistic undertakings"; and that businessmen should not play the dominant role in aid to the cities because "whatever other qualifications they may have, businessmen are not competent to design a new civilization"—and "have no democratic right to do so."

It is reasonable to contend that business should not play the dominant role in solving urban problems. But this is different from saying that business should play one of the major roles. In our complex pluralistic system there are many problems that will require concerted and cooperative attention of all major social institutions. If problems are to be defined, objectives formulated, and solutions implemented, no single major social institution has the capabilities to carry out fully the whole job. It is even doubtful whether any single major social institution has the capabilities to perform one of these functions by itself.

Therefore, it seems apparent that if our national social problems are to be solved, all social institutions must participate cooperatively and collectively. This means that government, business, and labor (as three major institutions) must find ways to work together which capitalize on the strengths of each.

It does not necessarily follow that ". . . satisfying social needs and making money are two . . . antagonistic undertakings." On the contrary, utilizing the strengths of each major institution in the right way, at the right time, and in the right combinations will produce gains for all in an expanding and rapidly changing social system. And certainly the social payoffs for society should be tremendous. The contributions of business must be much greater than mere financial donations. What is needed is a commitment to improving the quality of urban life. Business is the principal institution that has the managerial, innovative, and technical capabilities to respond to the challenges and solve the urban problems defined by society. And it can do these things within the framework of the existing system.

In this chapter we will discuss the role of business as it relates to the problems of urban deterioration and urban sprawl, and the goals of rebuilding cities and adapting to expanding population.

[3] Michael Harrington, *Toward a Democratic Left,* quoted in Robert C. Albrook, "Business Wrestles with Its Social Conscience," *Fortune,* August, 1968, p. 90.

URBAN SPRAWL

The city is one of man's greatest achievements. It has now become one of his greatest challenges. One observer has commented, "It is to a large extent ungovernable, uninhabitable, and unamiable."[4] But the city is not likely to disappear. Rather, there is every indication that the city of tomorrow will be larger and more complex. What has happened is that growth has occurred in concentric rings which encircle the city, leaving at the center an island which is isolated politically and culturally from the rest of the metropolitan area.

Causes

There has always been a tendency for the most affluent people to move to the outskirts of the city where they could enjoy less congestion, more private space, and cleaner surroundings. Increasing affluence in America has enabled the large middle class also to desert the congestion of the cities for the amenities of the suburbs. The rapid growth of population along with rising prosperity has created suburb after suburb which has resulted in urban sprawl.

Business, too, has followed somewhat the same pattern. Anxious to escape the stultifying effects of city traffic, to enjoy lower taxes, or to move closer to adequate labor supplies, or for other reasons, many businesses have deserted the cities. Thus sometimes business has led and sometimes business has followed the exodus from the cities.

A national manufacturer of consumer goods had grown from a small company to one of the major corporations of America. Many of the component parts of its final product were purchased from other manufacturers. Other component parts were manufactured by the firm itself. The company had grown and prospered in a large Eastern city.

The company was faced with a major decision concerning plant expansion and modernization. The complex of buildings which it occupied was old and needed major renovation. Additional space was also required, and the property surrounding the plant was extremely high priced.

The president had obtained an option for the company on a large piece of vacant property several miles outside the city and urged the board of directors to build a new plant on that property. He argued that:

1. The entire tract would cost little more than obtaining additional property at the present location.
2. Building a new plant would be no more expensive in the long run than modernizing existing facilities.
3. Taxes would be less on the new facilities.
4. Since the new property was close to two major highways, trucks could have easy and quick access to the plant, thus eliminating many difficulties now experienced in shipping and receiving by truck.

[4] Heckscher, op. cit., p. 14.

5. There would be little difficulty in obtaining a rail spur from the nearby railroad.
6. Many employees presently commuted from the suburbs. They could move to a small city near the new location. Or if they chose not to move, they could commute to the new location.
7. The new plant could be architecturally in keeping with the countryside and the grounds could be well landscaped, thus adding to the beauty of the area and satisfaction of employees.
8. There was an ample supply of labor in the small communities near the new site.

How would you evaluate the president's arguments?

Results

Movement to suburbia has had two major results. First, movement of population away from cities has created an inner core whose major characteristics are different from anything we have experienced. This will be discussed more fully in a later section. But it is important to note here that the inner city has changed character—a busy and bustling thing by day, and an empty shell by night.

Second, suburbanization has created rings of "outer cities" around the central core. As these outer cities have aged, they are beginning to experience the same problems as the central core, that is, traffic congestion, air and water pollution, poverty, slums, crime, and physical deterioration.

URBAN DETERIORATION

From a sociological viewpoint, cities have changed from places to work and live to places only to work during the day. City streets during the day are crowded with people and traffic snarls, and buildings teem with activity. At night those same streets and buildings are nearly deserted. Proportionately, few people live in cities *by choice*. Those who have "made it" move out, leaving behind those who have not. Those who remain in the cities are usually the most recent immigrants.[5] They are usually poor, have less education, and are unskilled.

At the same time, businesses that have remained in the cities or move to them require many employees with rather high skills. Most people having the required skills live in the suburbs, thus creating a daytime commuting population that depends on the city for a great number of services, but they make little contribution to maintaining those services.

The urban crisis is not exclusively the fault of business, as some would like to believe. Rather, the crisis is a result of a number of socioeconomic factors. However, business has contributed (in most cases passively) to a number of urban problems, although at the same time it often tries to help solve these problems. In this section we will mention some of the problems and some of the ways that business contributes to these prob-

[5] For a discussion see Irving Kristol, "The Negro Today Is Like the Immigrant of Yesterday," in Nathan Glazer (ed.), *Cities in Trouble*, Chicago, Ill.: Quadrangle Books, Inc., 1970, pp. 139–157.

lems. In the next section we will discuss business involvement in solutions to some of these problems.

Transportation

Over sixty percent of our population lives in metropolitan areas. The convenience, productivity, and income of these people depend on systems for moving in and around the cities. Yet, cities have been unable to correct the inadequacies of their transportation systems.

The two major problems of urban transportation are handling the rush of commuters to and from the city and providing the proper land use to accommodate needs of transportation systems. Most urban transportation facilities—rapid transit railways, public intracity transportation, and highways—are subject to maximum use only during the peak hours at the beginning and the end of the workday. Operation of commuter railroads, for example, requires high concentrations of labor and capital that are largely idle twenty hours out of each twenty-four hour working day. It has been observed that:[6]

> About 50 percent of all daily travel by rapid rail transit occurs in the four peak hours. On many motor-vehicle arteries congestion is the main deterrent to the use of autos and buses during peak hours.

The second problem is land use. Congestion is caused by too many vehicles competing for too little space. Most cities were not designed for the tremendous volume of motor vehicles in use today. The consequence is traffic snarls and slow movement which result in higher costs of deliveries, additional expense of operating vehicles, and inconvenience and frustration for the people who must work in the cities. It is virtually impossible, in most cases, to increase road space in the cities. Also, valuable space must be set aside for parking, train tracks, and the like. Often this space could and should be put to more productive use.

Business contributes to the problems of traffic congestion just by being there. Traffic problems are created by people going to and from work and by going about the tasks of conducting business. It is not suggested that all business should desert the cities. But a question does arise—should businesses move into already congested areas, thus bringing even more people to add to congestion?

A major U.S. business announced that it planned to move its corporate headquarters to a large Eastern city. The company boasted that several hundred people would be employed in the new headquarters. It was well aware of the congestion and transit problems that existed.

A by-product of motorized traffic is the intensification of air pollution. It is estimated that "the proportion of existing air pollution attributable to

[6] Lyle C. Fitch and Associates, "The Urban Transportation Problem," in Jeffrey K. Hadden, Louis H. Masotti, and Calvin J. Larson (eds.), *Metropolis in Crisis: Social and Political Perspectives*, Itasca, Ill.: F. E. Peacock Publishers, Inc., 1967, p. 332.

motor-vehicle exhausts reaches 40 percent in New York City."[7] Much of this contribution to air pollution is generated from business-oriented traffic. But business is now applying its technological expertise to the problem of developing pollutant-free engines and fuels.

Physical Deterioration

Physical deterioration of the inner cities is much less a function of business activity than a function of social movement of population. As the more affluent have moved to suburbia, much housing has been taken over by the poor who cannot afford to maintain dwellings themselves. Landlords also often cannot afford to maintain property, thus causing a blighted area. It is reported that: "In recent years, some 12,000 buildings that once housed 60,000 families in New York City have been abandoned."[8] Blighted areas sometimes are caused by the new location of a factory or failure to maintain and modernize existing facilities, which causes the area to be less desirable for residences. Government, too, causes urban blight by building transit systems or highways.

The highway department in one state announced the location of a new three-mile stretch of highway to be built through a residential neighborhood.[9] After ten years the highway had never been built. But as leases expired tenants of property in the highway path and in neighborhoods adjacent to the proposed path moved out and could not be replaced by landlords. Landlords could not meet taxes nor could they maintain the houses. Some buildings have been abandoned and have rapidly decayed.

Another evidence of physical deterioration in cities is seen in inadequate garbage removal and treatment facilities, which leads to pollution of water by dumping garbage. Large chuckholes and broken paving in streets stand as testaments to the inability of cities to cope with the problem of decay.

Poverty and the Ghetto

The flow of people to the suburbs has not relieved urban crowding. But suburbanization has changed the socioeconomic character of city population. As has been mentioned earlier, most regular residents of the inner city are poor. And as this population increases, both from natural causes and from other poor people moving to the cities, they have fewer places to live. Abandonment of buildings, destruction of buildings by fire, and government urban renewal projects have combined to compress more and more people into fewer places to live. Eventually ghetto cores turn into ghost towns as the poor move to ghetto fringes, thus creating additional ghettos.

At the same time, business—especially businesses offering the kinds of jobs most ghetto dwellers could perform—has fled from the ghetto

---

[7] *Ibid.*, p. 336.
[8] Gus Tyer, "Can Anyone Run a City?" *Saturday Review*, Nov. 8, 1969, p. 24.
[9] "Specter of an Unbuilt Road," *Business Week*, May 2, 1970, p. 104.

leaving little or no chance for employment. Business has sometimes complicated the plight of the ghetto dweller in other ways. Several studies have shown that prices are higher in poor neighborhoods than in middle-class or upper-class neighborhoods.[10] In addition, the poor appear to be more susceptible to unethical or dishonest business practices than their more affluent neighbors. For example:[11]

> A couple who signed a paper to buy a "custom-made" orthopedic mattress and box spring for $22 each did not know until too late that taxes, carrying charges, delivery charges, and other fees brought the total cost to $247.

Rising insurance costs have also added to the problems of ghetto property owners and businesses. In some cases insurance costs have risen as much as five times in riot areas or potential riot areas. To help alleviate this problem for those in the ghetto, Congress in 1968 passed the Fair Access to Insurance Requirements Act (FAIR). Under this plan each state is to join with private insurers to provide insurance for those who cannot get it elsewhere. Companies that participate are eligible for federal reinsurance so that each company will bear only a small part of losses caused by riots.

Crime in the Cities

Another evidence of urban deterioration is reflected in rising crime rates. Some argue that there has been little or no increase in the crime rate.[12] They contend that the number of reported serious crimes per capita has remained somewhat constant. But two things seems to be important. First, the absolute number of serious crimes has increased substantially. Second, a high proportion of crime used to be confined largely to poor neighborhoods. Today the mobility provided by the automobile has diffused the incidence of crime over greater areas of the city.

Like most social problems, solutions cannot come from any single social institution. The President's Commission on Crime states, "Controlling crime is the business of every American Institution."[13] How can business participate? It can enlarge programs of vocational training and job opportunities for prisoners. And perhaps even more important, it can apply technical abilities to problems of crime prevention and apprehension.

Perhaps even more important is organized crime's involvement within legitimate businesses. There appears to be increasing evidence of organized crime's infiltration into business. Legitimate business sometimes offers opportunities to organized crime for investment of surplus funds. On other occasions legitimate business offers fronts for illegitimate activi-

[10] Esther Peterson, "The Poor Pay More," in Hadden, Masotti, and Larson, op. cit., pp. 284–289.
[11] Ibid., p. 286.
[12] James Q. Wilson, "Crime in the Streets," in ibid., pp. 305–315.
[13] "Summary of President's Commission on Crime," in ibid., p. 330.

ties. And sometimes illegal gambling is established through company employees. In addition, businessmen are often forced to pay graft or protection money.

Businessmen sometimes become directly involved in business dealings with members of the underworld. More often they are unwilling victims of corrupt city government. But from both a social and business viewpoint the biggest difficulty seems to be apathy within the business community concerning the problem of organized crime. Where organized crime has made penetrations, it appears that business must share at least a part of the blame.[14]

BUSINESS AND LESS-ADVANTAGED CITIZENS

There is a strong conviction in America that society should provide more opportunity and help for less-advantaged citizens. And while there are many groups of less-advantaged citizens, such as the rural poor, we seem to have given priority to the urban poor. Rebuilding the ghetto is high on the priority list of urban problems.

There is an old saying that slums are made by slum dwellers, not the other way around. What this means is that in the effort to rebuild slums, social and economic factors as well as physical factors must be considered. Even black leaders of business development groups report problems in communicating this idea to slum dwellers. One black leader commented that: "All they [slum dwellers] want to talk about is housing. We think if we get economic development, housing will take care of itself."[15] Government, business, and labor, cooperatively and individually, are directing resources toward a variety of problems of less-advantaged citizens.

Employing the Hard-core Unemployed

A key problem of the less-advantaged citizen is his high rate of unemployment. To a large degree many of these people have been deprived of social, economic, and educational opportunities. In a way they have been programmed out of society. In an attempt to bring them back into society, substantial efforts are being made to provide basic education and training which can lead to steady and productive employment.

The National Alliance of Businessmen (NAB) has been a partnership effort between business and government to provide jobs for hard-core unemployed. According to the NAB *Employers' Digest:*[16]

> Its implementation combines government resources with business know-how. Its goal is to find permanent jobs for the hard-core poor in the nation's largest cities and summer employment for in-school youth from the inner city.

[14] Stanley Penn, "Mafia Inroads: Business Shares Blame," *Wall Street Journal* (Midwest edition), Jan. 27, 1970, p. 18.
[15] "Black Capitalism Gets a Test in Pittsburgh," *Business Week*, Oct. 5, 1968, p. 58.
[16] *Employers' Digest*, Washington, D.C.: National Alliance of Businessmen, undated, p. 2.

Under this plan government agencies locate, identify, and recruit potential employees. Business hires, counsels, and trains recruits. Government also pays for the additional expenses incurred by business in hiring and training hard-core employees.

In general, business has been well satisfied with the results of programs to hire hard-core unemployed. Although training problems are different and often more difficult than for non-hard-core employees, business is finding that these people can become productive employees.

The Move Back to the Inner City

A serious problem has been that as industry moved out of slum areas, slum dwellers either could not, or would not, travel long distances to jobs in suburban plants. Businesses both on their own and through government prodding are now opening or planning plants in ghetto areas. Many large companies as well as small companies are making the move back to the slums.

Many companies have purchased existing buildings, but many more are moving into new facilities in new industrial parks being built in the inner cities.[17] Some industrial parks are being built on already vacant property. In other cases tracts are being cleared specifically for industry. As an example, Flatlands Urban Industrial Park in Brooklyn, New York, is expected to employ about 7,000 people. And New York City has several other similar parks in the planning or building stage.[18]

Aid to Minority Group Businessmen

Not all ghetto dwellers are poor, nor are they all less-educated. An increasing number have college degrees. Many of these people are moving into the management ranks of corporations.[19] Many others, sometimes with the help of more experienced and financially stronger businessmen and with the help of government, are establishing businesses of their own.

Menswear Retailers of America has established a program to help less-advantaged persons become store owners.[20] The kinds of help extended are market feasibility studies, training in small business and retail store operation, assistance in obtaining government financing, and special extended-credit opportunities.

Also, some commercial financial institutions[21] have invested capital in minority-owned businesses that could not meet normal loan requirements.

In addition to large corporations establishing subsidiary or branch plants in ghetto areas, many companies are attempting to establish manu-

[17] "New Plants Dot the Black Slums," Business Week, Mar. 22, 1969, p. 100.
[18] "Parking Place for Industry," Business Week, Sept. 20, 1969, pp. 120–124.
[19] The April–May, 1970, issue of The MBA is devoted to the subjects of black entrepreneurship and black manager in the corporate structure.
[20] Action Report, Vol. 2, No. 1, p. 1, New York, The Chase Manhattan Bank, Winter, 1968.
[21] Ibid., p. 4.

facturing plants and promote ownership of these plants by minority groups by selling stock to employees and other residents.

Business is active also in education of the socially less advantaged. In addition to on-the-job training of hard-core unemployed, some businesses are trying to reach the young before they become dropouts.

A large California aerospace company[22] has been experimenting with ways to motivate eighth-grade and ninth-grade students. Much of the learning process takes place in games and simulation exercises which enable the student to focus on specific goals and to see how gaining knowledge will help achieve these goals.

Much of the preceding discussion has stressed business efforts to aid less-advantaged citizens, but government contributions and cooperation with business should not be minimized. The federal government through the Department of Health, Education, and Welfare has assisted in financing training efforts. Federal money has become available for college scholarships for the less-advantaged. The Small Business Administration, both through direct loans and through guarantees to banks, has increased the capital available to less-advantaged citizens. State and city governments are also actively contributing to solutions. One thing seems to be clear: the greatest successes have come from cooperative efforts of business, government, and others—not from isolated individual activities.

Housing

Many persons believe that low-cost housing should receive the highest priority in the scheme of rebuilding cities. And indeed it appears evident that the need for housing is great. Housing is being allowed to deteriorate faster than it is being rebuilt.

Congress has indicated the housing shortage to be in the area of 26 million units between 1968 and 1978.[23] This is the estimated number of new or rehabilitated homes needed to take care of people between 1968 and 1978 and to replace substandard units.

Government has been involved in public housing for many years, but government efforts have sometimes intensified the shortage. Urban renewal and attempts by government to provide low-cost housing have not always worked well. Urban renewal has sometimes created more problems than it has solved. Clearing areas of substandard buildings has often replaced slum dwellings with vacant lots. The result has been additional crowding as displaced residents moved into other slum areas, thus adding to already overcrowded conditions. As older parts of cities are torn down, many elderly poor also have been deprived of low-cost housing and low-cost places to eat, thus increasing the welfare burden of government.

[22] *Ibid.,* p. 3.
[23] "The Breakdown in Our Cities: Interview with the Secretary of Housing and Urban Development," *U. S. News and World Report,* July 28, 1969, p. 49.

Long delays are common in urban renewal. According to one report, New York [State] had 2,741 acres under urban renewal, of which 198 acres were completed projects, 280 acres were in advanced project states, while the remaining 2,263 acres were in limbo, lacking feasible plans and viable sponsors.[24]

Most urban renewal projects have focused largely on commercial buildings. A more recent thrust, however, has been to give more consideration to housing for low-income and moderate-income families and to avoid past mistakes in developing public housing. Past records of public housing built solely on the criteria of functionalism and lowest cost have not been good. Much of the older public housing suffers from greater-than-average deterioration and high vacancy rates in spite of housing shortages. Three explanations seem to emerge. First, public housing became a symbol of poverty. Those who lived in these housing projects were marked with the social stigma of poverty and clearly set apart as an identifiable group. Second, design dictated by economy often produced unwanted and unexpected results. For example, elevators that stopped only on every third floor sometimes offered convenient settings for crime. Third, because accommodations were low in cost and low in rent, a sort of reverse pride in ownership or pride in tenancy occurred. Broken windows, unattended lawns, and vandalism often reduced public housing to undesirable living quarters at any price.

Aware of the consequences of earlier public housing policies, the new governmental thrust focuses on aesthetics as well as utilitarian considerations, and it is putting much greater emphasis on ownership of single-family dwellings and apartments.

If adequate housing is to be made available to less-advantaged citizens in sufficient quantities and at prices they can afford to pay, both central government and city government will need to lead the way by establishing objectives and policies. City government will need to reevaluate building codes and zoning regulations. Business will need to direct innovative efforts toward new materials and new ways of financing, designing, constructing, and selling. And labor will need to discard obsolete work rules and help develop new and better ways of performing work so that new materials and building techniques can be effectively utilized. Through pluralistic cooperation these groups can develop a better quality of life for the urban community.

THE NEW URBAN CENTER

It is generally accepted that city ills stem from the inabilities of cities to adjust to changing political, social, and economic requirements. Political boundaries which fragment governmental effectiveness, social mobility of higher income groups, and economic entrapment of less-advantaged citizens have all contributed to the urban crisis.

[24] Samuel Kaplan, "Bridging the Gap from Rhetoric to Reality: The New York State Urban Development Corporation," *Architectural Forum*, November, 1969, p. 70.

If the problems of urban America are to be solved, it will take a great deal of thinking about what a city is and what its purposes should be. There are many who believe that traditional approaches to city planning and development are obsolete in our modern social system and that trying to rebuild cities in the traditional patterns will not solve the problems. One observer warns that "as the world becomes urbanized, the city must be organized on new principles, but ultimately the choice is not merely between different kinds of cities, but different concepts of man."[25] And Peter Drucker has observed:

> One reason for the misery and disorganization of megalopolis is that it has outgrown what we still consider modern technologies . . .[26]
> To organize megalopolis we need a new perception. . . . The lack of such a perception makes all efforts at "city planning" futile.[27]

Planners and critics alike seem to agree on certain requirements. To be healthy, viable, and strong, a city must have two basic ingredients—density and variety. It must have a variety of buildings for different uses and a variety of people performing a variety of functions.

Two solutions suggest themselves. The first is to build entirely new cities based on concepts and technology never before used in city planning. The second is to work with metropolitan areas that presently exist, creating new centers and new individuality as one moves outward and at the same time rebuilding the dying central cores according to some master plan which takes into account all the variables and the relationships between these variables.

In either case solutions are likely to require cooperation between the major social institutions to a degree which has seldom been achieved. Government's role will need to be largely that of setting objectives, planning, and financing. The role of business will need to be that of providing government with tested planning techniques, such as systems analysis, and of applying technical expertise and capability to urban problems. Labor's contribution must come from accepting and even initiating new ways to organize and perform work.

The Dilemma of Government

Unfortunately, many government efforts have been of questionable value because they have been organized on a vertical basis, with little or no communication or coordination between various agencies. Work has been organized on a project basis and assigned to various government agencies which operate as semiautonomous units. One author cited three representative examples of the problem.[28]

[25] Heckscher, *op. cit.* p. 10.
[26] Peter F. Drucker, *The Age of Discontinuity: Guidelines to Our Changing Society,* New York: Harper & Row, Publishers, Incorporated, 1969, p. 33.
[27] *Ibid.,* p. 35.
[28] "Private Responsibility for Public Management, a Special Report by the Editors," *Harvard Business Review,* March–April, 1967, p. 7.

One agency may be building roads to bring more cars into the city, while another agency is developing mass transit systems to keep them out.

Recently the Federal Aviation Agency awarded money for modernization of an airport in Massachusetts, while the Civil Aeronautics Board was denying certification of the only commercial flights into the city served by the airport.

When the bill to create the Department of Housing and Urban Development was before Congress in 1965, it was being touted as the coordinating unit for all urban programs. In reality it was to have jurisdiction over only a handful of the more than scores of federal programs then in existence.

Uncoordinated activities such as those described can only lead to fragmented effort and to divergent and often conflicting objectives.

Business Efforts Are Also Often Isolated

Business efforts in many cases have also suffered from the same fragmentation that has plagued government efforts. Businesses have tried to contribute positively and actively to solutions of urban problems on an individual basis. But many of these efforts have been hampered by lack of cooperative effort between business, labor, and government, and where some form of cooperative effort has occurred, these efforts have been hampered by the project organization of government activity. Businessmen, too, are often disenchanted by endless forms, reports, and inspections required by government. But in spite of many obstacles, business is attacking city problems in a variety of ways that are likely to have far-reaching results.

Rebuilding Downtown

Unlike the slum areas and the ghettos, the central business district of most American cities has not suffered from neglect. On the contrary, over the past twenty-five years, business has been busy transforming the business district into a collection of shining office buildings. But even by day, cities have become forbidding and inhospitable places. In New York a committee of executives reported that the pleasures disappearing from Manhattan were diversity, coherence, grandeur, style, and humanness.[29] And these criticisms apply equally to most other American cities.

Through extensive planning which emphasizes a systems approach, planners are trying to control development, so that the central business district will again become a friendly, human, cohesive whole. Some of the ingredients seem to be open spaces devoted to fountains, small plots of grass, trees, outdoor sitting areas, arcades, a variety of attractive stores, outdoor cafes (weather permitting), theatres, few automobiles, and people living in the city.

[29] Quoted in Walter McQuade, "Downtown Is Looking Up," *Fortune*, February, 1970, p. 133.

There is little question that all these things and more will be necessary to revitalize the central business district. The key to success will be the correct balance of components. Based on computer simulation models one expert[30] suggests that the key to economic and social health of cities lies in the balance between jobs and housing. For most cities this would mean emphasis on professional and managerial jobs and on premium housing that would be attractive to people holding these kinds of jobs. This means finding ways to encourage people to move back to cities to live. And in addition to the correct balance between jobs and housing, all of the supplementary services that together make up the "good life" must be provided in the correct balance.

Obviously, American cities cannot be rebuilt overnight. The rebuilding must occur a bit at a time. But most cities are formulating long-range plans, based on a systems approach which attempts to relate, coordinate, and control rebuilding efforts. Most rebuilding and modernization in central business districts is being accomplished through cooperative efforts of federal government, city government, and private capital.

A new development in San Francisco is an example of how this cooperation in downtown reconstruction works. The new project will occupy three blocks and will contain a convention center and commercial complex. The key to this undertaking is the city's right to condemn land and write down the cost with the aid of federal funds under urban renewal and to have private capital build and operate the facilities.

Not all businessmen are convinced that government money or extensive government cooperation is necessary to rebuild cities. Many believe that it is the responsibility of business leaders to take the initiative in planning and building well balanced improvements in the central business district. Some have emphasized developing sites just outside the central core.

The planning and development of a large tract a dozen blocks outside the central core of a large Midwestern city is a good example.[31] Over a period of fifteen years one business leader acquired nearly a hundred acres surrounded by parks and hospitals. The first building to be built was the corporate headquarters of the company owned by this business leader. Developmental plans for the area call for concealed parking, 1,100,000 square feet of office space, 2,200 apartments, motion picture theatres and restaurants, many special shops, plazas, and ample well-planned space for pedestrian circulation.

There is one danger, however, with independent developments such as the one mentioned above, and that is the danger that these projects may be difficult to integrate into a comprehensive pattern of development. Especially careful planning will be needed to ensure compatibility with overall redevelopment of a city.

[30] Jay W. Forrester, *Urban Dynamics*, Cambridge, Mass.: The M.I.T. Press, 1969; reviewed in "A Daring Look at City Ills," *Business Week*, June 14, 1969, pp. 142–146.
[31] McQuade, *op. cit.* p. 136.

The Traffic Problem

From both technological and social points of view, the movement of people may be the most difficult problem facing the cities. Cities have always been built around the need to transport merchandise and people—that is, a need for a central marketplace and a need for people to make the marketplace function. Continued belief in this need to transport both commodities and people to a central gathering place has produced the congestion problems of which we are all aware.

Technologically we have most of the know-how to eliminate the need for central gatherings and the excessive movement of goods and people. The new technology emphasizes the need to transport information and knowledge, not people and things. With the electronic communication techniques available today, there are few technical reasons for an executive to be in face-to-face contact with subordinates, customers, secretaries, or associates. Technically, people could shop, go to theatres, and visit friends without ever leaving their own home.

But from a social point of view we are not yet ready to surrender our mobility and flexibility to communication media. We are basically social animals, and the urge for social contact is strong. The need to move people for social, if not for business, reasons will remain. Therefore, the challenge will be to find new ways of moving people that will preserve the flexibility provided by private automobiles and at the same time eliminate or reduce our dependence upon the automobile. Rapid transit systems as they are being developed will undoubtedly provide part of the answer, but a complete answer will need to go far beyond the limits of contemporary public transportation systems.

THE NEW CITY CONCEPT

There are strong feelings that efforts to rebuild our cities, no matter how great, will not be enough to cope with problems caused by rapidly expanding population. If growing population is expected to be absorbed into already existing cities, the result will likely be further urban sprawl and intensification of already existing problems, such as smog and traffic congestion. To avoid urban paralysis, many believe it will be necessary to build completely new towns.

Dozens of new towns are in the planning stage and arrangements are being formulated to make possible their completion. Most of the schemes for building new towns consist of some form of partnership between business and government. Both federal and state governments are joining with business to make possible new urban developments. Technically there will be few problems in building a new town. All the technology that is needed is already available, and, indeed, there are single companies large enough and sufficiently diversified to build an entire city. The major problems are in financing the developmental costs. Few, if any, companies can commit the needed amounts of capital for the long period of development. To overcome financial problems, the federal government, through the Department of Housing and Urban Development, is guaranteeing long-term loans for the purpose of new city development. Loans of up to sixty years, along with deferred payment provisions, relieve developers of the heavy debt-service burden until the town becomes established and starts to pay off. It also has been suggested that private corporations be allowed to sell tax-free bonds to finance construction of public facilities such as schools, parks, and playgrounds.

Undoubtedly the new city concept, as it is being developed, will do much to overcome urban problems, particularly if the factors vital to the city are well planned and well balanced. There are some, however, who view the new cities (particularly those located close to existing cities) as being at best only a temporary solution to urban problems. There is a conviction on the part of some that we will need to look for entirely new places and new ways to build cities. There are many unique possibilities. Cities which float on the ocean or on our rivers have been suggested. Subterranean cities have been a practical reality for centuries, and technology for building cities on the ocean floor is not far off. Similarly, it seems likely that research will soon provide answers which will make it possible to build cities in space.

SUMMARY

Whatever direction urban development takes, one thing is certain. As population continues to increase, urbanization will also increase; and urban problems will increase rather than decrease. Business can and must play an active role in improving the urban quality of life. Business is the principal social institution capable of providing the managerial and technical skills needed to implement plans for the city. But business cannot play the leading role in areas such as goals and social priorities. Solution to urban problems will require coordination among all major institutions in a magnitude and to a degree never before achieved in our social system.

STUDY GUIDES FOR INTERPRETATION OF THIS CHAPTER

1 Contact the nearest representative of the National Alliance of Businessmen. Learn from him how many businesses in that community are hiring and training hard-core unemployed. Contact a business that has had experience in hiring hard-core unemployed. Report to the class the experience of that company.

2 Write to your Congressman or Representative and ask him to provide you with information about existing and proposed federal government activity in planning and management of urban land use. What roles do government and business play in planning and management of land use?

3 How do you explain the willingness of some major companies to establish business in the inner city and then transfer ownership to members of minority groups?

4 In what ways can business best contribute to the solution of urban deterioration?

PROBLEMS
THE INFORMATION SERVICE CENTER

Corporate headquarters of a large firm were located on the edge of a fifty-block concentration of urban blight in a large Eastern city. Most of the residents of the area belonged to minority groups. For many years the company had been making substantial financial contributions to various local welfare agencies.

One day a young executive suggested to the president that the program of financial grants be largely discontinued, and he recommended an alternative program in its place. The residents of the area, the young executive contended, needed what he termed administrative support more than they needed financial support. While financial support should not be withdrawn completely, emphasis should be placed on providing information, guidance, and assistance that would help residents of the area solve their own problems. The key to the proposed program was an information service center which would direct people to help that is available, help them prepare complaints or requests, and make appointments with the right people. In extreme cases the center could assist directly with such activities as emergency requests for food and clothing, or negotiating out-of-court settlements with a finance company. Other activities might include help with neighborhood improvement projects and help in organizing Boy Scout troops or similar groups.

1 If you were the president would you favor substituting the proposed plan for the old one? Compile arguments both for and against the new plan.

THE CITY PLANNING COMMISSION

Mr. Brown, a prominent business leader in a large city, was asked to serve as a member of the city planning commission. Mr. Brown's city was experiencing most of the urban problems faced by other cities. Among these problems were movement of more affluent residents to suburbs, movement of business out of the city, loss of tax revenue, increasing cost of municipal services, urban deterioration, slum crowding, increase in crime, and traffic congestion.

At his first meeting Mr. Brown listened to a fellow commissioner urge adoption of programs which would implement recommendations made by Professor Jay W. Forrester in his book *Urban Dynamics*.[32] These recommendations suggested that a city should do the following:

[32] Jay W. Forrester, *Urban Dynamics*, Cambridge, Mass.: The M.I.T. Press, 1969; reviewed in "A Daring Look at City Ills," *Business Week*, June 14, 1969, p. 142–146.

1. Tear down 5 percent of its already scarce low income housing every year.
2. Clear away an equal volume of aging business enterprises.
3. Spurn programs for housing, job training, and outside financial help.

In many ways these recommendations seemed attractive to Mr. Brown, particularly since they seemed to place the burden of city revitalization on business. On the other hand, Mr. Brown found it difficult to understand how business could assume the entire burden.

1 If you were in Mr. Brown's position, how would you analyze Professor Forrester's recommendations?

2 What functions or activities of urban revitalization can best be performed by labor, assuming a community follows Professor Forrester's recommendations?

CHAPTER 18

THE INTERFACE BETWEEN BUSINESS AND HIGHER EDUCATION

In short, what is needed is a marriage between
learning and leadership.

L. F. URWICK[1]

At the beginning of the 1970s at a distinguished university in the eastern United States a noisy band of 200 demonstrators, ignoring an order of the university provost, battered through a door and seized the offices of top officials of the university. The locked door to the president's office was broken in by four men wearing ski masks and using a battering ram made of heavy pieces of pipe welded together with hand holds on the sides. Obviously they had prepared in advance for violent action. The group, consisting of both students and nonstudents, demanded abolition of the university discipline committee and cancellation of disciplinary action given to students who took part in an earlier violent demonstration. The group chanted slogans, such as "Power to the People" and "Smash GE." "GE" was General Electric Company, which had a strike in some of its plants at the time.[2]

Only a small minority of students is represented by the kind of demonstration just described; however, their influence on student learning patterns and attitudes toward business can be far greater than their number. The fact is that similar demonstrations with slightly different plots in each case had occurred on leading campuses around the world and were to be repeated many times. On a number of occasions business activities, such as recruiting, pollution, and profits, were a target of the demonstrations.

[1] L. F. Urwick, "Learning and Leadership," *Columbia Journal of World Business*, July–August, 1969, p. 73.
[2] Associated Press release, *Arizona Republic*, Jan. 16, 1970, p. 20; and *New York Times*, Jan. 16, 1970, p. 10.

Since business employs the majority of college graduates and draws its leadership from them, the relationship of the college campus to business is a significant factor in business viability; hence it is the focus of this chapter. First, we discuss how a knowledge-oriented society affects the interface of business and higher education. Then we examine the various ways in which business and universities work together and the university climate for business. Discussion in this chapter is limited to education beyond high school.

BUSINESS AND EDUCATION IN A KNOWLEDGE-ORIENTED SOCIETY

The close and relevant interface of business and higher education is a new development. Centuries and even mere decades ago each had a somewhat hands-off attitude toward the other. A relatively small intellectual elite maintained their seclusion in ivied university halls, educating a few selected students to become intellectual and social leaders of their nation. Education was not for the masses who labored in factories, fields, and stores. University educators had little interest in business, and businessmen had little interest in educators. Each lived in a different world. Many educators showed an elitist disdain for businessmen who were perceived as less nobly motivated than educators. Most businessmen admitted that the disdain was mutual, since the men in the ivory tower had little that was practical to offer business.

The separation of business and education gradually waned as higher education expanded in accordance with democratic ideals of equal opportunity, but the real breakthrough came with development of a knowledge-oriented society.

A Knowledge-oriented Society

A *knowledge society* is one in which knowledge rather than manual skill becomes the principal means of serving human needs. Therefore, the society which wishes to serve human needs and to advance civilization requires a large proportion of educated, knowledge-oriented citizens. No longer can it afford the luxury of a small and isolated intellectual elite. Knowledge must be widespread, and *the interface between higher education and the world of work must be active and close.*

In economic terms, knowledge has become the chief factor in production; however, it is important to realize that the idea of a knowledge society is more than a narrow business or economic concept. It applies to the entire social system.

Just as it is almost impossible to run a productive large business without a computer, it is also nearly impossible to provide advanced hospital care without an elaborate collection of complex electronic and chemical apparatus. The country doctor of two generations ago would not know what to do with this equipment. Moreover, most of the equipment is operated and maintained by a broad array of new knowledge workers who usually are not physicians. Though these knowledge employees may work with their hands, they are applying knowledge derived from education, instead of a skill learned by a tradesman's apprenticeship.

In the knowledge society the term "knowledge" has a special meaning. The distinction between it and traditional learning of an intellectual elite is explained by Peter Drucker as follows.[3]

"Knowledge" as normally considered by the "intellectual" is something very different from "knowledge" in the context of "knowledge economy" or "knowledge work." For the intellectual, knowledge is what is in a book. But as long as it is in the book, it is only "information" if not mere "data." Only when a man applies the information to doing something does it become knowledge. Knowledge, like electricity or money, is a form of energy that exists only when doing work. The emergence of the knowledge economy is not, in other words, part of "intellectual history" as it is normally conceived. It is part of the "history of technology," which recounts how man puts tools to work.

Effects of a Knowledge Society

We shall discuss effects of the knowledge society in terms of its primary influence upon each of the three groups involved in the business-education interface. These are business, educational institutions, and students.

1. BUSINESS   The main educational effect of the knowledge society on business is to require a close and active interface between business and higher education, as mentioned earlier. Since business as an institution is committed to fulfilling certain areas of human need, it requires large numbers of knowledge workers to function effectively. It secures these from educational institutions; hence, it becomes more dependent on them to prepare knowledge workers capable of making useful social contributions through the institution of business. Even more significant is the need for business to work closely with knowledge-oriented faculty for research, consulting, and continuing education of business's knowledge employees. This faculty-business relationship is distinctly new.

2. EDUCATIONAL INSTITUTIONS   The main effect of the knowledge society on education is to change curricula and power alignments within educational institutions. With regard to curricula, major new knowledge disciplines have been created. In other instances, traditional courses have not been brought up to date and thus have lost their relevancy to the world outside the university and, consequently, to many students who take these courses.

With regard to power alignments, a century ago liberal arts dominated education; there were only a few peripheral areas such as law. Since that

[3] Peter F. Drucker, *The Age of Discontinuity: Guidelines to Our Changing Society*, New York: Harper & Row, Publishers, Incorporated, 1969, p. 269. Drucker estimates that the knowledge industries (those producing and distributing ideas and information rather than goods and services) will provide one-half of the gross national product by the end of the 1970s; see p. 263.

time most university growth has been in knowledge-oriented areas—most of which are new—such as computer technology, engineering, nursing, and business. For the first time the traditional academic groups find themselves outnumbered in university councils and their elitist intellectual status threatened by the new, successful, knowledge-oriented faculty. To make matters worse, businessmen and other institutional leaders are giving much of their attention to knowledge-oriented faculty, because they want men who can help them solve problems in the large organizations they manage.

A survey of chief executives of *Fortune*'s top 500 companies shows the degree to which liberal arts now shares with knowledge-oriented disciplines the responsibility for developing business leadership in a knowledge society. The executives were asked, "If you had the opportunity again to prepare yourself for the position you now hold, or if you were advising your son who aspires to a role of leadership in management, how would you rate the educational preparations listed below?"

Only 28 percent of respondents rated four years of liberal arts as good or excellent, and five or more years of liberal arts fared even worse. On the other hand, both of the following programs were rated good or excellent by 94 percent: (1) four years of liberal arts combined with two years of business, and (2) four years of engineering combined with two years of business. Clearly over three times as many executives opted for some or even dominant knowledge-orientation in preference to straight liberal arts.[4]

3. **STUDENTS**   The main effect of the knowledge society on students is that for the first time they have such a complex variety of specialized career choices that some of them become confused and insecure. As Drucker explains, "There are so many choices, so many opportunities, so many directions, that they bewilder and distract the young people."[5] In addition, new knowledge convinces students that mankind possesses the ability to solve most of its social problems quickly if only its institutional leaders cared. Some leaders may not care, but it is also true that many students do not understand the difficulties and dangers of introducing change in a real world. In effect, the students have been taught the problems, but not the realities of how to solve them.

The psychological dissonance between "what is" and "what ought to be" is so great in the minds of some students that they drift into insecurity and alienation.[6] They become impatient with the realities of introducing social change and want action *now.* This situation is particularly diffi-

---

[4] James W. Kelley, "Management Grades the Graduate Business School," *Personnel,* September–October, 1969, pp. 16–26.

[5] Drucker, *op. cit.,* p. 274.

[6] The focus of this discussion is the role of higher education in affecting student attitudes. It is also clear that at the time many students enter higher education they already are insecure and alienated, or have predispositions toward being so, because of earlier experiences. Although higher education became the locus of student alienation and militancy in the 1960s, this is not proof that it is the primary cause of these conditions. Our discussion, however, suggests that higher education is a contributor to these conditions, and conversely it could be a stronger bulwark against growth of these conditions.

cult for students in liberal arts and other less applied disciplines, because their program often is intentionally idealistic without a counterbalancing career preparation to help them apply their idealism in the complex institutions of a knowledge society.[7]

Eventually some alienated students develop an antiestablishment attitude and say, "A plague on all your institutions because they don't fit my values." Thus, the seeds are sown for student militancy and violence such as that described at the beginning of this chapter. Even though only a small proportion of students may be involved, this condition disrupts the whole system. It suggests that the students, even though "educated," lack an understanding of the way that a knowledge society works through large organizations to create multiknowledged teams to serve mankind's needs. Lacking this understanding, they in frustration abandon hope of working within the system and resort to radical and sometimes violent action.

C. Heavier Responsibilities on Business, Education, and Youth

The knowledge society has imposed heavier responsibilities on business, education, and youth (as well as other institutions and groups) to manage change successfully. Consider, for example, the effects of only *one* technological development on *one* of the groups mentioned. This is the effect of television on youth.

For the youth of the 1950s and 1960s, television collapsed both space and time. It brought the world right into their living rooms so that distant events could be known and seen, thus collapsing the parochial walls of home and community which bound youth in earlier generations. It also collapsed time by showing these events as they happened. There is a difference between seeing something as it occurs and reading about it later in a newspaper or history book. Under these conditions the face and ideas of a spokesman for a pluralistic group two thousand miles away often became better known than the face and ideas of the local mayor. Youth were socially conditioned for change and for having it now. Why not now? If society could bring instantaneous news and instant coffee, why not instantaneous social action? (Hence, they are sometimes called the "Now Generation.") The inevitable result was a weakening of parental, religious, and community restraints, plus a stubborn impatience with the normal change of traditional institutions.

The knowledge society can be used to improve the quality of life, but only if the components of a pluralistic society can agree on social priorities, because all problems cannot be solved at once. Next it will be necessary for these groups to marshal resources to deal effectively with the

---

[7] Research shows that the less applied disciplines in higher education have a proportionately larger number of alienated and militant students. For example, see Seymour M. Lipset (ed.), *Student Politics*, New York: Basic Books, Inc., Publishers, 1967, especially pp. 199–252. Although it can be argued that a larger proportion of alienated students chooses to enter the less applied disciplines, there is also evidence these disciplines are a causal factor in alienation. For example, see Figure 18–2 and related discussion later in this chapter.

priorities they have selected. Finally, they need to educate themselves regarding how to *solve* problems rather than just *find* them,[8] and then to show the patience and cooperation to work successfully in the system of organizations which a knowledge society requires. Business, education, and youth have key, cooperative roles to play in improving the quality of life in a knowledge society, but in order to achieve their potential they need to give more emphasis to their mutual goals and responsibilities instead of their differences and rights.

D. A Concluding Statement

Without a doubt, the knowledge society and the Now Generation have introduced ideas and practices which will affect the long-run life style of civilization. What society wishes to assure is that unfavorable proposals are weeded out, while favorable and constructive changes are accomplished with minimum negative side effects. If activism leads to increasing polarization of pluralistic groups, social instability, and violence, then its worthy intentions will become socially worthless.

The knowledge society frees modern youth to move out of the restricted environment of the primitive tribe or the small town, but this freedom and mobility also impose on youth a heavy burden of choice. A young person has many occupations, many locations, many types of institutions, and many life styles which he can choose. Thus, there is forced upon him a responsibility for deciding what he wants to become and how he wants to live. In essence, more than ever before, he has to decide how he will apply his abilities to help his fellowman. He has freedom, choice, mobility —and responsibility. No wonder some youth have tried to escape this awesome responsibility by withdrawing into a hippie culture or the dreams of psychedelic drugs.

II. BUSINESS RELATIONSHIPS WITH UNIVERSITIES

A. Encouragement of Continuing Education by Employees

Business in a knowledge society needs educated employees. Employees as persons want to keep growing and increasing their opportunities, but education takes employee time as well as money. The result is that business and employees join together to encourage continuing employee education and to share the costs. Companies have a variety of plans. Some pay tuition and book costs. Others pay only tuition, rationalizing that books become personal property of the student. Occasionally firms pay just part of tuition, expecting the student to share economic costs. Some give released time from work to attend a course at a nearby college, while others emphasize off-duty education. Regardless of the rules, the key

---

[8] The perception of problems without a counterbalancing perception of how to solve them leaves youth with a feeling of inability to cope with life. As stated by one observer, youth of the 1970s "... have become *the first generation in American history to graduate into adult life without optimism.*" See Louis Banks, "The View through Youthful Eyes," *Fortune*, April, 1970, p. 77. Italics in original.

point is that most large firms strongly support higher education for employees because they recognize its significance in a knowledge society.

Two-year community colleges are an area of special interest because they have both academic and vocational courses. Employees can attend these colleges either to upgrade specific vocational skills or to prepare for a degree program in a senior college. These colleges are often available near residential neighborhoods or downtown business areas, so that travel time and costs are reduced compared with senior colleges and universities. Many community colleges will arrange work-study programs so that an employee may pursue a long-run vocational program while maintaining his employment.

B. Television Education

Many major universities provide educational television courses, and this type of education gradually will expand. It brings education into the home or business classroom, but one limitation is that a student cannot engage in direct discussion with his instructor. Advanced electronic systems overcome this limitation, and some firms with substantial educational needs are using these.

In the Dallas-Fort Worth industrial area a number of companies have established a microwave television network which brings graduate courses from nearby universities directly into electronic classrooms in their plants. The classrooms have television screens which show the instructor, and each desk has a telephone which a student can pick up for direct voice connection with his instructor. This system permits questions and back-and-forth discussion even though it is not face-to-face. The company-university system carries engineering, science, and business courses, and students may register for credit toward a degree.

This complex system is expensive, but firms which use it believe it is more economical and practical than sending students to a distant campus or bringing faculty to the plant. It also allows students to use top-quality courses from several universities rather than just one, in accordance with each student's needs.[9]

C. Management Development Programs and Conferences

Annually thousands of managers temporarily abandon their jobs and families in order to attend live-in executive programs at major universities. In addition there are thousands of special university conferences and short courses heavily attended by business specialists of all types. Most of these courses are not restricted to businessmen, so they give business people an opportunity to share ideas with representatives of other pluralistic institutions. The magnitude of this continuing education movement is illustrated by the enrollment figures in a metropolitan college of business. Although its regular student enrollment was large, each year it had a larger number of participants in programs sponsored by its Center for Executive Development.

[9] "Bringing Graduate School to the Plant," Business Week, Jan. 10, 1970, pp. 64–65.

An approach which can be used by a large company or group of companies is to establish its own management development facility and then bring university instructors to the facility to teach in-company programs.

The Pepsi-Cola Management Institute is an example. It was established by the Pepsi-Cola Company in cooperation with Pepsi-Cola bottlers. Although the parent company does operate some bottling plants, most bottlers are independent businessmen operating their own franchised plants having from 10 to 250 employees. Bottler personnel come to the Institute from plants throughout the world in order to attend courses taught by faculty from a number of major universities. Each classroom in the $2-million facility is equipped with a full range of teaching aids including television.

The underlying concept of all of the programs discussed is that business people in a knowledge society need continuing renewal and upgrading in order to retain their personal effectiveness and keep business viable. The ancient statement that "old dogs cannot be taught new tricks" has been turned to state that "old dogs keep young by learning new tricks." Even more, "there are some tricks that only old dogs can learn," because they are able to interpret theory in terms of experience.

The training institute of an international drug company illustrates the variety of university-business interface required in a knowledge society. While one of the authors discussed management with executives in one conference room, across the hall in another room there was a company symposium on genetic factors involved in the conception of twins. The symposium was directed by a panel of renowned scientists from universities in several nations. The company was studying drugs related to fertility and birth control, and apparently it believed the large cost of this private symposium was worthwhile for its scientists working on this project.

Other Relationships

Faculty consulting with business has proved an effective instrument for mutual benefit of faculty, students, and business. The faculty member learns more about the realities of business, which should improve his teaching and research. The students benefit from a better teacher who can more realistically interpret business to them. Finally, the business which initiated the relationship expects to gain from the faculty member's aid and advice.

A partial reversal of this relationship is the executive-in-residence program of some universities. In this instance a leading business executive is brought to a business school for a week or more in order to exchange ideas on a face-to-face, give-and-take basis with students. He is in a sense a consultant to the students, giving them direct interaction with "a real, live executive," not a retired one or one who comes to make a public relations speech and then hastens away. The experience is rewarding to students, faculty, and the executive. Each learns more about the other. In the words of one executive in residence, his revelation was that "businessmen are likely to be appallingly ignorant of what business students want and need to know before they can perform any satisfactory service."[10]

Another way in which business and the university interpret their needs to each other is through school of business advisory committees. Functions of an advisory committee include comments about the relevance of proposed curricula, aid in fund drives, cooperation with field research programs, and contact with faculty and students.

The knowledge society had caused a major expansion of business recruiting on campus. During the economic depression of the 1930s a graduate had to seek his own job, and he felt lucky to get one. Now business recruiters along with recruiters from other institutions seek the graduate, and competition is keen for qualified persons. With rising student activism in the 1960s, militant groups on campus began harassing and threatening both job seekers and recruiters from companies which they felt were not socially responsible. This militant interference caused the American Association of University Professors in its 1969 meeting to reaffirm its view that the free environment of a university requires that any recruiting facilities should be available to all recruiters and job seekers.[11]

Business Gifts to Higher Education

About four-tenths of one percent of corporate profits are given to support higher education. Since public gifts of corporations total about one percent of profits before taxes, this means that higher education receives a large share (two-fifths) of corporate gifts. This proportion of giving to education shows that business has a serious interest in upgrading the education of citizens and potential employees.[12] Gifts include scholarships, research grants, capital grants for buildings, endowed professorships, and outright grants for general expenses. (Educational payments for present employees are recorded separately as a fringe-benefit cost.)

Figure 18–1 shows that from 1950 to 1960, as the effects of the knowledge society became evident to business, the proportion of gifts to higher education more than tripled. Since that time the proportion has remained relatively stable. The claims of other social needs such as urban problems and the disadvantaged became so important in the 1960s that business was unable to give a larger proportion to higher education. It appears likely that this proportion will stabilize around 0.40 percent or even decline as other social claims are made on business.

[10] James E. Patrick, "Bridging the Student-business Gap: The Role of the Executive-in-residence," *Business Horizons*, April, 1969, p. 59.
[11] Official Resolutions, Fifty-fifth Annual Meeting, American Association of University Professors, Minneapolis, Minnesota, May 2–3, 1969.
[12] In spite of business's general interest in higher education, it has been especially unresponsive to the needs of university business schools, allocating them only 2 to 4 percent of its gifts. This figure is much less than the proportion of business students among all students enrolled in higher education. For an early study see *Educating Tomorrow's Managers: The Business Schools and the Business Community*, New York: Committee for Economic Development, 1964, Appendix A, pp. 43ff.

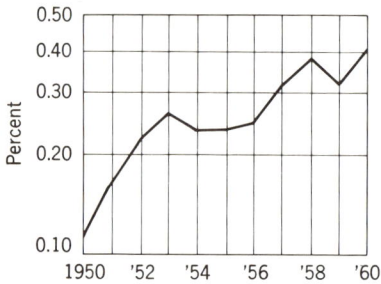

Figure 18-1 Percentage of corporate profits before taxes contributed to higher education. Adapted from *Business Week,* Apr. 3, 1965, p. 132. Data from Council for Financial Aid to Education, Inc., and U.S. Department of Commerce.

Different Gift Practices

A greater proportion of large companies give to higher education than small companies. Perhaps one reason is that larger businesses tend to employ more specialized college graduates. Another is that small businessmen usually have no established policies of gift giving. Since there are not many planned campaigns by those needing educational gifts, small businessmen simply forget to give. Since local charity drives usually bring a knock at the door, there is more direct motivation to give in these circumstances. Small businessmen could benefit from planned giving according to policy just as much as larger businesses do. Otherwise the "squeaky wheel" gets the gifts.

Companies which are large enough to give substantial sums usually establish carefully developed policies, just as they would for any other expenditure. When General Electric Company developed its policy toward gifts to education, it took a four-page advertisement in a national magazine to explain the policy. The advertisement was written as an article rather than in the usual advertising style. At that time college graduates on its payroll numbered about thirty thousand persons from 760 institutions. The article began: "By now, most responsible people in industry are convinced that, both as individuals and as corporate citizens, they have some obligation to help American education solve its growing problems." Several principles for giving were emphasized, among them the "multiplication factor," which is that the company tends toward giving to the need which probably will have the widest effect. "For example, in the choice between helping to pay a faculty member a higher salary, or assisting a student with a scholarship, the advantage lies clearly with the professor, whose improved teaching can influence a whole generation of students."[13]

Some employers give to both private and tax-supported institutions because they hire employees from both and feel that both have similar

[13] "One Viewpoint on Corporate Aid to Education," *Harper's,* December, 1957, pp. 19-22.

objectives. Other companies, while not prohibiting gifts to tax-supported institutions, give priority to private ones. They do so because the private institution depends on private society for nearly all its income, while tax-supported institutions can call upon government taxing power over the whole society, including the corporation. Further, aid to private institutions keeps that sector of education viable in the face of encroachments from tax-supported higher education. Thus, private aid further supports pluralism in society.

Business aid to education is typically justified under the investment philosophy of giving. It is considered to be an investment in educated citizens (some employed by business), in advancing technology which business uses, and in a better public climate for business. All these objectives can be demonstrably related to business's long-range well-being.

It seems certain that business aid to education will continue. It is founded on basic values of pluralism. First, there is support by one institution (business) for another institution (education) which provides useful services to business. Second, both business and education have a mutual interest in a free society (free business decisions on the one hand and free inquiry on the other). Third, regarding private educational institutions, there is the further point that one private institution wishes to help another keep viable in order to balance pluralistic interests better, especially to offset greater government control of education. Wherever businesses have examined policy implications of business giving to education, they have supported it. They are not, however, opposing tax-supported education. They recognize that the entire educational job is beyond their capacity, but they do wish to play a role in it to confirm their pluralistic interest therein.

III. THE UNIVERSITY CLIMATE FOR BUSINESS

In a pluralistic knowledge society which depends on the effective functioning of many institutions, society needs to ask the question: Are universities educating students with a sound understanding of business's role as a social institution serving human needs? If students graduate without understanding business but have to live with it for the remainder of their lives, they may become less effective citizens, in the same way that a citizen may be less effective if he does not understand another major social institution such as government or education. In addition, business could become less effective if universities direct students away from business, drying up its proportionate share of potential leaders.

A. Business in the University Curriculum

With the financial aid of James Wharton, the first academic business school was established in 1881 as the Wharton School of Commerce and Finance at the University of Pennsylvania. By the 1950s there were over five hundred collegiate business schools in the United States, and graduate schools of business were well established in major universities. In the

United States business was a popular subject. In other nations business schools developed more slowly, but interest quickened in the 1950s as nations began to see business schools as a means of providing leaders to make better use of limited resources.

As business schools gradually proved themselves in the university community, their curriculum gained academic stature, particularly graduate business education and the M.B.A. degree. However, some academic areas with a longer and richer heritage still look on business as a newcomer of dubious reputation. Though business is a major social institution, educators in areas such as science, liberal arts, fine arts, and education are reluctant to have their students take even one business course before graduation. Even in 1970 the majority of college graduates entered the world of work (and voting citizenship) without a course in business.

B. Student Attitudes toward Business

In long-run terms, during the last century student attitudes toward business seemed to improve gradually as business gained academic respectability, but there have been cyclical swings based upon economic and social conditions. The 1960s provided a major downward swing as student idealism and unrest grew. For example, a study of Princeton University seniors showed that the percentage of those planning to enter business dropped from 13 percent in 1961 to 7 percent in 1966.[14]

Since Princeton is a single institution, broader surveys give a more representative view of student attitudes.

The Research Institute of America surveyed about five thousand students in a dozen universities in 1967. One question asked was, "Where do you see the most promising opportunities for yourself, in terms of your own personal fulfilment?" Twenty-four percent of students chose business. It was the students' first career choice, well ahead of government and education.[15]

On the other hand, a 1965 Harris poll of 800 college seniors throughout the nation reported that business ranked below government and education as a career choice. Only 12 percent of seniors made business their first choice, although 31 percent were seriously considering business as a career.[16]

Both surveys reported that the predominant student view was either one of vague dissatisfaction or substantial ignorance about business. Since these students were the educated elite of modern society, the data suggest that somehow the educational system failed to clarify for students the social role of business.

Further insight into this issue is obtained from a survey at the Sloan School of Management, Massachusetts Institute of Technology. Students,

[14] George Olmsted, "The World Community and the Need for Improving Management Techniques," *Advanced Management Journal*, October, 1968, p. 13.
[15] Leslie M. Dawson, "Campus Attitudes toward Business," *MSU Business Topics*, Summer, 1969, p. 37.
[16] *Ibid.*; and Olmsted, *loc. cit.*

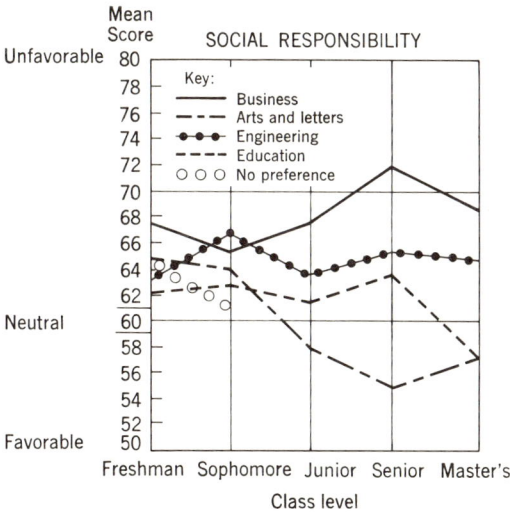

Figure 18–2 Attitudes of 581 students toward how well business meets its social responsibilities, classified by student's academic major. From Leslie M. Dawson, "Campus Attitudes toward Business," *MSU Business Topics*, Summer, 1969, p. 40. Reprinted by permission of the publisher, the Bureau of Business and Economic Research, Division of Research, Graduate School of Business Administration, Michigan State University.

faculty, and executives in a Sloan executive program were given a survey which included the following statement: "Corporations have a definite obligation to be actively involved in community affairs." Only about 54 percent of both students and faculty agreed with this statement, but *84 percent* of executives agreed with it. Even though this was a school of *management*, not liberal or fine arts, a substantial portion of students and faculty still apparently held the classical economic doctrine that business has no *obligation* (this is the word used in the survey) in community affairs. However, the executives—the men with experience—saw an obligation. For other questions concerning "business in society" students and faculty maintained their joint disagreement with business executives, and the executive viewpoint was consistently more oriented toward social responsibility. Somehow the university people did not see business in society in the broad way that executives saw it.[17]

Influence of Faculty and Curricula on Students

Figure 18–2 shows the influence of faculty and curricula on student attitudes concerning how well business meets its responsibilities to society. The research covers 581 students at Michigan State University. Students in all curricula start as freshmen with approximately the same attitudes. Engineering and education majors retain their beginning attitudes for

[17] Edgar H. Schein, "Attitude Change during Management Education," *Administrative Science Quarterly*, March, 1967, pp. 601–628. This article also reports substantial differences among faculty subgroups such as marketing, organization, and finance.

their entire undergraduate program, which suggests that the instruction they receive is approximately neutral toward business. Business students gain about four points between their freshman and senior years. This improved attitude should be expected since business is their chosen field of study. Arts and letters (liberal arts) students, on the other hand, suffer a strong drop of about *ten points* between their freshman and senior years. Their attitude toward business shifts from favorable to unfavorable beginning with their junior year. Their fast decline, in the absence of decline by others, suggests that there is something in their specific program which increases their dissonance with business. At the graduate level all other student attitudes decline (perhaps representing a more questioning point of view), while arts and letters students increase slightly (perhaps representing broader insights).

The pattern of difference between business and liberal arts is maintained for all four other areas of the survey: economic attitude, ethical norms of business, status of business careers, and worth and quality of collegiate-level business education. In each instance attitudes of liberal arts students toward business move from a favorable freshman attitude to an unfavorable one in their senior year. (No other group is unfavorable toward business in its senior year, except education majors regarding ethical norms of business.)

When the same survey form was given to university graduates working in business, it showed that experience tempered their collegiate differences. After two years of business experience, attitudes of all groups toward social responsibility were about the same, and all were favorable. (Education majors were excluded because not enough were in business.)[18]

In general, the evidence indicates that business in the long run is gaining academic status, but the total university climate discourages many students from wanting to enter business. Many academic attitudes toward business represent traditional classical economic doctrines, rather than modern corporate business in a pluralistic social system.

SUMMARY

A knowledge society requires an active and close interface between business and education. It has given students a bewildering number of occupational choices and alternatives for solving social problems, thereby increasing student alienation, activism, and doubts about business as a career. Although business education gradually has gained academic stature, the general university climate has not strongly encouraged business as a career. Nevertheless, business and higher education tend to work cooperatively because of their interdependent needs and mutual interest in a free society.

[18] Dawson, *op. cit.*, pp. 36–46. There are also substantial differences in attitudes of entering freshmen concerning status of business careers and worth of business education, with business majors highest and arts and letters majors lowest in each instance. Another study confirms this entrance difference regarding status of business occupations. See Andre L. Delbecq and James Vigen, "Prestige Ratings of Business and Other Occupations," *Personnel Journal*, February, 1970, pp. 111–116.

STUDY GUIDES FOR INTERPRETATION OF THIS CHAPTER

1 Following a collegiate speech by the president of a large chemical firm, a student directed the following question to the president: "You businessmen could solve the world's hunger problem if you would release your secret patents to the people; why don't you do it?" As president, how would you respond?

2 In the same discussion another student commented, "Business does not care enough about higher education. I have read that business gives only 0.39 percent of its profit for this purpose." As president, how would you respond?

3 Another student asked, "Why are profits necessary? Our state university does not have to make a profit each year to be successful." As president, how would you answer?

4 Discuss the effects of the knowledge society on student educational plans and occupational choices.

5 What business actions do you propose to get more university students interested in business as a career?

PROBLEMS
THE FABIAN COMPANY

Management of the Fabian Company, a drug manufacturer, has decided that it wishes to give four student scholarships in support of university education. Among the alternatives it has considered are the following:

1. Give scholarships to children of employees, allocating them on the basis of need, a competitive screening process, or a chance drawing.

2. Give scholarships to students who live in the plant community and who wish to study any field allied with medicine.

3. Give money to the local university to grant to any student taking any field allied with medicine. The university would select scholarship recipients based upon other criteria which it determined.

4. Give money to the community high school system with the specification that scholarships be given to deserving disadvantaged students who probably could not otherwise go to college.

1 Appraise in pluralistic terms each of the alternatives considered. Then offer your own best scholarship proposal to the management, giving a full explanation of why your proposal is superior.

THE WEAPONS MANUFACTURER

During a recruiting trip a recruiter for a chemical manufacturer talked before a senior class in chemistry, explaining the many advantages of working for his company. During the discussion period one of the seniors stated, "Why should I want to work for your company? It produces chemicals for rockets used by the U.S. military, and I abhor war." The recruiter knew that the statement was true, because 2 percent of the company's sales were to the federal government. Some of these products had military uses, while the remainder were used in other governmental functions.

1 As the company's recruiter, how would you respond to the statement made?

CHAPTER 19

BUSINESS INVOLVEMENT WITH CULTURAL AFFAIRS AND COMMUNICATION MEDIA

The basis for the new power is information, not money or force.

PETER B. CLARK[1]

As reporters, we have always been falsifying issues by reporting on what goes wrong in a Nation where, historically, most has gone right. That is how you get on page one, that is how you win a Pulitzer Prize. This gears the reporter's mind to the negative, even when it is not justified.

HOWARD K. SMITH[2]

The story is told that businessman-philanthropist Andrew Carnegie grew weary of being called upon each year to make a gift to cover the large deficit of a community symphony orchestra. Finally he refused to pay the deficit again. With his strong work ethic he felt that the fund committee should invest some of its own efforts by going to other wealthy people in the community. In order to encourage the fund committee to try this approach, he said, "If you raise half the money from other donors, then I will donate the remaining half."

A week later the committee returned and informed him that the other half had been raised. Mr. Carnegie was very pleased and wrote his check for the balance. As he handed his check to the committee, he inquired, "Would you mind telling me where you got this amount of money so quickly?"

"Not at all," the fund chairman replied with a grin. "We got it from Mrs. Carnegie!"

Business has always had some involvement in cultural affairs and communication because of its wealth, power, and commercial trading, but during the last ten to twenty years it appears that this involvement has increased. Both business and society are recognizing the system relationship which business has to all elements of a pluralistic culture. Business

[1] Peter B. Clark, "The Reporter and the Power Structure," *Editor & Publisher*, Dec. 7, 1968, p. 10.
[2] Howard K. Smith (national television newscaster), quoted in Edith Efron, "There *Is* a Network News Bias," *TV Guide*, Feb. 28, 1970, p. 11.

and culture are tied together in many ways. Business is a major supporter of community cultural projects, and it is probably the largest employer of performing artists and of journalists in communication media such as radio, moving pictures, records and tapes, television, and newspapers. It also provides the advertising revenue which maintains most of our free newspapers, magazines, radio stations, and television stations. From another point of view, business health and growth depend on a balanced society which includes widespread cultural activities and open communication.

In this chapter we discuss business's increasing role as a participant in the cultural life of society, as exemplified in gifts for cultural projects and business's beautification of its own properties. We also discuss the role and responsibilities of business as the chief operator of mass communication media in society.

BUSINESS PARTICIPATION IN CULTURAL AFFAIRS

Support of Cultural Activities

A growing area of business giving is community cultural activities. Throughout the centuries, art has been heavily dependent on some form of patronage for support. Pharaohs, noblemen, the church, and the state have all provided patronage because the market could not be depended on to support culture to the extent sought by societal leaders. Traditionally in Europe, deficits are made up by state subsidies. In the United States wealthy persons have supported culture; but with greater tax restrictions on accumulation of wealth, this source has declined, requiring a broader base of support. Cultural organizations have sought support from business and, in small amounts, from today's more numerous middle class. Over five percent of the business gift dollar now goes for cultural activities. The list of business donors to operas, art shows, symphonies, and ballets is gradually expanding. In Detroit, for example, twenty-six companies gave $10,000 each for a reorganization of the symphony. And 362 companies gave $9.5 million to New York's Lincoln Center for the Performing Arts, with individual corporate gifts reaching as high as $450,000.[3]

Business justifies its gifts in terms of a higher quality of life in the community. In turn, this quality of life improves recruiting and retention of employees. It also improves satisfaction of employees with their community, provides a better place for their children to grow up, and encourages each employee's own cultural growth. The system effects continue in many directions. If, for example, the firm sells its products locally, a community with a better cultural life should have improved chances for growth, thus providing more customers. Further, culture should attract a better quality of citizen, thus improving the quality of the labor pool from which the firm recruits. Cultural opportunities also may challenge youth in the community, raise their achievement drives, and provide favorable

[3] "Performing Arts Find an 'Angel' in Business," *Business Week*, Mar. 13, 1965, pp. 52, 55.

outlets for their energies, thereby reducing tendencies toward delinquency. In turn, less crime and delinquency may reduce the tax burden. When a systems view such as this is taken, it can be argued that an investment in community culture tends to improve the entire social system.

Limitations on Business Giving

There are, however, limitations on business giving. One point is that business needs to exercise caution that it does not overcommit itself to cultural activities alone, because there are many alternative social needs for business funds, such as education and the disadvantaged. A second point is that business support depends upon genuine community participation in the long run. Business may be the primary initiator of a project, but strong community support is needed to keep a project going and to carry its intended effects into the community.

The Minnesota Theater Company performs in a very stylish playhouse built primarily with business funds, although school children and others gave to the project. Its performances have received high ratings from critics. During a period of seven years it has received normal gifts, plus $400,000 through a federal school program and a grant of $870,000 from the Ford Foundation (the Andrew Carnegie of modern times!). In spite of these advantages, it had a record deficit of about $365,000 in its seventh year. Community interest and attendance declined, and the theater was not yet able to pay its own way. The theater company asked businessmen for gifts to make up the annual deficit.[4] (If you were a community businessman, how would you respond?)

Another point is that, although business may occasionally support a risky venture in art just as it does in commerce, generally it should be sure that financial planning for the project is sound. In fact, because of business's special expertise in finance, it may be argued that it is the responsibility of business to insist that major projects to which it contributes will have sound financial planning. If planning is inadequate, then business may find itself saddled with requests for substantial additional funds which it feels it cannot afford, but which it feels it must give in order to salvage the cultural investment it has already made.

The Spanish Pavilion was a key attraction of the New York World's Fair in 1964; therefore, it was reasoned that the pavilion should be an equally important attraction in dressing up the St. Louis, Missouri, waterfront. The Spanish government donated it to St. Louis, and a public foundation was set up to operate it. Estimated costs of bringing it to St. Louis and setting it up were $3 million, but actual costs were about $6 million.

St. Louis businessmen originally contributed nearly $2 million of the funds. When costs began to rise far above estimates, the mayor appealed to businessmen for more help. According to one business leader, "The same companies contributed reluctantly the second time, despite the fact

[4] William Glover, "Can Community Theater Live without Subsidy?" *The State Journal* (Lansing, Michigan), Dec. 21, 1969, p. E-17.

we didn't think it was a very sensible project. The only reason we went along was that we felt the mayor had gotten himself into a mess and needed help."

When the pavilion opened, the anticipated visitors failed to show up and the pavilion had an average monthly deficit of $35,000 for the first seven months. At that point the mortgage holder filed a lawsuit, and cultural leaders came to business asking for more gifts to help bail them out of their financial morass.[5] (If you were a businessman in this situation, what would you do?)

A final point is that business giving should not be so total that it makes the individual artists dependent upon business support. Both the artist and the businessman have a mutual interest in maintaining independence and a climate of freedom in which each can makes his own type of social contribution. One businessman observes, "I believe that corporations should give more money than they have been, but there is such a thing as smothering. Art should not be *encouraged* too much. Art is the expression of individuals with independence of spirit. These people should not be captured by the Establishment."[6]

Cultural Affairs in the Individual Business

Concurrently with their gifts for cultural activities, businessmen have discovered art as a means of creating a desirable in-company environment for employees and customers. Banks were among the first to move art from the museum to the office. Many banks and other offices today are, indeed, places of beauty with tastefully presented art collections that might even arouse envy in a museum director.

The business interest in art and other cultural affairs is worldwide. Italy's largest steel company, a state-controlled business, has supported a distinguished program of art, even commissioning the best Italian artists to illustrate its publications and decorate its buildings.[7]

It is popularly thought that businessmen are less interested in art and cultural affairs than the typical citizen, but this seems mostly to be a myth created by people who perceive businessmen in terms of the theoretical model of economic man. Businessmen throughout history have shown a strong interest in art, beauty, and cultural affairs. They developed great collections of art which they gave to public museums, gave land for public parks, supported symphonies, and created libraries (for example, Carnegie libraries). As explained by one businessman and art fancier:[8]

The pseudo-highbrow notion that the businessman is uninterested in the artifacts of life and unmoved by beauty is unhistorical and increas-

[5] "The Mayor's Tilt with the Windmills," *Business Week*, Jan. 31, 1970, p. 105.
[6] Armand G. Erpf, "Interface: Business and Beauty," *Columbia Journal of World Business*, May–June, 1967, p. 88. Italics in original.
[7] "A Steel Company in a World of Culture," *Fortune*, October, 1963, pp. 138–141.
[8] Erpf, *op. cit.*, p. 86.

ingly baseless. It is being recognized as a stale caricature that has enjoyed quite excessive longevity. Some of the great creators of business were men of magnificent, multifaceted artistic taste. Perhaps that's why they were great builders in their own fields. The creative instinct of a businessman may well be comparable to the creative force of an artist; it is just that the two are working with quite different materials and in different media.

An example of the cultural interest of one businessman at the beginning of the twentieth century is the magnificent Huntington Library in the Los Angeles area. It was formerly the home of Henry E. Huntington, a Western railway executive and community developer. Huntington spent many years assembling a choice art collection and an outstanding library which is especially rich in early English and American editions. The house itself is a work of art, and the grounds are beautifully landscaped with plants from around the world. In 1922 Huntington gave this entire collection and estate to the American public and included an $8-million trust fund to support and expand it.

Beauty in Business Building Design

From ancient times to the present, attention has been given to beauty in the design of many public buildings, but this idea did not carry into the design of factories in the Industrial Revolution. Generally, factories and many other business buildings have focused strictly on utilitarian function. The result was not just an absence of beauty, but a genuinely distasteful ugliness. As a result, in recent decades many manufacturers have encountered zoning opposition when they tried to move into a community. The potential factory's neighbors had images of factory blight, noise, smoke, and lowered home values. They wanted the factory's economic contribution, but not its social by-products.

In response to pressures from a pluralistic society and their own expanded view of their factories' effects, businessmen began giving more attention to combining beauty with utility in business buildings. In the words of one writer, "The Nineteenth Century Ugly school of factory design is finally dying out."[9] Many factory sites today are genuine industrial parks, often more attractive than their surrounding neighborhoods. The effect is to upgrade, rather than to blight, the neighborhood.

The cost of a factory "beauty treatment" is usually 1 to 5 percent of factory cost, but firms which have tried it usually report that it is worth the cost. These firms expected a better public image from beautification, but some additional effects were less expected. Improvements reported are higher labor productivity, decreased absenteeism, lower turnover of good employees, and improved recruiting. In addition, some firms report a heightened spirit of mutual interest, creativity, and job satisfaction. In other words, employees seem to feel better and work better in aesthetically pleasant surroundings.

[9] Steven M. Lovelady, "A Thing of Beauty . . . Handsome Factories Yield Unexpected Joys," *Wall Street Journal* (Pacific Coast edition), Dec. 1, 1965, p. 1.

A cement plant in the bleak Mojave Desert, for example, maintains that employee absenteeism and turnover became significantly lower after it landscaped its plant. The plant site is landscaped with $150,000 of plum, olive, elm, and peach trees, and it has colorful year-round gardens of flowers. The result was so impressive that the company set aside a larger amount for landscaping a new plant in another location.

An unusual case is that of a steel-strapping plant which built on 60 landscaped acres in a rich suburb of $50,000 to $80,000 homes. In the beginning the plant's neighbors opposed it, but once they saw its parklike landscaping, they considered it an asset to their neighborhood. The plant was so good-looking that its wealthy neighbors asked it to expand into an adjoining tract to prevent a real estate developer from building lower-priced homes on it. They felt that the lower-priced homes would depreciate the neighborhood more than the factory![10]

Costs of Securing Aesthetic Beauty

Costs of beautifying a building site may be considered a nominal capital investment which can be recovered because of the benefits mentioned, but there are other beautification costs which are more substantial. They also create major questions of public policy concerning who should pay for them. Overhead electric utility lines are certainly unsightly in metropolitan areas, but they are also expensive to place underground.

In a metropolitan area an electric utility company faced the choice of building a new high-voltage line overhead for $15 million or placing it underground for $160 million. This difference is substantial and would affect consumer cost of electric power. Who should pay this cost? Should it be the people who live near the line and would directly benefit from its being underground? Should it be all customers served by this line? (If so, in this case, they are at the end of the line, so those along the route would pay nothing.) Should it be all persons in the metropolitan area served by the line? Should it be all persons served by the utility in the state? Should it be government at the local, state, or national level? These answers do not come easily.

Furthermore, any rate increase required by the underground line will have to be approved by the public utility commission. This problem, therefore, is a matter of politics and public policy, as well as a socioeconomic decision for the firm. However, since the transmission line will exist for many years, the company must look ahead and develop a strategy that will be publicly acceptable for twenty years. It would be an economic and social waste to build an overhead line now and then in a few years be required by public pressure to place it underground.

Perhaps a rational strategy in this instance is to place low-voltage neighborhood lines underground as quickly as possible, because these affect more people and an acceptable technology is already available. Since underground high-voltage lines are very costly and affect the neighborhoods of fewer people, perhaps the placement of these lines underground may need to await a technological breakthrough or a more affluent society which can afford the cost. In the short run, society probably has

[10] *Ibid.*

more desirable alternatives for use of its limited capital and labor. (If you were the utility executives, what strategy would you decide? Or, as a citizen, what strategy would you desire?)

A costly strategy already decided is found at the Henderson mine of American Metal Climax, Inc., in the Colorado wilderness. Mine tailings (ore waste) are normally stored in ponds near the mine, but the mine in this instance is near a major highway. For this reason the mine is spending $25 million to tunnel more than nine miles through a mountain so that it can deposit its tailings out of view in a relatively inaccessible area. This arrangement increases the cost of the mine nearly fifteen percent, and there will be continuing operating costs to transport the tailings to this area. However, since the mine is a long-run investment, a preconstruction strategy was required which hopefully will meet aesthetic and conservation requirements for several decades.

In addition, the company is designing and coloring buildings to blend with the landscape in order to improve the usual drab appearance of mines. It is also building access roads which preserve as many trees as possible.[11]

A Look Ahead

It seems certain that the interface of business and cultural affairs will increase in future years. The systems model of business and society makes it clear to businessmen that the aesthetic and cultural quality of society does have an effect on the quality of business practice.[12] For these new conditions business needs to develop strategies which will be consistent with future expectations of society. Business needs to lead, rather than reluctantly back into the future.

One of the most advanced experiments in the interface of art and business is the Art and Technology project in the Los Angeles area. Through arrangement with the Los Angeles County Museum of Art, artists are working *within* business itself. They are not employees but are free artists experimenting with artistic implications of technology in areas such as electronics, cement, and aircraft. The artists work directly with employees, and companies spend thousands of dollars aiding them with time and materials. For example, one artist is working with laser beams and mirrors in closed space, another with light modulation, another with steel forms, and so on.

In the words of one artist, "This isn't oldtime patronage. It's like I'm a professional working here on a project." Another comments, "Probably for the first time, companies are actively participating in the art process. It's no longer passive patronage."

In the beginning this arrangement was difficult for companies to understand, but they now are enthusiastic about this kind of interface. For example, they talk about the catalytic effect scientists and artists have on each other's ideas.[13]

[11] "The War That Business Must Win," *Business Week*, Nov. 1, 1969, p. 71.
[12] For an extensive discussion see Richard Eells, *The Corporation and the Arts*, New York: The Macmillan Company, 1967.
[13] "Artists Use an Industrial Palette," *Business Week*, Nov. 8, 1969, p. 96ff.

BUSINESS AND MASS COMMUNICATION MEDIA

In the philosophy of democracy, a free society depends on open communication. This means that in the free world a large proportion of mass communication media, such as book printing, newspapers, motion pictures, radio, and television, are operated by independent business organizations, most of them operating on a profit-making basis. In each of these areas the state performs a regulatory role and produces some output itself, but the dominant operation is typically by free business (with the probable exception of television).

Business's operation of communication media places upon it a heavy burden of responsibility. It must assure a high quality of output, else the quality of society itself may deteriorate. It must assure reasonable saturation of its market so that all citizens are informed and have a chance to develop their potential. It must maintain an open system (free speech), but at the same time it must assure that the most outspoken groups do not dominate because this becomes de facto restriction of the openness of the system. Not only must it tell the truth, but it must tell the whole truth to assure that citizens have a balanced view of reality as it exists— and of future aspirations of both the common people and society's most capable idealists. The power of business is great in mass communication; therefore, in accordance with the Iron Law of Responsibility the responsibility of business is also large. It takes great institutions and noble business leaders to bear these substantial responsibilities, especially during a fast-changing age of discontinuity.

The subject of free mass communication and business's role in it is worthy of many books. In this chapter we briefly discuss certain key issues in the business-society interface. In discussing these issues we shall apply the criteria just mentioned: quality of output, reasonable saturation of market, open system with balanced representation of different views, the whole truth, and the Iron Law of Responsibility.

Freedom with Responsibility

Freedom of the press and other mass communications is not an end in itself but is a means to an end of a free society. Obviously mass communication is not set up simply for the profit of business. Business's social role is to provide the people a valuable service which helps maintain their freedoms. Since this service has deep ethical and political significance, business has special obligations to assure that it performs this service responsibly. Irresponsible abuse of free communication would threaten the foundations on which a free society is built. This condition is aptly phrased in a section of the Constitution of the State of Connecticut written in 1818. It provides freedom of speech and press but states that all citizens are ". . . responsible for the abuse of that liberty."[14]

In a similar manner free communication does not exist just for the pleasure and profit of communication professionals such as journalists

[14] Richard L. Tobin, " 'Responsible for the Abuse of That Liberty,' " Saturday Review, Jan. 13, 1968, p. 107.

and authors. They, like business, are the servants of the people. They have a deep ethical obligation to society to provide communication which meets the criteria mentioned earlier. Since they are the ones who actually produce the service which business sells, they have a responsibility to provide quality of output, balanced representation of views, and the whole truth. If journalists engage in irresponsible abuse of free communication, they—like business—will threaten the foundations on which a free society is built.

It is evident from this discussion that freedom of mass communication also implies some responsibility for the abuse of that liberty. The Iron Law of Responsibility applies equally to journalistic "producers" of communication and to business "sellers" of it. As a matter of fact, both journalists and businessmen have a mutual interest in developing open, responsible mass communication, because both know that their own freedoms depend on maintenance of a free society.

Who Controls Mass Communication?

Business's role in mass communication can be better understood by examining the centers of control of mass communication. At first glance, the answer may appear obvious. It can be said that, since business owns and controls the economic assets of communication such as printing presses and broadcasting studios, it must certainly control mass communication. However, ownership of assets in our complex, pluralistic society does not mean complete control of how these assets are used. In the highly interdependent structure of mass communication, many groups in addition to business owners and managers apply their control and influence.

Government, for example, controls the limits of communication through its court decisions on obscenity and on mergers which lead to monopoly of the press. It controls other communication media through administrative agencies such as the Federal Communications Commission. At the local level it exercises control through censorship boards and local laws.

The consumer also controls mass communication. He decides which books and magazines to purchase. He chooses which moving pictures to attend, and he is the one who turns the dial on his television set to select the program he desires. However, certain communication media such as newspapers, motion pictures, and television offer only a limited number of outlets, so he can choose only from the alternatives offered him. If both local newspapers are conservative or if both are liberal, then his choice is limited. Similarly, if all three motion picture theaters in his neighborhood are showing X-rated films, he cannot take his children to the neighborhood theater; but he may go elsewhere or choose another form of entertainment.

In addition, advertisers exert control on media which depend on advertising for their support. If a television producer cannot find an advertiser to support a specific program which he desires to produce, he may have to give up his project regardless of how worthy he thinks it is.

Similarly, various partisan groups control communication media by means of their information inputs into the system. Normally they issue information releases which are favorable to their points of view. In other cases they bring social pressures on newsmen to present their points of view, or they plan meetings or protests in terms of attracting news coverage.

Another major control group is composed of those who write and edit mass communications, as will be discussed in the next section.

The purpose of this discussion of control is to show that, although business owns communication assets, it is only one of many influences on the content of mass communication. What is evident here is the normal operation of a pluralistic society in which many semiautonomous groups are influencing the quality and content of communication. Pluralism helps keep the system free of monopoly and open to different points of view. It encourages development of different types of media and different types of output. In this manner it helps achieve the free society which is the ultimate objective of free and responsible mass communication.

Keeping in mind the basic ideas which have been discussed, we will examine three situations in which business encountered difficulty in its operation of mass communication media.

The Crisis in News Coverage

A normal model of pluralism assumes that social equilibrium is maintained by balanced influences of many interest groups. If one group gains excessive power which primarily serves only its interests or values, social disequilibrium develops, and quality of output tends to diminish. Further, in order to restore a balance considered more "just" or "right" by the parties involved, countervailing pressures will develop. This is the situation which developed with news coverage in the late 1960s. The public began to feel that they were not getting the whole story, that news coverage was negative in tone, and that it consistently followed an ideological bias. (These objections applied to news only; bias on the editorial page was generally accepted as part of a free press.) Some of the public blamed business (the managers of news media) for this condition, but most of them centered their dissatisfaction on reporters and television newscasters. These men play a key role in the powerful technostructure of modern mass communication.

For decades, news has typically emphasized disaster, violence, and problems. In the heritage of journalism, these conditions make news. As stated in one of the quotations introducing this chapter, "That is how you get on page one, that is how you win a Pulitzer Prize." However, the public reaction was caused by two additional factors. First, many persons felt that news coverage was dominated by journalists with a common ideological viewpoint; consequently, news tended to carry a uniform ideological bias. The situation was interpreted by a representative of a national broadcasting company as follows: "Men of like mind are in the news. It's provincial. The blue- and white-collar people who are in revolt now do have cause for complaint against us. We've ignored their point of view. It's bad."[15]

A second cause of dissatisfaction was that some persons believed that careless journalism was contributing to public problems. One publisher explained that off-target journalistic criticism can intensify social problems rather than solve them. He added:[16]

> For example, many write as if the federal government, or state government, or local government, or big business firms, or *somebody,* has it within their power promptly to "solve" what we call the urban crisis.
> Certainly each of these institutions must do everything it can to help.
> But given the best of intentions, the largest budgets, and the most skillful of executives, it may just be beyond the capability of all of these institutions to "solve" the problem in a reasonable period of time.

Looking at the situation in general terms, another journalist said that "the words and pictures that flow from the instruments of news media do, *without question,* structure the world for the beholder. The consumer of our products can only react to and accept or reject the material we allow him to read or hear or see. And so, in our editorial function, we make the world after our own image. The world is as we say it is."[17]

The public's fundamental conclusion in this situation was that journalism had exceeded the bounds of justice, balance, and representativeness. Excessive power had drifted into the hands of a small elite which was unduly influencing public thought patterns. In pluralistic terms, journalists had acquired power which they were not using responsibly. Consider, for example, the following rather routine situation.

The U.S. Department of Labor released annual figures of per capita income and employee wages for each of the fifty states. The figures reported that a certain state had per capita income below the national average. Under the news heading "State Income Below Average," a reporter in that state built a two-column article criticizing business for being a low-wage employer and not caring about worker economic needs. He reported an interview with the State Director of the AFL-CIO who condemned business for economic exploitation of workers. He also interviewed two workers who reported dissatisfaction with their income. No economist or businessman was interviewed.

As a matter of fact, if the reporter had examined the Department of Labor report more fully, he would have seen that manufacturing wages, construction wages, and other major wage classifications in the state were substantially *above* the national average. Had he consulted an economist he could have learned that per capita income is affected by many variables such as number of children in families and income from sources

[15] Fred Freed, quoted in Edith Efron, "The 'Silent Majority' Comes into Focus," *TV Guide,* Sept. 27, 1969, p. 7.
[16] Clark, *op. cit.,* p. 10. Italics in original.
[17] John R. Rider, "The Moment of Truth," *The Quill,* October, 1969, p. 28. Italics in original.

other than wages. In this particular state, even though wages were above the national average, per capita income was below average, in particular because of a high proportion of large families with children not working and a low proportion of very rich persons receiving income from nonwage sources.

This example suggests that a considerable part of the bias attributed to journalists may result from shoddy research and inadequate knowledge of the subject being reported.

A Rise of Countervailing Power

Regardless of the rightness of the public's conclusion about journalism, the widespread existence of this kind of public opinion was the cause of a gradual buildup of countervailing power, as might be expected in pluralism. Countervailing pressures developed toward both journalists and business as the employer of journalists. Pressures came from a variety of sources such as public personalities, journalism teachers, comedians joking on the subject, advertisers, and community action groups.

For example, under the leadership of a Stanford University professor of communication two experimental community press councils were established in the West. Their purpose was to review the fairness of press coverage in their community. When the mayor of Honolulu was asked his attitude toward this approach for his city, he approved and commented, "I think that it is always healthy for a citizens' committee on their own to call to task a newspaper article or a newspaper generally for not reporting the news without bias."[18]

At the national level the National Commission on the Causes and Prevention of Violence early in 1970 proposed a national independent center to evaluate the manner in which news is being presented. Dr. W. Walter Menninger, a psychiatrist on the Commission, went even further and suggested government licensing of journalists similar to the licensing of lawyers and psychiatrists in order to weed out ". . . individuals who are totally inept." He believed this approach would restore public confidence and ". . . assure the public that the practitioners of the art are qualified practitioners." He also suggested that news media provide a system for the public to gain redress for what it considers improper handling of news.[19] (As a citizen, what is your response to Dr. Menninger's proposal? How would you respond as a journalist?)

Proposals of this type are extreme, and they raise a cry of "censorship" from journalists, but they also indicate the seriousness of the rift between journalism and some segments of society.

[18] "Conference to Study News Media Quality," *Honolulu Advertiser*, Dec. 10, 1969, p. C-20; and "Fasi Gives His View on Press," *Honolulu Advertiser*, Dec. 9, 1969, p. A-12.
[19] "Licensing of Newsmen Asked," Associated Press Release, *Arizona Republic*, Feb. 5, 1970, p. 12.

During this conflict the chief criticism of business has been that it could have acted more responsibly to keep this situation from getting out of hand. As an employer of journalists, it could have encouraged more self-development and broadening of background, challenged careless or biased news reporting, and given assignments more suited to each journalist's capabilities. There is no suggestion that business managers tell journalists how to write the news. Professional independence of journalism is essential to a free society, but independence does not relieve journalists of responsibility for the abuse of their liberty. Nor does it relieve business of its obligation to operate mass communication responsibly.

The Fairness Doctrine in Federal Regulation of Broadcasting

The issue of fair news coverage is related to the *fairness doctrine* of the Federal Communications Commission in its regulation of the radio and television industry. This doctrine applies across the board to all broadcasts, rather than to news alone. Essentially the doctrine states that stations have a public obligation to air both sides of important public issues and to allow free time for persons or groups to reply if their "honesty, character or integrity" is challenged on the air. The Commission has applied this doctrine to political candidates, public controversy presented in an unbalanced way,[20] editorial attacks on individuals, and even cigaret commercials. For example, if an editorial favors a political candidate, opposing candidates must be given free and equal time to reply. As another example, until radio and TV cigaret commercials were banned by law on January 2, 1971, the Commission applied the fairness doctrine to them, requiring that stations which carried these commercials had an equal duty to inform listeners of the health hazards of smoking.

Broadcasters have opposed the fairness doctrine on the grounds of interference with rights of free speech, added broadcasting costs, and the fact that the doctrine may tend to suppress discussion of controversial issues or personalities. In June, 1969, however, the U.S. Supreme Court in the Red Lion Broadcasting Company case in a rare unanimous decision sweepingly upheld the Federal Communications Commission's constitutional and statutory right to apply the fairness doctrine.

Why does the fairness doctrine apply to broadcasting, but not to other mass communications such as newspapers and magazines? The reason is that broadcasting is a restricted marketplace, while printing provides a fairly free marketplace. For technological reasons, there are only a limited number of broadcast channels available, and this fact requires the Commission to choose among applicants who promise to meet public interest, convenience, and necessity. The granting of a broadcasting license, therefore, imposes on the licensee a responsibility to serve the public interest fairly. In the words of the Supreme Court a licensee has no right ". . . to

[20] For example, the Commission declared that a 1969 broadcast on a national news program violated the fairness doctrine by maligning private aircraft pilots without presenting news favorable to them. See "Huntley-Brinkley Hit by FCC as Unfair to Private Pilots," *Wall Street Journal* (Pacific Coast edition), Apr. 1, 1970, p. 31. However, the Commission reversed this decision on Sept. 25, 1970.

monopolize a radio frequency to the exclusion of his fellow citizens. It is the right of the viewers and listeners, not the right of the broadcasters, which is paramount.''[21]

In the case of printed media a variety of options are available to the public, so the normal workings of pluralism in a free society should assure a reasonably open presentation of different points of view. This concept does not deny that on some occasions ideas will be suppressed and bias will predominate; but viewed as a whole, open communication will tend to prevail. Thus, the *Chicago Tribune, Time, Look,* and *Playboy* can go their merry ways without cautiously having to balance points of view among their contents.

Motion Picture Self-regulation by Means of a Rating System

Another area of business difficulty in mass communication is motion pictures which have undesirable qualities for some of the population, particularly young persons. Motion pictures serve a broad audience ranging from young children to mature adults. In order to serve that audience, pictures of different maturity regarding sex, obscenity, and violence are produced. The maturity level, however, is not easily identified by the title of a movie, so children and others might attend movies which were unsuitable for them. The result was a growing disenchantment with motion pictures by a substantial portion of the public. Various citizen rating groups arose and community censorship increased, threatening chaos in the industry.

Recognizing its responsibility, the motion picture industry moved toward self-regulation. Since it had no power to prevent filming of any picture which met the minimum standards of the U.S. Supreme Court, it established in 1968 a rating system to designate the maturity level of films produced by its members. The president of the Motion Picture Association of America explained the reason for the rating system as follows:[22]

> We can and ought to be concerned for our children and what they read and see. That's what the film-rating system is all about.
>
> The great majority of film-makers and movie executives are true professionals, creative men and women, who are earnest workmen. But there are a minority who are not. The producer or director who inserts senseless violence and useless sex into his film so that he can lure more restless youngsters (and grown-ups) into the box office is a faker and a fraud, and he ought to be so labeled.''

[21] *Red Lion Broadcasting Co. vs. Federal Communications Commission,* 395 U.S. 367, June 9, 1969; and "Radio, TV Stations Have to Air Both Sides, Justices Decide in Upholding FCC Doctrine," *Wall Street Journal* (Pacific Coast edition), June 10, 1969, p. 4. Looking toward the future, television violence is receiving increased attention. It may be further regulated either by the industry itself or by government guides such as the fairness doctrine.
[22] Jack Valenti, "Motion Picture 'Czar' Reports on Ratings," *TWA Ambassador,* November–December, 1969, p. 36. Some films, especially foreign ones, remain unrated because the marketer does not seek a rating, often because of poor quality or obscene content.

The following rating system is used. "G" films are recommended for general audiences of all ages. "GP" (formerly "M") films have unrestricted admission, but they are mature films for which parental discretion is advised. The "GP" code refers to the words "General—Parents." "R" films are restricted admission films which do not admit persons under sixteen unless accompanied by a parent or adult guardian. They are clearly adult films. "X" films do not admit anyone under age sixteen, and in some states the age limit is higher by law. Their adult content may be offensive to some adults.

In the short run the rating system has been effective in meeting public needs, thereby reducing pluralistic pressures on the industry. The rating system's long-run capability is still to be tested. During its short existence, unrated "art films" have expanded dramatically. If a situation develops in which the majority of films become unrated, then the rating system will probably collapse, and new public pressures will develop.

SUMMARY

Business interface with cultural affairs is increasing. There are, however, limitations on business involvement in cultural affairs, because there are many alternative needs for business's efforts. Community cultural affairs are most likely to be successful when they have strong community support, rather than business dominance. Business's proper role is secondary; both the artist and the community need to retain their independence.

Free mass communication is a necessary means for achieving the social goal of a free society; consequently, business's operation of communication media places upon it a heavy burden of social responsibility. Business needs to provide a high quality of output, reasonable saturation of its market, open and balanced communication, and the whole truth. These responsibilities have proved difficult to meet in an age of discontinuity, as business works with independent journalists and strong pluralistic pressures.

STUDY GUIDES FOR INTERPRETATION OF THIS CHAPTER

1 The River City Fine Arts Association has proposed to the local chamber of commerce that businessmen build and support a community playhouse in order to upgrade community cultural life. As chamber of commerce president, how would you respond?

2 Discuss how large a percentage surcharge you would permit on your electric utility bill in order to pay for placing high-voltage trunk lines (not neighborhood lines) underground.

3 Choose a two-column news item from the *New York Times* or other major newspaper and critically appraise it for journalistic bias.

4 Attend a GP-rated motion picture and appraise why it was not rated G.

5 In response to a citizen complaint about biased news coverage of a certain event, a television executive commented, "Your complaint is not relevant. Our journalists are all qualified professionals and men of good intentions." Appraise this statement.

6 The United States Constitution, Amendments, Article I, reads in part as follows: "Congress shall make no law . . . abridging the freedom of speech or of the press. . . ." Discuss in terms of this provision of the Constitution: (a) the fairness doctrine of the FCC and (b) the proposals for local and national independent centers to evaluate news presentations.

PROBLEMS
THE BUILDING DESIGN REVIEW BOARD

An attractive suburban community strongly emphasized beauty in new building construction. The city established a design review board to approve building designs and specify changes required for total attractiveness of each building and building site.

In this city a nationwide retailer proposed to build a department store, garden shop, and auto service center on a major commercial street near a residential area. The design review board approved the plan including the following conditions:

1. Buildings shall cover not more than 25 percent of the land, and the site shall be landscaped throughout, including landscaping 10 feet deep along all street frontages. Interior boundaries shall be marked with a 6-foot wall properly landscaped.

2. All outside sales, service, and loading areas shall be screened from public streets.

3. No signs shall be on the side of the building facing residences, and any lights located there shall be directed away from residential areas.

4. No windows shall be above the ground floor level.

Residents in the neighborhood protested that these requirements were inadequate, requiring reconsideration by the board. The board then added the following additional conditions:

1. The building shall be located at least 100 feet from residential property. This change placed the building nearer the front of the lot, requiring substantial customer parking at the rear of the store.

2. Fences shall be 8 feet tall, with landscaping having an initial height of 12 feet.

3. Any open sales area shall be screened on all sides by a decorative masonry wall 8 feet high.

4. The automobile entrance doors of the auto service building shall be screened from the street by walls and/or landscaping.

5. Unpaved areas reserved for future buildings shall be turfed or otherwise treated attractively.

The retailer protested that major customer parking at the rear of the store was unworkable. Several builders and businessmen protested that the new requirements would drive this needed retail store out of the city into a nearby suburban city. The local newspaper editorialized, "Stop the harassment that will paralyze business in our city. We need to shop here as well as live here."

1 Appraise the new specifications of the review board. Do you consider them reasonable requirements for business construction in this attractive middle-class community?

2 A homeowner commented, "The protests of other businessmen not directly involved in this dispute are an unreasonable interference with our rights." Appraise this comment and prepare a reply to it.

THE PORNOGRAPHIC FILM

Warren Wilson has been in the theater business for thirty-three years, most of the time working for a national film distributor and theater operator. He is now sixty years old and regional manager for this firm. The four theaters which he supervises in the town where he lives are top-quality theaters. A month ago when he reviewed his booking list he learned that an unrated foreign film had been booked into one of his theaters. He viewed the film, which had already been banned by censorship boards in several cities, and judged it to be base pornography not suited to the quality theaters which he managed. He agreed in principle with Supreme Court rulings allowing controversial films to be shown to adults, but he felt that managers should have the right to apply common sense and make local interpretations of appropriateness. At that time X-rated films were showing in two of the four theaters he managed.

Wilson protested the film's bookings to higher management, giving his reasons, and two weeks later he was notified the film had been dropped from his booking list. Then, only a few days before the opening date originally scheduled for the film, he received a telephone call from the parent company which owned the national firm for which he worked. The top official who called him said the owner of the film would file a lawsuit for damages if the film was not shown, so it would have to be shown. Wilson objected, but the official said the film would be shown.

1 In the role of Wilson analyze the situation and determine what course of action you will take.

2 Appraise the parent company's decision.

THE TELEVISION CODE

A part of the Preamble of the Television Code of the National Association of Broadcasters (thirteenth edition, August, 1968) reads as follows:

Television and all who participate in it are jointly accountable to the American public for respect for the special needs of childen, for community responsibility, for the advancement of education and culture, for the acceptability of the program materials chosen, for decency and decorum in production, and for propriety in advertising. This responsibility cannot be discharged by any given group of programs, but can be discharged only through the highest standards of respect for the American home, applied to every moment of every program presented by television.[23]

1 Note the clear focus on the *home* in this Preamble. Discuss the reasons for this focus and its implications for the content of television programs compared with the content of motion pictures prepared for showing in commercial movie theaters.

[23] *TV Guide,* Aug. 23, 1969, p. 4.

CHAPTER 20

ECOLOGY AND ENVIRONMENTAL POLLUTION

All this talk about ecology: What the world needs is grass to lie on and people who will help keep it clean.

A SIGN POSTED ON A LAWN IN THE
HONOLULU, HAWAII, ZOO

An activist is the guy that cleans up the river, not the guy that concludes it's dirty.

H. ROSS PEROT[1]

Ecology is concerned with the relationships of living things and their environments. It provides a framework by which we can see that all living things are related to other living things, and they are all likewise related to their physical environment. Thus, a dry season may reduce vegetation, which affects the population of rabbits, thereby affecting the population of wolves. Likewise, the amounts and kinds of air pollution in an area may affect the health of orange trees—and of people.

Ecology and environmental quality are of interest to all people. It appears that quality of environment will be in the 1970s and 1980s a genuinely populist movement, appealing to people regardless of political views, religious beliefs, ages, or income levels. Probably pictures of earth from space did more than anything else to convince people that the earth is a tiny planet covered with a thin sheet of life-giving air and orbiting in hostile nothingness. If so, then this idea alone was perhaps worth the cost of all space exploration, because it may have saved mankind from extinction by irreversible pollution.

There is little doubt that mankind is facing an ecological crisis of various proportions around the world. It is easy to paint a bleak picture of man's senseless struggle against nature—a struggle which he cannot win. However, we believe that the systems concept of ecology requires man to think beyond the bleakness of defeat toward how mankind may apply his

---

[1] H. Ross Perot, quoted in Christopher S. Wren, "Ross Perot: Billionaire Patriot," *Look*, Mar. 24, 1970, p. 32.

intellect to use the system for improvement. This is what man has done historically. He has improved his environment through harnessing natural forces, such as water power, improving on nature as in hybrid seeds, and developing a technology which enables him to live in houses instead of in caves. It is significant that in the Chinese language the ideograph for "crisis" consists of two symbols: *danger* and *opportunity*. We believe this symbol represents the true proportions of the ecological crisis.

Most readers of this book are already knowledgeable about ecology and pollution, so this chapter will focus on selected broad ideas relating to business in an ecological system, a historical perspective of pollution, and approaches toward pollution control.

BUSINESS IN AN ECOLOGICAL SYSTEM

Complexity of an Ecosystem

An ecosystem is a total ecological community, both living and nonliving. The key point about an ecosystem is its immense complexity and inter-relatedness. Mankind is just now coming to understand that each act he takes is intricately tied to many other events in the chain of life of an eco-system. Since these intricacies have not been understood by the experts, businessmen likewise often have not realized the effects of their actions. This lack of understanding means that even the best of intentions may have unforeseen and undesirable results.

For example, Egypt sought for years to build its great Aswan Dam on the Nile River because it was seen as a benefit in countless ways for Egyptians who needed flood protection, a more stable water supply, and irrigation for parched desert farmlands. Predictions indicated that the entire lower Nile Valley would be a better life area because of the dam. Further, protective measures were taken to overcome negative effects of the dam. Valuable animal life was saved from areas to be covered by the lake, and important archaeological specimens were either protected or removed.

Now that the dam has been built, unforeseen negative effects on the ecosystem are being discovered.[2] The stabilized water flow prevents buildup of silt dunes at the end of the delta as the Nile enters the sea. These dunes formerly kept the sea away from rich delta farmlands, but now sea erosion is overcoming these dunes and flooding 1 million acres of farmland with salt water.

An additional problem is the spread of water hyacinths which evaporate large amounts of water in the lake above the dam. It appears that the lake may lose by evaporation about as much water as it was supposed to send down the Nile for irrigation. Of course, the hyacinths could be poisoned, but this would mean poisoning the lake.

Another danger predicted by an eminent zoologist is that a disease-carrying snail may spread through 500 miles of new irrigation canals below the dam. Peasants using the canals may catch the painful and normally incurable disease it carries.

[2] David Perlman, "America the Beautiful?" *Look*, Nov. 4, 1969, p. 25.

Thus, we must ask, was the ecological system of the Nile improved or deteriorated by the Aswan Dam? The answer hinges on whether the possible negative effects can be overcome by man's ingenuity.

Now let us look at two projects more directly involving business. Both had unforeseen outcomes. One was favorable and the other was unfavorable.

Oil and gas drilling expanded rapidly in the Gulf of Mexico beginning about 1957.[3] One predicted negative effect was damage to marine life by oil spills, so controls were established to minimize damage. There have been oil spills, some receiving much publicity, but damage has been relatively minor. Meanwhile, an unforeseen effect has been produced by the thousands of docks, platforms, and pipes. These structures provide a better place for lower forms of sea life to attach themselves than the silt-laden sea botton in this area. In a sense, the structures operate like a coral reef. Through supporting lower sea life, they attract and support larger quantities of desirable fish. Consequently, since oil expansion began, the commercial fish catch has doubled in this area, while it has declined as a whole in all other United States fishing areas. The Department of Interior gives credit for this increasing catch to the increase in these undersea structures.

Meanwhile, in the scenic Santa Barbara Channel of California the effects of oil drilling have been worse than expected because of oil leakages from geologic faults in the sea bed. And lower sea life did not need the underwater oil structures, because it already had an adequate supply of rock formations to which it could attach itself. As a result, President Nixon in 1970 asked Congress to cancel offshore leases in the area and create a 198,000-acre marine sanctuary in their place. Again, the evidence is clear that each ecosystem presents complex *individualized* factors, many of them beyond man's present capacity to foresee.

Social Trade-offs

Man's actions in an ecological system usually involve social trade-offs. These social trade-offs are of two types. First, there is the *priority choice.* All things cannot be done at once. If man allocates his time and resources to, let us say, reducing air pollution, then he has less time and resources for reducing water pollution, improving education, or recreational travel. Just how much, for example, are we willing to give up to achieve a cleaner world? Will we give up individual automobiles and accept public transportation? Will we give up our right to leaf burning in autumn, to smoking, or to backyard steak broils? Will we pay for the new municipal sewage system and the new street- and park-cleaning labor force?

The international Organization for Economic Cooperation and Development estimates that among the developed nations approximately four percent of gross national product is required merely to hold the line against more pollution.[4] That is tens of billions of dollars *annually* in the

[3] Ruth Sheldon Knowles, "Oceans of Resources—and Questions," *Wall Street Journal* (Pacific Coast edition), Sept. 30, 1969, pp. 22. You may wish to compare the following illustrations with our discussion in Chapter 1 of the public visibility of oil spills, particularly the one in the Santa Barbara Channel.

[4] "The Rhetoric of Ecology," *Life*, Mar. 6, 1970, p. 36.

United States. More important, many times that much will be required to make inroads into pollution existing from past causes. Is this a more important priority than poverty reduction, education, housing, or crime control? If it is, what pollution problems should be dealt with first? Should we tackle the easier problems with greater net returns or the harder ones that are more serious? Should *you* have to pay for cleaning up water pollution in New York or Colorado, if you do not live there? The choices are numberless.

A second kind of trade-off is what some have chosen to call the *gross national by-product* in order to contrast it with the gross national product (GNP). The idea of a gross national by-product implies that any major action which mankind takes for its benefit will also offer some negative results in the total ecosystem. For example, when slums are cleared for urban renewal, people are displaced, social communities are changed, and some historical heritages are destroyed. Or, if a mine is opened in a rural area, it brings truck traffic, night work, the probability of air, water, and solid waste pollution, perhaps an earth-jarring dynamite blast at noon each day, and a host of other changes that some persons will judge to be negative.

Many of the conditions mentioned can be controlled by allocating enough time and money to them, but there is no doubt that any major business or social action produces some gross national by-product. Man's choice is to make sure that, considering the system as a whole, he takes one of the alternatives with the greatest net benefits. We believe it is idealistic to insist that the one "best" choice be taken because there are too many intangibles and unpredictible future events in most social choices. Mankind acts wisely when it chooses one of the better alternatives on the basis of careful research of the whole ecosystem and cautious prediction of the unknown.

Public Visibility

From the point of view of business, a notable quality of ecology is the public visibility of some dysfunctions within the ecosystem. It is easy to see a coal mining scar on a green hill, the ugliness of a factory yard, and street trash in a downtown commercial district. A person can smell the stench of paper mills, untreated sewage, and dead fish from water pollution. These situations make humorous jokes, as shown in Figure 20–1, but they are also quite serious in their effect on business's image if there is any way that the public can connect the visible pollution with business.

In general, business is more visible in its pollution than other institutions and thus more vulnerable to public criticism. It is easier to see the black or yellow smoke coming from a factory smokestack than the wastes from thousands of home oil furnaces which actually may be polluting the air more than the factory. The same reasoning applies to mostly invisible pollutants coming from hundreds of thousands of automobiles in a large city. It took a great amount of scientific research to identify automobile exhaust (aided by photochemical action from sunlight) as the primary

FUNNY BUSINESS   By Roger Bollen

Figure 20–1 The seriousness of pollution is sometimes communicated through humor. Source: *State Journal*, Lansing, Michigan, Dec. 8, 1969. Reprinted by permission of NEA.

source of Los Angeles smog. Then major publicity was required to con-vince the people that the research was accurate. "The factories and refin-eries must be causing our smog," the people insisted. And, of course, they were partly right; the public visibility was there. However, by 1969, with normal regulation, combined industrial-residential-commercial sources caused only about ten percent of air pollution in Los Angeles County. The remaining ninety percent came from motor vehicles, even though some emission controls were already required on vehicles.[5]

A HISTORICAL PERSPECTIVE OF POLLUTION

Pollution needs to be seen in its historical perspective in order for it to be understood with a balanced view. It is not something new to the twentieth century. Mankind has dumped its trash into the soil and water since the beginning of civilization. Archaeological excavations show the trash of sev-eral civilizations (not generations) dumped one on top of the other. Smoke from man's fires has polluted the air since the Stone Age. Citizens of early Rome complained that soot from fires dirtied their clothes, and London was described in 1660 as covered with "clouds of smoke and sulpher."[6]

[5] Louis J. Fuller (Los Angeles County Air Pollution Control Officer), "As I See It," *Forbes*, Dec. 15, 1969, p. 55.

[6] M. A. Wright, *The Business of Business: Private Enterprise and Public Affairs*, New York: McGraw-Hill Book Company, 1967, p. 27. London endured these "clouds of smoke" for 300 years until the Clean Air Act was passed in 1956. Under the law gov-ernment authorities could set up tight standards for emission of dark smoke. Since much of the smoke came from home heating, householders were given subsidies of up to 70 percent to pay for conversion of heating equipment to take smokeless fuel. A report released after thirteen years of experience with the law showed that it was immensely effective. For an annual per capita cost of 36 cents the average Londoner received 50 percent more winter sunshine, and visibility was increased from 1.4 miles to 4 miles. Respiratory diseases also declined, indicating the complex ecology of the community. See "London Sees the Light, Thanks to Its Clean-air Law," *Washington Post*, Mar. 17, 1970, p. A3.

Natural Pollution

Nature, as well as man, also pollutes the air. Dust storms toss dirt and debris into the air, natural forest fires cast a pall of smoke over mountain valleys, and lightning creates certain chemical compounds. The director of the United States Geological Survey estimates that more than one hundred million tons of nitrogen in the form of ammonia and nitrates are precipitated on the earth each year.[7] In the United States alone, 36 million tons of calcium compounds fall on the earth in rain.

The pollution from volcanoes is phenomenal and puts modern pollution clearly in perspective. The director of the Geological Survey states that only three eruptions in the last one hundred years—Krakatoa in Java in 1883, Mt. Katmai in Alaska in 1912, and Hekla in Iceland in 1947—have produced more air pollution than mankind in all of his history. From these three eruptions, "More particulate matter in the form of dust and ash, and more combined gases were ejected into the atmosphere than from all of mankind's activity."[8]

Perhaps the most uncomfortable and irritating of all natural pollutants, as many persons with allergies can testify, is the pollen released every day by trillions of plants. This pollution causes great human suffering.

Although pollution has existed since the early history of man, it was usually of minor significance. Only a few serious problems developed such as polluted drinking water near metropolitan areas, destruction from volcanic eruptions, and allergies. Since 1700, however, three additional causes have arisen which have fundamentally altered the seriousness of pollution. They have upset the delicate balance of nature which allowed men to live comfortably in their environment.

The Industrial Revolution

A primary cause of air and water pollution has been the Industrial Revolution. Its factories spread first across Britain and then the rest of the world, with smokestacks belching contaminants into the air. Industry requires power, much of which is secured from incomplete combustion which releases pollutants of various types. The complex chemical processes of industry produce undesirable by-products and wastes that pollute land, water, and air. Its mechanical processes often create dust, grime, and unsightly refuse. More recently, the Agricultural Revolution as an adjunct of the Industrial Revolution has produced overkill with pesticides, odors, refuse from cattle feeding "factories," and other unpleasant conditions.

The International Council for the Exploration of the Sea reports that the Baltic Sea is becoming polluted from agricultural pesticides and fertilizers, industrial wastes, and sewage.[9] Phosphate concentrations, which

[7] "Geologist Says Nature Equals Man as Despoiler of Earth," United Press International news release, Arizona Republic, June 8, 1970, p. 14.
[8] Ibid.
[9] "Pollution Threat to Baltic Sea," London Times News Service, Arizona Republic, Mar. 6, 1970, p. 19.

are especially hazardous to sea life, are three times higher than fifteen years ago. Mercury pollution is so high that there is a ban on fish caught in some areas of the sea. DDT concentration in seals is ten times that of nearby North Sea seals, and scientists fear that reproductive ability of some fish species is being reduced.

A Higher Standard of Living

Industrialization has raised man's standard of living enormously. As man consumes more, his consumption tends to create more wastes. The more elegant his tastes for food become, the more garbage and other refuse he produces. The more he buys, the more paper and packaging are required, most of which become refuse. When he buys a car to replace his horse and buggy, he travels more and the engine he uses leaves more airborne pollution. As he travels, he leaves a trail of debris such as cans, bottles, and wrappers.

Every rise in the standard of living means a related rise in pollutants produced by the individual person. Further, as his consumption increases, his economic demand requires an increase in industrial production with its related pollutants. For example, solid wastes discarded in the United States are nearly a ton a year *per capita*. These wastes are distributed as follows: household, 44 percent; industrial and construction, 30 percent; and commercial, 26 percent.[10]

Bottles and tires discarded illustrate the enormity of solid wastes.[11] In order to use these wastes it has been suggested that bottles be ground into particles to replace gravel as a base for highways. Tires could be mixed with asphalt to make a road that is better able to withstand cracking. The result is a "glasphalt" highway. However, if this method were used completely, the bottles and tires disposed of in 1970 alone could pave a freeway that would cross the United States twenty-three times!

The Population Explosion

The ultimate time bomb in pollution is a speedup in population growth.[12] This has happened mostly during the last 200 years as a result of economic and medical progress which allowed people to live longer. Every additional person adds pollutants to land, air, and water, although the amount of these vital natural resources remains the same. The result is more intensive pollution of these existing resources, unless mankind takes steps to reduce pollution. In the year 1900 in the United States, for example, about three million square miles accommodated less than eighty million people. By 1970, this area, and the air and water that go with it, had to accommodate over two hundred million persons. It should, therefore, not be surprising that the environment is becoming more polluted.

It is estimated that the population rate is doubling every thirty-five years. If existing rates continue, the 1970 population of slightly over

---

[10] "Cash in Trash? Maybe," *Forbes*, Jan. 15, 1970, p. 20.
[11] "Riding on Wastes," *Time*, Mar. 16, 1970, p. 62.
[12] Paul R. Ehrlich, *The Population Bomb*, New York: Ballantine Books, Inc., 1968.

3 billion will be 6 billion by the year 2000. If this rate continues for a few hundred years, the earth will be covered with people with standing room only. This is obviously an impossible situation, so eventual pollution control must rest on a base of realistic population control.

A Worldwide Problem

Pollution is, indeed, a global problem. In Russia the Volga River boatmen are charging that chemical plants are discharging wastes which kill sturgeon and threaten Russia's caviar supply. Scandinavian paper mills are poisoning the Baltic Sea. Japanese traffic police have oxygen masks available to wear during rush hours in certain busy street intersections. Cities of the western United States are imperiled by smog. Italian paintings and monuments are being eroded by fumes from industrial plants. Even in poor areas of the world, such as a slum in an Indian city, the crowding of people creates a polluted land, polluted water, and the stench of refuse and filth.

APPROACHES TOWARD POLLUTION CONTROL

As one of the authors approached Honolulu on a commercial flight, the pilot announced that the airplane was tenth in the "stack" awaiting landing because the airport was under ground-controlled landing conditions. The view below as one looked out the window was a deep black like a dark rainstorm viewed from above. No land was visible. Finally we moved through the blanket of black and to an easy landing. Only then did we learn that the city was blanketed with "vog" (volcanic fog). A volcano on another island had a minor eruption the day before, and unusual winds had blown the suspended ash to this spot and held it there. The condition was strictly temporary and unusual. The next morning there was no trace of it; and the ash, wherever it had blown, would soon be carried to the ocean in rain squalls.

A few weeks later one of the authors approached St. Louis, and the pilot made a similar announcement. The air below was a brownish black, and again no land was visible. As he descended through the brown blanket his eyes began to burn, and he knew he was in smog. On the ground the newspaper reported that this was the third day of a smog alert, and no relief was in sight for two more days.

Whether the pollution is water, air, solid waste, noise, sight, or something else, some of it is transitory, like the Honolulu vog or a mountain stream clouded by a spring flood, and will soon by solved by normal ecological processes. Other pollution is man-made and tends to be more permanent or to recur frequently, unless man does something about it. Almost without exception, a preventive approach is better than a remedial approach.

Pluralism in Action

Efforts toward pollution control provide an excellent example of pluralism in action, showing both its faults and strengths. There are duplicated efforts, confusion, and slow responses; but there are also wise countervailing powers, an array of different talents and approaches, and the creativity and enthusiasm that come from active participation. Among those involved are different branches of government, professional groups such as architects, labor, business groups with different interests, conservationists, and neighborhood groups. Several approaches toward pollution control used by these groups and others will be discussed in the following paragraphs.

The Search for Technological Breakthroughs

Perhaps the most exciting approach to pollution control is the search for technological breakthroughs which turn potential pollutants into harmless or desirable by-products. As population increases and standards of living rise, man's need for power for his machines and equipment increases dramatically. The difficulty is that power sources tend to cause polluting by-products such as fly ash, gases, heat, and radiation. Atomic energy was once seen as the solution to most of these problems, but its by-products of thermal pollution and radiation have not been solved. Another solution with much potential is the fuel cell, which makes electricity directly through chemical reaction, usually with harmless by-products of carbon dioxide and water; however, the fuel cells that have been developed are costly and low in power output.

On a more imaginative level a director and former president of the Solar Energy Society of Phoenix has proposed a 25-square-mile solar energy cell operating in earth orbit.[13] It would produce more power than is used by the entire New York City area. The power would be beamed by microwave to a 36-square-mile field on the earth. Wires spread over the field would collect the waves, convert them to electricity, and feed the electricity into the existing power grid. The wires and microwaves would make the field unsafe for housing, but it would be suitable for farming.

This unique plan is feasible with existing technology, and it would avoid all present forms of pollution from power generation. (However, would the microwaves create a new form of pollution or some unforeseen ecological imbalance?) At any rate, it is a creative approach. Its originator points out that, contrary to the argument that space funds could be better spent on earth problems, he is perceiving that "space technology might save life on earth," because of the superior capacity of space to generate pollution-free energy.

Voluntary Business Response

Another approach to pollution control is voluntary business action to prevent pollution or remove it. Hundreds of millions of dollars annually are being invested in this way. It can be argued quite properly that business action is not wholly "voluntary," because business is responding to countervailing pressures. This is correct in many cases. Business typically recognizes pollution control as one more cost of doing business in a par-

[13] "How to Get Sun Power for New York," *Business Week*, May 9, 1970, p. 128.

ticular environment. As stated by one businessman, "We used to consider mostly minimum capital and maximum efficiency in our plant design, but now we have a third ingredient, pollution costs." These costs can run as high as 10 percent for a paper mill and 20 percent for some chemical plants, but typically they are in a more reasonable range of 1 to 5 percent of capital and operating costs. An example of the complexities and costs of pollution control is the experience of Mobil Oil Company with its Ferndale refinery.[14]

> To combat air pollution Mobil engineers designed many refinery units in a way that minimized emission of mist, sulfur dioxide, petroleum vapor and other chemical compounds. A special incinerator was installed to convert smelly compounds to less objectionable materials. A smokeless flare and blowdown system was provided to insure that all hydrocarbon releases were properly burned. Oil storage tanks with floating roofs were selected to minimize evaporation losses. These and more design innovations put a tight clamp on air and plant pollution.
>
> Control of water pollution turned out to be an even tougher nut to crack. . . .
>
> The men who designed Ferndale planned six separate sewer systems to handle different types of waste. Expensive—but effective. These systems separately accommodate oil process waste, sanitary waste, phenolic process waste, normal storm drainage, emergency storm drainage and ship's ballast discharge.
>
> "We even have educated 'bugs' to help us decontaminate the first three types of waste water" [said a process engineer].
>
> Ferndale's bugs are fussy. Once they get accustomed to a certain concentration of phenol, they die or quit eating if served up a different diet of phenol. The waste water that goes into their tanks is, therefore, carefully controlled, and a reserve supply of sludge is always maintained just in case the main floc overeats. . . . When they're through, phenol in the water is nil.

A somewhat different response is the design of pollution control into a product in order to improve its desirability for customers. The quieter engines of Rolls Royce, Ltd., were said to be a factor in its winning the engine contract for the Lockheed airbus. However, even when the product is more desirable, if it costs more, it may have difficulty gaining acceptance until this cost is worked into the whole social structure.

Air compressors at construction sites are unpleasantly noisy, and people agree that quieter ones should be used. Ingersoll-Rand designed a quiet "Whisperized" air compressor, partly to meet requests of New York City for this type.[15] Contractors agree that the quiet compressor is a substantial improvement, but it costs 25 percent more. Unless quiet compressors are specified in construction contracts, contractors using quiet compressors are at a disadvantage in bidding on contracts, because a quiet compressor does no more work than a noisy one. The result is that broad acceptance of the product eventually will depend on city noise ordinances

---

[14] "Ferndale Refinery: Profile of a Good Neighbor," *Mobil World*, February, 1965, p. 7.
[15] "The Trade-offs for a Better Environment," *Business Week*, Apr. 11, 1970, p. 66.

and the government's willingness to specify this type of product in its own contracts. Even after the product was available, the City of New York continued to order more of the noisy compressors.

A direct business approach is to design and market pollution control equipment and services. This is a standard business practice in existence for decades, and a few companies earn most of their income from this type of operation.

Countervailing Powers among Businesses

Like most other groups, businessmen do not have uniform attitudes toward the environment. Different types of business want different conditions in the environment; consequently, powerful countervailing pressures arise within business itself. For example, commercial fishermen filed a damage suit against certain chemical companies for polluting Lake Erie with mercury compounds. The fishermen wanted to make profit from their fish catches, and the chemical companies wanted an economical dumping ground for their wastes. These two goals finally came into conflict, so the fishermen instituted countervailing pressures through the legal system.

In a Midwestern city, three property owners in the downtown business district failed to maintain their property adequately. Major shops in this area believed that the shabby appearance of these buildings drove shoppers from the area, so they worked through their retail merchants' association to bring pressure on the owners either to sell or to improve their property. In another instance, a large chemical plant wanted to build near an area that real estate developers believed was prime residential land, so the latter used publicity to build enough opposition to block the necessary zoning permit for the plant.

Since most of these cases involve pressures rather than legal rights, the outcome can go either way. However, with society's strong interest in pollution control, the business group which takes action against a polluter or potential polluter has a powerful ally in the form of public opinion. Therefore, the antipollution group is the typical winner, and this is encouraging more businesses to take action against their polluting neighbors. The general conclusion which this discussion suggests is that if the public will give strong support, business groups with antipollution interests will force other businesses to reduce their pollution.

Conservationists

Strong allies in any drive for a cleaner earth are the conservationists, such as fishermen, campers, boating enthusiasts, and nature lovers in general. The largest and most influential of these, and one of the most militant, is the seventy-seven-year-old Sierra Club. It has worked to save redwood forests and block the building of dams in the Grand Canyon of the Colorado River. It has lobbied against the supersonic transport (SST), because of possible noise pollution and ecological damage from its supersonic shock waves.

Court decisions have established that the Sierra Club and similar groups have legal standing to sue in court on behalf of the public interest.[16] Accordingly, the club is pursuing legal actions such as the following: preventing construction of a pulp mill in Alaska, stopping a mining company from dumping taconite tailings into Lake Superior, preventing a six-lane expressway along the banks of the Hudson River, and stopping construction of a $35 million ski resort in California. The club also is seeking a national corporation code which would require corporations to protect the environment.

A major difficulty with conservation groups is their singular interest in almost a pure, pristine, back-to-nature environment. Through legal actions they may bring long delays in projects which, on balance, serve human needs. These kinds of delays have already prevented necessary power plant construction, leading to the probability of major power brownouts or blackouts in the 1970s.

Government Regulation

Government cannot watch all of us to determine whether we toss our candy wrappers into the gutter, but certainly it has a major role in pollution control. In terms of functional analysis, it has strong capabilities for setting general policies and minimum standards for pollution affecting interstate commerce. It also can provide economic incentives to encourage businesses, communities, and regions to reduce pollution, and it can offer just legal and administrative systems for resolving disputes about pollution. For example, air moves freely. Regulation in the corporate limits of one city will not stop pollution; therefore, the national government needs to establish minimum standards for air quality. Eventually international standards may be established. On the other hand, since each region's air pollution problem is different, national minimum standards should not preempt the authority of states, regions, or communities to set more stringent standards within the bounds of reason to meet local problems.

National government has control of navigable waterways and may set standards for their use. The Refuse Act of 1889 shows that water pollution was a substantial concern of citizens at that early date, because it allows fines of $2,500 for each day or incident of discharging wastes into a navigable stream without a permit from the Corps of Engineers. An interesting part of the law is that it grants the reporting individual a bounty of one-half the fine. If the government fails to prosecute, the citizen may sue the violator in the name of the United States and collect the bounty. Perhaps if this law had been better known to citizens and enforced by the courts, water pollution would not have become the problem it is.

More recently there has been the Water Quality Act of 1965, which sets up machinery for eventual establishment of pollution standards and their court enforcement. The Air Quality Act of 1967 takes somewhat similar action regarding air. There are many other laws, such as the Solid Wastes Act of 1965 concerning research and demonstration grants for

[16] "Sierra Club Mounts a New Crusade," *Business Week*, May 23, 1970, pp. 64–65.

solid waste disposal, and the number of laws is sure to increase in the 1970s.

A survey of the chief executives of the largest United States firms shows that they favor more government control.[17] In response to a question about federal government regulation, 57 percent favored an increase in regulatory activities while only 8 percent favored a reduction. A major reason for this view is that cessation of pollution by one firm does not noticeably affect the quality of life nationally; therefore, large firms feel the need for national minimum standards. Unless all firms go along with pollution abatement, the remaining pollution will continue to give even the nonpolluting firms a "black eye" in the public image—and the nonpolluting firm will have a competitive disadvantage because of the cost of his control equipment. Clearly, this is a situation requiring government policies and minimum standards.

Administrative Controls

In 1970 a three-man Council on Environmental Quality was established by law within the Executive Office of the President. The law is similar to the one creating the Council of Economic Advisors in 1946. The 1970 law declares that it is the policy of the United States to use all practicable means to maintain conditions of productive harmony between man and nature and to fulfill the social, economic, and other requirements of the people. The principal duties of the Council are: (a) to assist and advise the President in preparation of an annual report on environmental quality, (b) to develop and recommend national policies which promote environmental quality, and (c) to accumulate data for continuing analysis of trends in the national environment.

In addition, President Nixon in 1970 established a National Industrial Pollution Control Council consisting of about fifty industrialists. The purpose of the Council is to chart plans for cooperative industry-government efforts to improve the quality of environment.

Ways of Applying Government Controls

The preceding discussion shows that government will make its influence felt *in a variety of ways* in pollution control. This is the key thought. Government will not follow just one approach, because the situation is too complex and variable. Following are some of the approaches that are likely to be used, including those already mentioned.

1. Legislative standards enforceable in courts of law
2. Administrative boards which may set standards enforceable in courts of law
3. Zoning and other regulations which require new construction or new products to meet certain pollution standards (such as waste discharge of new plants or exhaust emissions of new automobiles)

[17] Robert S. Diamond, "What Business Thinks," *Fortune*, February, 1970, p. 119. This issue of *Fortune* is devoted to "The Environment: A National Mission for the Seventies."

4. Tax incentives for pollution control equipment (such as faster depreciation or tax credits)

5. Matching grants or subsidies for installation of pollution control equipment

6. Monitoring and investigative bodies which make reports, recommend legislation, and use the pressures of publicity (such as the Council on Environmental Quality)

7. Cooperative groups for research and policy guidance (such as the National Industrial Pollution Control Council)

8. Denial of government contracts and other privileges to violators (or perhaps privileges to nonpolluters, similar to veterans' preference in government employment)

9. Research grants for development of new control methods, and demonstration grants to test them in service

10. Fixed charges for pollution emissions (such as a certain number of dollars for each ton of noxious fumes from a smokestack or each gallon of a chemical waste dumped into a river), an approach effective in reducing pollution of certain European rivers

A Concluding Statement

Two points derive from this discussion. The first is the complexity and variety of ecological problems. There is no easy solution. There is no economical solution. Since there are many unknowns in the situation, a variety of approaches and the best of man's creative talents are required. Research needs to precede action whenever possible, as the following incident illustrates.[18]

Kaneohe Bay is an ocean jewel nestled against green hills on Hawaii's windward coast. It is surrounded by small boat docks and the town of Kaneohe. Concern gradually arose among citizens that the bay was becoming polluted by wastes from boats and homes, along with commercial and residential sewage released into the bay after processing. When most of the clams in the bay suddenly died, the people became alarmed, and a government-financed ecological study of the bay was initiated.

With the aid of $90,000, twenty-three scientists, and one year of research, the study concluded that ecological conditions of the bay were in "exact balance." That is, organic matter (including sewage) going into the bay was consumed as fast as it entered; hence, the organic matter was needed to supply the large amount of sea life in the bay. The only spot where the water did not meet the state's stringent water standards was directly over the main sewer outfall. (Since large population increases could upset the existing ecological balance, periodic future studies were recommended.)

Then what killed the clams? Research disclosed that they were killed by a prolonged rainstorm which flooded the bay with so much fresh water that the clams could not survive in the less-saline water. Human wastes had nothing to do with their death.

[18] Claude Burgett, "Water Pollution Study Finds Kaneohe Bay in 'Exact Balance,' " *Honolulu Star-Bulletin*, July 19, 1969, pp. 1, A-7.

A second point derives from the first. Since ecology is complex, mankind did not recognize impending problems soon enough to take corrective action, so a crisis developed. Massive efforts, education, and resources will be required to overcome this crisis. Successful action will require the cooperation of all segments of pluralistic society. On the other hand, we must be cautious not to become so frantic that we impose harsh, unrealistic standards[19] or take well-intentioned actions which accomplish nothing, or even increase ecological problems.

SUMMARY

Ecology furnishes a framework by which we can interpret man's relation to his environment and the developing crisis in environmental pollution. The ecological system is complex, requires social trade-offs which result in some gross national by-products, and gives high public visibility to some polluting acts of business.

Three conditions have accelerated pollution. They are the Industrial Revolution, a higher standard of living, and the population explosion. The approaches to pollution control are an example of pluralism in action. Government's role is primarily that of setting policies, establishing standards, and providing incentives to reduce pollution.

STUDY GUIDES FOR INTERPRETATION OF THIS CHAPTER

1 Study the Water Quality Act of 1965 and the way it has been implemented. Then report to your group your judgment, with reasons, regarding the effectiveness of the act.

2 A group of militant environmentalists has proposed to the board which governs the city-owned convention center that the board deny use of any of the center's facilities to any business or business group which "contributes to ecological imbalance" of the world. They have specifically mentioned mines, agribusiness groups, chemical firms, automobile firms, and petroleum firms. You are chairman of the governing board and vice-president of a local chemical plant producing industrial chemicals. How would you respond?

3 Based on research and statistics, give a report to your group concerning your interpretation of the seriousness of the population explosion and what control measures should be taken, if any.

4 Study information about noise pollution, including its possible effects on health, and report your conclusions.

5 Study news releases concerning the Council on Environmental Quality and the latest annual report of the Council. Then give your interpretation of the Council's effectiveness.

[19] For example, note the copper industry's claim that technology is not available to meet requirements in some states for control of smelter emissions of sulfur dioxide, as reported in "Copper Men See Red over Pollution," Business Week, June 13, 1970, p. 31.

PROBLEMS
"THEY CAN'T PUT US OUT OF BUSINESS"

The manager of a metalworking firm in a city of 50,000 persons has defied pressures by various groups to stop the factory's cyanide pollution of a river which runs through the town. The manager commented, "Pollution control is money down the drain, because it adds nothing to the product. All you get is a little local goodwill, and we sell our products nationally. They know they can't put us out of business, because we employ 1,500 people in this plant."

Investigation shows that available cyanide control equipment would cost $50,000 for installation and $15,000 annually for operating expenses.

1 You are president of one of three other major employers in the town, and you believe that you have considerable influence with the manager of the metalworking firm. Your firm releases no pollutants into the river. Pollutants from your firm's smokestacks are moderately controlled, but better equipment is now available. Your firm's products are sold nationally and are not in competition with those of the metalworking firm. What would you do, if anything?

2 Assume you are a banker who is president of the local chamber of commerce. The metalworking firm has its account in your bank. What would you do, if anything, in your role as president of the chamber of commerce?

THE REPUBLIC OF NAURU[20]

The Republic of Nauru is situated on a small island of 5,263 acres in Polynesia near the equator. It is 2,600 miles southwest of Hawaii. The republic has a population of 3,304 persons. These people may be the richest in the world, and they are getting richer every day. Investment income and annual phosphate mining royalties paid to the government by the Nauru Phosphate Company, in which the British have an interest, amount to over $6,000 annually *for each Nauruan.*

Few Nauruans work because their affluent income does not require labor to support their needs. The phosphate mines are worked by Polynesians from other islands. The government, except for top positions, is run by employed civil servants mostly from Australia. They are paid such high salaries by the Nauruans that the Australian government is considering a special tax on their incomes. Most other work on the island is performed by Chinese.

There is enough phosphate on the island to last another twenty-five to forty years at the present rate of mining. If mining were stopped immediately, annual investment income for every Nauruan would be $1,200 for life. Nauru has no other significant source of income, although its color-

[20] Birch Storm, "South Sea Republic of Nauru Emerges," *Honolulu Advertiser*, Dec. 8, 1969, pp. D-4, D-5. The republic's name and the facts in this case are not disguised.

ful postage stamps are popular with philatelists. There is one beach area with possibilities for tourist development. There is no port; only open sea anchorage is available. Air transportation to the island is provided by Fiji Airlines once a week and Air Micronesia every two weeks. In order for planes to land, the phosphate mining operation is shut down the day before the plane is due. If it did not shut down, clouds of dust from the mining operation would obscure the runway and prevent the plane from landing.

1 Discuss ecological problems and decisions which Nauruans will face during the next ten years. How is business involved?

2 Discuss ecological problems and decisions which Nauruans will face during the next ten to forty years. How is business involved?

PART FIVE
BUSINESS IN AN INTERNATIONAL WORLD

CHAPTER 21

THE SOCIAL RESPONSE OF MULTINATIONAL BUSINESS

Managers of international companies, if they are to
do their jobs well, must not only be technically
competent in their field of work, but they must also
become deeply involved with the ideas and feelings
of the people around them.

DAVID A. SHEPARD[1]

The idea is gaining acceptance that multinational
industry is perhaps a more stabilizing factor than
government in international relations.

DANIEL PARKER[2]

Nations of the world as a matter of national policy are seeking to improve their social and economic development. Multinational business has
a significant and perhaps leading role in achieving these social goals. The
people have needs. Business has the know-how and resources to meet
these needs and perhaps to improve international cooperation at the same
time.

Some years ago a soft drink bottler entered a nation which was just beginning its development.[3] At that time the society was quite poor and
almost wholly agrarian. Even bottles and wooden bottle cases had to be
imported, but the company quickly started working with nationals of this
country who were community leaders to develop local supplies and
services related to its business. To secure a bottle-making facility, it
helped these nationals organize a company, gave them a large order,
helped them construct their plant, and advanced working capital to them.
This glass-making facility now employs hundreds of people and the
nation's glass container needs are served wholly by domestic ownership
and management.

The bottler translated its truck maintenance manuals into the local
language and taught a local truck operator how to maintain its trucks,

[1] David A. Shepard, "Statism, Nationalism and American Business Abroad," *The Lamp*,
Winter, 1962, p. 2.
[2] Daniel Parker, "To Improve the Conditions of Life for Everyone Everywhere," *Columbia Journal of World Business*, July–August, 1968, p. 22.
[3] J. Paul Austin, "The Management of Abundance," *Advanced Management Journal*,
January, 1968, pp. 9–10.

which at the same time helped him extend the life of his own equipment. His facility has now grown into a large automotive body works and maintenance business.

Other citizens were encouraged to make wooden crates for bottles and metal coolers for keeping drinks iced. Each later became a large factory owned and managed by citizens of the country. In this manner the multi-national bottler helped others serve human needs while it fulfilled its own goals of providing low-cost soft drinks for masses of people.

Based upon universal needs for development and the rising aspirations of people, modern business relationships have become worldwide. Expansion beyond national boundaries is much more than a step across a geographical line. It is also a step into different social, educational, political, and economic environments. Supply lines are lengthened, and control becomes more difficult. It is hard enough to run a business in one language and one culture, but when there are two, three, four, five—or seventy—languages and cultures, difficulties are compounded. Complex businesses of this type push men's organizational skills to their limits. The best of men's intellectual capacities and goodwill is called upon in order to make those organizations workable.

In the next two chapters we shall explore the international environment as it affects business, and vice versa. In the current chapter we discuss the nature of multinational business and the responses it is making to international needs. Then we discuss some of the major environmental constraints on business and relate them to a Law of Persistent Under-development.

MULTINATIONAL ENTERPRISE

The people of the world are organized into communities and nations, each in its own way according to its resources and cultural heritage. There are similarities among nations, but there are also significant differences which define the boundaries of business practice in each nation. Some nations have a customer-oriented economy, while others have a centrally planned economy, and there are various shades of practice in between. Some are economically developed, but others are just now developing. Some are political dictatorships; others are more democratic. Some are socially advanced, while others have minimum literacy and social development. And in each case the managerial conditions of work are different because of different expectations from participants.

Development of Multinational Enterprise

In an attempt to meet worldwide social needs, the traditional international business is changing into multinational enterprise. The traditional "international business" has been a predominantly national company which also operates in a limited way in a few other nations, such as having a mine, processing plant, or shipping office in another nation. This type of company viewed only one nation as its major area of operations, and it looked to that nation to provide its capital, markets, and even legal system for security and justice. It was *ethnocentric* in the sense that its standards were based upon its home nation's customs, markets, and laws.

The traditional international business is now becoming outmoded because developments in areas such as technology and communication have created an interconnected, worldwide social system. There are worldwide capital and market needs, and an ever-increasing flow of tourists and others among nations. People today are less inclined to accept the restrictive economic and export policies of self-centered nations. As a consequence, the world's largest businesses need to operate multinationally with their full line of services in order to remain viable. "The real point is that business *everywhere* is outgrowing national boundaries and, in so doing, is creating new tensions between the way the world is organized politically and the way it will be increasingly organized economically."[4]

This more modern type of international business is typically known as *multinational enterprise* because it is truly multinational in its markets, sources of managers, communication flow, and other activities. Since it centers upon the world as its area of operations, it is geocentric in its outlook, as shown in Figure 21–1. This figure can be interpreted as showing the headquarters orientation of a firm as it moves from traditional ethnocentricism to polycentric attitudes and eventually to a multinational, geocentric outlook. The ethnocentric attitude is represented by the attitude, "These managerial practices work in our nation; therefore, they are also best for your nation." It says, "We will supply the leadership and management, but we can use the foreign nationals to do the more routine work."

The multinational, geocentric attitude, on the other hand, recognizes that practices must be adapted to different cultures, but it still maintains worldwide identity and policies for the firm. It develops leadership among all nationals and truly seeks to use the best man for the job regardless of his country of origin.

Forms of Multinational Enterprise

Different forms of multinational enterprise are being explored in order to achieve better adjustment to the variety of business conditions in other nations. Since nations do feel concern about direct foreign investment, some firms are adopting a policy which shares ownership with host countries. The firms establish joint ventures or other arrangements which have substantial local ownership, even more than fifty percent. Then the business is looked upon not as an intruder but as a part of the host country's business system.

A variation is to acquire overseas subsidiaries in exchange for stock in the central corporation. Nationals then become multinational *owners*, reaping dividend benefits based upon the whole business's success internationally. This approach is rather different from that of having nationals

[4] Robert Lubar, "The Challenge of Multinational Business," *Fortune*, August, 1969, p. 73. Italics in original.

ORGANIZATION DESIGN	ETHNOCENTRIC	POLYCENTRIC	GEOCENTRIC
Complexity of organization	Complex in home country; simple in subsidiaries	Varied and independent	Increasingly complex and interdependent
Authority; decision making	High in head-quarters	Relatively low in headquarters	Aim for a collaborative approach between headquarters and subsidiaries
Evaluation and control	Home standards applied for persons and performance	Determined locally	Find standards which are universal and local
Rewards and punishments; incentives	High in head-quarters; low in subsidiaries	Wide variation; can be high or low rewards for subsidiary performance	International and local executives rewarded for reaching local and worldwide objectives
Communication; information flow	High volume to subsidiaries: orders, commands, advice	Little to and from head-quarters. Little between subsidiaries	Both ways and between subsidiaries. Heads of subsidiaries part of management team
Identification	Nationality of owner	Nationality of host country	Truly international company but identifying with national interests
Perpetuation (recruiting, staffing, development)	Recruit and develop people of home country for key positions everywhere in the world	Develop people of local nationality for key positions in their own country	Develop best men everywhere in the world for key positions everywhere in the world

Figure 21–1 Three types of headquarters orientation toward subsidiaries in an international enterprise. From Howard V. Perlmutter, "The Tortuous Evolution of the Multinational Corporation," *Columbia Journal of World Business*, January–February, 1969, p. 12. Used with permission.

share ownership in the success of the subsidiary alone. A subsidiary could fail or be manipulated by the persons who control it, but multinational stock ownership brings to owners the full security of the whole company. It is likely that multinational ownership of businesses will continue to grow.

The multinational enterprise which comes closer to an ideal form is one with truly diversified ownership, management, markets, and operations, without domination of any of the four features by one nation. Its managers look at the world as an operating unit, and they are capable of managing in more than one culture. Nestlé International (Nestlé Alimentana S. A.) is one of a few firms that have already developed a multinational image. It sells in most nations and manufactures in many. In addition, its managers and shareholders are from many nations.

Supranational Enterprise

Perhaps a further development will be the *supranational enterprise*. It is a worldwide enterprise charted by a substantially nonpolitical body such as the International Monetary Fund or the World Bank. It operates as a private business without direct national obligations. Its function is international business service, and it remains viable only by performing that service adequately for nations which permit its entry. With its integrative view, it should be able to draw the economic world closer together. It could serve all nations without being especially attached to any one of them. Because of its independence of any nation and its universal outlook, it is also called the extranational enterprise, the "geocorp," and the "cosmocorp." Somewhat related supranational organizations out of the business area are the International Red Cross, religious bodies, and scientific associations.

This kind of organization may sound ideal, but it does have limitations. It is still an outsider to any nation, and it probably will be dominated by people from certain nations compared with others. It will be essentially sovereign unto itself with little direct control by persons other than its management cadre and its board of governors. Would it really be more responsible and responsive to human needs than modern forms of multinational enterprise? From his wide experience in international management, John Fayerweather comments as follows:[5]

> Furthermore, for all their negative comments about foreign capital, many nations may have considerably more confidence in the beneficence and responsibility of highly developed business communities than in the qualities of a floating corporation chartered by a very weak government institution and presumably virtually free of overall government control. This is not to say that the concept may not in fact prove sound, but only to emphasize at the moment it is unduly favored by the age-old advantages of "the grass in the next pasture."

[5] John Fayerweather, "19th Century Ideology and 20th Century Reality," *Columbia Journal of World Business*, Winter, 1966, p. 81.

THE RESPONSE OF MULTINATIONAL BUSINESS TO HUMAN NEEDS

Upgrading Social and Economic Systems on a Worldwide Basis

In our time the central international responsibility of business is to extend its productive capacities throughout the world to upgrade developing countries. The problem is not so much a shortage of capital as a need for productive use of capital which is available. Multinational business's "track record" in this area is excellent. In the words of one observer, "It is the most effective medium for spreading technology, management skills, and capital around the world. It is a far more effective force for development than government-to-government aid, which often gets dissipated in politics and bureaucracy, and in any event represents only the transfer of money, with little accompanying knowledge about how to put it to work and make it productive."[6]

There is, however, no simple formula for economic and social development. Each country, region, and industry is different. There are widely varied stages of development with an infinite variety of cultural backgrounds. The only fruitful approach to these varying conditions is to work step by step to solve specific needs, and this is the kind of role in which business has proved historically that it can produce results. In fact, it leads in this role because of its singular focus on making things work.

Building World Cooperation and Peace

People tend to look to governments, religious bodies, and philosophical groups for improving world cooperation. Are they overlooking perhaps their strongest ally—business? Multinational business thinks globally. Its effectiveness depends on rational cooperation and the honoring of agreements. It requires stable political systems in order to perform its long-range planning. Since this is its pattern of life, it may spread, by its own example, ideals of mutual cooperation and constitutional government throughout the world. One international business specialist comments, "It seems inevitable that international economic integration, satisfactory investment climates, and constitutional government will follow. . . . These concepts can be transmitted most effectively by socially responsible business enterprise."[7] Another adds, "Finally, the multinational corporation is the only institution so far—and the only one visible on the horizon—that creates a genuine economic community transcending national lines and yet respectful of national sovereignties and local cultures."[8]

For a long time the philosophers and international specialists have overlooked the potential of business in building worldwide cooperation and peace. Business was either ignored or viewed as an exploiter which led to conflict. Certainly this view has been accurate on numerous occasions; however, world conditions change and so do business practices.

[6] Lubar, op. cit., p. 74.
[7] Richard D. Robinson, *International Business Policy*, New York: Holt, Rinehart and Winston, Inc., 1964, p. 222.
[8] Peter F. Drucker, *The Age of Discontinuity: Guidelines to Our Changing Society*, New York: Harper & Row, Publishers, Incorporated, 1968, p. 97.

Perhaps now the situation is different. Hans B. Thorelli comments, "Whatever it does, the cosmopolitan corporation should be mindful of the fact that it represents a more successful instance of international cooperation and a closer approach to global thinking than we have thus encountered among governments. It is the torchbearer of One World."[9]

Helping Develop Local Business

Another social response of multinational business is to encourage more locally owned, progressive businesses. Sears, Roebuck and other firms, such as the soft drink bottler described at the beginning of this chapter, have actively encouraged local suppliers to develop when they move into a country. Sears's program has been especially successful in Latin America, leading to the establishment and growth of hundreds of companies. In the beginning, Sears could purchase within a country only a small percentage of the merchandise it sold there, but now in Latin American countries, such as Mexico and Brazil, over ninety percent of its merchandise is made within the country.

In addition to encouraging suppliers and commercial associates, business may also work directly to develop new enterprises in unrelated business areas, thereby helping upgrade the general community in which it operates. In Venezuela, Creole Petroleum Corporation formed a subsidiary investment firm to supply new risk capital to stimulate local investment and expand opportunity. Creole limits its ownership interest to less than fifty percent to make clear that its purpose is to support local enterprise rather than dominate it. Other Standard Oil affiliates are taking similar steps in other countries.[10] The purpose is strictly to supply risk capital in new areas of business. This objective is entirely different from the common practice of forming a joint venture with a local firm for business purposes in product areas where the two firms normally conduct business.

Supporting International Management Groups

Another social response of business is to support different types of international management groups to aid in world development. Many persons are not aware of the extent and diversity of these organizations. Several of them follow.

INTERNATIONAL EXECUTIVE SERVICE CORPS   A unique approach is the *International Executive Service Corps* (IESC) formed in 1964 as a nonprofit corporation. It consists of volunteer managers who are available to enter nations by invitation to assist an individual business or an entire industry with a difficult project. Its modest operating costs are supported by gifts from business and government. The volunteers include both retired executives and managers on leave from their jobs, and they serve

[9] Hans B. Thorelli, "The Multi-national Corporation as a Change Agent," in Richard N. Farmer, *International Management*, Belmont, Calif.: Dickenson Publishing Company, Inc., 1968, p. 73.
[10] Robert H. Scholl, *International Business and the Community*, New York: Standard Oil Company (New Jersey), 1963, pp. 1–10.

without charge. This kind of arrangement gives business and individuals a stake in world development, and it permits nations to call upon specialists *outside their company roles* when needed.

In the first five years following its creation the IESC operated over 750 assistance projects in over forty nations. According to its president, its two most distinguishing features are:[11]

1. Its volunteers function as professionally competent private citizens doing a professional job.

2. Its form of organization permits government and business to cooperate in providing international aid without that aid being officially attached to either of them. The volunteer does not act as a representative of a business or a nation. His work has no economic or political strings attached to it, so a local business finds him more psychologically acceptable. As explained by the president of IESC, it is in a sense a "third force" in international development, additional to both government and business.

An example of an IESC project is a Middle Eastern firm which had an urgent need for improvement to avoid collapse.[12] The firm manufactured fertilizer and insecticides essential for the war on hunger. In the beginning the IESC volunteer made no progress because he encountered reserve and hostility in the plant. He soon realized that no one except top management knew that he was there to try to save this company and its 1,000 jobs, so he asked management to explain his mission to supervisors and employees. Top management was astonished because it had never recognized the need to communicate with its people on *any* subject.

Finally, a memo was written, and the people began to accept him. He helped make many improvements in operations, but perhaps his most significant improvement for the long run was the establishment of a minimum amount of communication between top management and its operating people.

Several other nations have adopted organizations similar to the IESC. In Japan, for example, volunteer executives are provided by the *International Management Cooperation Committee* (IMCC) founded in 1966. As explained by the vice-chairman of the IMCC, "I feel that 'the advanced countries' should exert all their efforts to elevate the living standard of the people in the developing countries, as well as to help them improve their social and economic conditions."[13]

COUNCIL FOR INTERNATIONAL PROGRESS IN MANAGEMENT An other coordinating group which responds to worldwide needs is the *Council for International Progress in Management* (CIPM). Membership consists of management associations (such as the Academy of Management),

[11] Frank Pace, Jr., "Prescription for an Ailing World: Management," *S.A.M. Advanced Management Journal*, January, 1969, pp. 4–9.
[12] *Ibid.*, pp. 6–7.
[13] Sohei Nakayama, "IMCC Training Business Managers in Developing Countries," *Management Japan*, vol. 3, no. 1, 1969, p. 12.

corporations, and universities. Somewhat similar management groups exist in most of the other nations of the world which are industrializing. Each of these groups has an avenue for cooperation with other nations through the international management association, Comité International de l'Organisation Scientifique (CIOS), to further management ideals of productivity and rational cooperation throughout the world. CIOS has been effective in uniting both government and business managers in improving management internationally. It is the coordinating body for the International Management Congress which is held every third year in a different nation and is attended by business and government managers from over fifty nations.

INTERNATIONAL MANAGEMENT DEVELOPMENT PROGRAMS   The CIOS and its affiliates such as the American Management Association have been active in supporting international management development programs that draw their participants from many countries so that no nation's executives dominate. This kind of program is entirely different from a local executive program dominated by nationals of one country.

Universities and businesses have also created effective international executive development programs. University programs include those sponsored by Harvard, Stanford, and Hawaii. One of the most successful business programs is IMEDE (the Institut pour l'Etude des Méthodes de Direction de l'Entreprise) in Lausanne, Switzerland. It is a Swiss foundation established in 1957 by Nestlé International in cooperation with the University of Lausanne, and its purpose is to develop top-level multinational managers. Its two principal programs are its extensive annual program of *eight and one-half months* for middle managers and a summer program of three weeks for top managers.[14]

THE ENVIRONMENT FOR MULTINATIONAL BUSINESS

Having discussed the social role and response of multinational business in world development, let us examine some of the environmental constraints that restrict business's social response, especially in the developing nations. We will examine this environment by discussing some of its major social, educational, political and economic aspects. Although we discuss these items separately, it should be understood that all of them are bound together in a complex social system.

Social Environment

The most evident and widespread factor in the social environment is the variation in culture among peoples. It makes each operating situation unique, creating both opportunities and problems; and it is discussed throughout the next two chapters. Two other significant social factors follow.

[14] *Fourteenth Annual Program, 1970–1971*, Lausanne: IMEDE, 1969.

SOCIAL OVERHEAD COSTS   Social overhead costs are public and private investments which are necessary to prepare the environment for effective operation of a new business unit. When a business moves into a developing area, it normally finds that support facilities such as schools, hospitals, roads, and public utilities either are not available or are in such short supply that efficient operation of the business is prevented. A productive business system cannot simply be grafted onto the emaciated body of a poorly developed society. The whole system must be upgraded, and this action takes substantial social overhead costs as well as additional start-up time.

When Indonesia's Gresnik cement plant was built, for example, a village had to be constructed to house imported scientists and administrators and also local skilled workers.[15] Schools and recreation facilities were built, police and fire protection established, and a bus system started for transporting workers. Ocean dock and oil storage facilities were acquired, a diesel power station constructed, a bag factory built, and railroad equipment added. The cost of these social overhead items was nearly $15 million. This sum was approximately the amount by which the cost of the Gresnik plant exceeded the cost of a similar plant in the United States.

PUBLIC VISIBILITY   Not only must a multinational business live up to different standards in each country, but it also must be prepared to meet these standards with more perfection than national businesses are expected to do. As an interloper from afar, its public visibility is greater than that of local businesses. Nationalism, love of one's own people, and desire to protect national business make local citizens more sensitive to the effects of a foreign business. They know that its whole loyalty—or even its primary loyalty—is not to their economy and their people. They are quick to condemn its indiscretions and hesitant and faint in their praise of its benefits.

Of equal importance is the tendency of critics, when they observe an indiscretion of a foreign business, to generalize therefrom to condemn all businesses from that same country. Native businesses are not subject to this kind of generalization.

A country in Asia serves as an example. When one of its national businesses acts in a way considered contrary to the national interest, it is merely regarded as a bad citizen. But when a German subsidiary misbehaves according to those same standards, its record is used to condemn the whole group of German businesses in that country. Managers who make decisions in this climate of public visibility must actually pay more attention to local standards and national objectives than purely local businesses need to do.

---

[15] Leonard A. Doyle, "Some Problems of State Enterprises in Underdeveloped Nations," *California Management Review*, Fall, 1963, p. 27. See also Leonard A. Doyle, *Intereconomy Comparisons: A Case Study*, Berkeley, Calif.: University of California Press, 1965.

Insight into all these variations of social conduct is difficult for even the best-qualified manager. He needs to be broad in his thinking and highly sensitive to political and social trends. If he comes from outside the host country, he cannot by himself sense all the fine points that should bear on his decisions; therefore, he depends on the counsel of local associates who are loyal and communicative. If they understand that above-average behavior is required because the business is a foreign one, they can be quite helpful in counseling toward responsible decisions. Unless they do see the situation broadly, they may for reasons of national pride be hesitant to help an "outside" business conduct itself better than national businesses do.

Educational Environment

The educational environment is usually a major handicap in upgrading developing nations.

SCARCITY OF QUALIFIED HUMAN RESOURCES   An evident characteristic of developing nations is the scarcity of human resources qualified to serve social and economic needs in an advanced society. There are major shortages of managers, scientists, and technicians, and these deficiencies limit business's ability to employ local labor productively.

In the absence of sufficient human resources, people with needed abilities are temporarily imported, while vast training programs prepare local workers. In fact, the lending of trained people to a nation may be of more lasting benefit than the lending of capital because of the *multiplier effect* by which these people develop a cadre of qualified nationals, who then become the nucleus for developing more nationals in an ever-widening arc of self-development.

UNDERDEVELOPED EDUCATIONAL FACILITIES   The shortage of qualified human resources would be less serious if excellent educational facilities were available to prepare people quickly; however, these facilities normally are also inadequate. There are shortages of schools and equipment for them. In turn, there are not enough qualified teachers to supply an expanded educational system, so either existing universities must be expanded or new ones established to train teachers. All of education is tied together in a system relationship, requiring a nation to start at the beginning of the sequence in order to be successful. Economic and social growth are difficult until human resources have been developed.[16] As stated by one economist:[17]

Although it is obvious that people acquire useful skills and knowledge, it is not obvious that these skills and knowledge are a form of

[16] Harbison and Myers spell out the needs for, and strategies of, human-resource development in Frederick Harbison and Charles A. Myers, *Education, Manpower, and Economic Growth,* New York: McGraw-Hill Book Company, 1964.
[17] Theodore W. Schultz, "Investment in Human Capital," *American Economic Review,* March, 1961, p. 1.

capital, that this capital is in substantial part a product of deliberate investment, that it has grown in Western societies at a faster rate than conventional (nonhuman) capital, and that its growth may well be the most distinctive feature of the economic system.

Political Environment

The social and political environment are closely related. The political system influences attitudes of citizens, and the citizens concurrently have a substantial influence on the kinds of political leaders and policies which exist.

NATIONALISTIC DRIVES   As has been mentioned, many people have strong nationalistic attitudes. They want their nation and their economic system for themselves without substantial interference by foreign nationals. In Burma, for example, a visiting professor presented a case problem where there was conflict between a British shipmaster and a Burmese crew. Expecting a human relations discussion, the professor was surprised when his class focused on how to train Burmese to take over from the British master so that they would not have to deal with him.

GOVERNMENT CONTROLS   When a multinational firm does enter another nation, it often is subject to a variety of special controls, licenses, foreign exchange rules, and sanctions supplied by government. These are complicated by the fact that the government itself is sometimes unstable, inconsistent, and bureaucratic, though well-meaning. Decisions are made on a political basis with little thought given to business needs. The state normally plays a major role in central planning in both developing and developed nations. With regard to developed nations, for example, at the thirteenth International Management Congress an Italian industrialist explained the situation this way: "While in the United States the 'homo-economicus' is still nowadays the protagonist of economic events, in Europe he has somewhat faded and has been replaced by a type of economic subject who practically acts as the main character in a play written by the state."[18]

With regard to developing nations, although heavy state planning can give direction to the system, it also can be so restrictive that it wastes scarce resources and interferes with social effectiveness. After a study of his own nation an analyst in India concluded, "The system of excessive regulation and overcontrol of private business has proved to be self-defeating and unworkable in India to the extent that it has forced the government to retreat from its original stand."[19]

In most nations there is also heavier government involvement in social welfare than exists in the United States. This affects a foreign business in a number of ways. Fringe-benefit costs as a proportion of wages will be

[18] Guido Zerilli Marimo, "Management and the International Arena," *Proceedings of the Thirteenth International Management Congress*, New York: Council for International Progress in Management (United States), Inc., 1963, p. 416.
[19] Amar N. Agarwala, "The Government-business Relationship in India," *MSU Business Topics*, Spring, 1968, p. 26.

high, running as much as 50 percent of wage costs. Layoffs of employees may be restricted and made expensive. And taxes are likely to be high to support government welfare payments. In fact, excessive welfare costs beyond a nation's economic capacity have been one cause of economic chaos and inflation in South America and elsewhere.[20]

JOINT OWNERSHIP WITH GOVERNMENT   In many nations, particularly with regard to basic industries, the government will insist on being a partial owner in a foreign business which it admits. In other cases it is a full competitor, owning and operating a business selling the same type of product. The market may be allocated with a certain portion going to the state and another portion to the foreign business. The general conclusion is that in nearly all countries outside the United States, the government is more involved in business than is the case in this country. Businessmen in these nations have to be actively interested in government affairs in order to operate successfully. Sometimes they must give political considerations priority over economic and technical values when they make decisions.

A complex example of joint government ownership and control is the Scandinavian Airlines System (SAS).[21] One airline each from Sweden, Norway, and Denmark have joined together under the symbol SAS. They share operations, flight equipment, and ground facilities, even though each airplane is owned separately by only one of the three airlines. To further complicate the situation, each of the three member airlines is owned 50 percent by its respective national government and 50 percent by private business. Net proceeds of operations are divided according to a negotiated ratio. This complex arrangement allows three smaller airlines to operate as one large international airline.

The various types of government involvement in business may be summarized as follows:

1. Government ownership of an industry; other firms not allowed
2. Government ownership of a firm in an industry having private firms in competition with government
3. The arrangement described in item 2, with the market allocated
4. Partial government ownership of a private foreign firm
5. Government economic planning with sanctions applied to private industry to assure compliance
6. Routine government licensing and control only

EXPROPRIATION AS A SPECIAL POLITICAL RISK   When a government nationalizes or expropriates the business of a foreign company, this means that it assumes ownership and control of the property. The govern-

[20] Frederick Harbison and Charles A. Myers, *Management in the Industrial World: An International Analysis*, New York: McGraw-Hill Book Company, 1959, especially p. 172, concerning Chile.
[21] Donald M. Barrett, "Multi-flag Airlines: A New Breed in World Business," *Columbia Journal of World Business*, March–April, 1969, p. 9.

ment may or may not pay for what it takes. One study identified at least 187 United States companies which had experienced an expropriation since World War I, and it reported that only a minority of them received any compensation for asset losses. United States assets expropriated by Cuba in 1959–1960 amounted to nearly one and one-half billion dollars.[22] Assets of companies from industrialized nations other than the United States have been similarly expropriated at various times.

The risk of expropriation is a strong deterrent to investment in nations which have a history of expropriation, have an unstable government, or have hostile attitudes toward private industry; consequently, many underdeveloped nations fail to get needed capital because there are no international assurances protecting against expropriation without compensation. The United Nations or some other international organization could make a substantial contribution to world economic stability and free flow of capital into underdeveloped nations if it could develop some reliable plan for controlling expropriation.

When expropriation does occur, an equal or greater loser tends to be the expropriating nation itself. It can only expropriate the property. It cannot expropriate managerial skills, technical know-how, international markets, and the many other benefits which a multinational business offers a developing nation. The multinational business is needed in most cases because, through its multiplier effect on local people and businesses, it becomes an effective medium for spreading management skills, capital, technology, and market opportunities worldwide. Many nations are voluntarily recognizing the benefits of multinational enterprise and are entering into joint ownership agreements rather than taking the self-centered and risky route of expropriation.

Economic Environment

Business is so thoroughly involved in the economic life of a nation that it would take an entire economics textbook to discuss thoroughly the international economic environment of business. There are high interest rates, capital shortages, unstable economic systems, and restrictions on repatriation of profits; however, inflation is the one item selected for discussion because of its widespread social influence and its severity in many nations which most need development. A high level of inflation creates so much instability and social unrest that it restricts business's capacity to respond to human needs.

In the United States, which has had mild inflation for decades, the value of the dollar was cut more than half in the generation from 1940 to 1965, but in other parts of the world currency has been cut to one-hundredth or even *one-thousandth* of its value since 1940, as reflected by cost-of-living indexes. What used to cost one unit of currency now costs 1,000 or more. In terms of dollar currency, an ice-cream cone that

[22] Franklin R. Root, "The Expropriation Experience of American Companies," *Business Horizons*, April, 1968, pp. 69–74.

originally cost 10 cents would now cost 10,000 cents, or $100! In Brazil in 1963–1964 the increase in cost of living was running at about 100 percent annually, meaning that an item which cost 10 cruzeiros in one year will cost 20 cruzeiros the next year. As explained by a Brazilian government official, "There must be some recognition of the problem that battling a runaway inflation such as those that Brazil, Argentina and Uruguay have experienced in the recent past, is not less serious than a civil disorder or a war-like engagement."[23]

With high inflationary conditions, such matters as inventory policy, sales policy, and cash discounts are guided substantially by the state of inflation. Interest rates run as high as 5 percent monthly, which is 60 percent yearly; yet borrowing can be economical if the inflation rate runs higher, such as 8 percent monthly, permitting the debt to be repaid with cheaper money. An entire year's profit can be wiped out by a currency devaluation or some other development external to the firm. Typical "good management" through long-range planning is very difficult, and even regular operations become unsettled.

Just as business operations are unsettled, so is the worker's economic life. He must spend quickly lest his money lose its value. Savings payable in fixed currency units become meaningless because they lose their value; hence, he seldom plans for his own security, as workers do in the United States. He develops more dependence and more anxiety, and he becomes more politically volatile. As a worker's money income increases, his aspirations naturally rise; however, since there is inflation, his standard of living does not significantly rise. The result is increasing unrest. This condition can be stated as a formula $(A - S) + I = U$, where "A" is the worker's aspirations, "S" is his standard of living, "I" is his insecurity, and "U" is his level of unrest.

In other words, as the difference between aspirations and standard of living increases, unrest also increases. When this is added to the unrest caused by insecurity in the system, the result is a general measure of social unrest. Inflation contributes significantly to this condition. As interpreted by one observer, "The cost of living spirals up each day and as the gap increases between income and cost of living, tension and unrest continue to rise. The political and social stability of a country depends upon its success in curbing inflation. It is a problem which spares no one, whether he be a poor man or a rich man."[24]

Since inflation weakens confidence in money, it often causes capital to flee from the inflated country to one with a more stable currency. This condition increases capital shortages and further limits business growth. In summary, high inflation tends to perpetuate underdevelopment and a low growth rate because it creates substantial economic and social dislocations which interfere with business efforts to develop productivity.

[23] Roberto de Oliveira Campos, "Rising Expectations: With or Without Revolution," *Columbia Journal of World Business*, May–June, 1968, p. 12.
[24] Juan Aranda, "The Latin America Dilemma: Industrial Development," *Advanced Management Journal*, July, 1968, p. 31.

The Farmer-Richman Model of Environmental Constraints

Farmer and Richman have developed a model for comparing environmental constraints on managerial efficiency in different nations.[25] They reason that efficiency is substantially affected by constraints imposed on management by the external environment. That is, if the external environment does not permit and encourage internal efficiency, it will not be forthcoming. Constraints are grouped into four classes which are approximately the same as those we have discussed: sociological, educational, legal-political, and economic. Each class is divided into weighted subclasses which are rated for each nation to determine that nation's total constraints. A high constraint score indicates that external constraints are giving high support to efficient management.

Sociological constraints will serve as an example. Their maximum weight is 100 points out of 500. The subclasses and maximum weights are as follows: view of managers as an elite group, 10; view of scientific method, 40; view of wealth, 10; view of rational risk taking, 10; view of achievement, 20; and class flexibility, 10. The sum of constraint scores is the constraint index. This index is related to the nation's gross national product and its growth rate during the last decade in order to determine an efficiency index. The index expresses the efficiency with which a country converts its inputs into production outputs. Efficiency indexes for five nations in the early 1960s were as follows: Saudi Arabia, 20; Mexico, 38; United Kingdom, 178, Russia, 273; and the United States, 405. This type of analysis helps pinpoint reasons why a country is low in efficiency because a low score on a particular constraint shows that it needs improvement in order for there to be a gain in efficiency.

A study of Russia by Richman shows how the four classes of environmental constraints operate as a system to suppress productivity. Richman found that "problems of inefficiency, waste, and opposition to innovation in production are serious, widespread, and as yet unresolved. . . . So far the Soviets have not been able to devise a system that effectively combines central planning with local decision-making and initiative."[26] Soviet managers are therefore more interested in making quotas than in producing goods and services for use. They resort to "storming," which is a mad rush to fill quotas in the last days of a month or quarter. They are dubbed in slang as "heroes of the twenty-ninth day" because most of their output is shipped in the final hours of the month. Richman believes that the lack of market standards, local initiative, and reward systems, as well as other factors, is a major deterrent to management effectiveness. He concludes that reform in the external environment of business would greatly improve Russian productivity. The restrictive external environment is the central productivity problem, rather than untrained managers and workers.

[25] Richard N. Farmer and Barry M. Richman, "A Model for Research in Comparative Management," *California Management Review,* Winter, 1964, pp. 55–68; and Richard N. Farmer and Barry M. Richman, *Comparative Management and Economic Progress,* Homewood, Ill.: Richard D. Irwin, Inc., 1965.
[26] Barry M. Richman, *Soviet Management, with Significant American Comparisons,* Englewood Cliffs, N.J.: Prentice-Hall, Inc., 1965, p. 253.

The Law of Persistent Underdevelopment

The many constraints on productive enterprise in developing nations lead to the general conclusion that an underdeveloped nation's cultural foundation for productivity is as underdeveloped as its economy is. Cultural factors operate in an interacting system to suppress both social and economic growth. The nation becomes locked into a self-perpetuating cycle of low development, and it has difficulty breaking out of this imprisoning cycle without outside help or unusual effort on its own. We call this system relationship the Law of Persistent Underdevelopment. It is not a "law" in the sense that it forever condemns a nation to underdevelopment. Rather, it is a law in the sense that it is self-perpetuating unless some *new force* is added to break a nation out of its grasp. It gives notice to nations that intentional, determined effort is necessary to initiate a cycle of development. The Law of Persistent Underdevelopment simply states that an underdeveloped social system is locked into self-perpetuating low development until new social forces can be introduced to break the cultural chains which bind it.

The key cultural and economic components of the Law of Persistent Underdevelopment are shown in Figure 21–2. Cultural factors, represented by the larger circle, and economic factors, represented by the

Figure 21–2   The Law of Persistent Underdevelopment: Tandem cultural and economic chains perpetuate underdevelopment.

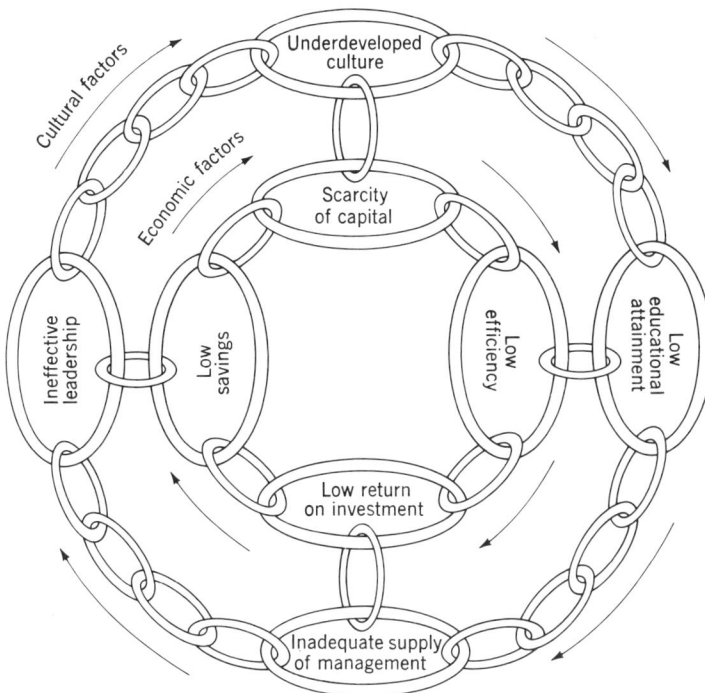

smaller circle, operate in tandem to perpetuate underdevelopment. As shown by the larger circle, in the beginning an underdeveloped culture leads to low educational attainment, which causes an inadequate supply of management, resulting in ineffective leadership, which perpetuates the underdeveloped culture. In the economic sphere a similar perpetuating chain exists. The scarcity of capital causes low efficiency, which leads to low return on investment, causing low savings, which perpetuates the scarcity of capital.

A country which is caught in these self-perpetuating tandem chains requires large economic and cultural inputs to generate a takeoff force which will break the circle and head it toward a more advanced social condition. Business managers are a key factor in this takeoff force because they provide leadership to overcome inefficiency and cultural lag. By making a society productive enough to reward those who qualify themselves, management motivates citizens to upgrade their skills and education. Without advancement opportunities provided by successful business, citizen educational lethargy persists. People seek education as a result of self-motivation, not because of public exhortation to become educated.

A study of Mexico shows how a high level of educational attainment may be used to generate progress in a developing area.[27] Excluding the federal district in which Mexico City is located, the industrial state of Nuevo León has the highest percentage of population with twelve or more years of education. This percentage is over *ten times* that of several less-developed states. There is immense variation in the quality of management systems among Mexican states. Business development is by region, rather than being general throughout the nation. Generalizing for the benefit of other nations, the study suggests that efforts to develop all Mexican states equally will spread resources so thin that underdevelopment will persist. The "only feasible procedure" for getting the very poor states developed ultimately is to concentrate limited resources in the advanced regions where management is already productive. This procedure will temporarily widen the contrast between states, but it will produce a growing surplus which then can be applied to bringing up the less-advanced states. Thus, the restrictive fetters of the Law of Persistent Underdevelopment can be overcome.

System Development toward Industrialism and Professional Management

As nations reduce their environmental constraints on business and become relatively developed and affluent, their advanced system is called industrialism. *Industrialism* is defined as social organization in which both service and manufacturing industries, especially large-scale ones, are dominant forces in the conduct of the social system. It is comparable to the term "agrarianism" to describe a nation's social system several hun-

---

[27] Charles Nash Myers, *Education and National Development in Mexico*, Princeton, N.J.: Princeton University, Industrial Relations Section, 1965, p. 147. Statistics are from p. 27.

dred years ago. Based on extensive international research, Harbison and Myers have identified three types of management which develop in a nation's march toward industrialism. These are patrimonial, political, and professional management.[28]

Patrimonial management is the common first stage in a nation's march toward industrialization. It is management in which ownership, the major policy-making positions, and other key jobs in the business are all held by members of one extended family. In this manner they control the business, and its goals are oriented toward their interests and aspirations. In Europe, India, Brazil, Japan, and many other countries patrimonial management continues to be active. It does have its advantages. In developing industrial cultures where forms of industrial organizations are not sophisticated, it encourages teamwork, loyalty, and mutual interest. Where controls are not well established, it provides some trustworthiness in handling finances and protects trade secrets from prying outsiders.

Patrimonial management can be dynamic and effective, but it usually runs into difficulty in the long run. Heirs tend to lose interest, lacking the personal commitment of founders. They tend to become conservative with their acquired assets, not willing to take the entrepreneurial risks that they once did. With advancing industrialization they sometimes lack the capacity to grow in their technical and organizational skills. And as the business grows it becomes too large to be staffed with one family, even including distant cousins. The house of Mitsui, in Japan, for example, finally expanded its patrimonial group to eleven families very loosely defined. Even these were not enough as the firm grew, so it started hiring outside managers. Because of the limitations of patrimonial management, it usually tends to move toward professional management as industrialization advances.

Political management is often a second stage in industrial development, although it is less common than patrimonial management and some nations essentially bypass it. It is management in which ownership, the major policy-making positions, and other key jobs in the business are all held on the basis of political affiliations and loyalties. Access to leadership is dominated by political considerations, and management decisions are colored by political goals. Political management is commonly associated with government operation of enterprises. India, European countries, and others have political management in state-owned enterprises. Russia is an extreme example of political management. In the 1930s not only were party members established in key managerial positions, but they also shared power equally with purely political commissars who were in each plant to assure political obedience. The inefficiency of this system finally forced its abandonment, but party membership and loyalty are still important criteria in Soviet management.

Political management has approximately the same hazards as patrimonial management, with the additional hazard of diversion of resources and interests toward political goals rather than economic goals. Loyalty to

---

[28] Harbison and Myers, *Management in the Industrial World: An International Analysis,* chap. 4.

an abstract party is also harder to maintain than the personal family loyalty of patrimonial management.

Advanced industrial societies move toward *professional management*, in which major policy-making positions and other key jobs are held by leaders on the basis of competence. It is similar to the term "career management," which we have been using. Unlike patrimonial and political management, the location of ownership is of no consequence in professional management. Ownership may continue to reside in a family, state, or other group, but if managers rise to leadership by competence and make decisions free of external domination, then professional management exists. It is a distinct career requiring advanced training and continuing self-development. It will thrive in various economic and political systems, as evidenced by its success in Great Britain, Germany, Japan, Russia, and the United States. Professional management is the direction in which advanced industrial nations find it necessary to move in order to maintain their social progress. Among the three types of management, it can deal most successfully with the complexities of advanced industrial civilization. As stated by Peter Drucker, "Management is fast becoming the central resource of the developed countries and the basic need of the developing ones."[29]

SUMMARY

As a result of worldwide needs for economic and social development, major businesses are moving rapidly into multinational operations. Ethnocentric ways of looking at the world are being discarded for more global, geocentric attitudes. Major social responses which multinational business is making include upgrading social systems, building world cooperation and peace, helping develop local business, and participating in international management groups which seek to improve world development.

In its multinational operations business is required to work with a variety of environmental constraints in different nations. Major social, educational, political, and economic constraints were discussed, along with the Farmer-Richman model for evaluating them. In many nations the combined conditions are so severe that they tend to bind a nation in a self-perpetuating Law of Persistent Underdevelopment. A number of other nations have achieved a relatively advanced system of industrialism and professional management, and most nations are progressing in that direction.

STUDY GUIDES FOR INTERPRETATION OF THIS CHAPTER

1 The United States automobile manufacturer of which you are international vice-president owns the plant of a long-established automobile manufacturer in England. Recently, as you spoke at a civic association

[29] Peter F. Drucker, "Management's New Role," *Harvard Business Review*, November–December, 1969, p. 54.

meeting in a city near the plant, a member of the audience challenged you as follows: "Your ownership of our plant means foreign control of one of this region's largest employers. In case of a real crisis in the industry, we will see that you hold the whip and we are the slaves." How would you respond?

2 Discuss the social effects of high inflation on business environment in a developing nation.

3 Explain how the Law of Persistent Underdevelopment may operate to lock a nation into low development.

4 You are general manager of a genuinely multinational company operating in an African nation. Eight hundred and seventy of the nine hundred employees are black. The other thirty employees are North Americans, Asians, and Europeans. They are mostly in professional and managerial occupations. The African nation's minister of labor has contacted you, saying that it is the government's "urgent request" that the nonblack work force be reduced to ten persons within six months. How would you respond?

5 Survey three university students from other nations and learn their attitude toward a business from an advanced nation which is operating in their country.

PROBLEMS
"NATIONALIZATION BY AGREEMENT"

The Anaconda Company is a worldwide producer, fabricator, and marketer of metals, especially copper and aluminum. In 1969, two-thirds of its copper production came from its large mines in Chile. Since the price of copper was relatively high that year, its Chilean operations (primarily copper and mineral by-products of copper refining) contributed about three-fourths of worldwide earnings for the company.

On June 26, 1969, Anaconda released a two-page statement to the press and its stockholders concerning acceptance of a Chilean offer to "nationalize by agreement." Major paragraphs relating to ownership in the statement are as follows:

> In order to avoid expropriation by the Government of Chile through legislation, the Board of Directors of The Anaconda Company has agreed to recommend to the directors and stockholders of Chile Exploration Company and Andes Copper Mining Company the acceptance of an offer to nationalize by agreement the operations of these two companies operating in Chile.
>
> The Anaconda Company announced that its two subsidiary companies, Chile Exploration Company and Andes Copper Mining Company, operating in Chile, have reached an understanding with the Chilean Government, subject to corporate legal requirements and stockholder approval of the respective companies, whereby the Chilean Government will acquire the properties of these two companies in an arrangement in two stages.

Effective January 1, 1970, the assets and liabilities of these two subsidiaries will be transferred to two new Chilean mining companies. On that date 51% of the stock of the two new companies will be purchased by the Chilean Government. The purchase price will be the book value of these subsidiaries payable in dollars in semi-annual installments over a period of twelve years commencing January 1, 1970, with tax free interest at the rate of 6% per annum.

The Chilean Government will purchase the remaining shares of the two new companies after the Chilean Government has completed payment for 60% of the unpaid balance of the purchase price of the first 51% of the shares and, in no event before January 1973 nor later than the end of 1981. The purchase price per share for the 49% interest shall be determined by multiplying the average annual net earnings from January 1, 1970 to the date of purchase by 8 for 1973, $7\frac{1}{2}$ for 1974, and reduced accordingly and progressively to a minimum of 6 by 1977 or thereafter.

1 Comment on the social response of Anaconda's management in its action "to nationalize by agreement." Give both favorable and unfavorable aspects from the point of view of the pluralistic investment groups involved.

2 Study current information in order to determine how equitably the Anaconda nationalization has been handled. Then comment on the long-run effects which this nationalization may have on industrialization and the standard of living in Chile.

BANKRUPTCY FOR THE SUBSIDIARY

Flagstaff Company, a major electronics manufacturer operating primarily in the United States, owned a subsidiary in a poorly developed city in Southern Europe. Ownership developed gradually during a period of twelve years through purchase of a locally-owned company using some of the Flagstaff Company's technological know-how. The original plant grew until it employed over one thousand workers by the time Flagstaff assumed complete ownership. During the twelve years the plant had rarely been profitable; so when Flagstaff bought full ownership, it dispatched a management team to bring up the plant's profitability. During the following year the plant's losses were greater than ever.

To improve the situation management decided to close its most unprofitable operation, laying off 275 workers. As a result of the layoffs, there was heavy labor strife. There were two or three wildcat strikes a week, which further reduced productivity; management threatened to close the plant unless the strikes stopped. Because the strikes continued, management closed the plant a few weeks later. To the surprise of management, the mayor of the city, using an obscure law, physically seized the plant and locked out management supposedly to prevent the company from liquidating its assets. (There was also some evidence he used the seizure as leverage to try to force management to reopen the plant.) Shortly thereafter the subsidiary filed for bankruptcy.

One major issue is that the subsidiary owes banks in the nation about $6 million in unsecured loans which were made without any bank request that the loans be guaranteed by the parent company in the United States.

1 Identify and explain any apparent errors in judgment made by parent-company management in operating this subsidiary.

2 Does the parent company have a responsibility to pay the unsecured loans? What are the implications of (a) paying the loans or (b) not paying them?

CHAPTER 22

BUSINESS ENCOURAGEMENT OF SOCIAL CHANGE AND PRODUCTIVITY

The success or failure of a change agent's project will ultimately depend on the motivation of individuals; therefore it is worth considering what makes individuals desire an innovation.

CONRAD M. ARENSBERG AND
ARTHUR H. NIEHOFF[1]

It can be said without too much oversimplication that there are no underdeveloped countries. There are only *undermanaged* ones.

PETER F. DRUCKER[2]

Consider the following chilling prediction made in the 1960s.[3]

If present trends continue, it seems likely that famine will reach serious proportions in India, Pakistan and China in the 1970's, followed by Indonesia, Iran, Turkey, Egypt and several other countries within a few years, and then followed by most of the other countries of Asia, Africa and Latin America by 1980. Such a famine will be of massive proportions affecting hundreds of millions, possibly even billions, of persons. If this happens, as appears very probable, it will be the most colossal catastrophe in history. . . . This is the Malthusian Doctrine finally coming true after 170 years.

The prediction begins with an "if," so birth control and other developments may prevent the occurrence of all these predictions. Nevertheless, a rapidly expanding world population does create an urgent need for nations of the world to make productive use of their resources. As a major change agent for productivity, business can contribute toward serving this need.

Even if population could be controlled, the aspirations of people

[1] Conrad M. Arensberg and Arthur H. Niehoff, *Introducing Social Change: A Manual for Americans Overseas*, Chicago: Aldine Publishing Company, 1964, p. 101.
[2] Peter F. Drucker, "Management's New Role," *Harvard Business Review*, November–December, 1969, p. 54. Italics in original.
[3] Raymond Ewell, Editor, *Population Bulletin*, quoted in *Columbia Journal of World Business*, January–February, 1967, p. 89.

378

around the world have risen dramatically. Generally speaking, impatient society does not wish to wait for slow, generation-by-generation improvement, like the drip-drip of a cavern stream forming a stalagmite. In its concern for others and for "progress," society is in a hurry—perhaps too much so for its own good. Nevertheless, it wants progress now. It is depending on business to introduce quickly and effectively many of the changes it wants.

Business is only one of many organizations serving human needs internationally. In fact, the various institutions serving international development provide an excellent example of pluralism in operation. All of them are bound together in a complex system relationship. These organizations include private business, labor unions, venture capital organizations, foundations, religious groups, universities, local governments, and foreign governments. Essentially, each institution is following the idea of functionalism, performing its special functions to contribute to the mutual objective of international development.

In this chapter we discuss the way in which business encourages cultural changes toward more productive patterns of life. After some introductory observations, discussion will be in terms of integrating social systems, introducing change, developing productivity, and motivation in a less-developed environment.

SOME GENERAL OBSERVATIONS

Business is a major change agent in relatively developed nations as well as developing ones. Its influence in developed nations is illustrated by two forceful books on the challenges of development in Europe and Japan.

"The American Challenge"

In 1967 in Paris Jean-Jacques Servan-Schreiber published Le Défi américain (The American Challenge), which discussed the successful "invasion" of Europe by productive United States business.[1] Although written as a popular book rather than an academic analysis, it is full of valuable cultural insights about business practice. It quickly became a best seller, being translated into English in 1968. Servan-Schreiber maintained that United States business learned how to use the opportunities afforded by the European Common Market better than European business did. The result was that most European companies, when faced with the need to strengthen their competitive position, preferred to join with American multinational companies rather than other European firms. He concluded that the success of United States business resulted primarily from its productive management culture and extensive education of knowledge workers. Europe could meet this challenge of business "colonization" only by adopting this management culture and abandoning its elite concept of education for a few intellectuals.

[1] J.-J. Servan-Schreiber, Le Défi américain, Paris: Editions Denoel, 1967. See also J.-J. Servan-Schreiber, The American Challenge, New York: Avon, 1969, and other editions of the book.

The thesis of *The American Challenge* has itself been challenged in many ways. It has some truth and some exaggeration. Nevertheless, it presents many interesting differences among business practices in developed nations.

The possibilities for increases in productivity in Europe are illustrated by one report.[5] Through better management practices, many European factories routinely have increased productivity 20 to 30 percent. One electrical components firm doubled its output in three years without increasing its labor force. Another firm increased productivity of casters 400 percent, and another increased typewriter productivity 770 percent!

"The Japanese Challenge"

In 1969, Haakan Hedberg published *Den Japanska Utmaningen* (*The Japanese Challenge*) in Stockholm. This book presents the thesis that in the late 1980s Japan will have the largest per capita income of any nation, thus becoming the affluent society's first "economic superpower."[6] The Japanese are moving toward this position through close business-government cooperation, superior long-range planning, large investment programs, and loyal semipaternalistic cooperation.

In the Matsushita Electric Industrial Company, workers can receive medical care in a company hospital, be married in a company chapel, purchase a home with company financing, and vacation at company resorts. As explained by the company's founder, "I have impressed on the employees that each must perform his task or the system breaks down. Each man is taught that he is managing the company through his own work, and that with this work he is doing something for society."[7] The success of this philosophy is reflected in the company's growth in worldwide markets and profitability. In addition, in only one year the company's 55,000 workers submitted 420,000 ideas through the employee suggestion program.

In its rise toward advanced industrialization, Japanese business has been able to retain much of its old culture and still be competitively productive. Japanese workers are hired virtually for life, and managerial promotions are often based on seniority. However, most of the technological improvements of modern business have been introduced into this cultural context. What Japanese business loses in production rationality, it seems to gain back in employee stability and loyalty. Culture is used to reinforce productivity rather than to interfere with it. Meanwhile, the culture is gradually adapting to industrialization. At Matsushita Company, for example, a manager who operates an unprofitable operation may not hold his job just because he has seniority. But neither is he fired, as is often the case in the United States. Rather, he is moved to a less demanding job, often with a large bonus for "past contributions."

[5] James H. Duncan, "Old and New Productivity Techniques Start Closing Gaps," *Columbia Journal of World Business*, January–February, 1969, pp. 69–70.
[6] Haakan Hedberg, *Den Japanska Utmaningen*, Stockholm: Albert Bonner Publishing Company, 1969.
[7] "Japan's Remarkable Industrial Machine," *Business Week*, Mar. 7, 1970, p. 64.

The Convergence Hypothesis of Industrialization

The experiences of both Europe and Japan[8] provide support for the *convergence hypothesis* of industrialization, and trends in less-developed nations are additionally supportive. The convergence hypothesis holds that as societies industrialize they are inevitably pulled toward similarity. There are factors inherent in industrialization, such as rationality, responsibility, and long-range planning, which in effect require some degree of cultural accommodation. They make convergence *necessary* if industrialization is to be successful.

An example of convergence theory is the trend toward professional management discussed in the preceding chapter. As nations industrialize, they tend to emphasize professional management regardless of earlier practices, because professional management proves necessary for effective use of socioeconomic resources.

The convergence hypothesis illustrates the significant effects of environmental constraints on productivity, as discussed in the Farmer-Richman model in the preceding chapter. The environment is a key input into an industrial system; therefore, it must gradually adapt in order to allow industrialization to advance effectively. Since business is a principal change agent for industrialization, it constitutes a strong pressure for more education, social development, dependable law, rational cooperation, and other conditions of industrialism. Improvement in these environmental inputs is necessary for continued growth in outputs of goods and services, both material and cultural.

This input-output relationship of environment and productivity in the social system has been proved countless times when technologically advanced businesses entered developing countries. A well-equipped plant is not enough. The whole society needs to adapt in terms of education, health, respect for contracts and obligations, view of quality, and so on.

The following experience of one of the authors emphasized the relationship of environment and productivity in a developing country.[9] Visiting that country's modern rayon plant, he noticed that sheets of cellulose (the main raw material) were made in Canada, 9,000 miles away. He asked why this was so because he knew that this developing nation had vast forest reserves and some cellulose plants. The reply was, "We have the proper equipment, but we haven't been able to operate it well enough to make the high quality of cellulose needed for the rayon plant."

Since less-developed nations typically provide the greatest lack of convergence and, therefore, the most difficult environment for industrial change, the remainder of this chapter will focus primarily on conditions which arise when a firm from a more advanced nation enters a developing nation.

[8] Bernard Karsh and Robert E. Cole, "Industrialization and the Convergence Hypothesis: Some Aspects of Contemporary Japan," *Journal of Social Issues*, vol. XXIV, no. 4, 1968, pp. 45–64.
[9] Both authors of this book have participated in development programs in other nations.

INTEGRATING DIFFERENT SOCIAL SYSTEMS

Understanding Social Systems

The overriding factor in all international business is that it operates within different social systems. The amount of difference between any two systems may be called *cultural distance,* and in many situations this distance is substantial. As concisely stated by a citizen of an Asian country, "We are two days and 200 years distant from Washington."[10] Whatever the amount of cultural distance, it does affect the responses of all persons to business. Imported managers naturally tend to be ethnocentric and to judge conditions in a new country according to standards of their homeland. Although this way of perceiving conditions is very human, it will thwart understanding and productivity. In order to perform effectively an expatriate manager will need cultural empathy for local conditions. Having this empathy, he must then be adaptable enough to integrate the communities of interest of the two (or more) cultures involved. But cultural adaptation is not easy.

When a manager enters a developing nation to install advanced technological equipment and get it operating, his role is that of a *cultural catalyst* to accelerate change in the developing nation. He will need to make adjustments in leadership techniques which he employed in the advanced economy from which he came. Also, local employees in this new installation will find that they can no longer follow the ways of their less-productive culture. In other words, both the manager and the employees must change. There must be a fusion of cultures in which both parties adjust to the new situation of seeking greater productivity for the benefit of both the enterprise and the citizens of the country in which it operates.

Culture Shock

A manager or technician who enters another nation without adequate cultural preparation may suffer *culture shock* and be unable to perform effectively. His surroundings appear to be behavioral chaos. He becomes disoriented and retreats into isolation or wants to return home on the next airplane. But a different culture is not behavioral chaos; it is a systematic structure of behavior patterns, probably as systematic as the culture in the manager's home country. It can be understood if the manager has a receptive attitude. But there *are* differences, and these differences strain a person, regardless of his adaptability.[11] One observer comments about United States managers in Europe as follows: "Some operate in a continuous, though mild, state of shock—at how the market systems, distribution, and thought patterns they must deal with differ from those

---

[10] Jose de Cubas, "Let's Call 'Time,'" *Columbia Journal of World Business,* November–December, 1967, p. 7.

[11] For a major study of different managerial values see Mason Haire, Edwin E. Ghiselli, and Lyman W. Porter, *Managerial Thinking: An International Study,* New York: John Wiley & Sons, Inc., 1966. See also David A. Heenan, "The Corporate Expatriate: Assignment to Ambiguity," *Columbia Journal of World Business,* May–June, 1970, pp. 49–54.

in the U. S."[12] Similar difficulties in adjustment were reported by a research study of United States managers in joint ventures with Japanese in Japan.[13] What an expatriate manager soon learns is that it is irrational to expect workers in the host culture to act "rationally"—that is, according to his ethnocentric standards of rational conduct.

One study of thirty-four technical advisers from the United States judged that twenty-six of them lacked cultural insight about the country in which they were working.[14] The customs which frustrated them the most were those which were substantially different from practices in the United States. The three customs mentioned most frequently were orientation of the people toward life, nature, and behavior (mentioned ten times); lack of individual responsibility and initiative (ten times); and concepts of time and punctuality (nine times). Examples of "lack of individual responsibility and initiative" are failure to accept blame, reluctance to face facts, avoidance of work by educated men, and hiring people to work without training them. The Americans adjusted by trying to change themselves, trying to change the situation, accepting the situation, retreating from it, or marking time. The first two changes were attempted most.

Managers and technicians who have the ability to operate effectively in more than one culture are truly *transcultural* employees. They are low in ethnocentrism and adapt readily to different environments without culture shock. Usually they can communicate in more than one language. They are a vital asset to multinational business.

Organizational Design to Accommodate a Culture

There is a natural tendency for firms operating in advanced nations to want to install advanced business and production systems in a developing nation. The host nation readily agrees because it wants "the latest and best equipment." Though this kind of policy sounds like a desirable one, it is often a mistake. A simpler system may get better results because the advanced system is beyond the capacity of local managers and workers.

In one nation a smaller, slower paper-making machine produced at a lower unit cost than a modern, high-speed machine. Reasons were that the slower machine could employ less-skilled labor, breakdowns could be more easily repaired by nationals, and when breakdowns did occur they were less wasteful of time and material. For example, paper breakage on the high-speed machine wasted paper at the rate of nearly a mile a minute until it could be rethreaded through the rolls of the machine, and the threading process required more skill. When the machine itself had major breakdowns, it often lay idle for days while specialists from other nations were brought in to make repairs.

[12] Edward A. McCreary, "Those American Managers Don't Impress Europe," *Fortune*, December, 1964, p. 187.

[13] M. Y. Yoshino, "Administrative Attitudes and Relationships in a Foreign Culture," *MSU Business Topics*, Winter, 1968, pp. 59–66.

[14] Francis C. Byrnes, "Assignment to Ambiguity: Work Performance in Cross-cultural Technical Assistance," *Human Organization*, Fall, 1964, pp. 196–209.

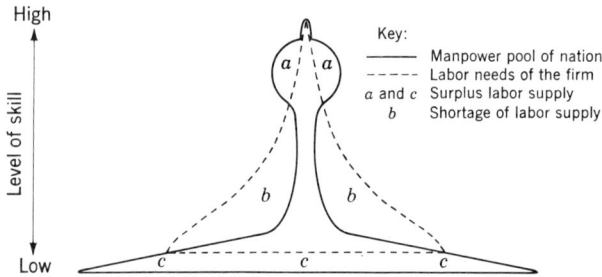

Figure 22-1   Comparison of a developing nation's available manpower pool and the labor needs of an advanced business entering the nation. Adapted from Richard N. Farmer, "Organizational Transfer and Class Structure," *Academy of Management Journal,* September, 1966, figures 2 and 3, pp. 209 and 211.

The significance of equipment breakdowns is illustrated by the experience of three factories producing similar products and with comparable technology.[15] The factory in the United States had breakdown time of less than 1 percent. In India, on the other hand, the subsidiary plant of a United States firm had a breakdown rate of about seven percent, while a comparable native Indian plant had a rate of fifteen to twenty percent. With breakdown differences of this magnitude it is evident that simpler equipment could result in greater net productivity if it could be kept operating more of the time.

The same kinds of comments which apply to factory machines also apply to office systems, accounting controls, organizational design, and other components of an advanced business system. The system can be too difficult for effective operation by the supply of labor available. Figure 22-1 shows the potential mismatch between an advanced firm's labor needs and the available labor pool in a developing nation. At the top there is often a surplus of available high-level people, as represented by area "a" in the chart. Even though these people are educated in subjects such as law and political science, rather than needed disciplines such as engineering and business, many can eventually be developed to meet company needs. Meanwhile, top-level specialists can be brought to the nation to fill in the manpower gaps.

As one approaches the middle of the organization, large shortages appear, as represented by area "b." The nation usually has a small middle class, and there are major shortages of technicians, middle managers, and skilled workers. This shortage is substantial and is the principal reason why simpler organizational systems may be more productive in the beginning. To overcome this shortage, large social overhead investments in training and education are required. As the labor force is upgraded,

[15] Barry M. Richman, "Empirical Testing of a Comparative and International Management Research Model," in *Academy of Management Proceedings* (1967 Meeting), Bowling Green, Ohio: Academy of Management, 1968, p. 47.

then organizational processes can be upgraded also, eventually approaching the system design and productivity achieved in an advanced nation.

Area "c" on the chart represents a large group which is unsuitable for employment. Some are illiterate, others lack social adaptability to rigorous work, and others are in poor health. This group typically needs the aid of government programs directed toward improving the whole social system. Business can cooperate with government in these programs.

INTRODUCING CHANGE

The Social Nature of Change

Whether the changes required are large or small, the work culture of a nation tends to change slowly, and in so doing, it gives stability and security to society. This is an advantage. However, there is an offsetting disadvantage; this very stability makes changes more difficult to initiate. As we have learned from both experience and research, change is a social problem as well as a technological one. The technological part of change is usually solvable by the logics of science, but the social part is more dependent on the uncertainties of human nature.

A point of major significance is that top management or lower management may block change. It is a mistake to consider that only technicians and workers are culturebound by tradition.

A United States consulting group, for example, made a detailed productivity study of a French shoe factory.[16] In presenting their report to the factory owner they showed how certain changes would increase both his income and that of his employees. He shrugged his shoulders and rejected the report because it would require him to make changes he could not socially accept. His family had owned the factory for three generations. If he installed new machinery, it would cause unpleasant stress on faithful older employees who had worked for his family all their lives. He also might have to work harder, and his wife would object to his longer hours. Why risk this much when he already had a pleasant life and sufficient income for his needs? (If you were "in his shoes," how would you respond?)

In another French firm the president accepted a consultant's changes, but his associates and middle managers blocked it.[17] After making a methods study in one small section of the plant, the consultant was able to increase productivity by 60 percent. The president was impressed, but his other managers finally persuaded him not to extend the study to the remainder of the plant.

Even changes designed for employee or customer service, rather than the company's benefit, will fail unless they integrate with the customs of the people affected. For example, a United States bank had a successful branch in the principal town of a small Polynesian island. Management

[16] Donald C. Stone, "Bridging Cultural Barriers in International Management," *S.A.M. Advanced Management Journal*, January, 1969, p. 57.
[17] Duncan, *op. cit.*, p. 71.

sought to improve customer service by installing a drive-in window. Customers failed to use the window, and it was finally abandoned. Investigation revealed that "going to the bank" had become a mark of status and a major social event in the community. Customers wanted to be seen by others at the bank and have an opportunity for social visiting. The bank had become the social center of the community somewhat in the manner of the general store or post office in rural America years ago. If customers used the drive-in window, they denied themselves these social amenities, so they declined to use it!

Encouraging Support for Change

Since management initiates most changes, it has the primary responsibility for handling them in such a way that there will be satisfactory adjustment. Although management initiates change, employees control the final decision to accept it or reject it, and they are the ones who actually accomplish it. Under these conditions, employee support becomes vital.

Most people in less-developed countries are not accustomed to the rigid demands of an industrial system. They are not prepared for the rigorous timing and discipline, precise division of labor, rational forms of action, and impersonal styles of supervision and control that prevail in advanced work systems. And they cannot be so prepared by a speech or two and a few haphazard instructions. Long-run environmental forces are required to establish cultural changes of this magnitude.

USING COMMUNITY FORCES   Even experienced multinational firms often overlook the power which community forces have in influencing the acceptance of changes *within* the firm. When certain changes are essential for productivity, it is desirable to enlist the support and participation of all possible community status groups, such as government leaders, unions, church dignitaries, mayors, universities, prominent social clubs, and others. This action helps each worker understand that people he respects are supporting this particular improvement. A business is one part of a community system; so the more support it can get from that system, the better are its chances for success.

USING GROUP FORCES WITHIN THE FIRM   Although most changes probably are introduced by management authority and staff persuasion, internal group forces are more effective when it is possible to use them. This process uses participation and group discussion to help people understand the need for change and to apply their own ideas to make change more workable on the job.

The British refinery of Esso Petroleum, a subsidiary of Standard Oil Company (New Jersey), has successfully used the group approach to achieve a major change in work rules.[18] Working with the union, a joint consulta-

---

[18] "How to Change Work Rules," *Business Week*, Mar. 31, 1962, pp. 50–52.

tion committee, and a consultant from the United States, major changes in archaic rules were made which increased efficiency substantially. For example, overtime was abolished, tea breaks and clean-up time were reduced, and the system of three mates (craftsman's helpers) for each five craftsmen was abolished.

BEGINNING AT THE TOP   Since we have already discussed how top managers can block effective change, it is evident that their support is vital to a new project. In developed nations there is often substantial decentralization of authority, so a project may succeed in spite of some opposition from the top manager. On the other hand, the management structure in most developing nations is authoritarian. If the top management does not approve, the project will probably gain little support at lower levels.

One highly successful development project in the Cauca Valley of Colombia combined all three approaches which have just been discussed.[19] This was a community development project, rather than one by an individual firm, but it was spearheaded by businessmen. This program focused on the "movers and shapers," who were the few people at the top of the human resource pyramid in the community. These men were at policy-making levels, had proven competence, and already had some desire to improve their society. They had both the capability and the power to make productive changes if their energies could be focused on this goal. The men primarily used group discussions to develop long-run plans for improvement, aided by a local university and an outside consultant. The improvements initiated by these men brought a dramatic upsurge in development of the Cauca Valley. Further, by means of the multiplier effect, the developmental spirit of these men spread to others in the valley.

UNLEARNING OLD HABITS AND REINFORCING NEW ONES   Productive change requires the unlearning of old habits, instead of simply adding new habits on top of the old ones. Take the situation of a local supervisor who is taught by an overseas management new ways of leading employees. What sometimes happens is that he retains most of his old approaches also, so that now he has a strange mixture of newer, positive practices which are substantially offset by holdover practices from his old habit patterns. As a consequence, there is little net benefit from his new practices. If he does not substantially believe in these new practices, he tends gradually to return to his old ways of doing things because these ways are more secure. Even when he does believe in his new practices, he may become frustrated because his old habits (and those of his manager) interfere. This condition means that any changes which are introduced require regular social and economic reinforcement to keep them going until they become firmly established as new habit patterns.

[19] Described to one of the authors by Professor Roderick F. O'Connor of Georgia Institute of Technology, and reported in Roderick F. O'Connor, "This Revolution Starts at the Top," *Columbia Journal of World Business*, Fall, 1966, pp. 39–46.

DEVELOPING PRODUCTIVITY

The Social Goals of Work

There are essentially three ways of perceiving the goals of one's efforts in a social system. Usually a single goal dominates, and when it does, it substantially determines how people use resources within their society.

One goal is *to work competitively to redistribute* power, income, property, or some other desired resource in the society. This means that a person is trying to get from others some of what they have, or trying to keep them from getting more. This goal is usually selfish, though it can be an effort to get more for someone else with whom one does not personally identify (i.e., not one's group, class, or craft). A typical example is workers in a developing nation who assume that there is a static pool of economic resources and the only way they can get more for themselves is to take from others. In popular terms, they try to take a larger slice of a static economic pie. Their main efforts are diverted away from trying to increase wealth and toward utopian equalitarian schemes which promise to redistribute it. Wealth could, of course, be more easily redistributed *as it is increased,* but the dominant worker attitude is simply getting a larger slice of a static pie.

A second goal is *to work more of the time* in order to have more of what one wants. For example, a person may work longer hours or may decrease absenteeism. He may also put his wife and children to work, thus increasing the wealth of his family.

A third goal is *to work more productively.* Productivity is an input-output relationship which implies a larger value of outputs in relation to inputs. It provides for more effective use of resources, whatever their amount. It is normally the most rewarding of the three choices from the point of view of the whole society.

All three goals may be pursued at the same time. A worker may be more productive through increasing his skill, but also work longer hours and through his union seek to raise wages at a rate greater than productivity gains. The important point is that the view which predominates will color strongly his attitudes toward work and the society in which he lives.

Social emphasis in most of the developed nations is upon the third goal, with moderate additional emphasis on the first goal in order to achieve a better balance of income and power among people. In less-developed nations the first goal often dominates, with minor emphasis on the second and rare attention to the third.

Building the Idea of Productivity

With few exceptions, a society is poor not because it lacks resources, but because it is unable to organize and use its resources productively. This means that productivity is the central idea which the people of a nation need to absorb in order to develop the spirit to rise above poverty and inefficiency. Without a devotion to productivity, new capital inputs are dissipated. Without a belief in productivity, more education merely increases the demand for wasteful personal aides, attendants, and helpers. Without productivity, achievement drives merely increase competition for resources that are not growing. These drives cause the achiever to step harder on his neighbor's shoulder as he climbs to the top, and since national resources are not expanding, whatever one gains is at the expense of the other.

It often comes as a surprise to uninitiated observers to discover that the majority of workers in a developing nation do not really understand the idea of productivity or identify with it in their work. This lack of understanding even extends to managers. One study of local citizens who were managers in ten Latin American nations reported that "only a minority of the managers interviewed had a reasonably clear concept of productivity."[20]

The idea of productivity includes quality of output as well as quantity. Less-developed nations too often emphasize amount of output regardless of quality in order to make their record look favorable. Any other characteristic of either inputs or outputs may also be considered. Thus, productivity can apply to social inputs and outputs just as much as it does to economic values. The point is that productivity is an all-encompassing idea for effective use of resources. *Society chooses* the types of inputs and outputs it will emphasize and value more highly in the input-ouput model.

Indirect approaches seldom work in conveying the productivity idea. It does little good to change organization forms in the hope that workers will somehow come to understand productivity as a result. In Israel, for example, workers own and control many business firms through their labor union, Histadrut. Planners hoped that workers would take an ownership interest in making these firms productive and that the firms would then serve as models of efficiency for the nation. Derber's study, however, reports an opposite result. He comments:[21]

> Socialist idealists had expected that workers in Histadrut-owned plants would view these plants as their own and would take an active part in their development and operation. They found, to their chagrin, that workers did view the Histadrut enterprises differently from private enterprises but mainly in the negative sense of expecting better economic returns and employment conditions rather than of promoting efficiency and production.

Another influence on productivity is the existence of *counterproductive factors* in a nation. Counterproductive factors are those which harm productivity instead of merely failing to contribute to it. For example, one of

[20] Albert Lauterbach, "Executive Training and Productivity: Managerial Views in Latin America," *Industrial and Labor Relations Review*, April, 1964, p. 366. Our experience shows that a number of students in developed nations also lack an understanding of productivity, because they are unable to distinguish between "an increase in production" and "an increase in productivity," even when they have formerly studied this difference.
[21] Milton Derber, "Plant Labor Relations in Israel," *Industrial and Labor Relations Review*, October, 1963, p. 58.

the authors observed in an Asian nation that university students are taught not to do production work because it is beneath the dignity of an educated person. The university system emphasizes law, theoretical economics, and political science; and most graduates seek work in the government bureaucracy. Most of the nation's talented manpower is tied up in government, so business and other applied areas do not have an adequate pool of talent for improving productivity. The result is that the whole nation is the loser.

A more complex system example of a counterproductive factor is government policy which funnels capital into urban housing and grandiose public buildings, giving an impression of wealth and comfort in the city. In turn, unskilled countrymen crowd into the city to "share the wealth," leading to urban unemployment, displaced persons, and rising crime. Crowded shantytowns and slums develop near the city, overtaxing the capacity of government to provide public utilities such as water, sanitation, and roads. The result is less productive employment of labor and increasing social unrest.

MOTIVATION IN A LESS-DEVELOPED ENVIRONMENT

In multinational management the most important idea regarding motivation is to apply it *in terms of the environment of the people involved* rather than in terms of an advanced industrial economy. Most companies desire to hire native supervisors, and there is little use trying to motivate workers until these supervisors can be trained and motivated. What is effective motivation in one environment may not be in another.

In a South American factory, for example, accidents were high. The six native superintendents were not following management's instructions for accident prevention. They seemed agreeable, but somehow failed to sell accident prevention throughout the organization. The overseas top management of the company then tried a high-powered safety publicity program of the type used in its own home plants. This was of no avail. Finally, a wise staff man found an effective solution. Paper-mâché heads of the six superintendents were molded and colored, the idea being that each week these heads would be arranged on a "totem pole" at the front gate in the order of the weekly safety rank of each man's department. No superintendent wanted to see himself as low man on the safety totem pole, so the accident problem was quickly corrected. In this case, management used existing cultural values of the country in order to accomplish the desired result of better safety.

Less-advanced Need Structures

Most workers in less-developed nations are correspondingly less advanced in their need structures. Modern psychology reports that new human needs take priority whenever former needs are reasonably satisfied. In other words, man is motivated more by what he is seeking than by what he already has. Human needs are generally recognized to be in some order, with physiological and security needs preceding social and ego needs. In less-developed countries, most employees are still seeking basic physiological and security needs. Hence, some of the more sophisticated and elaborate motivational devices of modern industrial management may not be appropriate in these countries. The needs of workers may be more simply reached by direct motivation. In many countries, workers have lived in economic systems in which there was little direct connection between their work performance and the amount of their rewards. Therefore, they require management to show them simple, direct evidence that if they work more effectively, they will receive more. In other words, work must be interpreted in terms of their immediate needs, rather than waiting for indirect results through a complex economic or social system. Accordingly, action which would be inappropriate in an advanced country may be workable in a less-developed country, as illustrated by the following events.

In South America, an international petroleum company employed about twenty local workers in an oil-well perforation team managed by an overseas executive. In spite of management efforts, each perforation job averaged nine days. Since a similar job with similar equipment was done in the United States in $1\frac{1}{2}$ days, management reasoned that—even considering the more primitive operating conditions in South America—the job could surely be done in six days or less. Since the job did require genuine teamwork and since the men worked in isolated locations less subject to direct supervision, management decided on a drastic step to break the cultural pattern. It offered nine days' pay for each job, regardless of the actual number of days worked. This dramatic economic incentive proved sufficient to alter long-standing cultural habits.

The employees' attitudes gradually changed. Within four years, they had reduced perforation time to $1\frac{1}{2}$ days, the same as in other efficient countries. Team members readily offered suggestions to improve teamwork and adapt technology to the special conditions of that area. On two occasions, the team encouraged transfer of men who would not change their habits and were thus holding back the team.

Research supports the view that workers in less-advanced countries have a less-advanced need structure and, consequently, require different supervisory approaches. A study of factory workers in India reports that security and wages to satisfy basic physiological needs are most important to Indian workers, although higher needs are important in the United States. The study concludes concerning the Indian worker: "Once his basic physical needs are satisfied his psychological-social needs will no doubt become more important, but today they are still of strictly secondary importance."[22]

To restate the basic point we are making, managerial practices from an advanced country cannot be transferred directly. They need to be adapted to the particular cultural practices, level of development, and employee need structure which a host country has. In effect, neither the advanced nation's nor the host nation's traditional practices are used.

[22] Paras Nath Singh and Robert J. Wherry, Sr., "Ranking of Job Factors by Factory Workers in India," *Personnel Psychology*, Spring, 1963, pp. 32–33.

Instead, a third—and situationally better—set of practices is developed which integrates the most workable ideas from both sets of traditional practices.

The Achievement Motive

Research by David C. McClelland discloses that emphasis on the *achievement motive* in a nation has an important influence on the drives of its people.[23] The achievement motive is present in everyone, but some people are consistently more oriented toward achievement than others. The achievement motive is a basic general attitude toward life, rather than a narrowly defined psychological need. It apparently can be stimulated by a nation's culture, for there are great differences in it among nations. McClelland found that the achievement motive is stronger in economically advanced countries and "growth" countries. As further evidence of cultural support of achievement, even children's books in the achievement-motivated countries give more emphasis to this drive, compared with books in nations low in achievement motivation.

People with strong achievement motives make accomplishment an end in itself, leaving in a secondary role the profit from accomplishment. They take moderate risks, rather than high or low ones, because they feel responsible for their decisions. They are realistic. They plan carefully and persist toward goals.

Research shows that achievement drives in a population are a useful measure for determining adaptability to economic development.[24] Fortunately achievement motivation can be developed. In India, which has a social climate lacking in achievement motivation, McClelland has been able to double the rate of entrepreneurial activity of persons who took a course in achievement motivation. He asks, "Why have policy-makers been so slow to act on this knowledge to invest in programs that would develop people's motives rather than merely their opportunities for work?"[25]

The achievement motive may be contrasted with competence, affiliation, and power motives.[26] These appear to be significant distinctions everywhere in the world. The achievement motive is more likely to develop the entrepreneur, innovator, and responsible leader. The achievers choose the best men to help them regardless of personal dislikes, while persons with affiliation motives choose their friends. The achiever works harder when he has feedback about progress, whereas the affiliator works best when he is complimented for his attitude and cooperation.

Perhaps the main point to be drawn from studies of motives is that there will be a different mix of them in different cultures. If an inter-

---

[23] David C. McClelland, *The Achieving Society,* Princeton, N.J.: D. Van Nostrand Company, Inc., 1961.
[24] Alan Howard, "Plasticity, Achievement and Adaptation in Developing Economies," *Human Organization,* Winter, 1966, pp. 265–272.
[25] David C. McClelland, "Achievement Motivation Can Be Developed," *Harvard Business Review,* November–December, 1965, p. 7.
[26] Saul W. Gellerman, *Motivation and Productivity,* New York: American Management Association, 1963.

national manager wishes to motivate local workers, he needs to learn the motive most emphasized in the local culture and try to use it constructively. Then he needs to try to interpret how motives vary among his people. For example, in South America the affiliation motives might be expected. Submanagers could be expected to hire, purchase supplies from, and otherwise bestow favors on their brothers, in-laws, cousins, and personal friends. However, a sample of 100 persons in the plant might be distributed by cultural motivation as follows: achievement, eleven; competence, thirteen; power, twenty-seven; and affiliation, forty-nine. If achievers can be identified and developed, they are likely to be responsible, innovating managers. The ultimate goal is to have many nationals managing operations as quickly as possible—and even moving to management positions in other countries, which would create a truly multinational work force for business.

SUMMARY

The nations of the world have urgent needs to make more productive use of their resources. Business is a major change agent and cultural catalyst in serving these needs. When an international business enters another culture, it is usually most effective when each culture adapts somewhat to the other. This idea especially applies when an advanced business enters a developing nation, but it also applies when both nations are advanced. The idea is reflected in the convergence hypothesis which holds that cultures tend to become more similar as they industrialize.

Multinational managers need transcultural capabilities in order to perform effectively without culture shock. Successful managers have the capacity to integrate social systems within a business context, introduce change, improve productivity, and motivate employees in a less-developed environment.

STUDY GUIDES FOR INTERPRETATION OF THIS CHAPTER

1 Marfa Electronics, a mutinational firm, is planning to build an assembly plant on a hill overlooking an Asian city with about one hundred thousand population. Local contacts have advised that many persons might refuse to work there because they believe the hill is haunted by evil spirits. The contacts have suggested that the city's leading medicine man be employed to hold a public ceremony to drive the evil spirits away before construction is started. They report that the medicine man's price, including decorations and refreshments, will probably be $5,000. As chief of the construction mission what would you do?

2 Read two articles or news items regarding international business and report whether they in any way support or refute the convergence hypothesis.

3 Choose another country, study its culture from books or personal contacts, and prepare a presentation telling a United States automobile

manufacturer how his company's managerial practices should be amended for the new branch it is starting in the country.

4 With the aid of the most recent information available, appraise the accuracy of J.-J. Servan-Schreiber's predictions in *The American Challenge.*

5 From the point of view of an advanced business entering a developing nation, discuss the significance of the chart comparing a developing nation's manpower pool with the labor needs of an advanced business. What major plans and policies does the chart indicate you should make?

PROBLEMS
HUMAN OR MECHANICAL POWER?

A. A multinational firm took 49 percent ownership in a joint venture with an Asian nation to manufacture a consumer durable good. One stated purpose in the venture agreement was that the multinational firm would provide its know-how to make the plant productive. The plant was to be located in a metropolitan center with substantial manufacturing. In planning for operations the multinational firm proposed using five mechanical forklift trucks to transport goods to and from production areas and in the warehouse. The government representative objected and proposed human labor with hand trucks. He gave the following reasons for his objections: (1) added capital costs, (2) difficulty of getting parts for the trucks and technicians to repair them, (3) difficulty of training qualified operators, and (4) unemployment in the city which made it politically essential for the plant to provide as many jobs as possible.

B. A multinational food producer took 49 percent ownership in a joint venture with a South American nation to process and can vegetables in a remote mountain region. One stated purpose in the venture agreement was that the multinational firm would provide its know-how to make the plant more productive than the typical local food processor in the nation. In planning for operations the multinational firm proposed five electric typewriters for office work. The government representative objected and proposed manual typewriters because (1) they tended to have fewer breakdowns, so they required less maintenance, (2) they could be maintained by less skilled technicians, available in a city 40 miles distant, and (3) electric service was unreliable, so the machines and their operators might be idled at times when they were needed.

1 In each instance, as the top local manager of the joint venture, how would you respond?

THE PAPER MILL IN BRAZIL

Olin Corporation had a two-page advertisement in *Business Week,* October 18, 1969. One page showed a picture of Karl Marx. The other page read as follows (reprinted with permission of Olin Corporation):

> *If Africa, Asia and South America go communist, don't blame him.*
> Karl Marx is not responsible for famines in Asia or epidemics in Africa. It's not his fault that the average South American earns 75¢ a day.
> All he did was predict the consequences.
> That a population living in misery will turn to communism as a way out. Unless something is done to alleviate these conditions.
> But the countries themselves don't have the economic resources to make these changes. The U. N. doesn't. Even the United States doesn't.
> They need the help of world industry. Particularly U. S. industry.
> Industry is in an ideal position to do this. It can deal directly with the people of a country. It can change their lives in a way no government can.
> A small case in point: in 1958, Olinkraft, a subsidiary of Olin, bought a paper mill in Igaras, a small town in the remote interior of Brazil.
> Igaras was the kind of town on which communism thrives—a declining mill, no doctors, shoeless children, men working an 84-hour week, etc.
> It wasn't hard to increase the production of the mill eight-fold, to lower hours and raise wages, to reforest the woodlands—but that wasn't enough.
> We hired a doctor, nurses, teachers; expanded the school; built a dispensary, a clubhouse; provided free medical and dental care (and medicines at cost to non-employees); financed housing loans and helped set up a cooperative store.
> And then the people joined in. They rebuilt their own homes, paid for their own teachers, built and operated their own store and, in effect, revitalized the whole town.
> But the people weren't the only ones to benefit. Olinkraft did well enough from the mill to start an extensive expansion program.
> Igaras, of course, is only one town. But Olin is only one company. Imagine this kind of success multiplied by tens of thousands of companies and towns all over Africa, Asia and South America.
> The deeds of industry may well be as important as the gospel of democracy.

1 Appraise this advertisement in terms of the multiplier effect, paternalism, the Law of Persistent Underdevelopment, the trusteeship role of management, equitable rewards to pluralistic investment groups, and other applicable ideas discussed in this book.

CHAPTER 23

LOOKING TOWARD THE FUTURE

Ours is not a finished society.

EMILIO G. COLLADO[1]

Progress doesn't happen; it must be made to happen.

CHARLES B. THORNTON[2]

New conditions bring new issues. Certainly a central issue of modern times is the relation of organizations to their external environment. In this book our focus is upon business and its external relations. The central issue—as with all organizations—is how to meet the needs of the organization (business, in this instance) along with the needs of its individual participants and of society in general.

In short, the issue is how to keep organizations viable along with man and his whole society. If we emphasize organization viability alone, society may become an organized monstrosity with human puppets dangling from its organizational strings. If we emphasize individual viability alone, we deny man the cornucopia of benefits that derive from organized activity. And if we emphasize only society as a whole, we deny man the individuality and freedom with which nature ordained him, and we reduce both organizations and men to servitude under the "plan." The only satisfactory answer is a balance which harmonizes all interests. The modern social balance is called pluralism. It is dynamic, not static, evolving into new forms that probably eventually will give it a new name also.

In this chapter we shall take a broad look at how the issues we have discussed are moving toward a more responsible business society in the future. We shall discuss how new relationships are evolving between busi-

---

[1] Emilio G. Collado, "The Central Problem of Our Times," *The Lamp*, Winter, 1963, p. 5.
[2] Charles B. Thornton, "The Challenge to Business Management," *The Deltasig* (Delta Sigma Pi), November, 1969, p. 21.

ness and society and how the business mission is being more clearly defined for society. Society is coming to understand the importance of business for achieving a better quality of life around the world, and the concept of a socially profitable business is emerging.

BUSINESS AND SOCIETY

Business in a Pluralistic Social System

The modern business is a social system in itself, but it is also part of a larger social system represented by society in general. Clearly there is a reciprocal relationship between business and this larger society. Society does affect business through religion, law, custom, and a host of other influences. But business is not a mute servant; it speaks with a voice of leadership in the affairs of society. It is a change agent influencing society in many ways. It is an important voice in a pluralism of many voices.

The society which created business could, of course, destroy its independence. Business is continually on trial before the high court of public opinion, but, in a free society at least, it is permitted to testify in its own defense by showing how its actions contribute to the general welfare. Except for the dark days of the Great Depression of the 1930s, business testimony has been effective. The public has little doubt about business's net contribution. The issue is not whether business should be stripped of power, but rather how its power and drive can be channeled into greater contributions. As explained by Taylor:[3]

> A pluralist society is obliged to proceed always on a principle of counterpoise: it discovers its equilibrium, not by eliminating oppositions, but by using them, by making them party to a larger design which exhibits the public dimension of every private act. . . .
>
> We do not solve the problem of governing the modern corporation by extinguishing its independence. We solve the problem by defining the limits within which its independence is admissible and beyond which its independence is an encroachment on the public interest.

We believe that the next few decades will be an era of pluralistic society. The idea of pluralism will tend to be used more and more to explain institutional conduct and analyze its consequences. As stated by one observer, "The trend has been toward a decidedly pluralistic pattern in which it is recognized that the existence of numerous decision centers throughout the social structure of the nation vitalizes the economy and is essential for the protection of basic liberties."[4] The idea of pluralism focuses on the social needs of many groups, the interfaces among them, and the system relationships that evolve from these interfaces. It increases the need to look upon conditions in terms of a whole.

[3] John F. A. Taylor, "Is the Corporation above the Law?" *Harvard Business Review*, March–April, 1965, p. 130.
[4] Richard Eells, "Beyond the Golden Rule," *Columbia Journal of World Business*, July–August, 1967, p. 83.

Dangers of Pluralism

Our discussion has treated pluralism as a fact of life for business in advanced free societies such as the United States, so our discussion has focused on how business can work within pluralism's constraints to serve human needs. However, like all social systems, pluralism has its faults, and these deserve recognition as we conclude the book. The principal dangers of pluralism include the following.

EMPHASIS ON INSTITUTIONAL POWER INSTEAD OF SERVICE In a system in which institutions have some freedom of action, there is always the possibility that institutional *power* will be overemphasized instead of institutional *service*. Institutions normally justify their existence by showing how they contribute to public needs. This is a positive, worthwhile measure of institutional performance. It is a valid social basis for granting power to perform designated institutional functions. However, in the absence of suitable checks and balances, this valid functional power can be diverted to power for its own sake; that is, "power to do" is diverted to "power over" others in the system. This kind of diversion makes organizations greedy for power and leads to power blocs and private wars among institutions for power supremacy. Power becomes the measure of success rather than the instrument by which service is rendered, and energies are diverted from more constructive public responsibilities.

As institutions become larger, there is the danger that they will lose sight of their service functions and rely on power to keep viable, unless constitutional provisions are established to limit power. Both the individual and total society need to be protected. The Labor-Management Relations Act, for example, has one set of provisions to protect the individual union member and another set to protect the public interest from union power.

SOCIAL FRAGMENTATION A second danger in pluralism is the possibility that so many different groups will arise that their objectives will overlap and they will dissipate their energies trying to maintain coordination and keeping off each other's toes. Just as too many cooks spoil the broth, too many pluralistic organizations could reduce progress to a quagmire of confusion and red tape. Each new institution further complicates the business environment. Since each institution is related to all others, the addition of one results in a geometric increase in complexity, rather than an arithmetic increase.

The fact that some pluralism is wise does not prove that more pluralism is wiser. At some point groups can be so splintered that each lacks the power to hold responsible leadership. Political parties in some European countries, for example, are so fractionated that none is strong enough to provide much-needed leadership. Divided responsibility and compromise become ends in themselves, while genuine political needs go unheeded for lack of leadership. In the business environment, government first moved in strongly. Then the unions came, followed by trade associations, professional and scientific societies, nonprofit organizations such as the Committee for Economic Development, and others. Recently we have added the institutional investor and social action groups. We must be cautious not to become so enamored with pluralism that we let complexity outstrip our capacity to coordinate society.

The point of diminishing returns in pluralism is the point where the increment from one more institutional finger in the pie is offset by the loss arising from additional complexity. Comparing pluralism with democracy, we recognize that an optimally free society is not one in which every citizen votes on every public issue regardless of its importance. Similarly, an optimally pluralistic society is not one in which every conceivable interest is represented by a separate institution competing for power.

Social fragmentation also has its effects on the individual. We can picture a situation in which a person finds his interests represented by so many hundreds of organizations that he feels close to none of them. Consequently, he can drift into a feeling of powerlessness, loneliness, and social alienation. He is like a person alone in New York's Times Square on New Year's Eve. Though he is surrounded by 100,000 people, he feels that none of them really care about him. He is alone in a crowd.

ELITISM   Technology and social systems are becoming increasingly complex, and it is inevitable that some persons should know more than others about these complex matters. These more knowledgeable persons are likely to rise within each organization. As they become more involved in abstract computer models, social planning, and decision making, they are likely to develop an elitist detachment from the persons they represent "who just don't understand the system." They come to the conclusion that they know what is best, because they alone can see the whole picture. If their group does not agree, it should be manipulated or coerced into agreement. Thus, the democratic basis of the organization becomes reversed. No longer are the leaders serving specific needs of individuals who comprise the group. This tendency can be observed in labor unions, minority groups, social action groups, and business trade associations. Controls are necessary to maintain democratic responsiveness to individual member needs.

In fact, individuality is the one "institution" not represented at the social-exchange table of pluralism. It stands to lose most if the institutional aspects of pluralism are overemphasized. Therefore, if individualism is a value which society cherishes (and we believe it does, within limits), then social controls and customs need to be established to obligate institutions to accept, respect, and even cultivate individualism (again, within reasonable limits).

FOCUS ON CONFLICT   It is sometimes said that pluralism focuses on conflict, since there are many autonomous organizations seeking their own goals. Certainly conflict does occur in pluralism, but it is not a special characteristic of pluralism compared with other social forms. In a pluralistic social system different groups can cooperate toward goals if they desire to do so.

If, for example, five groups on a hill want water from a well in a valley, they can argue about who will bring it up the hill or each can get its own or they can *cooperate* to combine this task with other tasks to bring more need satisfactions to all. We can even assume that there is not enough water in the well for all of them. In this case they can still cooperate to dig another well, dam a stream, or seek some other water source. Or, each group can try to keep the water for itself. This is a human choice, not a creation of pluralism.

WEAKNESS IN LONG-RANGE PLANNING Long-range planning is clearly a necessity in the modern world for such items as urban renewal, irrigation projects, and educational upgrading of people. Pluralism provides no special apparatus for interorganizational coordination of plans, so organizations may proceed with divergent approaches that will eventually come into conflict. On the other hand, variety in approaches is one of pluralism's strengths, because a single, rigid plan could lock a society into a wasteful course of action. Further, whenever interorganizational planning is definitely desirable, there is nothing in pluralism which blocks it. In fact, the basic model of pluralism suggests the opposite result: Where there are mutual interests, functional cooperation produces greater payoffs for all groups involved.

THE SOCIALLY PROFITABLE BUSINESS

In Chapter 3 we referred to the socially profitable business. In this kind of business various types of social investments are received from many claimants. Career management, acting particularly as trustee along with its other managerial roles, takes these investments and tries to develop payoffs to claimants that are greater than their investments. The payoffs cover all types of claimant expectations, including social and psychological rewards such as fulfillment, personal growth, social interaction, and opportunity.

The Nature of Social Profitability

When social and psychological goals become *a part of the organization's basic system of objectives,* rather than some thorn which must be tolerated to get the economic job done, then we have the foundation for a truly socially profitable business. Just as it is with economic profit, some businesses will do better than others, but the key point is that social profitability becomes part of the firm's basic objectives. Social goals are no longer a peripheral, nonbusiness item. When business accepts this expanded view of the social system, it will be released from its "economic ghetto" to play a larger part in the affairs of mankind than ever before.

Society's expectations of business are increasing dramatically—perhaps excessively. Not only does society expect business to take material goods and produce something better, but it also wants business to take employees and make them better. Society expects that a business which enters a community will make it better. In whatever business undertakes, the expectation is leadership toward improvement in the quality of life, rather than simply satisfaction of minimum standards of conduct. This high expectation places heavy responsibility on business to act in a socially profitable way.

To the extent that business fails to seek social profitability in accordance with human expectations, the Iron Law of Responsibility stands in the background to remind business of the urgency of its task. This law promises that a group which has power and fails to use it responsibly will eventually find its power slipping away to other groups which are ready to use it more responsibly. A number of years ago Berle stated clearly the alternatives available to business:[5]

> The choice of corporate managements is not whether so great a power shall cease to exist; they can merely determine whether they will serve as the nuclei of its organization or pass it over to someone else, probably the modern state. The present current of thinking and insistence that private rather than governmental decisions are soundest for the community are clearly forcing the largest corporations toward a greater rather than a lesser acceptance of the responsibility that goes with power.

The world of business is no longer just a technological and economic world—and probably it never was. Now, for sure, it is a social world also.

Social Profitability Includes Economic Profitability

Economic profit is basic to business success. Business deals with economic inputs, and if these resources are dissipated, the organization lacks the capacity to continue its services. Economic outputs need to exceed inputs, or else there is no reason for economic investors to allocate resources to the business. These economic facts of life are as true for publicly owned business as they are for private business. If the public invests its resources in a state enterprise, it expects a favorable return therefrom just as a private investor does. Therefore, when we speak of social objectives for business performance, we think of economic objectives as one part of this whole framework. We need businesses which are both economically and socially productive.

The business which achieves both objectives is the one which will be immensely stronger and better accepted by society. Looking at the situation this way, we see that the idea of social performance is in a sense a broadening of the profit idea to include social outputs as well as economic ones. Man seeks both social and economic returns from his business institutions, and he expects profitable outputs of each in relation to his inputs.

[5] Adolf A. Berle, Jr., *The 20th Century Capitalist Revolution*, New York: Harcourt, Brace & World, Inc., 1954, pp. 172–173.

The idea of mutual social and economic outcomes is consistent with the business mission of *productive implementation* discussed in Chapter 3. Society determines the priorities which are most important. Some of them are economic and some are social. Then business endeavors to serve these priorities *productively* in accordance with its resources and functional capabilities. Thus, in general terms the mission of business is *to create an environment for productivity and progress toward social goals.* Business approaches this mission with some self-interest and faults, but it is no different from other institutions in having these deficiencies.

The social goals of affluent nations are represented by the phrase "better quality of life." The ultimate social goals of developing nations are similar, but their interim goals more realistically are "social and economic development" to help them gain in their race with poverty and hunger. Business is especially prepared to help developing nations because of its proven record of economic productivity. Even poor nations can provide material goods, art, culture, education, and health for a chosen few, but they have learned that to provide these benefits for a substantial part of their people they must organize and manage their resources in the most productive ways possible.

An Appropriate Balance of Economic and Social Outputs

Business's difficult task is to balance economic outputs with social outputs in accordance with the priorities of each social system in which it operates. This task exposes business to the risk that its economic productivity will decline as it gives more of its energies to social outputs.[6] Nevertheless, in a world of rising social expectations, both outputs are required from business.

In order to perform their new socioeconomic role effectively, businessmen need to develop value systems which recognize responsibilities to claimants other than stockholders. There is strong evidence that many career managers and business owners have this kind of value system.

For example, a study of over fifty regional and national firms known to have social action programs showed that managers ranked responsibility to society a close second to traditional stockholder responsibility.[7] The weighted values for rankings of four groups covered in the survey were as follows:

Stockholders	237
Society	195
Employees	170
Management	125

[6] One study of seventy-two large industrial firms from 1952 to 1963 showed that those which were owner controlled (at least 10 percent of stock owned by one party) earned a substantially higher rate of return on investment; however, their dividend payments to stockholders were lower. See R. Joseph Monsen, "Ownership and Management: The Effect of Separation on Performance," *Business Horizons*, August, 1969, pp. 45–52.
[7] Fred Luthans and Richard M. Hodgetts, "Government and Business: Partners in Social Action," *Labor Law Journal*, December, 1969, pp. 763–770.

Furthermore, the managers showed a strong value commitment to their social action programs. When asked how they would respond to stockholder objections to a social action program, 90 percent said they would not abandon the program. Similarly, 95 percent would not abandon the program when faced with union objections. Clearly their commitment was to broader social responsibilities.

The Stockholder Role in Corporate Social Action

As a matter of fact, as social needs become more apparent to all citizens, there is declining opposition to business's efforts to achieve social outputs. Among stockholders, some perceive these outputs as a necessary activity in operating a business. To them it is simply good corporate citizenship in the way that they as individuals try to be good citizens. Other owners have strong social ideals, so they want some business efforts diverted to social interests. Others, taking a long look ahead, see social outputs as one of business's greatest opportunities for profitable service to humanity. They perceive that business will prove more productive of social outputs than other organizations; consequently, society will turn to it to produce social outputs *profitably* in its areas of functional capability, just as business has done with society's economic needs in the past. In this manner the activities of business will change gradually from economic outputs to social ones.

Another stockholder approach that is sure to expand is the purchase of stock by social action groups for the specific purpose of working through stockholder meetings to achieve social goals. One example is a group which purchased a few shares of General Motors stock in order to present to the 1970 stockholder meeting such proposals as the following:
    1. To amend the corporate charter to "limit the business purposes of the corporation to those purposes which are not detrimental to the public health, safety and welfare."
    2. To establish a shareholders' committee for corporate responsibility.
    3. To add to the corporate board of directors three members representing the public.
    The effort failed, but it received the broad publicity which its backers sought, and undoubtedly it made management more aware of the sincere interest of a broad segment of society in corporate social responsibility.

This discussion suggests that, instead of general stockholder opposition to business social action, there will probably be some stockholder pressure for social action. Even though the pressure groups may represent a minority of stock ownership, other stockholders will be sympathetic with their cause. The result is that conflict concerning social action will be as strong *within* the stockholder group as it is *between* stockholders and management. Thus career management will be left relatively free to follow its trusteeship role of providing both social and economic payoffs to various claimant groups.

    The kind of discussion which has been presented for stockholders could also be offered regarding employees, the community, and others.

There will be differences about *kinds* of social outcomes desired, and their *amount* compared with economic outputs, but the idea of business social outputs seems well established. The choice for business is, as it always has been, to work with the risks involved in order to produce the most productive and equitable outcomes possible. This is business's social response to the pluralistic claims made upon it.

EVALUATING THE SOCIALLY PROFITABLE BUSINESS

Throughout this book we have mentioned the quality of life and the socially responsive business which equitably distributes benefits to claimants in accordance with their investments in the situation. These are idealistic concepts. Are they also realistic? That is, can they be achieved, and are they specific enough to permit society to evaluate the performance of business, as well as other institutions? If society is to do more than simply rant and rave at the deficiencies of its institutions, it must offer specific, achievable goals toward which its organizations can work. And it must offer realistic criteria for evaluating progress toward objectives. In turn, business must use these goals and criteria (which it as one pluralistic institution has helped society set) to work toward socially profitable operations.

Definition of "Quality of Life"

Although the phrase "quality of life" is frequently offered as a social goal, it is rarely defined. We offer the following interpretation of what seems to dominate human thinking when this term is used. *Quality of life* exists when there is a free and affluent society in which people live compatibly with their inner spirit, their fellow man, and nature's physical environment; and a society in which motivation is self-generating because each person lives under equal justice and equal opportunity to become all that he is capable of becoming, through use of his different characteristics as well as his shared ones, to serve his own good as well as the common good.

"Quality of life" is unlikely ever to be obtained absolutely, but it does possess realistic measurable criteria such as amount of environmental pollution, morale of group members, capacity to cooperate, and justice through grievance and legal systems. Thus it is something toward which business and other institutions can work. For the individual it offers improvement, independence, and justice, which were discussed in Chapter 10 as claims which an individual makes on his organizations.

Social Criteria for Evaluating Organizational Performance

In Chapter 2 we discussed five basic criteria which society will use to evaluate the effectiveness of its institutions. These criteria are an open system, participative organization, productivity, distributive justice, and a power-responsibility balance. They are a nucleus around which society can build more specific social performance measures. For example, a firm which pollutes air others breathe is exerting power over them. Measures of pollution responsibility can be established, just as they can be for a man with a backyard barbecue grill. Furthermore, is the polluting firm exceeding the bounds of distributive justice? By not controlling pollution it is saving a few pennies for customers, owners, employees, or someone, but is it also unjustly distributing to its neighbors the negative output of pollution? If an open system is maintained, feedback and pressures will cause the firm to take appropriate corrective action to establish reasonable harmony among the pluralistic interests involved.

As the future unfolds, social performance measures are likely to increase in number and significance. National officials are especially interested in business's influence on economic growth and on ecology, its development of people, and its flexibility to absorb new federal programs. Social action groups are evaluating business on the basis of social justice and morality of conduct. Young persons are evaluating it on the basis of job freedoms and the opportunity to apply their unique ideals for social action.[8] Unions and others are evaluating it in terms of employment security, urban issues, and handling of technological change.

There appear to be about as many social-evaluation criteria as there are groups with claims on business. As with any developing social idea, most of the criteria are nebulous and poorly defined. At this stage of development, there are too many criteria and too few actual evaluations. As time passes, criteria will be sifted and combined into several key ones that can be better defined and measured. But even poorly defined criteria can be used by businessmen as guides to their decisions; hence, more emphasis will be directed toward educating businessmen about the external environment and encouraging them to consider social consequences in making decisions.

Public measures of social performance gradually are being developed. An early example was unemployment compensation laws, which give lower rates to the employer whose employment stability is greater. The same kind of arrangement exists in state workmen's compensation laws. Later examples are civil rights laws, pollution controls, and beautification controls on the issuance of building permits.

Even such a nebulous area as the effect of a business on the general well-being of people—society's human assets—may be carefully measured and evaluated in the future. The reason is that society stands to lose if human assets are used wastefully in the production of economic assets. Blum has described an experimental social audit of a business[9] and Likert concludes that social science tools are now available to make this type of audit.[10]

[8] For further discussion see Anthony G. Athos, "Is the Corporation Next to Fall?" *Harvard Business Review*, January–February, 1970, pp. 49–61.
[9] Fred H. Blum, "Social Audit of the Enterprise," *Harvard Business Review*, March–April, 1958, pp. 77–86.
[10] Rensis Likert, "Measuring Organizational Performance," *Harvard Business Review*, March–April, 1958, p. 49.

Relation of Intentions and Results

An important issue in evaluating social responsibility is whether the evaluation must be made at the point of decision or whether effects of the decision are also to be considered. It is quite possible that socially desirable effects will occur even when social responsibilities are not considered at the time the decision is made. Even antisocial decisions may, because of external, unforeseen events, have socially desirable outcomes. McGuire makes the following comment:[11]

> Obviously, the social content of a corporate decision cannot be evaluated ex post by an examination of the social benefits stemming from its outcome, for in a business world dominated by uncertainly this outcome is often unintended. Any decision process, therefore, must be appraised for its social content prior to or at the decision point. A corporate decision is socially responsible when that alternative the decision-maker believes will result in the highest social benefit is elected.

McGuire goes on to explain that there are degrees of social responsibility and that a business may for other reasons choose an alternative that advances social welfare less than the maximum possible. But, nevertheless, the decision must be evaluated in terms of whether social responsibility was considered at the time it was made. Socially responsible action can hardly be evaluated in terms of the effects of some subsequent event which interferes with the desired outcome. This reasoning is sound if society is interested only in the *intentions of businessmen* with regard to social responsibility. But society historically also has been interested in the *performance of business*. To the extent that performance is involved, effects of a decision must be considered. Allowance can be made for unforeseen events, but the final test is the social effect of a decision.

It appears likely that both intention and performance criteria will be applied in the future. It is important to know that businessmen responsibly consider social outcomes when they make a decision, but it is also important to know that their intentions are producing worthwhile results. Consistently poor results might indicate poor judgment, inadequate education in social values, lack of sufficient power to bring about intended outcomes, or something else; but in any case society needs to evaluate *results* as well as *intentions* in order to take the necessary corrective action. It is said that the road to social chaos is paved with good intentions and bad decisions.

The Meaning of Work for Multiallegiant Men

Modern society is changing fast, and business is required to move with it. Work, for example, is becoming less important to some workers, compared with their other pursuits. A number of social analysts believe that society

[11] Joseph W. McGuire, "The Social Responsibility of the Corporation," in Edwin B. Flippo (ed.), *Evolving Concepts in Management*, University Park, Pa.: The Academy of Management, Pennsylvania State University, 1965, p. 21.

is heading toward a new bohemianism of plenty, in which leisure rather than work will be the center of life. The wants of man will be so bounteously met by a technological society that little work will be required of him. On the other hand, man by his nature seems to be oriented to curiosity and problem solving. He derives satisfaction from finding and overcoming challenges, so he may choose to continue creative, productive work, even though need for it declines in urgency.

Regardless of whether work is at the center or the periphery of life, the work environment is becoming more democratized. Workers are often as committed to their intellectual specialty and its norms as they are to their company and its norms, and they are committed in other ways to other groups. This is the concept of multiallegiant man in a pluralistic society. Having less commitment to employers and an intellectual skill usable in many ways, workers become more mobile, shifting from job to job with ease. Social complexities further encourage democratization, compelling decisions to be made more on the basis of data contributed and evaluated by groups of specialists, since no man can know enough about a problem to be an autocrat with it. Thus, in order to be effective, the organization needs to maintain an open system internally among its parts, as well as externally with society.

The multiprofessional, multiallegiant, college-educated student, because of his wider interests and idealism, tends to be more interested in society than his predecessors were. Therefore, he expects to find in his work a social purpose which he can support. The business which can tie this extra motivational dimension to his work will achieve better social profitability and probably more economic profitability also. Work in this instance will, indeed, be meaningful. It will be "where the action is."

The Challenge to Business Leadership

It is an age of discontinuity. There is a youth revolution, a moral revolution, an educational revolution, a technological revolution, a minority group revolution, and so on. The pressures for change come endlessly from all directions.

With so many changes coming, business leadership in the next generation will be an increasingly difficult task, requiring intensely prepared career managers. The task is enormous, so it is dangerous to expect miracles in a decade. But the challenges are exciting. The opportunities are substantial. The new emphasis on quality of life opens a whole new planet for development in the business universe. No one claims that in the physical universe the task of reaching the planet Mars is easy, but it is exciting. The same excitement applies to the new planet of social outcomes which business is seeking. The payoff may be far greater than that derived from reaching and developing Mars. Consider, for example, the influence of one businessman on the Renaissance:[12]

> One would like to have a record of the thinking of the great Italian banker, Cosimo de' Medici, in the mid-fifteenth century. His bank and

[12] Berle, op. cit., pp. 176–177.

his business had come to dominate Florence. He ran the little country, though he assumed no political title. He subsidized art and artists, and supported queer penniless refugees from Byzantium who insisted on copying and translating Greek classics. Did he realize he was laying one of the foundation piers for the Italian Renaissance, one of the greatest efflorescences of human spirit in the Christian era? He was a reflective man, and he may have speculated on the subject. There are some marked similarities between his situation and that of American business firms five hundred years later.

There are indeed some similarities between the fifteenth and the twentieth centuries. Business today is coming to an era of social response to create a better quality of life. Business is pushed by world events, so it really has no choice concerning whether to step into this era or not. The social results can be just as exciting and as beneficial as those of the Renaissance—or even more so. This is business's great challenge.

SUMMARY

Although a pluralistic social system has certain deficiencies, this type of system appears to be the one in which business in advanced societies will be operating for at least the next generation. This type of system offers risks and challenges to business because it is quite flexible and quickly allocates tasks to institutions which show capability to perform them responsibly. Since quality of life is now a primary social goal, business needs to "shift gears" in that direction. Society wants socially profitable businesses which incorporate social goals into their basic system of objectives. Business's challenge is to strike an appropriate balance of social and economic outputs in accordance with the needs of society, distributing these outputs equitably to claimants.

Criteria for evaluating the socially profitable business are emerging. These relate both to intentions at the time a decision is made and to the results of that decision.

STUDY GUIDES FOR INTERPRETATION OF THIS CHAPTER

1 What, in your opinion, is the essence of the social opportunities facing businessmen around the world?

2 With regard to business, do you see any dangers in the further development of pluralistic society?

3 Is the idea of a socially profitable business a useful concept (a) for businessmen and (b) for persons appraising business actions?

4 A study mentioned in this chapter reports that managers of over fifty firms ranked responsibility to society a close second to traditional stockholder responsibility. Assume that a similar study is made in 1980 and give, with reasons, your prediction of its results.

5 Discuss arguments for and against stockholders electing an independent Committee for Corporate Responsibility to audit and report on a

company's social actions in the same way that an accounting firm audits and reports on the company's financial actions.

PROBLEMS
THE FEEDBACK SYSTEM

Martin Sober is a bright young M.B.A. from a prestigious graduate school. He is now one of five executive assistants on the staff of the executive vice-president of a national manufacturer of home appliances. Since assuming this position six months ago he has regularly insisted that the company establish (a) a better system of feedback about the social effects of its actions and (b) "better mechanisms for receiving inputs about forthcoming social problems which may affect the company's operations." This morning the executive vice-president called Sober into his office and asked him to prepare within the next two weeks a five-page report proposing realistic and specific ways to accomplish the two items he had mentioned. The vice-president implied that Sober might be assigned to implement some of his proposals if they were accepted.

1 In the role of Sober, prepare the report.

THE DANGEROUS DRUG

Margarita Pharmaceutical Products manufactures a prescription drug which is the only known effective treatment for a debilitating, lingering, and eventually fatal illness which primarily affects older persons. The drug produces marked improvement for four of five users, so it is popular with both physicians and patients. However, the drug has discomforting side effects in three of five users, and these effects are severe in one of five users. Several deaths have been attributed to use of the drug. The drug is approved by the federal government for prescription use; however, it probably would not have been approved if other less dangerous drugs were available to treat this disease.

This morning the president of Margarita opened the newspaper and read that in a public speech a Congressman from another state had attributed seventeen deaths to the drug during the last year. He called the drug "an atrocity on mankind" and an example of the "collusion between federal enforcement officials and drug company exploiters."

The president believed the stated number of deaths was reasonably accurate. He estimated that about 400,000 victims of the disease used the drug in the United States. He was convinced that, on balance, the drug was beneficial and desperately needed. His research scientists said they could find no way to reduce side effects of the drug, and this view was confirmed by several research physicians working with the disease in medical centers. However, the president was concerned that adverse publicity for the company would harm sales of its other products. About 40 percent of its products were nonprescription consumer drugs.

1 As president, what alternatives are available to you and what are the advantages and disadvantages involved?

2 What are the claimant groups in this situation and what investments in this situation give rise to their claims?

3 As president, what would you do, if anything?

CASES

Cases provide a useful medium for testing and applying some of the ideas in this textbook. They bring reality to abstract ideas about business, society, and environment. The cases have a decision-making emphasis in the sense that they end at a point which leaves some participant with a decision to make. One question often is, "Do I have a further problem?" If that question is answered in the affirmative, then further decisions must be made and analysis undertaken regarding what problems exist, why they are problems, what claimants are involved, what the contents and validities of their claims are, what alternatives exist within the constraints of the situation, and, finally, what action should be taken and what its implications are. This is the reality faced by all persons in operating situations. There is no escaping it.

All case names and certain case details are disguised except for "The Denver and Rio Grande Western Railroad Company, Silverton Branch," and publicly available details concerning Goodyear Tire and Rubber Company in the "Solo Rubber Company" case. These real names are used with permission of the companies involved.

These cases are not presented as either good business practice or poor business practice. Perhaps each case incorporates some of both. Each person must make these judgments for himself.

CASE 1

THE DENVER AND RIO GRANDE WESTERN RAILROAD COMPANY, SILVERTON BRANCH[1]

On December 21, 1959, the Denver and Rio Grande Western Railroad Company,[2] a common carrier by railroad subject to Part I of the Interstate Commerce Act, filed an application under Section 1(18) of the act for a certificate of public convenience and necessity permitting the abandonment of that portion of its narrow-gauge line known as the Silverton Branch. Protests against the abandonment were filed by several city chambers of commerce, the county commissioners of two counties, the Colorado Public Utilities Commission, the Colorado State Mineral Resources Board, various railway labor organizations, the San Juan Wool Growers' and Cattlemen's Associations, and a number of ranchers and businessmen from the area.

The Silverton Branch of applicant's system is a narrow-gauge line that extends between Durango and Silverton, two towns in the rugged mountainous area of southwest Colorado. The Silverton Branch was constructed by applicant in 1881 and 1882 for the purpose of transporting ore and concentrates from many rich mines in the Silverton area to the smelter in Durango and also for the purpose of transporting passengers and freight between the two towns and intermediate points. Prior to completion of the Silverton Branch, freight could be transported only by pack animal or freight wagons.

[1] Adapted from the report and order recommended by the hearing examiner in interstate commerce, Finance Docket No. 20943. The true company name is used in this case.
[2] Hereinafter referred to as "applicant."

Over the years, mining operations in the Silverton district have gradually declined, and the demand for freight service to carry ore and concentrate to the smelter at Durango, and supplies and other freight to Silverton, has slowly decreased. In 1924, the railroad stopped operating separate freight and passenger trains and instituted a daily (except Sunday) mixed-traffic service.[3] The amount of service was gradually reduced over the years, although the railroad continued to offer year-round service. From March, 1949, to September, 1953, the year-round service consisted of one mixed train per week. However, beginning in 1951, triweekly round-trip mixed-train service was started in the summer. This service was designed primarily to accommodate tourists and sightseeing passengers who wished to ride on an antique, picturesque narrow-gauge train, pulled by an old-time steam locomotive through the beautiful Colorado mountains. In 1953, the railroad stopped providing any year-round scheduled service, confining its scheduled trips to the tourist season of June 1 to September 15.

The line is subject to maintenance problems characteristic of narrow-gauge lines located in the mountains. It is difficult to maintain and operate, particularly during the winter and spring months. Heavy snows block the tracks, snow and rock slides often occur, and flooding (particularly from fast and heavy thawing in the spring) causes washouts of tracks.

Applicant estimated that the cost of rehabilitating the line so that it would be suitable for year-round operation would total $447,400. Although the track between Durango and Hermosa (a distance of 11 miles) is low and subject to flooding, no damage from floods had been experienced in recent years. A number of culverts along the line need replacing, and some portions of the roadbed require ditching. Much of the existing light-weight rail needs replacing, and because of age, bridges need to be reinforced and strengthened.

Although no regular year-round service has been provided over the line in recent years, maintenance work has been on an accelerated basis for the past several years. This has resulted in a general upgrading of the bridge structures and in the restoration of the track to a level entirely satisfactory for the restricted use that has been made of it.

Applicant admits that without any increase in its regular maintenance program, the line could be adequately maintained to afford service during the summer and that the extensive rehabilitation work outlined would be necessary only if year-round service were rendered.

Each summer since 1951, the combination sightseeing and freight service has been provided from early June to the end of September. At the commencement of each summer season, triweekly service is provided. During the peak of the tourist season, it is increased to daily service and is then reduced to the triweekly basis toward the end of the season. The train, normally consisting of a coal-burning locomotive, ten passenger cars, and two freight cars, departs from Durango at 9:15 A.M. and arrives at Silverton at 12:40 P.M. After a two-hour lunch period, the train makes

[3] A mixed train is one which carries both freight and passengers.

the return run to Durango, arriving there at 6:00 P.M. Although the train normally accommodates a total of 385 passengers, including some standees, occasionally additional standees are permitted, thus increasing the passenger maximum to 485. Such freight as may be available for movement is also handled on the trains.

Since applicant's line is narrow-gauge from Silverton to Alamosa, any freight moving between points on the branch and standard-gauge-line points must be transloaded into the larger cars at Alamosa. While freight has continued to move over the branch in this manner, the volume thereof has been greatly reduced in recent years.

Prior to 1952[4] (when all passenger service over the narrow-gauge lines, other than that provided on the Silverton Branch, was discontinued), applicant rendered passenger service over the entire narrow-gauge line to Alamosa, where passengers transferred to and from trains operating on applicant's standard-gauge line. Through such service, some interstate passengers were handled, and some were moved to and from points on the Silverton Branch. Since the discontinuance of passenger service between Durango and Alamosa, only intrastate passenger service has been provided over the Silverton Branch. Applicant no longer holds itself out to provide an interstate service over the line, and no arrangements exist for the through movement of interstate passengers wishing to travel over the branch line. Tickets for transportation over the line are offered for sale at Durango only.

Although no regular service is provided after the close of the summer season, applicant does claim to hold itself out to transport freight over the line whenever a shipper has ten or more carloads to be transported at one time. Under an arrangement with its wholly owned subsidiary, Rio Grande Motor Way, Inc., less-than-carload freight moving on applicant's line to or from points on the branch line is transported by the motor carrier. Applicant asserts that this provides an adequate substitute for rail service during periods when no regular rail service is provided over the line.

Applicant has published no schedules since 1953 covering any of the services rendered over the line, and it has obtained no authority from any regulatory body authorizing any temporary suspension of service over it. Also, no adjustments have been made in its intrastate and interstate tariffs, placing any limitation on the traffic that would be transported or establishing a minimum on the volume of shipments that would be handled.

Over the years, mining operations in the area gradually declined, and in 1938 the smelter at Durango closed. After this closure the decline in freight traffic moving over the line became more pronounced. Finally, applicant concluded that the slight demand for service that existed did not justify the expenditures involved in attempting to keep the line in operation on a year-round basis, and in 1953 it abandoned any attempt to provide any regular service over the line, except during the summer

---

[4] After 1952 the Silverton Branch became the last regularly scheduled narrow-gauge line in the United States.

months, and established the arbitrary minimum carload requirement previously mentioned. Applicant made no attempt, however, to create any embargo on traffic but merely notified shippers in the area and posted notices in the stations at Durango and Silverton of the minimum rule it had established.

The number of round-trip passengers transported over the line has increased substantially from year to year during each of the past four years, increasing from approximately twenty-five thousand in 1957 to more than thirty-five thousand in 1960. During the same period, passenger revenues increased from almost $86,000 to over $163,000. In most instances the train was filled to capacity each trip, and at times the demand exceeded the space available. During the summer of 1960 there were at least twenty-five hundred persons, representing three times that number of prospective passengers (families), who were unable to obtain tickets to ride the trains because of the heavy demand.

The amount of freight transported over the line in recent years has not been substantial. In 1957 there were 277 tons of freight handled, and the revenue therefrom amounted to $1,997. In 1958 there were 371 tons of freight handled, and the revenue was $2,410. In 1959 the revenue from 444 tons of freight amounted to $5,499.

For the first nine months of 1960, the total branch-line revenue amounted to $168,216, the branch-line expenses were $76,605, and the net branch-line operating revenue was $91,611. The net revenue to the system for freight handled over the branch line amounted to $2,704, and the net return to the system from branch-line operations amounted to $94,315.

From time to time, applicant has, by license or agreement, permitted individuals to use the tracks. People having property located at points on or near the tracks have been allowed to operate small motorized vehicles over the tracks for limited purposes. Applicant considers that the agreements are a matter of private contract between it and the individuals concerned and that they are without significance insofar as the issues involved in the instant proceeding are concerned.

With respect to passenger service, applicant asserts that the line provides no service whatever to that segment of the public residing in the area and that the motor-bus service provided to and from points along its line is more than adequate to meet the needs of the public traveling to and from the area. It alleges that the only use to be made of the line in the transportation of passengers is as a mere tourist attraction, appealing to those seeking the novel and unique experience of riding on a narrow-gauge railroad but having no relation to what is considered public convenience and necessity. It admits that the potential for the continuation of this type of patronage is good; that, by leaving off the freight cars presently handled, one or two more coaches could be utilized, thus adding considerably to the revenue earned by the line; and that it reasonably may be expected that the summertime tourist service would continue to be profitable if continued. Applicant considers the service rendered the tourist trade to be a special service for the pleasure of the passengers, rather than a necessity, which it, as a common carrier, has no obligation to provide. It alleges that inasmuch as the public no longer needs the service, public convenience and necessity do not require continuance of the passenger-train operation.

If, however, it is concluded that the passenger service should be continued, applicant then requests that consideration be given to the fact it has entered into an agreement with a newly formed corporation, the Durango-Silverton Railroad Company,[5] whereby said company would purchase the branch line, if abandonment were authorized, and would undertake to render intrastate passenger service to the tourist trade over the line. Applicant recognizes that the charter of the new corporation does not authorize the performance of any freight operations or authorize the corporation to operate in interstate commerce; applicant also recognizes that the abandonment of the line is not authorized. Applicant admits that the sole purpose of the instant application is to free it from the obligation presently imposed upon it as a common carrier to serve the line, and it asserts that it is willing to lose all the net revenue now accruing to the system from the branch line in order to be relieved of all its responsibilities toward the line.

Protestants assert that applicant had no right to limit its service in the manner described without first obtaining appropriate authority from the Interstate Commerce Commission and the Colorado Public Utilities Commission, and they contend that applicant's act in so limiting its service was, in legal effect, an actual abandonment of the line without authority. They argue that applicant, having committed an illegal act, cannot now rely on it in any way to establish justification for the abandonment but, instead, must rely on the situation as it now exists, which, they assert, shows the line to be profitable and necessary in the movement of both freight and passenger traffic. They contend that no burden is imposed upon interstate commerce by the line and that the best interests of applicant will be served by requiring operations to be continued.

In brief, applicant concedes that operation of the line as it is presently conducted, and if rehabilitation is not required for year-round service, is not a burden on interstate commerce.

Highway 550 is approximately parallel to the railroad between Durango and Silverton. It is a paved, all-weather highway and is one of the principal north-south highways in western Colorado.

Rio Grande Motor Way provides daily (except Saturday and Sunday) common-carrier service by motor vehicle, transporting general commodities, with certain exceptions, in interstate and intrastate commerce between Durango and Silverton as a part of its through truck service over Highway 550 and other highways between Durango, Silverton, Ridgeway, Montrose, and Grand Junction, Colorado, and other points. Continental

---

[5] A group of local businessmen who organized a corporation for the purpose of purchasing the Silverton Branch (if abandonment was authorized) and operating it as a tourist attraction.

Trailways Bus System operates one bus schedule daily in each direction between Durango and Silverton over Highway 550 as part of its scheduled interstate service.

Occasionally truck and bus operations are interrupted because of weather conditions on the highway between Durango and Silverton. These interruptions, however, occur rarely and usually do not continue for more than one day at a time. Although most of the populated areas between Durango and Silverton are provided transportation service over Highway 550, between those towns there are portions of the canyon area that are not served by any motor carrier.

As mining operations in the Silverton area declined and as other means of transportation became available, the need for freight service over the branch line declined. By 1953 all mining operations in the Silverton area had terminated, and those mines which had formerly transported their ore from another mining district to Silverton for movement over the branch to Durango had begun transporting their concentrates by truck to a smelter at Leadville or to applicant's standard-gauge railhead at Montrose. Except for one 40-ton car of zinc ore transported in 1957, no ore or concentrates moved over the branch from 1953 to 1959. In 1960, there was renewed interest in mining operations at certain points along the branch, especially in the Silverton area, and one mining company became actively engaged in performing the preliminary work incident to placing one or more mines into production. This company does not intend, however, to utilize the branch line for the transportation of its ore and concentrates, but will transport its shipments by truck to applicant's railhead at Montrose.

There are other companies and individuals who own mining claims along the branch and who desire to institute production operations. The record does not indicate, however, when production at any of these claims may be expected to commence.

Although numerous shipments of livestock used to be transported over the branch line, such movements have now practically ceased. In former years applicant provided convenient service for shippers of livestock and furnished adequate loading and unloading facilities for such movements. When the service was no longer convenient and when the needs of the shippers and the loading and unloading facilities on the branch either were eliminated or, because of lack of repairs, became unusable, most of the livestock shippers found it necessary to use other means of moving their livestock to and from the feeding ranges in the area served by the branch.

In 1957, the only shipments of livestock were three carloads of cattle that moved between points on the branch and other points on applicant's system. In 1958, the livestock shipments consisted of fifteen carloads of sheep that moved to or from points on the branch. In 1959, the only livestock transported over the line consisted of two carloads of cattle and calves. No livestock was handled over the line in the period during 1960 when operations were performed.

Applicant takes the position that the transportation needs of the area are adequately served by the truck and bus service presently available therein and that, in view of the insubstantial use being made of the branch line, there no longer is any need for its continued operation.

A total of twenty-five witnesses appeared in opposition to applicant's proposal. With respect to the passenger service provided over the line, the executive director of the Colorado State Advertising and Publicity Department described the numerous activities of the state in publicizing the branch line throughout the United States and the favorable results flowing therefrom. He stressed the economic benefits accruing to the communities involved and to the state from the large number of tourists who came to Durango each year to ride the train and enjoy the scenic beauty of the area. The branch line has now become one of the most important tourist attractions in Colorado. Not only does the state of Colorado consider that the interests of the tourists are served by the operation of the train, but it also considers the continued operation of the service to be of extreme importance to the welfare of all residents of southwestern Colorado.

Applicant's passenger traffic manager, who was one of the officers of the Colorado Visitors' Bureau, testified, pursuant to subpoena, that it is the policy of the bureau to encourage tourists to visit various attractions in Colorado, including the narrow-gauge line here considered, and that the bureau's efforts had been very successful. He expressed the view that, to the extent that tourists come to Durango to ride on the train, the needs of the public were thereby served.

The Chambers of Commerce of Durango and Silverton and officials and businessmen in Silverton consider the passenger service provided over the branch to be essential to the economic well-being of these towns and of the surrounding communities. Several business establishments in Silverton are dependent almost entirely upon the trade from the tourists riding the trains, and all businesses in the town also derive substantial benefits therefrom.

Protestants contend that by virtue of the very substantial demand that exists for passenger service over the line, it must be concluded that its continuance is required by public convenience and necessity.

With respect to the freight service provided over the line, protestants refer to the fact that there are certain areas on the line which are not accessible by motor vehicle and which can be served only by the branch line. They also point to certain mines and mining properties along the line which are not now producing ore but which the owners are endeavoring to place in production. They assert that the value of these properties would be reduced by the elimination of the only transportation services available.

At present there is approximately 47 million board feet of commercial timber in the Elk Park area of the national forest available for cutting, and the branch line affords the only means available for transporting a large portion of that timber out of the area. The United States Forest Service, however, has not authorized cutting that timber or indicated that such authorization may be given.

Protestants refer to the fact that Rio Grande Motor Way is not authorized to transport all types of freight between Durango and Silverton and that it is not physically possible for it to serve certain points in the canyon area that are served by the branch line. They therefore assert that this establishes that the needs of the communities involved and of the public can be adequately served only by the continuance of the freight service provided by applicant.

Several sheep raisers testified to a need for freight service in the movement of sheep to and from the summer range areas in the national forest near Silverton. Because of a lack of convenient service and adequate loading and unloading facilities on the line, most of the sheep raisers in the area have not utilized applicant's service for the movement of their sheep for a number of years. Instead, they have utilized truck service or have "trailed" their sheep to and from the summer ranges. Trailing involves walking the sheep along the highway through the national forest to the range areas. Each spring the sheep are moved into the national forest near Silverton, and they are then moved out in the early fall. Approximately six days are consumed in trailing the sheep between Durango and Silverton.

Sheep do not readily adapt to travel by motor truck, and for that reason the sheep raisers prefer not to utilize that means of moving their sheep. Furthermore, the truck service that is provided in the area not only is expensive but, many times, is not available when required. As a result, most of the sheep are trailed to and from the summer ranges.

Apparently applicant's freight service from Durango to other points on its lines is utilized by some of the sheep raisers in moving their sheep to market. If adequate and convenient service were provided over the branch and if applicant would provide proper loading and unloading facilities at points along the line, rail service would again be utilized by the sheep raisers opposing abandonment of the line.

The United States forest ranger for the area involved, who appeared under subpoena, testified that consideration is now being given to the imposition of a ban on the trailing of sheep through the national forest to the summer ranges but that no decision had been reached on the matter. If such a ban were imposed, the sheep would be moved either by truck or over applicant's line.

With respect to use of applicant's service for the transportation of livestock, it should be noted that applicant has the obligation of providing service and facilities adequate to meet the needs of the public. If it is found herein that the public convenience and necessity require the continuance of freight service over the line, applicant, of course, would be required to provide service and facilities adequate to meet the needs of the aforementioned shippers of livestock, and any failure on its part to provide such service might, of course, justify appropriate action to obtain the service required.

Certain operators of coal mines in the Durango area opposed the abandonment of the line on the grounds that the service was required for the movement of coal to Silverton. Although some coal is transported over the line each year, the witnesses conceded that truck service is available for the transportation of coal from the mines direct to customers in the Silverton area. One motor carrier at Silverton who was engaged in the delivery of coal from the rail siding in Silverton to consumers in the area testified, however, that he would abandon his motor-truck service if abandonment of the line was authorized.

DISCUSSION QUESTIONS

1 List the business claimants in this situation and explain the social investment each claimant perceives. What are the payoffs or benefits each claimant seeks?

2 What obligations does the railroad have to the communities it serves?

3 Do the communities involved have any responsibilities to the railroad? If so, what? If not, why not?

4 If you were the Interstate Commerce Commission hearing examiner, how would you decide this issue? Substantiate your decision.

CASE 2

BETTER STEEL CORPORATION

The Better Steel Corporation is a large, international steel company incorporated under the laws of New Jersey. On April 10, 1965, Joe Jones received a notice of the annual meeting and a proxy statement from the company. Jones owned 1,000 shares of common stock in the corporation, valued at $45,000. This investment represented some 20 percent of his investment portfolio. Income from this portfolio had been his primary support since he had sold his store and retired five years before. He bought the Better Steel stock at that time. Since then, the stock had declined 40 percent in value, even though stock market averages had risen. Some of the reasons for the decline, according to Jones, were:

1. Technological changes in steel markets
2. Foreign competition
3. The pricing conflict between big steel and President Kennedy in 1962, which shook public confidence and was followed by a sharp stock market dive
4. Reduced company earnings since his purchase, even though sales had increased, especially in 1964
5. A dividend reduction of 33 percent three years before, due to reduced earnings

While reading the proxy statement, Jones came upon a stockholder proposal which particularly interested him. It read as follows:

STOCKHOLDER PROPOSAL NO. 3
RELATING TO CONTRIBUTIONS

Martha Masters, Grand Central Station, New York, N.Y., 10017, the holder of record of twelve shares of common stock of the Corporation, states her intention to propose the following resolution at the meeting:

"RESOLVED: That the corporation's certificate of incorporation be amended by adding thereto the following provisions: No corporate funds of this corporation shall be given to any charitable, educational or other similar organization, except for purposes in direct furtherance of the business interests of this corporation, and subject to the further provision that the aggregate amount of such contributions shall be reported to the shareholders not later than the date of the annual meeting."

and asks that the reasons for the resolution be stated as follows:

"REASONS: With the amount of money being contributed by the corporation increasing over the years, it is becoming more important that all know the amount. Your dividend has been cut, and yet your company gave away 7½ million dollars of your money to charity during 1963, money which belongs to you.

"If you agree, please mark your proxy *for* this resolution; otherwise it is automatically cast against."

A Vote Against this Resolution is Recommended by the Directors for the Following Reasons:

The amount of contributions is reported. The 1964 annual report of the corporation states: "Better Steel made contributions for educational and charitable purposes during 1964 of 7 million dollars. This sum included 6 million dollars paid in December, 1964, to Better Steel Corporation Foundation, Inc., a nonprofit corporation which was formed in 1953 to provide aid for charitable, educational, and scientific organizations and activities." It is the opinion of the board that such contributions advance the interests of the corporation as a private corporation and as a part of the communities in which it operates. A report of the foundation is available upon request to the office of the foundation.

Adoption of the proposal would not be in the interest of the Corporation. It might be difficult to establish affirmatively that contributions which are used for general support of universities, scientific research, and the like are in "direct furtherance" of the business interests of a corporation. Yet this corporation and all business corporations generally must depend upon the availability of highly trained people for the future well-being of their companies and hence of our economy as a whole. Support of education is one way of assuring this availability.

Also, the proposal would seriously limit the corporation in fulfilling its responsibilities to, and maintaining its position as a corporate citizen in, the communities in which it is located and conducts business.

Corporate support is well recognized as essential. There has long been legislative authority in New Jersey and many other states for contributions to community funds, hospitals, and educational and other instrumentalities conducive to public welfare. The New Jersey statute was revised in 1950 to give added emphasis to the public policy that

New Jersey corporations are specifically empowered to contribute such moneys as in the judgment of their governing boards are conducive to the betterment of social and economic conditions. The New Jersey courts have said that such corporate aid to charitable and educational projects "amounts to a solemn duty."

Corporate support is vital to charitable, educational, and other voluntary institutions if they are to avoid being instrumentalities controlled by government and entirely supported by taxation. The benefits to a corporation from such support are many and varied and frequently much greater than those from expenditures which can be more easily demonstrated to be in "direct furtherance" of the business interests of the corporation.

The directors believe that the restrictions proposed would be contrary to the corporate and stockholder interests of the corporation, and they recommend a vote *against* this proposal.

Since this year's annual meeting was scheduled to take place in his metropolitan area in May, Jones decided he would not mail his proxy statement but would vote his shares in person. In thinking about Stockholder Proposal No. 3, Jones remembered that during the past year he had received several reprints of management speeches from the company. He remembered that one of them was on the subject of corporate giving. In his files he located three reprints. One speech was by the director of the corporate foundation mentioned in the proxy statement. Speaking before a business group, the director had supported business giving. Reading the speech for the first time, Jones was especially impressed with the following comments:

It is time for all to realize that the existence of an economic unit in a local community, or its entrance into one, automatically set up its proportionate share of the responsibility for achieving the community's aspirations. Any business concern doing a sufficient volume to make it a primary economic unit in the neighborhood should, as a matter of purpose, make provision in its organization structure for proper attention to community affairs and leadership. . . .

The first suggestion is that you adopt a basic idea with which you undertake a large share of leadership. The basic idea is this: When dealing with all matters affecting community needs and aspirations, business should temper any concept of "taking out of immediate profit" with the concept of "putting in for ultimate benefit to all." This must follow, since the common good, typically, represents an area that is "off limits" so far as "taking out" or immediate reward is concerned.

In the second reprint Jones noted that the foundation director established seven major areas for corporate giving:

1. Private social welfare causes such as community chests and united funds.
2. Private health and medical care such as community hospitals.
3. Cultural needs such as symphony orchestras.

4. Civic needs such as urban renewal and public sanitation.
5. Citizenship-leadership training, such as public and private education.
6. Education in physical and social sciences.
7. International development in areas where business skills can help the development of a country. "Enlightened capitalism must evidence to the world, not only to the people who already enjoy its fruits, that it has demonstrable nonmaterial values to offer peoples who hunger for the freedom and individual dignity that raises man above the condition of peonage."

The director reported that the corporation foundation supported projects in all seven areas of assistance.

Jones then turned to the third reprint which reported a speech by the company president at a community awards dinner. The president mentioned the burden of corporate taxes and community responsibilities, commenting: "We need to understand that we cannot so burden any one element in our community as to make it impossible for that element to operate successfully and thus supply the lifeblood of the city."

In May, Jones attended the stockholders' meeting. He heard the corporation president in a prepared speech state that there was no near-term probability of a dividend increase because of capital needs and continued low earnings. Later in his speech the president reported that for eight months the corporation's production facilities had been operating near capacity. He said major capital improvements were needed to expand capacity.

The time for stockholder voting was approaching, and Jones wondered how he should vote his stock on Stockholder Proposal No. 3.

DISCUSSION QUESTIONS

1 If you were Jones, how would you vote on Stockholder Proposal No. 3? Explain.

2 Discuss pro and con the corporation's stated position on Stockholder Proposal No. 3.

3 Do you see any conflict of viewpoints between the president's statements and the foundation director's statements? Explain.

4 As a stockholder, would you favor this corporation's giving in each of the seven areas mentioned by the corporation foundation director? Support your view separately for each area.

5 Who are the claimant groups in this situation and what social investment does each claimant perceive? What are the payoffs or benefits each claimant seeks?

CASE 3

BENEFICIAL BUILDERS

Beneficial Builders is a major subdivision home builder in southern California. During the last fifteen years it has developed seven large subdivisions in the Los Angeles area. Its policy is to buy large tracts of land on the edges of suburbs and build good-quality, low-cost homes for working families. In order to keep costs low, Beneficial Builders uses only a few house plans in each subdivision, enabling it to precut lumber and subassemble walls, door frames, windows, cabinets, and other house parts in its shops. There are several variations of the front, or "elevation," of the houses, so that the streets are not identical in their appearance.

A shopping center and 800 homes had been planned for the Hills East subdivision, located in high foothills 50 miles east of Los Angeles. Over seven hundred homes had been built and sold when the heavy fall rains started. After the ground had been thoroughly soaked, an unprecedented 12-inch rainfall occurred on Monday night in the foothills just above the subdivision. A stream which drained these foothills ran through the center of Hills East. In planning this subdivision, Beneficial Builders recognized that heavy thunderstorms did occur in the area, so it widened and straightened the stream bed according to a plan approved by county engineers.

The rain sent torrents of water down the steep stream bed at an estimated 30 miles an hour. It appeared that the stream bed was adequate until the fast, high water uprooted a giant eucalyptus tree on the edge of the stream and carried it ⅓ mile to a highway bridge. The tree lodged against the bridge and held fast, soon collecting other debris until it blocked an estimated 60 percent of the streamflow. The lake created behind the bridge soon flooded a few homes, and even worse, it caused a major streamflow over a low spot in the highway 100 yards from the bridge. This overflow could not return to the stream bed, so it continued down a street for several blocks, horizontal to the stream but one block away.

Soon there was a torrent of raging water 3 to 5 feet deep in this overflow route. Homeowners were awakened suddenly about 5:30 A.M. by the sound of water running through their houses and cars crashing against carports and house walls. Water rose above 3 feet in over twenty-five houses, and occupants had to flee to roofs or to a second story if they had one. Walls and doors were torn away, but no house was swept from its foundation. Two persons were swept away by the current and drowned.

In a few hours the flood subsided, leaving a jumble of automobiles, uprooted trees, furniture, and house parts. Forty houses and thirty-five automobiles had damages estimated at $300,000. National Guard, civil defense, armed services, and city police helped restore order and provided trucks to haul away debris. Light showers continued, but the stream was back in its bed, and no further flooding was predicted. All utilities including water were disrupted, and none of the damaged homes could be occupied.

Glen Abel, president of Beneficial Builders, heard of the flood early in the morning and drove directly to his subdivision. He talked with public officials on the scene and with dazed and shocked residents. Although some were understandably bitter, there was no evidence that they thought the flood had been caused by poor design of the subdivision. Their homes had received the same heavy rains that hit the foothills, so they knew the rainfall was torrential. A flood victim described his experience to Mr. Abel as follows: "When I woke up, the water was leaking through the walls at the joints. We all started picking things off the floor so they wouldn't get wet, and then there was a crash as the water broke a plate-glass window and an outside door.

"The furniture started to float on top of the water, and big pieces like our dresser fell over. I knew then that we had to get out, but I didn't know how or where to go.

"I started to the boys' room, but before I got there the bedroom wall gave way and they came floating right by me out into the yard, both in their beds. I started after them, sort of swimming. Finally I reached one of the boys, still on his bed, and I handed him up to my neighbor on the roof of his house. I just handed him up; the water was so high, I didn't stand on a ladder or anything. Somebody else reached my other boy and put him on a roof.

"My house is still standing and the roof is good, but most of the walls are gone. I really don't know how it all happened, because you couldn't see anything in the dark."

Abel checked with city street engineers at the bridge, and they reported that the stream bed had proved large enough to hold the flood and that there was no overflow except that caused by the blocked bridge. On the basis of these discussions and all other evidence he had, Abel concluded that the subdivision drainage design was sound and that his firm had no liability for the damages.[1]

Although no company liability was evident, Abel was nevertheless distressed by suffering caused by the flood. He knew that there was no insurance protection against floods; hence many home buyers faced the loss of all their savings or might be forced into personal bankruptcy. He knew that these wage-earning residents, most with young families, were not financially prepared to cope with losses this large.

From a business point of view, Abel recognized that even though the Hills East subdivision was nearly sold out, any remaining sales would be handicapped by publicity about the flood. He reasoned that many persons would not be able to repair their homes, which would leave eyesores of wrecked buildings until mortgage settlements were made. He expected that various types of lawsuits and legal entanglements would develop among homeowners, automobile insurers, real estate mortgagors, chattel mortgagors (furniture and appliances), repairmen, finance companies, and others.

While on the scene Abel checked with city engineers and determined that they would work with civil defense and National Guard truckers to clear all debris and return furniture to homes. The city would rebuild streets. Abel also worked with officers of the Hills East Community Improvement Association to arrange for flood victims to live temporarily with neighbors. The improvement association was a voluntary community group encouraged by Beneficial Builders when the first home buyers moved to Hills East.

Later that afternoon Abel returned to his downtown office several miles from Hills East in order to discuss with his associates what might be done for the flood victims. They considered asking the state governor for state flood aid, but delayed for two reasons. First, they felt that government aid should be requested only when all private and public self-help, such as the American Red Cross, was insufficient. Second, government aid would probably require much red tape and delay, and action was needed now.

They were discussing what direct action Beneficial Builders might take, when Arch Smith, the union business agent for Beneficial workers, arrived and asked whether the union might help. He said that he had talked informally with several union leaders and could guarantee 200 volunteer carpenters and other selected skilled workers all day Saturday and Sunday to repair all structural damage to houses, if someone would supply materials, equipment, and supervision.

After extended discussion, Beneficial executives and Smith decided

---

[1] Weeks later a special engineering report requested by the city council and made by city engineers concluded that the flood was an "act of God" and that no negligence was evident.

they would take direct action to repair all flood damage with donated labor and materials, provided Apex Lumber Company would donate lumber and building materials. Apex was considered the key to this plan, for lumber was the main building material needed. If Apex agreed, Abel and Smith believed that all lesser services would "fall in line." Apex was one of the largest building suppliers in the West, and it had been the principal supplier of Beneficial Builders since Beneficial Builders was organized.

If Apex accepted, the following plan would be used. All services would be donated. All homes would be restored to approximately their original condition, except for furniture and household supplies. A newspaper release would announce that the restoration was a joint effort of businesses, unions, and community agencies. Appeals for help would be made privately through existing groups; there would be no public appeal playing upon emotions and possibly leading to disorganized action. Unions would provide sufficient skilled labor for ten hours daily on Saturday and Sunday (an estimated two hundred men) and the following weekend if necessary. Beneficial Builders would provide supervision, shop services, and construction equipment (worth an estimated $20,000 wholesale). Apex would provide all building materials (worth an estimated $30,000 wholesale). Community agencies would be asked to supply unskilled labor (about one hundred men). Other groups employed by Beneficial Builders to construct its subdivisions would be asked to donate services, such as plumbing and electrical work, appliance repair, landscaping, and painting. All services except painting would be donated for the forthcoming weekend so that homes would be livable on Monday. Painting would be donated the following two weekends. The Red Cross or some other service agency would be asked to provide food and coffee for all volunteer labor.

Abel and Smith were convinced that 95 percent of the repairs could be made in one weekend because of the fortuitous circumstance that Beneficial's shops had completed cutting and assembling all components for the last fifty houses in the Hills East subdivision on the Friday before the flood. These components provided a ready-made inventory matching most of the houses destroyed. In the few instances where necessary items were not assembled, Abel promised to work his shops overtime to assure that all needed precut materials and subassemblies would be delivered to the carport of each home by 6:00 P.M. Friday. This procedure probably would delay by ten days the completion of the remaining fifty houses because new lumber would have to be cut and assembled. Some persons who had bought one of these fifty houses might be inconvenienced or have added expenses if they had already promised to vacate their present residence and move to Hills East on a certain date, believing that their home would be available at that time.

By the time Abel and Smith completed their plans, it was 7:30 P.M. They telephoned Abe Silver, southern California manager of Apex Lumber, at his home near Los Angeles. When he learned the purpose of their call, he agreed to an appointment in his home at 9:00 P.M. that evening.

At 9:03 P.M. Abel and Smith rang the doorbell of Silver's palatial home.

DISCUSSION QUESTIONS

1 If you were Abel, what presentation would you make to Silver? If you were Smith, what would you do? Role-play the 9:00 P.M. meeting of Abel, Smith, and Silver.

2 What are the different investment groups in this situation, and what are the investments and payoff expectations of each?

3 Discuss this case in terms of business values, viability, and public visibility.

4 Discuss this case in terms of the Iron Law of Responsibility.

5 What are the possible risks and rewards of social involvement by Apex Lumber in this situation?

CASE 4

RODO CATTLE COMPANY[1]

The Rodo Cattle Company is located in the metropolitan suburbs of Pleasantville, a city of over six hundred thousand people in a Western state. The primary business of the Rodo Company is operation of cattle feedlots for fattening cattle for slaughter. Although cattle feedlots have been used for centuries, commercial development of feedlots as a large business operation is fairly new. The Rodo Company is a specialized business of this type. Its cattle pens cover 80 acres and will feed at one time over twenty-five thousand cattle worth several million dollars.

Rodo Company's feedlots are organized into separate pens of about 1 acre each, and modern, laborsaving methods are used throughout its facility. The pens are ringed with concrete feed bunks and water troughs. Feed is mixed from truckload batches in the company's feed mill at the feedlot. Mixed feed flows by gravity to other trucks, which distribute it to the feed bunks. The entire acreage is covered by an overhead water sprinkler system that reduces the amount of manure dust in the dry afternoons; this helps prevent cattle tuberculosis and other lung diseases. The sprinkler system also reduces the drift of dust from the feedlots to neighboring residential properties; however, the lots cannot be kept wet enough to prevent all dust, so there are many complaints from neighbors, as will be discussed later. If too much water is used in dust treatment, muddy conditions develop which increase both neighborhood odor and cattle diseases.

[1] All names are disguised.

The company regularly sprays its pens to control flies. Its monthly expenditure for insecticide exceeds $300, and both the county health officer and neighbors agree that flies are effectively controlled. Manure in the pens is mechanically handled. After it has accumulated in a pen for several months, it is scraped up by a bulldozer and mechanically loaded into trucks which take it to the edge of the property, where it is stacked in large, flat piles 30 feet high. Portions of this manure are occasionally sold to a processor who pulverizes and bags it for sale to home gardeners and farmers. The supply of manure is much greater than the demand for it, so Rodo Company has an inventory of thousands of tons, which is increasing by hundreds of tons annually. The general manager and principal owner of the company, Mr. Jesse Rodo, is not sure what to do with this growing inventory because he is running out of storage space.

What would you do w/ it then?

The Rodo Company does primarily custom feeding. This means that it accepts on consignment cattle owned by others, and it feeds the cattle until a proper slaughtering condition is reached. The company also feeds a few hundred or thousand cattle on its own account when market conditions are favorable.

The Rodo Company was established sixteen years ago on 120 acres purchased especially for feedlot operation. In the beginning there were pens for only 500 cattle, but its facilities expanded rapidly as the idea of custom feeding became popular with local farmers and business investors. At the time the feedlot was established there were three other feedlots nearby, so the property was already recognized as a stockyard area. The land was rocky and uneven, was located near a river bottom, and was unfit for residential housing. The property was 6 miles from downtown Pleasantville, and the nearest residential developments were 1½ miles away on either side. Pleasantville was toward the west, and a suburban town was toward the southeast.

The other three feedlots in Rodo Company's area have also expanded, until this area now has pens for nearly one hundred thousand cattle. Meanwhile, the Pleasantville metropolitan area has also grown, pushing residential suburbs closer to the stockyard area. One new residential area is within 500 feet of the edge of Rodo's property, and homeowners are complaining loudly about feedlot dust and odors. In fact, the whole stockyard area is surrounded on three sides by residential and commercial developments less than ½ mile away. The municipal stadium is only a mile away, and several fine motels are on the highway about the same distance. The city auditorium, the site of operas and other gala events, is slightly over 2 miles away. On winter evenings when the air settles, an intense odor from the stockyard area sometimes reaches the auditorium at about the time programs begin. This one fact has caused strong protests from several influential Pleasantville people.

The odors and dust produced by a feedlot operation are much different from those of the common farm barnyard. Because of heavy use of the ground (several hundred cattle on 1 acre), the type of odor is much more putrid, and it exists in a stronger concentration than it does on the farm. The foul odor causes nausea and illness in sensitive people. And if the pens are not properly sprayed with water when the cattle are milling about in late afternoon before bedding down for the night, clouds of unpleasant dust, similar to those which arise behind an automobile moving along a dusty road at sundown, cover the neighborhood.

This combination of factors has placed a large segment of the community in conflict with feedlot operators. Residents of the suburbs southeast of the Rodo feedlot have organized a Fresh-air Committee, whose purpose is to encourage community action to control air pollution. Committee members include many influential citizens of the suburbs. The group holds public meetings, and officers regularly attend city council meetings to offer proposals for feedlot regulation and city prosecution under nuisance laws, since three of the four feedlots now are within the city limits of the suburb. The group is also developing proposed city ordinances for control of feedlot pollution. The group has employed a photographer and a scientist to gather evidence of feedlot pollution, and members are outspoken against the odor and dust derived from feedlots. The committee had proposed that since the cattle feeders cannot or will not do anything about the offensive nature of the feedlots, they should move to a rural area zoned especially for long-run cattle feeding. A local journalist reported the proposal as follows:

> That hero of Western lore, the cattleman, could be headed for a reservation just like his predecessor, the Indian, if a group of unhappy citizens has its way.
>
> The reservation proposal is the brainchild of the Fresh-air Committee and is aimed specifically at cattle-feeding operations in urban areas.
>
> They propose that statewide zoning be initiated by the Legislature to provide a permanent area where cattle and dairy operators can work free from encroachment by residential areas. This zone would be buffered with a 5-mile ring of orchards to protect people against the cows, and vice versa.
>
> The Fresh-air Committee is only one of many groups troubled by the scent of "Corral No. 5" and the dust rising every evening from the community's cattle-feeding operations.
>
> The list of complainants is long. It includes hotel and motel operators, airport authorities, city officials, doctors, health officials, homeowners, and tourists. The airport manager commented: "During the height of the tourist season, the airport receives the full 'benefits' of the stockyards. People get off the plane, and they want to get right back on."

In addition, a few months ago residents of some of the worst fallout areas filed lawsuits against all four cattle companies, alleging that they were maintaining a public nuisance. Some eighty citizens filed suits asking for damages totaling $859,040. The suits allege that stockyard dust settles in homes even when they are closed, requiring more frequent cleaning than in other areas of the community. They complain that use of patios and yards is denied on many evenings, that extra money must be spent for air conditioning and filters to keep odors and dust out of homes, and that home prices have depreciated more than normal. They allege that odor and dust have become worse since they moved into their homes because more cattle are being fed and larger piles of manure are accumulating. Some also allege nausea and bronchial difficulties caused by the nuisances. One of the complainants, speaking to a reporter, warned persons interested in buying a home in the area not to close the sale in the daytime. "All the people around here bought their houses during the daytime, when the dust and odor do not settle so badly," the complainant said. "The real estate people either evade the subject or ignore it when they're selling a house."

The lawyer who represented most of the complainants in their lawsuits made the following comment to a reporter: "We don't mind the stockyards, but we do mind the dust and odor. The basic legal question as I see it is the right of habitation or the right of agriculture. I believe that human habitation is superior to that of livestock."

Meanwhile, the Citizens' Council for Beautification of Pleasantville was taking an interest in the feedlot problem. The council is a civic committee appointed by the mayor to coordinate work of all voluntary groups seeking to make the metropolitan area a more beautiful, cultured, and pleasant place to live. The council was particularly concerned because feedlots caused a large blighted area on the edge of town, several distinguished visitors had inquired about the odor when alighting at the airport, several cultural events at the city auditorium and other locations had been made unpleasant by stockyard odor, and a number of residents had complained. In fact, some businesses on the highway were so affected by the feedlots that their managers were writing letters to anyone who would heed them. Some dispatched letters to their United States senators and representatives. They also complained to the county health officer, but at one of the council meetings he told the group that his office had investigated the feedlots and was convinced that neither their dust nor their odor constituted a health hazard to citizens.

Jesse Rodo became embroiled in the feedlot controversy in two ways. First, as owner and manager of Rodo Cattle Company, he was the object of lawsuits (which included both the corporation and its manager in each complaint), and he was under pressure to move his feedlot or take corrective action, which would be expensive. Second, he was at this time serving a three-year term as president of the Cattle Feeders' Association, which was the trade association of the feedlot operators. The association was working hard to offset unfavorable publicity which feedlots were receiving.

Several years ago, when complaints first started to develop, the Cattle Feeders' Association took the position that the feedlot operators were there first; hence, anyone who built a home or business in the area did so at his own peril. As one operator stated: "An age-old concept in common law is 'Let the buyer beware.' It is the buyer's legal duty to be aware of environmental conditions which might affect his home or business prior to investing in it. The feedlots should not be blamed because people insist on moving closer to them."

This argument reduced complaints and probably would have worked for the long run, except that the feedlots continued to expand their facilities and pile their refuse. The result was that people who originally built in an odor-free and dust-free neighborhood soon found that these nuisances were reaching their neighborhood also. Then, when the Fresh-air Committee entered the controversy, its officials reported legal opinion that prior occupancy of the area did not give feedlots an easement to inflict obnoxious dust and odor on adjoining property. In other words, adjoining property owners had just as much right to use their property freely as the feedlot owners had to use theirs.

At about this time Rodo became president of the association, and he persuaded members to hire a public relations firm to improve the feedlot's public image. The firm recommended emphasis on the economic benefits of feedlots to the state. This approach gained support of operators outside the Pleasantville area because some of them were beginning to receive complaints from their neighbors also; however, nearly half the state's feedlots were in the Pleasantville area. The public relations firm prepared news releases for mailing to all papers in the state at least once a month extolling the economic virtues of feedlots. Releases reported that during the last year nearly 150 million dollars' worth of cattle were sold out of feedlots in the state. In terms of dollar value this was the second largest agricultural product in the state. Fresh-air Committee officials countered this argument by reporting that tourism brought 400 million dollars to the state and that urban feedlots were driving away tourists.

Another publicity release explained that the feedlot industry provided employment for over one thousand persons and had invested over 40 million dollars in land and equipment. Rodo and the public relations firm also persuaded leading feedlot operators to prepare speeches and seek speaking invitations to luncheon clubs and other meetings.

The number of complaints did not diminish, so association officials persuaded a number of the worst offenders to experiment with spraying a masking agent (offsetting perfume) in their lots daily. In most cases the cattle odor and masking odor seemed to combine to produce a third odor as obnoxious as the original one. In fact, the new odor aroused additional complainants not aroused by the original odor.

As a result of the failures mentioned, the Fresh-air Committee continued to gain strength and worked with the city council of the suburb where Rodo Company's pens were located to develop a stringent ordinance regulating feedlots. The ordinance required operators to remove all organic refuse at least once a week and to haul it outside the city limits entirely. The feedlot operators felt that compliance with this ordinance would be expensive and unduly restrictive; therefore, they proposed a program of self-regulation to the city council. They offered to use masking agents and sprinkler systems and to remove refuse twice a year. The council "took the proposal under advisement" and continued with its plans for an ordinance.

The council's action caused feedlot operators throughout the state to become concerned that each city might set up its own special ordinance for feedlots. Differences in ordinances might cause cost variations which would upset competitive conditions. Feeding costs now were about equal throughout the state, but a local ordinance might increase costs in one city, driving a feedlot's customers to another lot and eventually driving the feedlot from the city. One influential operator proposed that the association go to the State Legislature, which was then in session, and request a law requiring nuisance regulation by the State Livestock Sanitary Board. Since the board consisted mostly of cattlemen, this approach would put them in the position of regulating themselves; therefore, regulations could be kept reasonable. Another operator said he would move his feedlot from the state if the state law was passed.

Rodo decided to call a statewide meeting of the entire association membership to decide what the next move should be. He knew that a strong plea would be made for the law requiring regulation by the Livestock Sanitary Board. He also knew that association members were looking to him for leadership, but he was not sure what to propose next. He was further confused by the situation with his own company. He owned land elsewhere in the state and was about ready to move his feedlot from the Pleasantville area; however, whenever he hinted to other operators that a move might occur, they strongly objected. They said that all feedlot operators must "stick together and not retreat at this time." They felt that if one feedlot left, it would be an "admission of guilt" and would make it necessary for the other lots to move in a short time.

DISCUSSION QUESTIONS

1 In Rodo's role as president of the Cattle Feeders' Association, prepare his speech to the association recommending a particular course of action. Give reasons for the action chosen.

2 In Rodo's role as general manager and principal owner of Rodo Cattle Company, appraise the question of whether you should move your feedlot in the near future. What issues are key ones in making your decision?

3 Discuss the ecological aspects of this case.

4 Discuss the different investment groups in this situation and the countervailing powers, if any, which each sought to apply.

CASE 5

WAGNER CHEMICAL COMPANY

The Wagner Chemical Company was founded by Charles E. Wagner in Newark, New Jersey, in 1933, when the chemical industry was beginning to gain industrial prominence. Mr. Wagner, president and general manager, graduated from college summa cum laude in chemistry. He later received his Ph.D. in chemistry from one of the country's outstanding universities.

He began his career with du Pont as a research chemist working on applied research, where his achievements were recognized as outstanding. However, his desire was to perform pure rather than applied research. Subsequently, he left du Pont, and with the aid of money borrowed from his father, started what is now the Wagner Chemical Company. Because of his spirit of adventure, creativity, and fresh approach to complicated industrial chemical problems, his company soon became successful. Creativity became the watchword of Wagner Chemical and still remains today as one of the company's major objectives.

Some outstanding discoveries in the fields of synthetics, drugs, vitamins, pesticides, insecticides, and fertilizers were patented and contributed heavily to the early success of the enterprise. In the period just prior to World War II and during the war, top-secret work was done for the United States government. The most important contribution to the war effort was the work done in the area of gaseous diffusion used to separate uranium-235 from uranium-238.

Present Situation

The company is presently engaged in research and manufacture of a highly diversified line of products for home and industry. It ranks among the top fifteen chemical and drug companies, with an annual gross income in excess of 150 million dollars. Mr. Wagner has always surrounded himself with competent and respected businessmen and hired the finest chemical minds available. His director of research is John Gordon, a respected chemist, who is well known throughout the world for his knowledge, ability, and creativity.

Competition in the chemical industry is extremely severe, and the heart of any leading company is in its research department. Finding and developing new products is essential, and to accomplish this, Wagner Chemical is constantly engaged in both pure and applied research.

Heavy emphasis on research in the chemical industries causes rapid change and product obsolescence. In order to survive and prosper in this highly competitive industry, firms find it necessary to allocate a much higher percentage of gross sales to research than most other manufacturing industries.

Wagner's Philosophies

Mr. Wagner and Mr. Gordon share the philosophy that no expense restrictions should be put on the scientists who are engaged in pure research. The budget for this activity is generous, and some scientists are performing revolutionary experiments without regard for any ultimate financial return.

Relatively low earnings of the company reflect the large sums spent on research. However, since leading stockholders lack unity and organization, no restrictions have been placed on research expenditures. The board of directors, in conjunction with Wagner, also contribute a reasonable percentage of the earnings to hospitals, community service centers, universities, the Red Cross, and other charities.

In justifying large research expenditures at the last annual meeting, Mr. Wagner expressed the belief that: "In my judgment, contributions and research are in the stockholders' best interest because they help retain public goodwill." He further pointed out that these expenditures are encouraged by tax laws, sustained by the courts and legislatures, and endorsed by the public.

The Research Department

The research department has been a major department since the corporation was founded. Mr. Wagner has always inspired his scientists and chemists to be creative and has been financially generous in order to obtain the best personnel available.

He hired Mr. Gordon shortly before World War II and found him to be an ideal man to head the research department. During his association with Wagner Chemical, Gordon has discovered and improved a vast number of new products and has written numerous papers for the Manufacturing Chemists Association. Under his direction, the company has greatly diversified its product line and has steadily improved its image in the industry. Among the new and diversified products which Wagner Chemical has been actively working on are pesticides and insecticides.

Pesticides and insecticides and their use have recently attracted wide public attention. Growing concern over the harm which these products do to human beings, fish, and wildlife has been accentuated by the book *Silent Spring*, by Rachel Carson. In addition, the Department of Agriculture, the Food and Drug Administration, the United States Wildlife Bureau, and the Surgeon General have been reviewing the effects of these poisons. Several conclusions have been drawn from their studies. It is generally agreed that poisons do accumulate on the food people eat and that men, plants, and animals may be damaged by this accumulation; however, the long-range effects of pesticides are not known. On the positive side, it is further agreed that the yield of crops is higher, that the quality of the harvested product is better, and that insect control is necessary for human health.

Mr. Wagner's Problem

Mr. Wagner is a rational businessman. He is aware of the dangers of pesticides, and he is also aware that agricultural producers need them and that cities need weed and insect control.

The Department of Agriculture and the Food and Drug Administration have set standards concerning the maximum amount of poison allowable on food, and producers of pesticides must conform to these standards. These government agencies have been satisfied with the results obtained with the use of insecticides, but admit that they are not certain what long-range effects they may have. The Surgeon General has also voiced concern over the unknown harmful side effects of the use of these poisons.

The U.S. Wildlife Bureau has been studying the birth rate, the death rate, fertility, and changes in species of birds and other wildlife; they have found changes, but they cannot be certain of their causes or of how extensive the changes really are. There is also growing concern over water pollution due to pesticides and the harm it causes to fish and animals.

Mr. Wagner has had several meetings with his competitors, heads of government agencies, and personnel in his research department. He has authorized additional funds for research to be used to eliminate or reduce the harmful effects his products have.

There are other dimensions to the problem. Certain insects become immune to insecticides, and this increases the need for stronger poisons or new products. The cost of research is already high in the industry, and stockholders want higher dividends and less research expenditure.

Mr. Gordon has made speeches and written papers saying that the problem has been blown out of proportion by the book *Silent Spring* and that insecticides and pesticides produced by Wagner Chemical conform to government and company standards. He adds that to discontinue their use would endanger the health of the nation and cause a food shortage. He further contends that the real cause of harm to wildlife is *misuse* of the products and use of them too close to water and game reserves.

Mr. Wagner has evaluated his problem and finds that over one-third of his company's income is derived from insecticide and pesticide sales. He is convinced that his products conform to government standards, but he does not want to be responsible for the death of wildlife, pollution of streams, or possible damage to human beings.

He must also face pressures from stockholders to reduce research expenditures, from competition to keep costs down in order to get his share of the market, and from the public to make his products safe for general use. He cannot ignore these pressures.

Any research into the long-range effects upon plant and animal life is an extensive, formidable undertaking, and there is little chance of obtaining conclusive answers. He knows that competition would take over if he discontinued producing insecticides and pesticides. He feels that he is filling a need by producing them. Mr. Wagner wonders what he should do.

DISCUSSION QUESTIONS

1 Discuss the ecological aspects of this case.

2 Is Wagner Chemical Company responsible for damage to fish and wildlife by its chemicals? If not, who is?

3 To what extent should Mr. Wagner feel responsible for effects on human beings of his company's pesticides and insecticides?

4 Evaluate the arguments Mr. Wagner has been using in his speeches.

CASE 6

SOLO RUBBER COMPANY[1]

The Solo Rubber Company is the second largest tire and rubber manufacturer in the United States. Although its headquarters remain in Akron, Ohio, where it was founded, it is a multinational company whose operations extend around the world. It owns rubber plantations and factories in several nations, and its products are sold in all major countries of the free world. It is widely diversified into rubber, chemicals, merchandising centers, and allied products. Sales and assets exceeded $1 billion each in 1964.

On April 15, 1965, Mr. Dick Smith, president, discussed with his executive committee a decision which had come to be called the "Romanian deal" within the company. For several months it had generated vigorous discussion within the executive committee. The Romanian deal concerned efforts of Romania, a Communist satellite, to purchase in the United States for installation in Romania a full-scale synthetic rubber plant. The plant which the Romanians desired to purchase used confidential production processes not yet publicly known.

President Smith reported to the executive committee that two days ago in Romania a Solo Rubber negotiating team had signed a preliminary contract with Romanian officials for a $45-million plant. Solo was to do a "turn-key" job, meaning that it would design and build the entire plant, delivering it to the Romanians in operating condition. The contract also

[1] The Solo Company and its officers are fictitious, but the problems with which the company deals are real.

called for Solo to train Romanian operators and keep the plant in operating condition for one year after it began producing.

President Smith reported that the contract should provide a profit of several million dollars to Solo Rubber Company, for the Romanians were eager to have the plant and had been willing to pay a generous price. He then commented:

"This preliminary contract specifies that it is subject to final approval by higher Romanian government officials and by Solo management in our Akron headquarters. We are now going to have to decide once and for all time whether we want to go through with this deal. As our earlier discussions have pointed out, the Romanian deal does have both favorable and unfavorable aspects. It is much more than a strictly commercial transaction because it involves grave questions of business social responsibility, public policy, and international relations.

"Newspaper releases correctly point out that this is the first time private American industry has contracted directly with a Communist nation since World War II. We must be sure before we proceed with this historic contract. I am therefore appointing a subcommittee of this group to review the whole situation and present their recommendation to this group two weeks from today. For ready reference the subcommittee should include a summary of all reasons for and against this contract, giving particular attention to our public responsibilities. The subcommittee will consist of John Dye [director of marketing], chairman; Roger Slade [director of research and development]; and Samuel Ratliff [director of public relations]. The subcommittee's report and our decision two weeks from today will then be presented to our next board meeting for ratification."

President Smith then moved on to other matters before the executive committee. He did not invite further discussion of the Romanian deal because it had already been thoroughly discussed at several earlier meetings. The events which led to the preliminary contract signed in Romania were rather complex. It seemed to President Smith that because this was a new situation, not previously faced by American industry, Solo Company had drifted gradually into the Romanian deal without any understanding of what might develop.

The Romanian deal began in the spring of 1964, when a Romanian delegation visited the United States and toured some industrial facilities. They were particularly interested in rubber and chemical plants. At that time they visited the Goodyear Tire and Rubber Company's polyisoprene rubber plant in Beaumont, Texas. They were not permitted in the plant, but were driven around it. In the summer of 1964 Romanian officials held trade negotiations with United States government officials in Washington. An interagency committee, which included representatives from the State Department and the Defense Department, studied the question of trade with Romania to determine whether it would conflict with the security of the United States. At the conclusion of the meeting, Ambassador Averell Harriman and Gheorgho Gaston-Marin, vice-chairman of the Council of Ministers of Romania, issued a joint statement. It said that the United

States had agreed to issue export licenses to Romania for a number of industrial facilities, including those in the petrochemical field.

The reported reason behind the government's approval of these export licenses was that the creation of greater economic ties between the United States and Romania would encourage the Romanians to be more independent of the Soviet Union.

Shortly after the export licenses were approved, Romanian trade officials contacted the Goodyear Tire and Rubber Company, whose plant they had visited in Beaumont, Texas. They wanted to purchase an exact duplicate of its polyisoprene facilities at Beaumont, complete with the processes, machinery, and technicians to run it.

Early in October, Goodyear withdrew from further negotiations. Board Chairman Russell DeYoung wrote Secretary Rush of the State Department that Goodyear was withdrawing because the company felt it was not in the "best interests of the United States" to sell this type of plant to a Communist nation.

A company house organ, the Goodyear Triangle, later explained the company's decision as follows:

Goodyear feels that the dangers far outweigh the possible benefits in the proposed deal. For that reason Goodyear has no intention of being a party to it.

Why is Goodyear so opposed to the transaction?

Because we foresee the knowledge that [what] Romania seeks to purchase from the United States [may be used by Romania or another Communist nation] in the potential role of an international agitator, we don't believe that the United States should allow any Communist nation to acquire the know-how to produce a synthetic rubber which competes head-on with natural rubber.

And that's what Natsyn—Goodyear's polyisoprene—does. As you know, Natsyn is a duplication of natural rubber, offering natural's many desirable qualities that have eluded duplication in all other manmade rubbers.

While synthetic and natural rubber are now competitively priced, Goodyear believes the Communists could—if they wished—disrupt natural rubber markets in Malaysia, Liberia, and other so-called underdeveloped countries. The Communists are not governed by marketing conditions in setting their prices and in the past have, in fact, used cut-rate prices as an economic club [italics in original].

The State Department, in commenting on the situation, has said that the Romanians have assured the United States that they won't divulge the polyisoprene secrets they purchase from us to other Communist nations. With due respect for the State Department's belief in the Romanians' promise, Goodyear would prefer not to entrust its production secrets to the Communists.

What's to keep the Romanians from passing techniques developed in the Goodyear Research Laboratory on Goodyear Boulevard to Communist production geniuses in Moscow or Peiping? The why's and wherefore's of Natsyn might make an interesting "I'll trade you . . ." tool for the Romanians.

With regard to Goodyear's concern about Communist manipulation of rubber markets, F. D. Hockersmith, director of the Office of Export Control in Washington, acknowledged in the *Akron Beacon Journal,* on October 23, 1964, that this was "something that could be done." But he observed that since other rubbers compete with natural rubber, the Communists could not be stopped by Goodyear's refusal to sell them a polyisoprene plant if they really wanted to upset the world market. He said that government policy in dealing with Communist countries is ". . . to permit trade in non-strategic items where there is no threat to the national security and welfare." In this particular case, the Federal government had approved the sale of the plant to Romania.

At the time the Goodyear decision was made, details were withheld because of possible effects on the forthcoming November national presidential election in the United States. Philip Meyer, Washington correspondent for the *Akron Beacon Journal,* commented in the issue of October 24, 1964:

Goodyear officials have a reason for soft-pedaling their objections to selling a synthetic rubber process to Romania.

They are afraid the question might get embroiled in the political campaign. It is a fear shared by officials in the State Dept., and other Government agencies.

Both Goodyear and the State Dept. have declined to make public the contents of a letter from Board Chairman Russell DeYoung to Secretary Rusk early this month, but its general theme has leaked out.

Basically, the company's position—which it confirms—is that a technical process developed only after great expenditure of time and money should not be sold to Communists.

Meyer went on to explain that State Department policy favored trade with Communist satellites to encourage independence from Russian influence but that conservatives opposed industrial trade with Communists; therefore, the conservative presidential candidate might be able to use the Goodyear letter to say, "Here is an example of private industry making a financial sacrifice in order to take the firm position on Communism which the State Dept. refuses to take."

Following their rejection by Goodyear, Romanian officials contacted the Solo Rubber Company. Since Solo lacked know-how with polyisoprene rubber, the Romanians asked it to build them a copolymer styrene-butadiene rubber plant. Although this rubber lacked the exact characteristics of natural rubber, it blended well with natural rubber, and Solo Company's advanced know-how involved some secret processes. Romanian officials noted that they had arranged for commercial credit to finance the purchase, with the credit being guaranteed by the United States Export-Import Bank, so they were ready to make the purchase immediately for cash.

Since the sale was approved by the State Department and credit was guaranteed by the Federal government, Solo officials felt they could hardly refuse preliminary negotiations with officials of the Romanian government. They felt that a preliminary refusal would be an affront to the Romanians, since the Romanians were initiating contact with the approval of the United States government. Solo officials knew, however, that their final decision would be difficult because of the volatile issues involved.

The first time the executive committee discussed the Romanian deal, several strong views were expressed. The vice-president for international operations reported that anti-Communist feeling was very strong in some of the company's foreign markets. Part of this opposition was organized, and company products could be boycotted if the company finally made a sale to Romania. Another committee member mentioned the reasons Goodyear gave for stopping negotiations and said that these reasons also applied to Solo Rubber Company. But another member pointed out that the rubber produced by the Solo plant was not an exact substitute for natural rubber, so the decision Solo Company faced was not quite the same as the one Goodyear faced.

Another member stated that Solo Company was not engaged in international relations; consequently, whatever the United States government approved, Solo Company should feel free to do. The director of industrial relations insisted, however, that the limits of law or government policy are not necessarily the *best* public conduct for a corporation. These limits set the extremes to which a company can go, he said, but usually the best action is somewhat short of the extreme permitted.

The treasurer pointed out that Communists are unalterably opposed to private industry and that this view was confirmed by the fact that the Romanians were government officials seeking to set up a *government* plant. For the stockholders' sake, he said, Solo Rubber should not help a group which sought to abolish their way of life. But another member explained that the Romanian people should be free to make their own choice of industrial organization without interference from Solo Rubber. Another member, however, argued that the Romanians' choice of communism in the beginning was not a free choice; therefore, any support at this time would simply give a stamp of approval to the original tyranny.

One committee member, a strong humanist in philosophy, said that Solo Company must help the Romanians because they are human beings who need rubber as much as any other human beings do. He announced that no human being can refuse to help another human being for any reason. A Ph.D. scientist, another strong humanist, took an opposite view. He philosophized that he loved the Romanian people as he loved his own brother but that the pending decision concerned support of the Romanian government, not help for the people. To strengthen the government would strengthen oppression of human beings and would in the long run be antihumanistic. As long as communism supported dictatorship and emphasized the state above the person, a humanist could not support the government, regardless of how much concern he had for its people.

Then the committee returned to what one member called "good business" and discussed how the Romanian deal would affect other sales. Three members pointed to the favorable publicity received by Goodyear and argued that Solo's sales and earnings would improve if the Romanian deal were rejected. The treasurer observed that, assuming a normal 5 percent net profit on sales, $100 million in new sales would be required to replace the net profit of $5 million expected from the Romanian deal. He doubted that sales could increase that much. He predicted that any tendency for increased sales as a result of favorable publicity would be offset by rejection of company products by those who objected to the company's decision.

During the next several months, discussion of the Romanian deal took a total of six hours in the weekly meetings of the executive committee. Two staff reports on the subject were heard and discussed. After each report, committee views seemed about evenly divided, so Romanian negotiations were continued, since there was no clear reason to stop them. Finally, the preliminary agreement was signed in Bucharest, and Solo Rubber Company faced its decision "once and for all time," as the president had mentioned at the committee meeting of April 15, 1965.

John Dye, director of marketing and chairman of the final subcommittee to study the Romanian deal, walked from the committee room wondering how he should go about preparing his subcommittee report in the two weeks of time that remained.

DISCUSSION QUESTIONS

1 In the role of John Dye, prepare a detailed plan for your subcommittee's action during the next two weeks. Then prepare the subcommittee report as you think it should be prepared.

2 Is it really necessary or desirable for the Solo executive committee to concern itself with the social, political, and international aspects of the Romanian deal? Should they not confine themselves to whatever is "good business," that is, with what is reasonably profitable and within the law?

3 Discuss this case in terms of the opportunities and responsibilities of multinational business.

4 Looking backward from the present, has history shown the Goodyear decision to be wise or unwise (a) from Goodyear's point of view and (b) from the point of view of the national interest of the United States? Explain.

INDEXES

NAME INDEX

Adams, Velma A., 235*n.*
Agarwala, Amar N., 366*n.*
Andersen, Hans Christian, 59
Andrews, Frank M., 65*n.*
Anthony, Robert N., 13, 208
Aquinas, St. Thomas, 238*n.*
Aranda, Juan, 369*n.*
Arensberg, Conrad M., 378*n.*
Argyris, Chris, 17*n.*, 148*n.*, 152*n.*
Aristotle, 105*n.*, 237*n.*
Artz, Reta D., 154*n.*
Athos, Anthony G., 405*n.*
Austin, J. Paul, 355*n.*

Bach, George L., 226*n.*
Baker, James C., 49*n.*
Banks, Louis, 306*n.*
Barkin, Solomon, 252*n.*
Barnard, Chester I., 75*n.*
Barrett, Donald M., 367*n.*
Baumhart, Raymond, 133*n.*

Beard, Meriam, 104*n.*
Berle, Adolph A., Jr., 32*n.*, 210*n.*,
    218*n.*, 401*n.*, 407*n.*
Besnette, Frank H., 271
Bining, Arthur C., 124*n.*
Blough, Roger M., 169*n.*, 176*n.*,
    277*n.*
Blum, Albert A., 252*n.*
Blum, Fred H., 405*n.*
Bock, Betty, 193*n.*
Bonjean, Charles M., 273*n.*
Bowen, Howard R., 95*n.*
Boyd, Harper W., 229*n.*
Brayman, Harold, 180*n.*
Broehl, Wayne C., Jr., 126*n.*
Brookings, Robert S., 75*n.*
Brooks, John, 218*n.*
Brown, Courtney C., 176*n.*, 191*n.*
Bunting, John R., 171*n.*
Burck, Gilbert, 56*n.*
Burgett, Claude, 348*n.*
Burns, Arthur J., 184*n.*

449

Taylor, Stuart A., 16*n*.
Thau, Theodore L., 132*n*.
Thompson, James Westfall, 108*n*.
Thorelli, Hans B., 361*n*.
Thornton, Charles B., 396*n*.
Tobin, Richard L., 324*n*.
Townsend, Edward, 252*n*.
Toynbee, Arnold J., 96*n*.
Tyler, Gus, 288*n*.

Urwick, L. F., 301*n*.

Valenti, Jack, 330*n*.
Vigen, James, 314*n*.
Vogel, Al, 272
Votaw, Dow, 91*n*.

Walton, Clarence, 27, 28, 91*n*.,
   135*n*., 139*n*., 218*n*.
Ward, John William, 121*n*.
Warner, W. Lloyd, 267*n*.

Weaver, David B., 205*n*., 210*n*.,
   212*n*.
Weber, Max, 109*n*.
Weiss, Herbert K., 61
Weissman, Jacob, 217*n*.
Westin, Alan F., 159*n*., 161*n*.
Westing, J. Howard, 228*n*.
Wherry, Robert J., Sr., 391*n*.
Whyte, William H., Jr., 150*n*.,
   153*n*.
Wilson, James Q., 289*n*.
Wise, T. A., 23*n*.
Wood, Laurence I., 92*n*.
Wright, David McCord, 218*n*.
Wright, M. A., 339*n*.

Yohalem, Aaron S., 242*n*.
Yoshino, M. Y., 383*n*.

Zahren, Bernard J., 188*n*.
Zaleznik, Abraham, 150*n*.

SUBJECT INDEX